W0114304

The Right of the People

The Right
of the People

★

Democracy and the Case
for a New American Founding

Osita Nwanevu

RANDOM HOUSE
NEW YORK

Random House
An imprint and division of Penguin Random House LLC
1745 Broadway, New York, NY 10019
randomhousebooks.com
penguinrandomhouse.com

Copyright © 2025 by Osita Nwanevu

Penguin Random House values and supports copyright. Copyright fuels creativity,
encourages diverse voices, promotes free speech, and creates a vibrant culture.
Thank you for buying an authorized edition of this book and for complying
with copyright laws by not reproducing, scanning, or distributing any part
of it in any form without permission. You are supporting writers and allowing
Penguin Random House to continue to publish books for every reader. Please note
that no part of this book may be used or reproduced in any manner for the purpose
of training artificial intelligence technologies or systems.

RANDOM HOUSE and the HOUSE colophon are registered trademarks
of Penguin Random House LLC.

Hardback ISBN 9780593449929
Ebook ISBN 9780593449936

Printed in the United States of America on acid-free paper

randomhousebooks.com

2 4 6 8 9 7 5 3 1

First Edition

BOOK TEAM: Production editor: Evan Camfield • Managing editor: Rebecca Berlan •
Production manager: Angela McNally • Copy editor: Allan Fallow • Proofreaders:
Susan Gutentag, Barbara Stussy, Kevin Clift • Indexer: Stephen Callahan

The authorized representative in the EU for product safety and compliance
is Penguin Random House Ireland, Morrison Chambers, 32 Nassau Street,
Dublin D02 YH68, Ireland. https://eu-contact.penguin.ie.

To Dad, Mom, and Kelechi

Perhaps the sentiments contained in the following pages, are not yet sufficiently fashionable to procure them general Favor; a long Habit of not thinking a Thing wrong, gives it a superficial appearance of being right, and raises at first a formidable outcry in defence of Custom. But the Tumult soon subsides. Time makes more Converts than Reason.

—Thomas Paine, *Common Sense* (1776)

CONTENTS

INTRODUCTION

> We have frequently printed the word Democracy. Yet I cannot too often repeat that it is a word the real gist of which still sleeps, quite unawaken'd, notwithstanding the resonance and the many angry tempest out of which its syllables have come, from pen or tongue. It is a great word, whose history, I suppose, remains unwritten, because that history has yet to be enacted.
>
> —Walt Whitman, *Democratic Vistas* (1871)

OUR DEMOCRACY. NO PHRASE, SAVE *MAKE AMERICA GREAT again,* has rung as loudly in the ears of the American voter this decade. In 2019, Joe Biden began his run for the presidency with an announcement that framed the task of defeating Donald Trump—a wannabe authoritarian from the moment he entered politics—in existential terms. "The core values of this nation, our standing in the world, our very democracy, everything that has made America, America, is at stake," he said. After his victory in the Democratic primary, the party as a whole, and much of the press besides, took up that message. "This administration," former president Barack Obama warned at the 2020 Democratic National Convention, "has shown it will tear our democracy down if that's what it takes to win." "This election," Bernie Sanders said in his own speech, "is about preserving our democracy." "Speaking at a political convention is something I never expected to be doing," former acting attorney general Sally Yates said in her remarks, "but the future of our democracy is at stake." In

September, *The Washington Post*'s editorial board ran a series of essays headlined "Our Democracy in Peril." "A second Trump term," they wrote, "might injure the democratic experiment beyond recovery." Biden, *The New York Times* editorial board agreed in October, "would stand with America's allies and against adversaries that seek to undermine our democracy."

Proving his critics right, Trump responded to his loss in that election with a scheme to invalidate the results—an effort that culminated in the attack on the Capitol on January 6, 2021. "Our democracy," Biden told the country that day, "is under unprecedented assault." In the lead-up to the 2024 election, he would do all he could to drive that message home again. By one count, Biden used the word "democracy" nearly four hundred times across one hundred campaign events in 2023 and 2024; upon dropping out of the race, Biden argued that his stepping aside would give Democrats their best chance at defeating Trump again and protecting our democratic system. "I believe my record as president, my leadership in the world, my vision for America's future all merited a second term," he said in his address to the country, "but nothing—nothing—can come in the way of saving our democracy. That includes personal ambition."

The task of defending democracy from Trump then fell to Kamala Harris. "He is the person," she warned voters in a major address at the Ellipse toward the end of the race, "who stood at this very spot nearly four years ago and sent an armed mob to the United States Capitol to overturn the will of the people in a free and fair election—an election that he knew he lost." Over and over and over again in 2024, at every available opportunity and in every available venue, the American voter was told—by Joe Biden, Kamala Harris, and the Democratic Party as a whole—that democracy itself was on the ballot.

If so, democracy lost fair and square. Trump was reelected with not only an Electoral College majority but the Republican Party's first presidential popular vote victory in twenty years. That's not to say most who went to the polls in 2020 actively approved of Trump's postelection scheming or the events of January 6. But for the winning share of voters, Trump's antidemocratic actions clearly took a back seat to economic concerns, other policy issues, and distrust in the Biden administration. And, troublingly, many who did have democracy at front of mind when they went to the polls in November 2024 wound up backing Trump anyway—about a third of those who supported him, according to the Associated Press, singled out democracy as the most important factor in their vote. In a poll from Vanderbilt University in July of that year, 53 percent of Republicans had reported feeling that democracy was under attack—significantly more than the 35 percent of Democrats who felt the same. Those figures were unsurprising. After all, most Republicans believed—or claimed to believe—that Trump had been cheated out of winning in 2020. "Now it is up to Congress to confront this egregious assault on our democracy," Trump had told the assembled crowd on January 6. "I know that everyone here will soon be marching over to the Capitol building to peacefully and patriotically make your voices heard. Today we will see whether Republicans stand strong for the integrity of our elections."

Eight Republican senators and 139 House Republicans—more than 60 percent of the Republicans in that chamber—voted to overturn the election on Trump's behalf on that day. In the days and weeks prior, 44 percent of Republican state legislators in nine swing states had done their part to try to discredit or overturn the results. The violence of January 6 would do nothing to chasten the party. According to a survey later in 2021 by the American Enterprise Institute, 56 percent of Republicans reported believing that force might be necessary to defend "the traditional American way of life." During the 2022 primary season, Republican candidates showed off or fired guns in more than one hundred ads. "We can think of no other major party," the political scientists Steven Levitsky and Daniel Ziblatt wrote of Western governments in 2023, "in which candidates so openly embraced violence."

Undeterred, industry and corporate political action committees (PACs) donated more than $100 million to Donald Trump and candidates who either refused to certify the results of the 2020 election or ran on lies about it between January 6, 2021, and August 2024. More than two hundred donating companies—among them Microsoft, Meta, and Bank of America—had previously suspended their giving to election-denying candidates. Overall in the 2024 presidential race, nearly two-thirds of business donations went to Trump and other Republican candidates. And Trump also earned the backing of several billionaires who had condemned the January 6 attack, including Jamie Dimon ("I strongly condemn the violence in our nation's capital"), Nelson Peltz ("We condemn President Trump's efforts to overturn the election results which culminated in yesterday's shocking events at our Capitol"), and Stephen Schwarzman ("The insurrection that followed the President's remarks today is appalling and an affront to the democratic values we hold dear as Americans").

"What possibly could have produced such a change of heart within this cohort," asked Harold Meyerson of *The American Prospect* in May 2024, "understanding as they do that Trump poses a clear and present danger to America's democratic values? Just between us, it's money. In 2025, the Trump tax cuts on individuals—more than 80 percent of which went to the wealthiest Americans—will expire. Trump has vowed to continue those cuts if he's elected, which would increase the nation's deficit by a cool $4 trillion."

Of the many billionaires who backed Trump in 2024, none received quite as much in return for their contributions as Elon Musk. Having spent more than $260 million to reelect the president, Musk was rewarded with an extraordinary role in his administration—leadership of an agency, the Department of Government Efficiency (DOGE), that immediately and illegally began cutting government programs and firing thousands of federal workers upon Trump's inauguration. Whole agencies, including USAID, the Consumer Financial Protection Bureau, and even the Department of Education were gutted. Federal scientific research on conditions like cancer and Alzheimer's was upended. And government services and grant-making were thrown into politically motivated chaos. Meanwhile, Musk companies like Space X and Tesla—regulated by the very agencies being undermined by DOGE—remained eligible for federal contracts, an obvious conflict of interest the Trump administration claimed Musk could be trusted not to exploit. Evidently unsatisfied with the extent of his influence, Musk also barged into a 2025 Wisconsin Supreme Court campaign in a remarkable fashion—not only spending some $25 million total in an ultimately failed effort against liberal nominee Susan Crawford, but offering gifts, including two $1 million dollar checks, directly to voters in the race.

This, as many Americans know, is how "our democracy" has come to function—the wealthy and corporations leverage their resources to have an outsize say in elections and the policy process. Given the dissatisfaction that sets in when one's party is out of power, and the persistence of congressional gridlock on issues that matter to many voters, it can hardly be a surprise that ambivalence about "our democracy" was widespread enough for Trump to prevail. In early 2024, Gallup reported 71 percent dissatisfaction with the way democracy is working, the highest level of dissatisfaction on record since they began asking the question in 1984. Only 19 percent of Americans believe democracy in America is a good example for other countries to follow. And 45 percent of Americans believe American democracy does a poor job representing the interests of ordinary people.

The facts and figures above lend themselves to a simple story: Backed most strongly by voters who measure the health of "our democracy" by their own power, financed by billionaires and businesses who care less about "our democracy" than their own wealth and profits, and at a moment when many Americans have come to doubt whether "our democracy" works in their own interests, Donald Trump and the Republican Party have managed to push "our democracy" to its breaking point, undermining our democratic norms and institutions in ways that may outlast what remains of Trump's political career.

There is truth to all of this. But no analysis of all Trump has done to and meant for "our democracy" should elide the fact that "our democracy" brought Donald Trump to office in the first place—over the opposition of most Americans. In 2016, he was sent to the White House by an Electoral College victory despite losing the popular vote to Hillary Clinton. In two impeachment trials, he was acquitted thanks to the high threshold for conviction set by the Constitution and despite public support for his removal. At no point during his first term did he earn the approval of a majority of the American public. In 2024, his third race, Trump finally won the support of a plurality of the American electorate—a normal victory, yes, but one that wouldn't have been possible if the basic structure of "our democracy" hadn't strengthened and secured a place for him in our politics. This was the fundamental irony of his triumph—the final victory of a candidate who ran against the institutions of "our democracy" despite having benefited from them profoundly.

The circumstances of Trump's rise—and the difficulty, after his defeat in 2020, that Democrats had in passing much of their agenda—have brought a growing chorus of political commentators to a striking conclusion: Some of the major and defining features of "our democracy" are not democratic at all. For most, that's nothing that a political tune-up of sorts can't fix. But to some on the right, those calls for restoration and repair miss the point of our system. "Democracy is a bad idea," the conservative pundit Charlie Kirk said flatly in 2022. "We are not a democracy. Democracy is unsustainable. They always say *our democracy, our democracy, our democracy.* We're not a democracy and we never should be a democracy." Conservatives of a certain bent have been saying this openly for decades. Robert Welch, the candy magnate responsible for Junior Mints, was also responsible for popularizing the familiar line "We're a republic, not a democracy" as founder of the far-right group the John Birch Society in the 1950s and '60s. But in recent decades, that view has spread far beyond the margins of the movement. "Democracy," Utah senato," Mike Lee wrote in the final weeks before the 2020 election, "isn't the objective. Liberty, peace, and prosperity are. We want the human condition to flourish. Rank democracy can thwart that."

As widely as Lee's comments were condemned, Trump's victory in 2024 deepened doubts about the democratic ideal even among its defenders at the other end of the political spectrum. We're told daily that misinformation and the dynamics of social media have worsened the long-standing problem of public ignorance. Even offline, experts insist, polarization has made the civil conversations and debates that sustain democracy impossible, from the halls of Congress to our own Thanksgiving tables. What's more, those most enthusiastically committed to the democratic ideal have competing visions of it. Democrats who've spent much of the last decade organizing against voter ID laws and other conservative efforts to restrict the franchise have been animated by the idea that voting isn't just a hard-won right, but a moral duty—to believe in democracy is to accept the responsibility of choosing your representatives, even if you don't like the options before you. Meanwhile, the mounting distrust of politicians and institutions has inspired a wave of protest movements over the last fifteen years that have vested their hopes in direct participation and action—bringing about change by bringing power back to the people themselves. "This," demonstrators have chanted from the streets, "is what democracy looks like." Is it?

Widen your lens beyond politics a bit, and the picture begins to lose all focus. Consider the word *democratize*, a verb that has found a remarkable variety of uses beyond reports on political events in places such as Myanmar or Hong Kong. On any given day, for instance, one might come across a piece about how generative AI is "democratizing creativity" or how NFTs "democratize the very essence of art." A post might inform you that "cryptocurrencies are democratizing the financial world" or that Amazon has "democratized online retail." "Social media," *Glamour* adds, "has democratized beauty in a way that is unique to this decade." In the financial pages, you might discover a start-up hoping "to democratize private flying by making it more afford-able." *Forbes* has doubts: "Is Democratization of Private Jets Dead?" it asks. On space tourism, *Smithsonian* has fewer: "Weightlessness is not only about to be democratized. It's about to become a lifestyle." A luxury magazine tells you that McLaren, Ferrari, and Porsche have worked to "democratize their hybrid performance powertrains across more affordable vehicles." In *Southern Living,* an article on tea towels notes that the mass production of cotton goods during the nineteenth century "democratized the dish-drying tool." *The New York Times,* for its part, has covered "the democratization of plastic surgery," "the democratization of airport lounges," and the efforts of a late sporting-goods executive to "democratize the world of fly casting." "Can Scent Be Democratized?" The Institute for Art and Olfaction would like to find out: "The balance of power is off in perfume," reports the institute's founder, "and it's off in the world."

I can't speak to perfume, but the balance of power is indeed off in the world. As rightly appalled as we are by the particular circumstances of Trump's rise here, we'd do well to remember that authoritarianism is on the rise just about everywhere. From 2020 to 2024, one in five elections worldwide was legally challenged and another one in five saw a losing presidential candidate or parliamentary party reject election results. Surveys tell us that many countries share our declining confidence in democracy—a degree of cynicism that aspiring autocrats just like ours have been able to take advantage of. And though the global democratic crisis that experts have been warning us about has surely been brought on by a complicated tangle of factors, one worth dwelling on is that we seem to have forgotten not only what makes democracy important, but what it even means. In the absence of clarity from its defenders and amid the failures of our putatively democratic institutions, democracy has become a specious and suspicious platitude, equally useful to marketers and would-be dictators—a hollow idea for a hollow, unserious time.

★ ★ ★

This book was written out of boredom. I have been covering American politics for just under ten years—not an especially long time, but enough to be dog-tired, already, of the habits of mind that shape American political journalism and wearied by the ways this industry has failed to meet this political moment. All that could be the subject of another book, or several, but the specific problem of relevance here is the way the economics of our profession force writers to engage with the fundamental questions shaping politics today—"What does it mean to be an American?" "How much inequality can or should a society abide?" "What is democracy, anyway?"—in thin, repetitive, ephemeral, and social media–optimized ways. Being given the time to consult a book and think about what you've read before firing off an opinion on the events of the week is an exceptionally rare privilege; being given the time and opportunity to write one is, of course, even rarer.

This particular one was motivated by the hunch—as I covered Trump's rise, his first presidential term, and the 2020 election—that for all our talk about democracy, our grip on the concept was loose and getting looser. And trying to get to the bottom of it, I figured, would be more interesting than contenting myself with dozens more pieces predicting, correctly, that a Democratic majority in Congress under Biden would fail to pass nearly the entirety of its legislative agenda unless it eliminated the filibuster, thanks to the design of the Senate. Given this and other realities those who cover politics are well aware of, the paeans to "our democracy" came to seem substantively untenable to me. In 2024, they also proved broadly unsatisfying to the American voter.

The truth is that those of us committed to defending democracy have more work cut out for us than we tend to acknowledge. You wouldn't know it reading most of the op-eds and columns of the last decade, but democracy is damned complicated—a frustrating, maddening, mathematically vexing thicket of competing ideas. For those of a certain cast of mind, it is also a thrilling problem—the kind of rabbit hole one can spend a lifetime in. This book might send some of you on your way down. But if nothing else, my hope is that readers come away understanding the danger of a political discourse that presumes the case for democracy is simple and obvious. It is neither—to take democracy for granted as an ideal is to leave it vulnerable. We're going to have a hard time defending democracy if we can't define it; we will surely fail to restore confidence in democracy if we can't engage and defeat its critics head-on. And with that basic ground cleared, we'll have a better understanding of what democracy might still be able to do for us—much more, I will argue, than we've been encouraged to imagine.

Let it not be said that our political leaders haven't made an effort to bring some rigor and clarity to our conversations about democracy themselves. A week after the 2024 election, for instance, House Minority Leader Hakeem Jeffries released a picture book called *The ABCs of Democracy,* derived from the first floor speech he'd made as the leader of the Democratic Party in the chamber. *A* is for *American Values* over *Autocracy.* Helpfully, a boy is pictured wearing an American flag as a cape. *B* is for *Benevolence* over *Bigotry.* *C* is for *The Constitution* over *The Cult.* And the *D* of *Democracy,* rather disappointingly, is *Democracy* itself, placed over *Demagogues.* Here, we see a crowd of hands pictured, some carrying flags representing the Democratic and Republican parties and others holding buttons bearing words such as *vote* and *equality.*

There are no pictures in *The Right of the People.* But one advantage it might have over the minority leader's book and the many gloomy titles on democracy for adults already crowding shelves is that it considers democracy from a philosophical standpoint first and foremost. In *Democracy in America,* Alexis de Tocqueville observed that while nineteenth-century Americans loved discussing politics, they had an allergy to abstractions—even to philosophical ideas that might have had some bearing on their debates and deliberations. As it happens, this is one of the precious and few things in that venerated tome that still holds water. In our most high-minded moments and in our deepest debates about the future of this country, we find ourselves narrowly asking what the Founders intended or would have wanted—this is about as high as we'll generally allow our imaginations to soar. What we tend to forget, though, is that when the Founders set about founding this country, they themselves asked not what their own inherited institutions and history bound them to, but what people are entitled to as human beings:

> We hold these truths to be self-evident, that all men are created equal, that they are endowed by their Creator with certain unalienable Rights, that among these are Life, Liberty and the pursuit of Happiness.
>
> That to secure these rights, Governments are instituted among Men, deriving their just powers from the consent of the governed,
>
> That whenever any Form of Government becomes destructive of these ends, it is the Right of the People to alter or to abolish it, and to institute new Government, laying its foundation on such principles and organizing its powers in such form, as to them shall seem most likely to effect their Safety and Happiness.

Next year will mark the 250th anniversary of those words; we've just marked the same anniversary of the beginning of the revolution that brought them about. We're rarely encouraged to remember that they established not just a country but a test—per the Founders, a standard set by reason for all societies, including the republic they themselves crafted, to meet. Life, liberty, and the pursuit of "Happiness"—both material security and flourishing, as the Founders meant it. A government that cannot secure our rights to these, or flouts our ability to achieve them, may be altered or abolished by the people subject to it in favor of a new government "most likely to effect their Safety and Happiness."

In the spirit of the Declaration, this book moves from first principles—an exploration of what democracy means—through

three main ideas: that democracy is good, that America is not
a democracy, and that America should become a democracy
through the transformation not only of our political institutions
but of our economy—a gradual transition significant enough in
scale that we might as well consider it a *new founding.* That language is derived from the work of the historian Eric Foner, who
has argued that the post–Civil War Reconstruction amendments
to the Constitution—the Thirteenth, abolishing slavery; the
Fourteenth, defining and granting citizenship to freed slaves and
establishing equal protection under the law; and the Fifteenth,
banning racial discrimination in voting rights—fundamentally altered the country's existing political order. "So profound were
these changes that the amendments should be seen not simply as
an alteration of an existing structure but as a 'second founding,' "
Foner has written. "A 'constitutional revolution,' in the words of
Republican leader Carl Schurz, that created a fundamentally new
document with a new definition of both the status of blacks and
the rights of all Americans."

It is my contention that "our democracy" is due for another
constitutional revolution—one animated by the idea that American democracy is a promise we've yet to make good on, a project
that remains ours to define and complete. Nearly 250 years ago,
the men who founded America made a fundamental break not
just from their old country but from the past—casting off an
order that had subjugated them with worn and weak ideas for the
promise of true self-governance and greater prosperity in a new
republic. With exactly their sense of purpose and even higher,
more righteous ambitions for America than they themselves had,
we should do the same now—work as hard as we can in the decades ahead to "institute new Government" for the benefit of the
many and not just the few.

PART I

WHAT IS DEMOCRACY?

★

CHAPTER 1

THE MEANING OF DEMOCRACY

WHAT IS DEMOCRACY, REALLY? LET'S START WITH THE BA-sics, as most people understand them: A democracy is a form of government in which people come together every so often to decide, usually through elections, what should be done and who should do it. Elected officials—representatives, mayors, governors, presidents, whoever they may be—are then responsible for carrying out the will of the people. If they don't—or if they do and the people change their minds about what they want—they get voted out and other candidates get voted in. All of this should happen freely and fairly—no one's vote should be forced, and every vote should be counted equally by impartial authorities. And a framework of basic political freedoms should accompany and support the democratic process—people should have the right to speak openly about politics, to seek out information, and to organize themselves politically without undue interference.

This is an outline of democratic society that has long been intuitive to ordinary Americans and scholars of democracy alike. For instance, Robert Dahl, one of the twentieth century's preeminent political scientists and democratic theorists, argued that democratic countries have six simple characteristics: empowered elected officials; "free, fair, and frequent" elections; free expression; access to diverse sources of information; the freedom of political association; and "inclusive citizenship," by which he meant the granting of full political rights to all adult citizens. Today, Freedom House, an American nonprofit that studies and promotes democracy abroad, describes democratic government as a system "based on the will and consent of the governed, institutions that are accountable to all citizens, adherence to the rule of law, and respect for human rights." Each year, it awards countries "democracy scores" that measure whether they have free and fair elections and how well they protect political rights and civil liberties.

Similarly, the Economist Intelligence Unit, which compiles an annual "Democracy Index," says that democracy, at a minimum, means "government based on majority rule and the consent of the governed; the existence of free and fair elections; the protection of minority rights; and respect for basic human rights." The Intelligence Unit ranks countries in its Index based on a slightly more complex set of factors than Freedom House's—the health of a country's electoral process and the state of its civil liberties are taken into account, but so are how well its government actually functions, how actively its citizens participate in politics, and the state of "political culture," by which they mean whether citizens engage in the political process civilly and peaceably.

That's a longer list of boxes to check off than we began with, but most Americans would probably consider the Index's metrics reasonable. A government too dysfunctional to implement the policies people voted for wouldn't be very democratic after all, and a political system in which hardly anyone ever voted—or in which elections could be regularly overturned by violence— would hardly be much of a democracy either. Still, as basic as the Index's requirements might seem, only around 15 percent of the countries in the world today—containing only about 7 percent of the world's population—are "full democracies" by its standards. (Congratulations to Canada, Germany, Japan, the United Kingdom, and their peers.) Around 28 percent of countries—with about 38 percent of the world's population— are what the Index calls "flawed democracies," a category that has included the United States since 2016. While our report card shows high marks for political participation, civil liberties, and even our electoral process—President Trump's coup attempt evidently notwithstanding—gridlock, polarization, and new voting restrictions have been dragging us down lately.

The Index's analysis of our current political situation is hard to argue with. But is it really fair to say American democracy is "flawed" overall? That depends on whether we buy the way the Index, and most of us, have chosen to define democracy in the first place.

Defining Democracy

As obvious as the norms underpinning electoral democracy might seem to us today, we should remember that the very concept of democracy was forged in societies with norms and political practices we'd find unrecognizable. Anthropologists believe early human bands of hunter-gatherers also made decisions by a kind of group consensus—albeit through processes led, surprise, surprise, by male elders. From there, the historical record suggests isolated pockets of proto-democratic governance developed just about everywhere humans settled—from the Middle East to the Americas. But the word *democracy* itself comes to us from Ancient Greek—*demos* meant *the people, kratos* meant *power,* and *demokratia* described the form of popular rule that probably governed about half of Greek city-states by the third century B.C.

Athens is the most famous of them. Historians believe democracy in Greece was preceded by a murky, predemocratic politics—there were city-states where chosen leaders ruled like kings. Then, in the sixth and fifth centuries B.C., political tumult and the reforms of three visionary leaders in particular—Solon, Cleisthenes, and Ephialtes—produced a new system of self-government. There was a democratic Assembly open to all full citizens—a legislature not of elected politicians, but of anyone who happened to show up. There was the Council of 500: a body that met nearly every day to set the Assembly's agenda and propose legislation, with its members selected annually from the citizenry in lotteries, a process political theorists call *sortition.* Then there were juries, also selected in lotteries, that ruled over court cases and reviewed the legality of the Assembly's decisions—a Supreme Court of sorts, with hundreds and occasionally thousands of ordinary citizens on its bench. Finally, there were officials responsible for implementing the laws—again chosen mostly by sortition, but with a set of top-level positions elected by the Assembly, which also chose the military's leaders.

Clearly, democratic government meant something different to the Athenians than it means to us now. Today, we elect politicians to act on our behalf—or hope they might, anyway, however dimly. But for the Athenians, democracy meant self-government in the most literal sense—the people participating in governance mostly without elected middlemen. It's not that the Athenians were unfamiliar with elections as a concept—again, they had them in limited form. But everyday Athenians also took it entirely for granted that they would be the first and final authority on all matters, no matter how complex—from foreign policy and commerce to basic municipal governance.

The structure and nature of Athenian democracy was a point of deep pride for Athenians such as the military hero and political leader Pericles. In his legendary Funeral Oration, delivered early in the intra-Greek Peloponnesian War, he rallied his countrymen with stirring odes to the distinctive character of Athenian government:

> Our constitution does not copy the laws of neighboring states; we are rather a pattern to others than imitators ourselves. Its administration favors the many instead of the few; this is why it is called a democracy. If we look to the laws, they afford equal justice to all in their private differences; if to social standing, advancement in public life falls to reputation for capacity, class considerations not being allowed to interfere with merit; nor again does poverty bar the way, if a man is able to serve the state, he is not hindered by the obscurity of his condition.

This is one of the passages that earned the Oration its reputation as one of history's greatest speeches. It's mostly nonsense.

"The people" who ruled in Athens were, again, full citizens—women, slaves, and free immigrants called metics were excluded, meaning that "the many" Pericles spoke grandly about were a minority of the population. And Athenian citizenship became only more exclusive over time—in the mid-fifth century B.C., a law backed by Pericles restricted that status to males with two fully Athenian parents.

Obviously, Athenian society lacked many of the social and political values we now take for granted—given the status of women, slaves, and immigrants, the "equal justice" Pericles spoke of certainly didn't mean "equal rights" for all. And even the supposed equality between individual citizens in the Assembly was undermined by the fact that some Athenians could afford to pay for instruction in rhetoric and the making of arguments. Moreover, though Athens lacked real political parties, supporters of the rich, the well-liked, and the well-connected were able to build important and influential political networks that shaped the city's politics.

As limited and unequal as Athenian democracy was in practice, many elites still believed the city's masses had been given an excessive and even terrifying amount of power. Plato, for instance, described democratic society as chaotic and decadent in *The Republic*, where he also predicted that the disorder in democracies would lead inevitably to the restoration of tyranny. But while democracy in Athens was overthrown twice, it was the subjugation of the city by the Macedonian king Phillip II in the fourth century B.C., rather than any internal tumult, that sent the system into a terminal decline.

The word *democracy* managed to survive that decline, though it was much abused with the rise of imperial Rome. "By the mid-2nd century A.D.," the historian James Miller writes, "Aelius, a famed orator, could declare, in the ode 'To Rome,' that 'there has been established throughout the world alike a democracy—under one man, namely the best ruler and controller.'"

That line would have baffled the Athenians—as would many of the other governments that have been labeled democratic since their time. By their lights, democracy by election—whether "flawed" or "full"—wouldn't have been democracy at all.

Still, there's a basic and broad definition of democracy that both we and the Athenians would likely agree upon if we could talk across time—collective self-rule. As the philosopher Joshua Cohen and the legal scholar Charles Sabel put it, a democracy is a system in which "the authorization to exercise public power—and that exercise itself—arises from collective decisions by the citizens over whom that power is exercised." The best plain-English version of that definition is still Abraham Lincoln's, delivered in the Gettysburg Address—democracy is government of the people, by the people, and for the people.

Different systems aim for that ideal in different ways, and arguments over what kinds of institutions best embody it have been ongoing for centuries. Much of this book will be dedicated to evaluating whether our system really embodies that ideal at all. That question aside, Lincoln offered us a definition of democracy we can work with. In a democracy, "the people" rule—the governed govern and power, as Pericles and Lincoln would have agreed, is wielded by and for the many rather than the few.

That understanding of what democracy's about, as rough as it is, should help us answer our next basic question: What's so great about democracy, anyway?

The Case for Democracy

One simple answer political scientists and economists are fond of is that democracy makes us rich and happy—the more democratic a society is, data suggests, the more stable and prosperous it tends to be. For most of the last eighty years, for instance, Western countries classified by researchers as democracies have accounted for the majority of the world's gross domestic product (GDP). Research tells us that the citizens of more democratic societies have better health outcomes too. And many scholars also believe that democracies are less internally violent and less likely to go to war with each other.

Of course, as we know from experience here in America, societies with democratic values can wage destructive wars against less democratic societies—and might even claim to do so in the name of spreading democracy. And beyond that wrinkle, there are basic questions of correlation and causation to untangle with the outcomes democratic researchers measure—figuring how much credit democratic governance deserves relative to other factors can be tricky.

Still, there does seem to be some connection between democratic governance and how well-off people are—a connection that might be as old as democracy itself. The classical scholar Josiah Ober, for instance, has argued that Ancient Greece owed much of its wealth, imperial power, and cultural achievements to its democratic norms and institutions. But even if it's true that democratic societies have been safer, healthier, and wealthier than others, that wouldn't be a very strong case for democracy on its own. If authoritarian societies managed to become as safe, healthy, and wealthy as democratic ones, democracy's advantages or each front would disappear.

This might already be happening. The share of world GDP held by Western democracies has decreased rapidly over the last few decades, due mostly to the economic rise of authoritarian China. "When China as a whole crosses above $20,000 in per capita income," the political scientists Roberto Stefan Foa and Yascha Mounk wrote in 2019, "1.8 billion people around the world will live in upper-income authoritarian regimes." Beyond material prosperity, Chinese society is, by all appearances, relatively stable and peaceful for most citizens—thanks, at least in part, to the Chinese regime's repression. Predictions from Western analysts that the Chinese people would demand democracy with time haven't yet borne out.

All told, the idea that democracies hold basic material advantages over other societies isn't a sure thing. History is littered

with examples of so-called "enlightened despots" who considered themselves committed to the well-being of the masses under
their rule. And in many cases, the masses agreed. Although
Americans tend to associate the phrase *a chicken in every pot* with
the promises made in modern political campaigns, for instance, it
was first credited to the popular sixteenth- and seventeenth-
century French king Henry IV, who reputedly wanted wealth to
be shared broadly enough that peasants could have chicken every
Sunday. Before we overthrew our own king, the British monarchy was popular and trusted enough on this side of the pond that
many American revolutionaries-to-be hoped King George III
would reassert control over an unpopular Parliament and its tax
policies. And back in Ancient Greece, Plato famously argued for
government by wise philosopher-kings capable of ruling more
justly in the best interest of the masses than the masses themselves.

Though China hardly resembles Plato's republic, its rise does
show that autocratic regimes can, potentially, secure the material
well-being of many or most of their citizens. But there are strong
conceptual reasons to doubt those kinds of regimes will do right
by their citizens for long.

For starters, autocrats often have few real incentives to act in
the interest of the people they govern—especially if the masses
have been subdued by the threat of violence or belief systems that
legitimize autocratic rule. Consequently, broad social uplift generally isn't on the agenda of most despots. And absolute authority is, ultimately, unaccountable authority—as generous and
enlightened as a despot or small cabal of elites might be toward
the people in one moment, nothing much binds them, or whoever
might succeed them, to be as generous and enlightened in the
next.

We also shouldn't assume autocrats would know how to govern in the interest of the people even if they wanted to. Advocates
of democracy tend to think about that point in two ways. On the
one hand, some democrats argue, for a variety of reasons, that the
people are more likely to know what's best for themselves than

higher authorities—especially ones who don't live ordinary lives. This was part of Thomas Paine's case against monarchs, for instance—"their minds," he warned in *Common Sense*, "are early poisoned by importance; and the world they act in differs so materially from the world at large, that they have but little opportunity of knowing its true interests." A century and a half later, the American philosopher John Dewey would say the same about educated elites. "It is impossible for high-brows to secure a monopoly of such knowledge as must be used for the regulation of common affairs," he wrote in *The Public and Its Problems*. "In the degree in which they become a specialized class, they are shut off from knowledge of the Needs which they are supposed to serve."

On the other hand, some democrats believe that "what's best" for the people is often difficult for *anyone* to know with real certainty—and that figuring it out is more a matter of wrestling with differing ethical perspectives than of discovering hard facts that can tell us, objectively, what the "right" or "wrong" thing to do in a given situation is. But where both democratic camps agree is that the judgments, beliefs, and values of one ruler or a few elites shouldn't be privileged over the judgments, beliefs, and values of the many.

All told, these are less arguments *for* democracy than arguments *against* autocracy. And really, a minimal defense of democracy might end here with Winston Churchill's famous quip: "Democracy is the worst form of government, except for all the others." The defects of the alternatives are so glaring, in other words, that we're stuck with democracy for better or worse.

But Churchill's full quote is more nuanced than that. "It has been said that democracy is the worst form of Government except all those other forms that have been tried from time to time," he told the House of Commons in a 1947 speech. "But there is the broad feeling in our country that the people should rule, and that public opinion expressed by all constitutional means, should shape, guide, and control the actions of Ministers who are their servants and not their masters." However undesirable the alternatives to democracy might seem and however flawed democracy might be in practice, Churchill was arguing, we've committed ourselves to democracy for its own sake nonetheless—not because it's the best of a set of bad options, but because we've genuinely come to believe in it. Should we?

★ ★ ★

As Churchill said, we've come to take for granted that the people we send into government are our "servants and not our masters." The basic democratic intuition, implied by that remark, is that the people shouldn't *have* masters—government, per Lincoln, should be *of* and *by* the people *for* the people's benefit, not *of and by* someone else the people hope will work in their interest. To make especially sure government would be *of and by* the people, as we've seen, the Athenian people put themselves directly into government. But they and those who believe today that the people can act through elections would likely both agree that "the people" should govern because "the people" are entitled to a measure of control over the conditions that shape their lives. Rather than being the helpless victims of circumstance or the obedient subjects of a powerful few, democratic self-governance lets us act at our own direction—being, in the words of theorist James Lindley Wilson, "coauthor, with others, of one's life and world" without masters and without minders.

For Dewey, one of the most moving advocates for democracy America has ever known, the promise of democratic self-government also carried within it the promise of self-improvement—of learning from those democratic interactions with others and fully developing the innate potential that lies within each and every one of us. Democracy, he wrote in his 1888 book *The Ethics of Democracy,* is "the form of society in which every man has a chance and knows that he has it and we may add, a chance to which no possible limits can be put, a chance which is truly infinite, the chance to become a person."

And as the philosopher Richard Rorty wrote in *Achieving*

Our Country, many American thinkers and reformers once took it as a given that the project of American democracy, in particular, would enable a new kind of human flourishing once fully achieved—the "Happiness" of the Declaration made manifest in the arrival of "a new sort of individual," democratically empowered and given more agency than all preceding generations. The poet Walt Whitman devoted his book *Democratic Vistas* to this vision:

> It is not that democracy is of exhaustive account, in itself. Perhaps, indeed, it is, (like Nature,) of no account in itself. It is that, as we see, it is the best, perhaps only, fit and full means, formulater, general caller-forth, trainer, for the million, not for grand material personalities only, but for immortal souls. To be a voter with the rest is not so much; and this, like every institute, will have its imperfections. But to become an enfranchised man, and now, impediments removed, to stand and start without humiliation, and equal with the rest; to commence, or have the road clear'd to commence, the grand experiment of development, whose end, (perhaps requiring several generations,) may be the forming of a full-grown man or woman—that is something.

It is to democracy's credit that it's had many visionaries like Dewey and Whitman willing to speak on its behalf. But whatever one chooses to believe spiritually or metaphysically about why democracy matters and what it might do for us, there's also a practical affirmative case for it—democracy offers us tools that should help us govern societies well.

One is *agency.* Democracy is based on the idea that if the governed want to be governed right, they should do it themselves instead of entrusting that responsibility to some other authority. As Dewey argued, it's important that we have the capacity to act on our own instead of waiting for a king or some other entity above us to decide that our problems are real problems. Again, for some democratic theorists, this is a matter of knowledge—of the masses knowing more and judging better than one ruler or a few elites.

A second tool is *dynamism.* A democracy, in theory, should be good at bringing about change. After all, each democratic contest offers a moment where the people can evaluate old ways of doing things and try new ones—judgments are made, previously chosen leaders and policies are evaluated and perhaps switched out. The most innovative and reform-minded authoritarians we might imagine still wouldn't be nearly as dynamic as a political system where competition and evaluation are built-in and no leader is above replacement.

And a third tool, related to the second, is *procedure*—democracies offer us stable, formal ways to make collective decisions and resolve disputes. As rough as politics can get, we're still better off having democratic debates over the issues than clashes in the streets. And while the tensions of democratic competition can obviously spill out into disorder and violence in broken societies or in places where democratic values have been weakened, democracy can help tame conflict when procedures are fair, routine, understood, and accessible. Under those conditions, even those who lose have good reasons to stick with the system—they'll get another shot in the next election or in another forum. For some theorists, this specific dynamic, "institutionalized uncertainty about the future," as some call it, is what democracy is fundamentally about—the knowledge that particular alignments of power will be challenged in fair processes and likely won't last forever.

Agency, dynamism, and procedure—the three pillars of a no-frills, brass-tacks case *for* democracy. But even if we buy that these are useful tools for governance, how, specifically, do democracies accomplish all we've just said they can?

How Democracy Works

Understanding how democracy actually works in practice is more than a matter of looking to governments we now call "democracies" as a guide. They won't be that helpful unless we're sure they really hold to the basic democratic principle we've established—that "the people" should rule, or, put another way, that the governed should govern. As we've seen, even Athenian "democracy" had serious problems in this respect—there, only a fraction of the population had political rights. And that minority governed not only itself but all of Athens, including women, slaves, and metics that couldn't participate in governance on their own behalf.

If we're being honest with ourselves, almost every "democratic" system in world history was like this until fairly recently. The political scientist Carole Pateman, in fact, has argued that democracy didn't arrive on the world stage until 1893, when New Zealand became the first country to give women the vote. Whether we agree rests on what democratic theorists call the "boundary question"—when we say democracy means rule of, by, and for the people who, exactly, are *the people* supposed to be?

That's a subject activists, scholars, and politicians in this country have taken more and more interest in lately; the voting rights of the imprisoned in particular have been a focus of reformers around the country. However broadly we might decide to construe "the people" today, it seems difficult to argue, to Pateman's point, that the broad exclusion of women and minorities from participation in premodern "democracies" was a mere shortcoming of systems that were otherwise democratic. It cannot logically be said that "the people" as a whole rule if only a particular slice of "the people" actually does; "democracy" isn't really democracy at all if it's working for only a minority of a given population. Otherwise, conceptually, we open ourselves up to the notion that a privileged 100,000 (or 1,000, or 100) might "democratically" govern millions with no political rights of their own. Even a dictatorship, in this sense, might be considered a democracy of one.

All told, the broad answer to the boundary question for those committed to democracy is that "the people" who govern has to include *at least* all who are directly governed themselves. But how can we tell when this is the case? In the simplest possible terms, a truly democratic system—where the governed truly govern themselves—will have three characteristics. The first is *equality*—rights within the system should be shared by and apply equally to all. This is what separates rule by "the people" as a whole from rule by "the people privileged or advantaged enough to matter"—constraining the rights of some, for whatever reason, would mean preventing them from fully taking part in democratic processes and their own governance.

For most, the idea that democracies should treat people equally is grounded by the idea that we're all equal in the abstract despite our outward differences. It follows that no person or group can claim the right to rule the rest on the basis of their supposed superiority. In *Democracy and Its Critics*, a classic text in democratic theory, Robert Dahl called this the "Strong Principle of Equality" and noted that early democratic processes, such as the assemblies convened by the Vikings, were used by many homogeneous communities where the equality of all participants would have been taken for granted.

Of course, equality for such groups wasn't the universal human equality most Americans believe in today. As we're taught, our Founders—who did not themselves believe that "all men are created equal" in the sense that we do now—played a significant role in getting us there. But there were many stops on the journey to the American Revolution. During the English Civil War, for instance, the Levellers, a faction of radical populists, demanded democratic reforms to Parliament in language quite similar to the rhetoric the Founders would later adopt. The pamphlet *An Arrow Against All Tyrants*, published by Leveller agitator Richard Overton in 1646, reads in some places like an early draft of the Declaration of Independence:

> For by natural birth all men are equal . . . born to like propriety, liberty and freedom, and as we are delivered of God by the hand of nature into this world, every one with a natural innate freedom and propriety, . . . even so we are to live, every

one equally . . . to enjoy his birthright and privilege, even all whereof God by nature hath made him free . . . ; every man by nature being a king, priest, prophet, in his own natural circuit and compass, whereof no second may partake but by deputation, commission, and free consent from him whose right and freedom it is.

Whatever we believe about whether and why we should be considered equals in the abstract, it's clear that democracies must at least treat people *as though* they're genuinely equals.

The second characteristic of a true democracy is *responsiveness.* Obviously, the governed can only govern if they have a political system that's responsive to them. And what distinguishes democracy from other forms of government is that the people are genuinely authoritative. While a king or a body of elites could take suggestions from the public if they really wanted to, the people actually *command* action themselves in democracies.

How responsive should a good democracy be? What's to be done, for instance, when injustices against some minority win out in the democratic process—if a hateful majority tries to disenfranchise or persecute some segment of the population? These are the kinds of outcomes commentators have in mind when they talk about the benefits of *liberal* democracy—democracies constrained by a framework of liberal rights, such as freedom of speech and religion, and a broad commitment to personal liberty. In the United States, the justices of the Supreme Court have been empowered, at least in theory, to act as our government's referees, responsible for ruling laws and policies out of bounds in keeping with the liberal rights enshrined in our Constitution.

That arrangement is democratically problematic: If the governed are to govern, how can a democratic system tolerate outcomes being overturned by an unelected and basically unchallengeable group of judges? The idea that some things should be taken off the table in any democracy we'd want to live in seems plausible. As much as we might want the people to rule, we might intuitively feel that they shouldn't be able to vote themselves or others into slavery, for instance. But the conceptual problem with "liberal democracy" as a solution for democrats is that *democracy* is the second, lesser half of the phrase—the *liberal* rights are a higher set of concerns, defined and defended by higher, likely flawed authorities who can overrule the democratic process when they see fit.

Importantly, though, many of the liberal rights we value can be derived from democratic principles. As the political scientist Corey Brettschneider has argued, if we want to restrict certain democratic outcomes—discriminatory laws, for instance—on the grounds that they're unjust, we can do so by appealing to the logic underpinning democracy rather than to an implicitly superior set of liberal principles: "Government policies themselves must reflect the status of citizens as the ultimate source of authority," he writes in *Democratic Rights,* "by respecting their interests and by ensuring that state coercion does not treat them in a manner that undermines that status." In other words, policies that fail to treat all the governed as equal governors cannot be understood as democratic.

As a practical matter, there might not be all that much of a difference between overturning democratically enacted policies for their illiberalism and overturning democratically enacted policies because they contradict democratic principles. But conceptually, the distinction does help rebut arguments that democracy is an inherent threat to the rights we value—arguments that might undermine support for democratic reforms and democratic governance more broadly.

In any case, democrats, their critics, and liberals would surely agree that democratic systems are responsive to the people. But how should democratic systems decide what the people want—especially, as is just about always the case, when the people disagree?

That question brings us to the third characteristic of a true democracy—*majoritarianism.* Of all the rules we might appeal to when we have to make a collective choice, the only one consistent with *equality* is majority rule, which is mathematically premised on the equality of every participant. Ask three people, each with an equal say, to cast a vote, and a majority of two votes will always beat one. Things can obviously get much more complicated than that—painfully so both theoretically and in the real world, as we'll explore in more depth later. But majoritarianism is the only principle for collective choices that even stands a chance of working democratically. The other alternatives are incompatible with all the considerations we've laid out so far. Unanimity is, of course, impossible to reach consistently—government would be totally unresponsive if we all had to agree to every decision that might be made. And requiring unanimity both advantages the status quo in any given situation and disproportionately empowers the most stubborn members of any given group. While all votes might *seem* like they count equally, unanimity, in practice, is *rule by the last holdouts.*

The same is true, albeit to a lesser extent, of supermajority requirements—the need to reach the support of more than a simple majority in an election or on a given decision. There can be no government of, by, and for "the people" if say, 55 percent of the people can be overruled by the other 45 percent. That much seems clear. But should the will of that 55 percent majority really be understood as the will of "the people" as a whole? Again, there'll be much more to come on that question.

Democratic Values

To sum up, democracy, whatever else we might say about it, offers us three valuable tools for governance: agency, dynamism, and procedure. And we know that any democratic system will have three basic characteristics: equality, responsiveness, and majoritarianism. But these are just foundations. Atop them, in practice, democracies can be designed and implemented in many different ways—depending, in part, on how a set of values democratic theorists argue intensely about are weighed. The first is *participation.* As we've discussed, Athenian "democracy" differed significantly from the forms of democracy we're most familiar with today. Athenians with political rights had the power not only to decide what their government should do but also to implement policies themselves. Again, for the Athenians, this system wasn't just a particular version of democracy—it *was* democracy. And elections, though they had them, were considered undemocratic. In a passage of his *Politics,* Aristotle offered a view that would have been typical: "The appointment of magistrates by lot is democratic," he wrote, "and the election of them oligarchical."

Today, the selection of juries by lot is the last vestige of this perspective—in America each of us understands that we might be called upon at random to render important and potentially life-altering judgments on our fellow citizens. That's a weighty responsibility, but the Greeks believed ordinary people were capable of doing much more. So too do today's participatory democrats. In the last few decades, some democratic theorists have revived arguments that we can govern ourselves more directly than by voting for or against politicians—through more policy referendums, for instance, or through policymaking bodies made up of self- or randomly selected people.

Whatever their specific recommendations, participatory democrats share a faith that ordinary people can and should participate in politics with fewer middlemen than we now have. "Participatory democratic theory is an argument about democratization," Carole Pateman writes. "That is, the argument is about changes that will make our own social and political life more democratic, that will provide opportunities for individuals to participate in decision-making in their everyday lives as well as in the wider political system. It is about democratizing democracy."

These reforms raise challenging questions for their advocates—beyond the questions that democratic skeptics raise about the public's competence. While it's true, as participatory democrats argue, that education and technology have made it more feasible for the mass public to participate directly in policymaking processes—a level of direct engagement long thought possible only on a small scale—contemporary society is much more complex than ancient Athens, with many more decisions for policy-makers to make. And although direct political participation may be easier for us all now in many ways, direct participation is still *easiest* for the well-off—comfortable retirees who might show up at a local hearing on an affordable housing project, for instance, while those who might benefit the most are busy working or tending to their children. "New and demanding opportunities to participate in democratic processes often come to be dominated by those with the greatest relevant advantages, including education, income, and status—as well as time and attention," the political scientist Kevin J. Elliott warns in *Democracy for Busy People.* "Instead of empowering the disadvantaged, they put more tools for maintaining power in the hands of the already advantaged members of society."

Clearly, the real promise of more direct participation today has to be balanced with a sensitivity to the social and economic inequities that participatory governance might replicate. And as a practical matter, any plausible large-scale democracy will have to rely substantially on delegated authority. That brings us to the second major value—*representation.*

While the Athenians might have scoffed at the idea, we take it for granted today that the people can govern through good representatives. As the theorist Hannah Pitkin argued in her 1967 book *The Concept of Representation,* political representation is based on the idea that the people can be made present in governance by representatives, even though they may be literally absent from the halls of power. "Insofar as this is a matter of substantive acting for others," she wrote, "it requires independent action in the interest of the governed, in a manner at least potentially responsive to them, yet not normally in conflict with their wishes."

The evolution in democratic practice from the Athenian conception of democracy to modern electoral representation was slow, fitful, and complex. As late as the eighteenth century, not long before the American Founding, electoral representation was still being called *antidemocratic* by a faction of Enlightenment figures such as Jean-Jacques Rousseau. "The English people thinks it is free; it is greatly mistaken," he wrote in *The Social Contract*. "It is free only during the election of Members of Parliament; as soon as they are elected, it is enslaved, it is nothing."

Historically speaking, Rousseau wasn't far off the mark in suggesting that modern forms of representation weren't fully democratic in conception. In Britain specifically, Parliament had been born from an administrative reform to the workings of the monarchy. A provision of the Magna Carta, first issued in 1215, stipulated that the English king had to summon nobles to court in order to justly raise taxes—practically speaking, those who showed up to what became Parliament were understood as representatives whose agreement at court contractually bound those in the regions they came from. Parliament's significance and power—and the power of British subjects to actually choose their representatives—grew very gradually from there.

It should be said, though, that representation—in the sense of making the absent present—had been a feature of even Athenian democracy. After all, as the political scientist Hélène Landemore has noted, Athenians with the right to participate in government weren't all participating at once—crucially, the Assembly, as a practical matter, could only seat a few thousand people at a time. "What is striking in this alleged direct-democracy institution is that, despite the fact that it was physically impossible for all to be present, the decisions of whoever showed up and managed to enter the Assembly place were taken to be those of the demos at large," she writes in her 2020 book *Open Democracy*. "In other words, the 6,000–8,000 who actually showed up de facto acted as representatives of the other 22,000–24,000 missing free Athenians, even as the legal and political concepts of 'representation' were not available just yet." This insight is one of the bases for Landemore's support, in the present, for a form of representation she calls "open democracy"—a system of representative lotteries and forums for ordinary people she champions as an alternative to electoral representation.

The scale and complexity of contemporary society makes representation, whatever form it might take, an inevitability for large democracies—this has long been obvious to democratic thinkers. "Since all cannot, in a community exceeding a single small town, participate personally in any but some very minor portions of the public business," John Stuart Mill argued, "it follows that the ideal type of a perfect government must be representative."

But the benefits of representation extend well beyond the bare practicality of representative government at scale. As Robert Dahl recognized, large societies governed by representation can pursue larger collective undertakings and draw upon more resources than societies with smaller democratic units. And while the forums envisioned in "open democracy" have much to recommend them, we shouldn't lose sight of everything that elections offer us, as cynical as we might be about the realities of electoral politics.

As the historian Jan-Werner Müller argues in *Democracy Rules,* elections give society's factions opportunities to present, compare, and debate their ideas. "Elections serve conclusively to process conflict: they generate winners and losers in an unambiguous manner," he writes. "If we assume, again in a hard-nosed-realist sort of way, that politics takes place in the permanent shadow of civil war, then elections are about potential parties to a violent conflict flexing their muscles; they'll settle the question of who's stronger without any shots being fired."

And beyond offering arenas for competition, elections are points of focus where societies can decide what problems they need to address in the first place and dream up solutions. They also, at least conceptually, offer the public more incentives to get engaged and organize around causes than sortition does. While it's impossible to know whether one might be selected in a lottery, there's always an election around the corner. And though it's true that elections as we know them have aristocratic origins, they remain the simplest, easiest, and most broadly accessible form of democratic participation today.

Some theorists, among them Nadia Urbinati, argue these aspects of electoral representation are so essential to democracy's proper functioning that representation should be considered integral to democracy rather than a mere practical alternative to its more direct and participatory forms. "Representation," she's written, "is a form of political creativity whose democratic character is not reducible to voting and the representative lawmaking function. It is synonymous with politics itself as the varied activities that people stage in the public arena when they stand against or for something and in so doing express themselves as political actors and modify or impact the overall political discourse of their society."

Still, representation is fraught with complications. How much independence, for instance, should representatives in a good democracy have from their constituents? For many Americans at the time of the Founding, the right answer was "none"—several early state constitutions said that representatives could be bound by specific instructions from their voters about what to support or oppose. That view of representation didn't win out at the Constitutional Convention and has been sidelined in most debates on the matter since.

Most of us feel intuitively at this point that representatives should have a measure of real freedom—partially because they have to address a wide variety of issues their constituents might not be fully attentive to. "Leadership, emergency action, action on issues of which the people know nothing are among the important realities of representative government," Pitkin wrote. "They are not deviations from true representation, but its very essence. It is often for that very purpose that people choose representatives." Pitkin also suggested that we should evaluate the representativeness of a system by thinking deeply about how well the system as a whole tends to work. "Representative government is not defined by particular actions at a particular moment, but by long term systematic arrangements," she wrote. "By institutions and the way in which they function."

The third and final value that shapes those democratic institutions is *deliberation*. As we've seen, there's more to democracy than the tallying up of votes. In any democratic system, whether representative or more directly participatory, the people are expected to come together in debates and discussions—in their homes and communities, through technologies such as television and the internet, and otherwise—about what should be done before moments of decision. Of course, political discourse is seldom as productive or informative as it should be. For deliberative democrats, who've dominated democratic theory as an academic field over the last few decades, that's a critical problem. And they take the need for better discussions seriously enough that they recommend the creation of special deliberative forums—spaces where participants would have to talk through and justify their political positions to each other as equals. "Not simply a form of politics," Joshua Cohen has written, "democracy, on the deliberative view, is a framework of social and institutional conditions that facilitates free discussion among equal citizens."

Ideally, those discussions would encourage participants to tune out manipulative rhetoric, set their particular interests on a given policy question aside, hear out all reasonable perspectives, and seek solutions to further the common good. When they accomplish this, James Lindley Wilson writes, deliberative institutions and practices respect the basic entitlement of all in a democratic society "to have their judgments receive appropriate consideration by others—that is, to have a fair hearing for their judgments."

But generating the kind of discourse deliberative theorists hope for would be much harder, obviously, than putting people together in big rooms. For one thing, deliberative theorists tend to underrate the extent to which discussions can pull people apart rather than bring them together—especially given how difficult it is to agree on what "the common good" might be when our principles clash. "[Deliberative democrats]," the political scientist Ian Shapiro has written, "sometimes write as if the activity of searching for the common good is itself the common good. Some deliberative democrats do not go this far, but usually they do assume that if people talk for long enough in the right circumstances, they will agree more often, and this is a good thing."

Moreover, as justly critical of political inequality in our status quo as deliberative theorists tend to be, they can be less attentive to how social and economic inequality—along with more basic inequities such as differences in public-speaking ability—might also shape outcomes in the forums they imagine, though, it should be said, more attention has been given to these questions in recent years. One problem even fully ideal deliberative forums wouldn't get around is that deliberation tends to be more productive with smaller groups. While it's easy to see how such forums might supplement other kinds of democratic institutions and practices, it's difficult to imagine them playing truly central roles in large, inclusive, and egalitarian democracies.

All of these values relate to and complement one another in certain ways. But there are also clear trade-offs between them—no democracy can be maximally participatory, representative, and deliberative all at once. This is one of the things that makes democratic theory so diverse, fascinating, and complex as a field—there's no shortage of intelligent opinions on what *democracy* should look like. But those disagreements have also driven some theorists to the idea that democracy, as an ideal, will always elude us—that it's less as a concrete idea we can pin down with any certainty than as a messy jumble of hopes and aspirations that different groups appeal to at different times for different purposes.

Theorists such as Philip Green, for instance, have argued that democracy is best understood not as a set of institutions and practices but, in Green's words, "a series of moments: moments of popular insurgency and direct action, of unmediated politics." Similarly, the progressive activist and documentarian Astra Taylor argued in a recent book that true democracy as a form of governance might be "a promise that can never be wholly fulfilled because its implications and scope keep changing":

Instead, the ideal of self-rule is exactly that, an ideal, a principle that always occupies a distant and retreating horizon, something we must continue to reach toward yet fail to grasp. The promise of democracy is not the one made and betrayed by the powerful; it is a promise that can be kept only by regular people through vigilance, invention, and struggle.

It may be true that the democratic ideal can never be fulfilled; if so, the reaching and struggling she describes will frustrate us constantly. But the ideal can still guide us—and must, if we take the words of our Declaration seriously. We must secure Safety and Happiness for ourselves through governing institutions we have the right to set up and take apart. And though the Founders themselves, as we will see, wound up doubting them, democratic institutions are the best means we've yet devised for pursuing our own interests. If we believe Dewey, democracy also happens to be the best means we've yet devised for our own self-development.

As appealing as democracy might seem in the abstract, of course, our faith in it has a way of faltering when we're disappointed on Election Day. The people make real and grave mistakes; on that basis, many still argue today, even if we reject rule by one or the few, that we shouldn't expect too much from democratic governance either. Are they right?

CHAPTER 2

DEMOCRACY'S CRITICS

Even more so than his victory in 2016, Donald Trump's reelection in November 2024—and, in particular, his victory over Kamala Harris in the popular vote—sent many of the country's political analysts and commentators into fits of despair. "Above all," *The Atlantic*'s David Frum lamented, "we must learn to live in an America where an overwhelming number of our fellow citizens have chosen a president who holds the most fundamental values and traditions of our democracy, our Constitution, even our military in contempt." "If you're accustomed, as I am, to believing that a critical mass of Americans embraces the values of freedom, pluralism, and common sense," the journalist John Harwood agreed, "the choice voters made defies comprehension." "Felon and President-elect Donald Trump did not conceal who he was," *The Washington Post*'s Jennifer Rubin added, "At some point, voters are responsible for their own decisions."

None of these voices, though, judged voters quite as harshly as voters have been judging themselves lately. In 2023, Pew Research found that 76 percent of Americans had little or no trust in the political wisdom of their fellow citizens. And the proportion of Americans who did trust the rest of the country had fallen 15 points in the previous two years. "As recently as 2007," their report read, "Pew Research Center surveys conducted by telephone found majorities of adults reporting at least a good deal of trust in the political wisdom of the American people. The share reporting this had declined precipitously by 2015 and remained low in phone surveys over the course of the next several years." It would surely tickle the cantankerous H. L. Mencken, one of the early twentieth century's most provocative pundits, that a majority of the American public today shares his disdain for their judgment. "Democracy," he once joked, "is the theory that the common people know what they want, and deserve to get it good and hard."

In Plato's *Republic*, Socrates takes the scenic route to the same dismal conclusion. One of the major turning points in the long and winding road to his case for rule by philosopher-kings instead is a tidy parable he offers to Adeimantus, Plato's brother. He tells Adeimantus to imagine a ship—clearly representing Athens—that's being steered by a "big and burly" but partially deaf and nearsighted captain. His sailors have had it.

> The sailors are quarreling over the control of the helm; each thinks he should be steering the vessel, though he has never learnt navigation and cannot point to any teacher under whom he has served his apprenticeship; what is more, they assert that navigation is a thing that cannot be taught at all and are ready to tear in pieces anyone who says it can. Meanwhile they besiege the master himself, begging him urgently to trust them with the help; and sometimes, when others have been more successful in gaining his ear, they kill them or throw them overboard . . .

All is not well on the SS *Metaphor*. Inevitably, "after somehow stupefying the worthy master with strong drink or an opiate," the sailors mutiny and "turn the voyage, as might be expected of such a crew, into a drunken carousal." What's worse, they also turn the ship over to a set of grifters—"anyone clever enough to lend a hand in persuading or forcing the master to set them in command."

"They do not understand," Socrates sighs, "that the genuine navigator can only make himself fit to command a ship by studying the seasons of the year, sky, stars, and winds, and all that belongs to his craft. And they have no idea that, along with the science of navigation, it is possible for him to gain, by instruction or practice, the skill to keep control of the helm whether some of them like it or not."

Socrates's parable reflected Plato's anxieties about Athenian democracy. To Plato's horror, in 399 B.C., Socrates had walked the plank, so to speak, of the Athenian Ship of State himself—after a legendary trial, he was executed for impiety and corrupting the city's youth. In killing Socrates and other follies, Plato believed the Athenians—intoxicated by their collective power, betrayed by their passions, and manipulated by savvy elites—had behaved like the tale's drunken sailors. Obviously, he thought, the Athenian people were too thick-headed to act in the city's best interest or to hand the reins over to those who would.

While democracy has managed to win the war of political ideas since then, Plato's line of criticism has survived. To this day, most of the arguments against democracy are arguments about you, reader. As educated and politically informed as you might think you are—and whoever you voted for in the last election—some who study and comment on politics insist nevertheless that you're probably too ignorant, too distracted, too emotional, and too easily manipulated to make good political decisions. And by their lights, many of your fellow citizens—most of whom don't spend their spare time riffling through books about democracy—are even worse. "There are plenty of people out there who have nothing useful or interesting to say, whose exercise of the franchise is only a great infantile 'I want!' endlessly reiterated every four years or so," the conservative author Kevin Williamson has written. "There is no special virtue in consulting morons and cretins simply because they exist."

"Morons and cretins" aside, the political economist Joseph Schumpeter influentially argued in the 1940s that politics can make even the reasonable among us unreasonable. "The typical citizen drops down to a lower level of mental performance as soon as he enters the political field," he wrote. "He argues and analyzes in a way which he would readily recognize as infantile within the sphere of his real interests. He becomes a primitive again." Democracy, he concluded, is less a way the public actually governs itself than a cover for "the rule of the politician," who, like the grifters on Plato's Ship of State, can manipulate public opinion for their own ends. And beyond political manipulation and propaganda, the journalist Walter Lippmann observed in *Public Opinion*, the sheer pace of modern life, with its new technologies and distractions, can make it difficult for us to get the information we need to make good decisions, leaving us grasping for stereotypes and easy answers instead. "Every man whose business it is to think knows that he must for part of the day create about himself a pool of silence," he wrote. "But in that helter-skelter which we flatter by the name of civilization, the citizen performs the perilous business of government under the worst possible conditions." In 1922, when those words were published, Lippmann had innovations like the radio in mind. One can only imagine what he would have made of smartphones and the internet.

Many serious analysts today aren't much more optimistic about politics than Schumpeter or Lippmann were. In 2014, the liberal commentator Ezra Klein launched *Vox*—a website dedicated, in part, to explaining the news to the politically engaged—with an essay on how "politics makes us stupid." "Washington," he wrote, "is a bitter war between two well-funded, sharply-defined tribes that have their own machines for generating evidence and their own enforcers of orthodoxy."

Political tribalism was also a major theme of *Democracy for Realists*, a 2016 book by the political scientists Christopher Achen and Larry Bartels arguing that deep divisions and irrationality might be features of democracy rather than bugs. Released in the thick of Donald Trump's rise to power, it was acclaimed by publications across the ideological spectrum, from *The New York Review of Books* on the left to *National Review* on the right. By the end of 2018, Klein's *Vox* alone had run at least a dozen articles referencing the book. CNN's Fareed Zakaria endorsed it. Jason Furman, chair of President Obama's Council of Economic Advisers, called it "essential reading." "It is impossible," the Brookings Institution's Thomas Mann added, "to overstate the significance of this magnum opus on democracy and democratic theory. Achen and Bartels lay waste to the folk theory of democracy through dazzling logic and rigorous empirical analysis."

The Folk Theory of Democracy

As Achen and Bartels describe it, that "folk theory of democracy" goes like this:

> In the conventional view, democracy begins with the voters. Ordinary people have preferences about what their government should do. They choose leaders who will do those things, or they enact their preferences directly in referendums. In either case, what the majority wants becomes government policy—a highly attractive prospect in light of most human experience with governments. Democracy makes the people the rulers, and legitimacy derives from their consent.

Political scientists and other researchers have been building evidence against the folk theory for many years. To begin with, many contend, most of "the people" in democratic societies aren't politically engaged enough to have real preferences. And those who do choose to vote are often woefully uninformed. "The political ignorance of the American voter," Bartels has said, "is one of the best-documented features of contemporary politics."

As he suggests, surveys tell us that some Americans can't identify their own representatives or answer basic questions about the Constitution and the structure of our government. What's more, voters can have a hard time accurately gauging what's happening in the world around them. Our ideas about how bad crime is in our neighborhoods Achen and Bartels write, for example, are more influenced by the tone of local news coverage than actual crime rates:

Thus, Gallup polls typically find majorities of respondents saying that crime is increasing, and pluralities saying that crime in their area is increasing, even though recent actual "rates of violent crime as well as property crime have generally leveled off at extremely low numbers." Misperceptions of this sort are probably common in domains where voters have very limited personal experience, even (and perhaps especially) when, as in the case of crime, they care a lot about the true state of the world.

Clearly, many voters who try to inform themselves wind up getting bad or slanted information. And many Americans aren't even trying. "Changes in the structure of the mass media have allowed people with an uncommon taste for public affairs to find an unprecedented quantity and variety of political news," write Achen and Bartels, "but they have also allowed people with more typical tastes to abandon traditional newspapers and television news for round-the-clock sports, pet tricks, or pornography, producing an increase in the variance of political-information levels but no change in the average level of political information."

The problem with democracy as we know it, they contend, isn't that voters are stupid. It's that they're too distracted to get good information and make good choices. In fact, some have argued voter ignorance might be rational given all the other demands on voters' time and attention. "If your only reason to follow politics is to be a better voter, that turns out not to be much of a reason at all," writes law professor Ilya Somin. "That is because there is very little chance that your vote will actually make a difference to the outcome of an election (about 1 in 60 million in a presidential race, for example). For most of us, it is rational to devote very little time to learning about politics, and instead focus on other activities that are more interesting or more likely to be useful." "For most, leisure time is at a premium," Achen and Bartels agree. "Sorting out which presidential candidate has the right foreign policy toward Asia is not a high priority for them. Without shirking more immediate and more important obligations, people cannot engage in much well-informed, thoughtful political deliberation, nor should they."

In his 2016 book *Against Democracy,* the philosopher Jason Brennan put all this more bluntly: "We should hope for even less participation, not more," he wrote. "Ideally, politics would occupy only a small portion of the average person's attention. Ideally, most people would fill their days with painting, poetry, music, architecture, statuary, tapestry, and porcelain, or perhaps football, NASCAR, tractor pulls, celebrity gossip, and trips to Applebee's. Most people, ideally, would not worry about politics at all."

That would be ideal because Brennan shares Klein and Schumpeter's concern that those who *do* worry about politics have been corrupted by it. Partisanship, he argues, has made us less willing and able to think for ourselves. In one experiment summarized in his book, researchers found that Republicans and Democrats were more likely to explain away contradictions from members of their own parties than those from their opponents. And in another where subjects were asked to analyze data on guns and crime, liberals and conservatives tended to interpret the results in ways that matched their preexisting beliefs. Remarkably, their interpretations were *more* biased the better at math they were.

Voters come away from all this looking a lot like sheep. And, as Achen and Bartels write, political campaigns, which "consist in large part of reminding voters of their partisan identities," are designed to move voters like herds, " 'mobilizing' them to support their group at the polls":

> They do not know the details of even salient policy debates, they do not have a firm understanding of what the political parties stand for, and they often vote for parties whose long-standing issue positions are at odds with their own. Mostly, they identify with ethnic, racial, occupational, religious, or

other sorts of groups, and often—whether through group ties or hereditary loyalties—with a political party. Even the more attentive citizens mostly adopt the policy positions of the parties as their own: they are mirrors of the parties, not masters. For most citizens most of the time, party and group loyalties are the primary drivers of vote choices. Thus, the folk theory of democracy fails. . . . The folk theory is like the ether theory of electromagnetic and gravitational forces: it is based on 19th-century intellectual foundations, and the empirical evidence has passed it by.

Brennan, going further than Achen and Bartels, argues that democracy as we know it is actually a moral injustice. "Most of my fellow citizens are incompetent, ignorant, irrational, and morally unreasonable about politics," he writes. "Despite that, they hold political power over me. These people can staff offices of great power and wield the coercive authority of the state against me. They can force me to do things I do not wish to do or have no good reason to do. They wield their power in ways that they cannot justify, and impose policies on me that they would not support if they were informed or processed political information in a rational way."

The case for democracy and granting all citizens the right to vote, Brennan concludes, rests solely on the idea that "we cannot produce a better-performing system." He spends much of *Against Democracy* arguing that we can.

What Voters Know

Is he right? Let's contend, first off, with the problem of voter ignorance. While many voters would agree themselves that they don't know as much as they should, pessimists like Brennan tend to read the data we have on this selectively. Take this passage, for instance, where he argues that voters who might know general facts about politics still don't have enough specific information to make good political choices:

> So, for instance, even though in AD 2000, most Americans knew that the federal deficit had decreased under Bill Clinton (in fact, there was a surplus), most were not aware how much it had decreased. Or while most Americans knew in 2000 that Gore was more liberal than Bush, they did not know how much more liberal he was. . . . Or even though many Americans in 1992 knew that unemployment had risen under George H. W. Bush, the majority of Americans were unable to estimate the unemployment rate within 5 percentage points of the actual figure. When asked to guess what the unemployment rate was, the majority of voters guessed it was twice as high as the actual rate.

Now, as useful as it might have been for voters to know the actual unemployment rate or exactly how much the deficit had gone down, that data is difficult to square with the idea that voters are *hopelessly* uninformed—if we believe Brennan's figures, most voters, as distracted and disengaged as they might be, are capable of understanding whether deficits have increased or decreased, whether unemployment has risen or fallen, and the rough ideological positions of presidential candidates. All of this is important, policy-relevant information. But for Brennan, it's not enough. What would be? How closely, for instance, *should* a well-informed voter estimate the unemployment rate?

Brennan buries this question under a barrage of embarrassing statistics. But the kinds of surveys he cites can be sketchy and inconsistent. Brennan writes, for instance, based on a single 2011 poll, that "seventy-three percent of Americans do not understand what the Cold War was about." In a nationally representative 2019 poll commissioned by the American Council of Trustees and Alumni (ACTA), 76 percent of respondents correctly said that the Cold War was a fight against communism. He writes, based on a poll taken ten years before *Against Democracy*'s publication, that "most Americans don't know what the three branches of government are." In 2021, the Annenberg Public Policy Center found that 56 percent of Americans could name all three. He writes that "less than 30 percent of Americans can name two or more of the rights listed in the First Amendment of the Bill of Rights." In 2019, the Freedom Forum Institute found that 40 percent could. "Voters generally know who the current president is," Brennan claims, "but they don't know much more beyond that." Yet in ACTA's 2019 poll, 74 percent of respondents correctly identified Nancy Pelosi as the Speaker of the House. And in its 2022 Survey of Civic Literacy, the American Bar Association (ABA) found that 57 percent of Americans could correctly identify John Roberts as the Chief Justice of the Supreme Court. The rest of the ABA survey, based on the naturalization exam given to those applying for American citizenship, also found that large majorities of Americans understood the separation of powers among the three branches of government (64 percent), the duties of the Supreme Court (81 percent), the president's role as commander in chief of the military (87 percent), and the Speaker of the House's place in presidential succession (70 percent).

The point here isn't that Brennan's figures are clearly wrong. It's that these surveys can be cherry-picked one way or another to make voters look better or worse. Brennan also points out, fairly, that multiple-choice surveys allow respondents to guess at the right answers, meaning positive figures might be overestimated to a certain extent. Nevertheless, the idea, in his words, that "most people know nothing, and many people know less than nothing" about politics and their government is pure hyperbole.

Even interpreting the surveys generously, though, their results are dispiriting—only 56 percent of Americans knowing all three branches of government, if we prefer that figure, still isn't great. But one solution to the problem of underinformed voters might be to better inform them. Achen and Bartels write themselves that political education has been shown to change minds and votes, while Brennan says social and cultural incentives encourage some voters to become highly informed. These amount to concessions that we could probably build a better voting public if we tried. Data from other countries also gives us reason for optimism—lest we forget, there *are* other voters in the world. Researchers have found, for instance, that European voters are substantially better informed than their American peers—a finding that's been attributed to Europe's public media outlets and lower levels of income inequality, which have been linked to smaller gaps in political knowledge between voters at different levels of education.

Ignorance, it seems, is less an insurmountable challenge for democracy than a problem policy can help solve. In a paper responding to critics of their book, Achen and Bartels briefly acknowledge this point before hand-waving it away. "While Americans' ignorance of basic political facts is symptomatic of the unrealism of the folk theory, it is not the heart of the problem in our view," they write. "Thus, comparisons of Americans' political-knowledge quiz scores with those from other countries with different media systems does not seem to us to shed much light on the extent to which citizens in those countries are likely to apprehend and act upon their 'real' political interests." Even if voters elsewhere are more knowledgeable, in other words, that doesn't necessarily mean that they're any more rational or any less driven by group dynamics than Americans are.

Before we turn to rationality and groups, we should consider another important set of counterarguments on the question of political knowledge. As said in the last chapter, many democratic theorists believe democracy has what are often called "epistemic" benefits—as uninformed or unwise as individual people might be, they contend, groups are more likely to know what's best for them than a single ruler or an elite few. Again, this is partially because elites are cut off from ordinary life. But there's also another reason—large groups might be better at making decisions than smaller ones or individuals. This argument is about as ancient as democracy itself. As Hélène Landemore notes in *Demo-*

cratic Reason, Aristotle makes it in his *Politics,* as he explains the virtues of democratic assemblies:

> Now any member of the assembly, taken separately, is certainly inferior to the wise man. But the state is made up of many individuals. And as a feast to which all the guests contribute is better than a banquet furnished by a single man, so a multitude is a better judge of many things than any individual.

Even Machiavelli—author of *The Prince,* and widely misunderstood today as a simple authoritarian—wrote rhapsodically about the wisdom of crowds, arguing in his *Discourses on Livy* that ordinary people were generally "more prudent, more stable, and of better judgment than a prince."

> Not without cause may the voice of a people be likened to that of God; for one sees a universal opinion produce marvelous effects in its forecasts, so that it appears to foresee its ill and its good by a hidden virtue. As to judging things, if a people hears two orators who incline to different sides, when they are of equal virtue, very few times does one see it not take up the better opinion, and not persuaded of the truth that it hears. If it errs in mighty things or those that appear useful . . . often a prince errs too in his own passions, which are many more than those of peoples.

While virtually no one today shares Machiavelli's remarkable faith in the public's judgment, most democratic theorists think there's something to his argument about collective decision-making. Democratic governance does, all told, seem to work better than we might expect given the ignorance and poor judgment we might see in individual voters. But why?

Nicolas de Condorcet, an influential mathematician and philosopher, and a leading figure of the French Revolution, offered one early theory in 1785. Mathematically, he discovered, a group that needs to choose between two options, one correct and one incorrect, is more likely to choose the right option by majority vote the larger the group is—as long as each individual voter has a better than 50/50 chance of making the right choice on their own. In fact, if each voter in a group of, say, ten thousand has just a 51 percent chance of choosing correctly, the group as a whole is nearly 100 percent certain to reach the right answer. Importantly, though, that bit of math doesn't work out when there are more than two options or if voters—due to bias or sharing bad information, perhaps—aren't actually more likely than a coin flip to choose correctly.

Theorists since have sought other explanations. We know, for instance, that when you ask a large group of people how many beans are in a jar, the average of their guesses tends to be pretty close to the right answer, even if some individual guesses are way off. Some think democratic judgments might work in roughly the same way. There's also the concept of *cognitive diversity*—the idea that large groups include people who think about problems in different ways, and are more likely to arrive at good solutions than smaller groups of people who think in similar ways.

In *Democratic Reason*, Landemore makes a case for this view with an allusion to the film *Twelve Angry Men*—a story about a jury that, one dissenter aside, is initially ready to convict a young man of murder. In the end, the case against him falls apart and he's acquitted thanks to the diversity of perspectives the jurors begin offering.

> Asking the other jurors to "talk it out" before making up their mind, juror number 8 takes the group on a long deliberative journey, which ultimately ends in unanimous acquittal. Whereas "Twelve Angry Men" has largely been interpreted as a movie about the importance of courageous, lone dissenters braving mistaken majorities, I take it to illustrate, rather, the phenomenon of collective intelligence emerging from inclusive deliberation. The brave dissenting juror, juror number 8, would not have been able to accomplish much left to his

own devices. In particular he would have been unable to substantiate his initial hunch and demonstrate that the sentence was beyond reasonable doubt. Only by harnessing the intelligence and cognitive diversity of the other members, often against their own passions and prejudice, does the group ultimately reach the truth.

These ideas from theorists are useful, but debates about the things "the people" know and how they might come to know them tend to miss something fundamental about the nature and purpose of politics. As important as facts and figures are, we make political decisions based on our principles and interests. There are important differences between trying to determine whether an accused murderer is guilty and trying to determine whether murderers should be executed as a matter of policy. Answering the latter question is a bit more complicated than trying to figure out how many beans are in a jar. And while relevant statistics and research might ground our intuitions on the ethics of the death penalty, it's entirely possible to develop a reasoned stance on it without knowing, say, how many people we put to death in a given year.

The truth is that as strongly as we might feel about the death penalty, or public education, or health care, or the purpose of government broadly speaking, there aren't, again, any ethically neutral, objectively correct answers waiting to be looked up or collectively discovered to many, if not most, of the issues we turn to politics to resolve. Instead, we resolve them largely by balancing and wrestling with principles even the least informed among us may hold.

★ ★ ★

Beyond our principles, many democratic theorists and political scientists argue that voters often *do* know a good amount about the material impact politics and policy have on their lives. "Are you better off than you were four years ago?" the question Ronald Reagan famously posed to voters in a 1980 debate with Jimmy

Carter, was an attempt to take advantage of what scholars call "retrospective voting"—the electorate's theorized habit of rewarding or punishing politicians based on their performance in office.

Achen and Bartels spend much of *Democracy for Realists* rebutting conventional wisdom on this. Though economic conditions matter, their research suggests voters tend to focus only on the state of the economy around Election Day and punish their leaders for bad times whether or not their policies were responsible for them.

> While we agree that voters' assessments of economic conditions play a substantial role in determining election outcomes, we part company with those who see retrospective voting as a mechanism for ensuring effective political accountability. The evidence presented in this chapter casts considerable doubt on the view that citizens can reliably form and act upon sensible retrospective judgments at election time. While they vote on the basis of how they feel at the moment, they forget or ignore how they have felt over the course of the incumbents' term in office.

While this seems true to the way elections often play out, the fact that voters do punish leaders for bad economic conditions come Election Day is, of course, an incentive for leaders to deliver real economic gains to them by campaign time. But Achen and Bartels also argue that voters often mete out punishment randomly or irrationally. And it's here that their critique of the average voter fully jumps the shark.

In July 1916, four people were killed in a series of shark attacks off the coast of New Jersey, creating a panic that grabbed the country's attention and severely damaged local tourism. Based on an analysis of local results in that year's election, Achen and Bartels argue that the attacks hurt President Wilson's reelection campaign in the area, despite "the fact that no government has any influence over sharks":

Every indication in the New Jersey election returns is that the horrifying shark attacks during the summer of 1916 reduced Wilson's vote in the beach communities by about ten percentage points. Shark attacks are random events in the purest sense of the term, and they have no governmental solution. If bathers insist on swimming in the ocean, governments then and now cannot save them, as subsequent attacks in New Jersey in 1960 and regular encounters in Florida, California, South Africa, and Australia demonstrate. Nor could the aftermath of the 1916 attacks be repaired by governmental action.

From the attacks and a similar analysis of the electoral impact of natural disasters, Achen and Bartels conclude that voters irrationally punish incumbents "with considerable regularity."

These findings on the 1916 shark attacks are among the most famous and influential in contemporary political science—by 2018, the 2002 paper they were originally presented in had been cited over four hundred times. But the story the paper tells should seem a little strange even to untrained readers. Even though Wilson obviously couldn't have prevented the attacks themselves, helping the local businesses hurt by the panic was another matter. And as Achen and Bartels admit, "letters poured into congressional offices from the affected communities demanding federal action" that never arrived. Importantly, Wilson did, in fact, convene a White House cabinet meeting to discuss a response to the attacks. If voters were delusional for judging the administration and thinking Wilson might have been able to do *something* . . . well, so was Wilson.

But, as it happens, it's unlikely that voters went to the polls with sharks on the brain at all. After correcting an important error Achen and Bartels had made in excluding one town from their data, comparing 1916 to a more representative set of election years, and trying to replicate the original paper's results with different sets of important variables, a pair of researchers found in 2018 that the attacks probably hadn't impacted the election much at all. "At best, the evidence is inconclusive, and any such effect, if genuine, is substantively small," the University of Chicago's Anthony Fowler and Stanford's Andrew B. Hall wrote. "The evidence on shark attacks and presidential voting is not strong enough to warrant dismay toward voters or the democratic process."

Groups and Polarization

Where does all we've said so far leave us? While voters are far from perfect, they're not quite as hopeless as cynics insist—they can roughly evaluate the ideological positions of candidates, the economic conditions at election time, and other policy-relevant information. While there's a lot they don't know, public knowledge might be improved by education, a better public media infrastructure, and social and cultural incentives. Moreover, many of the questions we face in politics are less simple questions of knowledge than matters of principle—each of us has values that we might bring to bear on our votes and political debates. And an electorate is more than the sum of its parts even as far as knowledge is concerned—we have good reasons to believe groups can employ a kind of collective intelligence to solve problems.

Still, we've also been warned that groups can undermine democracy—that, as partisans, voters substitute the judgments of their peers for their own. "For most people," Achen and Bartels write, "partisanship is not a carrier of ideology but a reflection of judgments about where 'people like me' belong":

> They do not always get that right, but they have much more success than they would constructing their political loyalties on the basis of ideology and policy convictions. Then, often enough, they let their party tell them what to think about the issues of the day. As a result, self-described liberals mostly wind up with the Democrats and conservatives with the Republicans. But the usual interpretation of that relationship supplied by the folk theory of democracy is quite misleading.

If election outcomes have policy content, it comes primarily not from voters, but from the relationships between parties and social groups.

Paraphrasing Achen and Bartels, Jason Brennan adds that those relationships have been formed mostly at random:

> Certain groups become attached to certain parties, but not because they believe in what those parties do or because those parties tend best to serve their interests and goals. Various identities or demographic groups become attached to particular political parties for largely *accidental* historical events or circumstances that have little to do with voters' underlying values or interests.

All of this is directly related to the widespread alarm, in recent years, over the polarization of the American electorate—our partisan identities have become powerfully and perhaps dangerously bound up with our personal identities. "Today the parties are sharply split across racial, religious, geographic, cultural, and psychological lines," Ezra Klein writes in his 2020 book *Why We're Polarized*. "There are many, many powerful identities lurking in that list, and they are fusing together, stacking atop one another, so a conflict or threat that activates one activates all." The result, we're told, is a political culture based on raw feelings and instinct—where voters inherit their political views from parties they feel socially attached to.

But there's a wrinkle or two to that story. There are more self-described independents than Democrats or Republicans in the American electorate today; as pundits have bemoaned the supposedly all-consuming tide of partisanship, fewer Americans have been affiliating themselves with the two parties. Importantly, most of those independents aren't down-the-middle moderates or mixed-up voters without a natural political home. More than 80 percent of them leaned toward either the Democratic or Republican party in 2019, according to the Pew Research Center.

And other research has shown that "independent" leaners vote for the party they prefer almost as reliably as self-described partisans. The independents just don't want to feel like they're rooting for a particular side. It's hard to account for their voting consistency if our political views really come from wanting to belong to a team.

Moreover, as ideologically polarized as the parties have become, there are still meaningful ideological differences not only within them—there are conservative Democrats and liberal Republicans, both of whom support their parties less consistently than their peers—but also within demographic groups. While it may not be true that voters arrive at their political beliefs and policy preferences as individuals thinking wholly on their own, it's also not true that voters just take marching orders from the parties and their leaders all the time. Instead, the relationships among the views we hold, the groups we belong to, and the parties and candidates we support are complex; influence runs in multiple directions. And there's nothing inherently problematic for democracy about voters taking some cues from politicians. At one point, *Democracy for Realists* highlights research on the 2000 election suggesting that many voters without strong opinions on privatizing Social Security adopted the views of the candidate they preferred as the race went on. It's not unreasonable, though, to suppose that a candidate you agree with on a lot of issues might reflect your principles on those you know less about.

Brennan tries to undermine this point by arguing that most issues in politics don't have much to do with each other. "If you want to raise the minimum wage, you probably believe global warming is a major threat, and that government needs to intervene to stop it," he writes as an example. "If you oppose raising the minimum wage, you probably believe global warming isn't real, isn't produced by humans, or isn't a big deal, and that government should do little or nothing about it. One political party and its adherents have picked one set of beliefs about these issues, while the other political party and its adherents have picked the opposite beliefs. There's rationally no reason why this should be so, since these beliefs are independent."

But they're not, actually. Conservatives suspicious of calls for government action can logically oppose both federally mandated wage increases and climate regulations for the same reasons; liberals more comfortable with government action can logically support both. And while it's true, as Brennan, Achen, and Bartels suggest, that groups influence our positions, the idea, in Brennan's words, that the resulting positions "have little to do with voters' underlying values or interests" seems highly questionable.

Democracy for Realists, for instance, features an important analysis of how Southern white voters gradually shifted toward the Republican Party. While conventional wisdom holds that those voters left the Democratic Party in opposition to civil rights, Achen and Bartels argue instead, based on survey data, that "these shifts in party identification were only weakly related to white southerners' views about specific policy issues."

As evidence, they point out that the shift among Southern whites began *before* Democratic leaders began pushing civil rights in earnest and also note that the shift happened slowly enough that people who opposed ending segregation "were still more likely to think of themselves as Democrats than as Republicans" as late as the 1980s. What's more, white Southern supporters of ending segregation *also* left the Democratic Party in significant numbers. From these observations, Achen and Bartels conclude the partisan shift was motivated not by policy, but by "white southern identity, a powerful force in southern culture at least since the antebellum period." "For most white southerners," they write, "policy preferences were probably of secondary importance."

But what does "white southern identity" really mean? They don't say. Is it really possible that "white southern identity," whatever it is, has nothing much to do with policy? Their case for that position is based on how Southerners responded to *a single set* of policy issues. States' rights, guns, education issues beyond desegregation, women's rights—none of the other issues that shaped Southern politics and the region's relationship to the Democratic Party in the second half of the twentieth century, often deeply connected to racial issues, were part of Achen and Bartels's analysis. And the story *Democracy for Realists* tells about civil rights specifically doesn't add up.

The most the book has to say about the content of "white southern identity" is that it was influenced by new black voters joining the Democratic Party, which encouraged southern whites, whether they opposed civil rights or not, to "think of the Republican Party first as a potential home and then as their natural home." But that backlash can be understood, obviously, as a response *to policy change:* the expansion of voting rights that brought more black voters into politics and the Democratic Party, which new black voters themselves chose *for policy reasons,* chief among them the Democratic Party's deepening support for civil rights. Additionally, while both proponents and opponents of civil rights left the Democratic Party in the South, other research suggests that white Southerners who supported or had no opinions on ending segregation left at only half the rate of those who opposed it.

The partisan shift in the American South wasn't just some "accident" of history brought about by random and arbitrary forces. It's a notable historical example of what we see groups doing in politics all the time: responding to changes in public policy based on their principles and interests. And the idea that voters can't have any real principles or understand their interests unless parties and leaders tell them what to think doesn't make any sense. Notably, Achen and Bartels don't even defend that argument consistently. "When coalitions shift," they write at one point, "politicians scramble to adjust their policy positions accordingly." But if groups have no real and deeply held views of their own, why would politicians shift in response to new coalitions of them?

Recent events have underscored the limitations of their analysis. The Democratic Party's loss of white working-class voters to the GOP—in the South and elsewhere—over the course of the last forty to fifty years helped send Donald Trump to the White House in 2016 and 2024. The afterword to the paperback edition of *Democracy for Realists* addresses the 2016 election directly; it contains more than three thousand words of analysis on the American political situation and why Trump won. The word *immigration* is not one of them. Instead, readers are told that voters demonstrated a "relative lack of interest in the candidates' policy proposals." Trump won, argue Achen and Bartels, because noncollege white voters saw him as "a strong leader, a man who spoke his mind without respect for elitist proprieties" and also because Trump showed them that he saw life "in terms of group antagonisms." Obviously, though, Trump would have had a much harder time connecting with them, and convincing them he cared about "group antagonisms," if he'd run on giving undocumented immigrants a path to citizenship and making it easier for foreigners to enter the United States. Instead, Trump made policy promises, on immigration and other issues, that made it clear he shared the "antagonisms" of the voters he wanted to win over. This worked because voters, for better and sometimes for worse, do have actual views on policy.

As you may have noticed by now, Achen and Bartels's account of how democracy works is marred by glaring contradictions. We're told that voters know next to nothing about politics and lack real policy views. Instead, things like very recent economic conditions "play a substantial role in determining election outcomes." "It is possible to account for recent presidential election outcomes with a fair degree of precision," they write at one point, "solely on the basis of how long the incumbent party had been in power and how much real income growth voters experienced in the six months leading up to Election Day." But we're also told that totally random and irrelevant events, like the odd wave of shark attacks, lead voters to punish incumbents "with considerable regularity."

Then it turns out that the economy and sharks might not matter so much after all. "Most of the time," Achen and Bartels write,

"voting behavior merely reaffirms voters' partisan and group identities." But by the end of *Democracy for Realists,* even the premise
that voters don't really follow the issues or want specific policies
has been fatally undermined—and not just by the book's confused
analysis of the South's partisan shift. In a chapter examining the
failures, in their view, of referendums and direct democracy initiatives, Achen and Bartels take voters to task for approving tax cuts
for themselves and, during the Progressive Era, taking more interest in liquor laws than in government reforms. "Clearly," they
write, "voters could be moved to vote on issues they viewed as
important in their day-to-day lives."

The truth is that voters can be moved by all kinds of factors—
not just by identity, economic conditions, and random events,
but by what they hear and personally know about the issues, as
well as the principles they think their communities and society
should be governed by. None of these factors are fully determina-
tive on their own; the mind of the average voter is a tangle of
competing ideas, instincts, and influences. Making sound decisions in the thick of all that is obviously difficult. But we've no
reason to believe it's as hopeless as democracy's critics insist.

Epistocracy, an Alternative

Jason Brennan, nonetheless, thinks we'd probably be better off
under an *epistocracy*—a system of rule not by the people as a
whole but by the most knowledgeable. "Democracy, as we practice it, is unjust," he writes. "We expose innocent people to high
degrees of risk because we put their fate in the hands of ignorant,
misinformed, irrational, biased, and sometimes immoral decision
makers. Epistocracy might be able to fix this problem. If epistocracy works better, we should go with epistocracy instead."

As we've seen already, doubts about the public's capacity to
govern wisely are very old—although Aristotle and Machiavelli
have shown us that confidence in the public *also* has a long history. In *Considerations on Representative Government,* pub-

lished in 1861, John Stuart Mill positions himself somewhere between the pessimists and the optimists on the public's reason. The ideal form of government, he writes, is a representative government elected by a mass electorate that should include even women—a radically democratic suggestion for the time. But crucially, he adds, the ideal government would also grant the educated more votes to reduce the influence of the ignorant:

> I do not look upon equal voting as among the things which are good in themselves, provided they can be guarded against inconveniences. I look upon it as only relatively good; less objectionable than inequality of privilege grounded on irrelevant or adventitious circumstances, but in principle wrong, because recognizing a wrong standard, and exercising a bad influence on the voter's mind. It is not useful, but hurtful, that the constitution of the country should declare ignorance to be entitled to as much political power as knowledge.

Conservatives today routinely defend testing voters on the same grounds. The pundit Ben Shapiro believes we should consider demanding a "minimum level of knowledge about the Declaration of Independence and the Constitution" from voters; Matt Walsh would "require that all voters take and pass a 5th grade civics exam." While conceding that such tests would be "a logistical nightmare," National Review's Jonah Goldberg has written that "expecting a certain minimal degree of education before letting citizens vote" makes sense in theory and that "literacy tests are the bare minimum." David Harsanyi, far more optimistic about the logistics of taking away the vote, thinks "we may be able to mitigate the recklessness of the electorate" by "weeding out millions of irresponsible voters who can't be bothered to learn the rudimentary workings of the Constitution."

Brennan is on board with this. "If the argument for regulating air pollution is sound, why not regulate votes as well?" he asks. "Why does the public goods argument justify regulating air pollution, but doesn't justify regulating voting pollution? Why is it legitimate to regulate pollution to protect us from ourselves, yet not legitimate to regulate voting to protect us from ourselves?"

One reason, of course, is that reducing "voting pollution" has historically meant discriminating against certain groups. The tests given to disenfranchise African Americans in the American South under Jim Crow, for instance, are an especially bad look for epistocracy and Brennan knows it. "These tests were administered in bad faith," he writes defensively in *Against Democracy.* "The fact that governments used to hide their racism beneath an epistocratic disguise does not show us that epistocratic exams are inherently objectionable." "It remains open," he argues elsewhere, "that there could be good grounds for restricting or reducing some citizens' political power. Perhaps some citizens are incompetent participants who impose too much risk on others when they participate. Perhaps some of us have a right to be protected from their incompetence."

As it happens, Brennan is especially interested in being protected from the "incompetence" of minorities, women, and the poor. Research on political knowledge, he writes, suggests that "whites on average know more than blacks, people in the Northeast know more than people in the South, men know more than women, middle-aged people know more than the young or old, and high-income people know more than the poor." "Most poor black women, as of right now at least," he continues, "would fail even a mild voter qualification exam."

Brennan goes on to say that these disparities reflect not the innate capacities of these groups, but societal inequities—and that the impact of those inequities would disempower minorities and the marginalized in an epistocracy even if tests and other methods of excluding the ignorant were designed fairly:

If the United States were to start using a voter qualification exam right now, such as an exam that I got to design, I'd expect that the people who pass the exam would be disproportionately white, upper-middle- to upper-class, educated employed males. The problem here isn't that I'm racist, sexist or classist. My moral credentials are of course impeccable, and on implicit bias tests, I score many standard deviations lower than the average person. Instead, the problem would be that there are underlying injustices and social problems that tend to make it so that some groups are more likely to be knowledgeable than others.

The arguments made earlier against the intractability of voter ignorance won't be repeated here. As far as social inequities specifically are concerned, one way to address their impact on voters would be to reduce or eliminate them. Brennan doesn't say much about this possibility, but he does suggest democracy can't make it happen—after all, the disadvantaged, as ignorant as they are, probably don't know how to improve their condition. "These voters might know what kinds of outcomes would serve their interests," he writes, "but unless they have tremendous social scientific knowledge, they are unlikely to know how to vote for politicians or policies that will produce these favored outcomes." They might be better off, he muses, trusting the educated members of society to act on their behalf. Given a large enough pool of qualified voters, "the evidence indicates they will likely vote sociotropically"—that is, for the common good. And that's especially fortunate for the disadvantaged, given that political participation makes us worse people: "Most common forms of political engagement," he writes in an earlier chapter, "are more likely to corrupt and stultify than to ennoble and educate people."

One habit of commentators who write this kind of swill is treating epistocracy as a hypothetical—a system that has never existed and must be imagined. But while excluding women and African Americans from the vote was rooted in prejudice, America before their enfranchisement really can be understood as a crude epistocratic state—obviously, groups banned from participating in politics would have known less about politics and policy than those with full political rights.

So what should we make of the historical record? Did politically educated and informed white men govern in the best interests of all who weren't politically educated and informed? If not, why not? And what should we make of all that's happened since we reached universal suffrage? Has it failed to improve conditions for women and African Americans? Has it made them more corrupt and ignoble people than they were before they gained the vote? And was America damaged in any measurable way—made less free, less strong, or less prosperous—when they, in their initial ignorance, entered the electorate?

Epistocrats and conservatives don't offer us answers to these questions. Instead we're asked to take it for granted that those who know more know better, and that they would vote accordingly, for the benefit of all, if they were the only ones with political rights. This is despite the fact, as research tells us, that the well-informed can often be *more* politically polarized in their beliefs and *as or more susceptible* to conspiracy theories than the average voter. One thing education might give voters, it turns out, is the ability to reconcile new and unsettling information with the positions they already hold and want to keep.

It hopefully goes without saying that experts and the well-informed or -educated can also just get things wrong. For one vast and influential study of expert competence conducted over the course of sixteen years, psychologist Philip Tetlock asked about three hundred experts on politics and economics to predict—given three potential outcomes—whether certain events, such as an American war in the Persian Gulf or a peaceable end to South African apartheid, would happen. After collecting more than eighty-two thousand such forecasts, Tetlock found that the experts were no better at making predictions than college undergraduates—and were, in fact, worse at making predictions than they might have been had they guessed at random. "Human beings who spend their lives studying the state of the world," *The New Yorker*'s Louis Menand wrote in a 2005 review summing up Tetlock's work, "are poorer forecasters than dart-throwing monkeys, who would have distributed their picks evenly over the three choices." Just a few years after Tetlock's study concluded, his findings were underscored by a global financial crisis most experts failed to anticipate.

Jason Brennan references Tetlock's work directly in *Against Democracy*, but he complains that Tetlock "only tested experts on what the experts themselves regard as the 'hard' questions." Most policy questions, he argues, are easier to resolve, and many good solutions have already been discovered by expert consensus. Among economists, for instance, there exists "a wide range of agreed-on views, such as that we should have free trade and avoid price controls." On the same grounds, Walter Lippmann argued for creating bodies of experts that would play a much greater role in shaping policy than the general public. "Representative government," he wrote, "cannot be worked successfully, no matter what the basis of election, unless there is an independent, expert organization for making the unseen facts intelligible to those who have to make the decisions." Voters, he hoped, would eventually come to realize that they'd be better off letting researchers and social scientists make most decisions for them: "The private citizen, beset by partisan appeals for the loan of his Public Opinion, will soon see, perhaps, that these appeals are not a compliment to his intelligence, but an imposition on his good nature and an insult to his sense of evidence."

Even so, expert consensus can only get us so far. In 2020, a global crisis underscored this painfully. The spread of infectious disease is one of the oldest policy problems around. In fact, one of the earliest pandemics we have on record happened in ancient Athens. In 430 B.C., the city was gripped by a plague that killed tens of thousands—including Pericles, whose death marked a turn for the worse in the trajectory of Athenian democracy.

Since then, we've gotten the basics of infectious disease prevention down, literally, to a science. But as straightforward as the question of how to prevent transmission of COVID during the pandemic might have been to public health experts—masks, social distancing, and vaccines—the realities of governance complicated the response considerably. Should the general public be encouraged to purchase masks needed by medical professionals? What risk of blood clotting should be acceptable in a vaccine, and how should that risk be communicated? What are the best ways to ensure that minority groups with long-standing health disparities get vaccinated? How many additional shots should be made available to Americans while millions remain unvaccinated abroad?

Whatever one thinks now, with half a decade's worth of hindsight, about how public health authorities handled these and other questions, it should be clear that resolving them wasn't merely a matter of turning to or "believing" the science—their data and their expertise produced conflicting, contestable, and often controversial judgments. And outside the medical field, many more calls had to be made by many more experts. Sociologists, economists, administrators, and regulators of all kinds debated issues ranging from the wisdom of closing schools and businesses to the inflationary potential of pandemic relief measures.

Yes, many lives would have been saved if more Americans had listened to basic medical advice. But no one expert knew all there was to know about the crisis. And there was no single expert consensus on how to address it. Instead, the most educated and knowledgeable people in the country offered a cacophony of different perspectives on different issues. Major disagreements were aired within and across various disciplines. And those disagreements, like many of the disagreements we encounter all the time in politics and policymaking, were, again, often about balancing competing principles and interests—a task that should be undertaken collectively by all in a society, experts and nonexperts alike.

All that said, Brennan is right that the views of those who study issues closely should weigh upon us, especially in areas where expert consensus seems clear. One such area is the study of democracy. By his own admission, Brennan's stance on democracy is deeply at odds with the opinions of most democratic theorists. "Political philosophers and theorists who specialize in democratic theory," he writes in one book, "often have a quasi-religious reverence for democracy." Even among democratic theorists more sober about the capacities of voters, few endorse the kinds of epistocratic measures Brennan defends in *Against Democracy*. What should we make of that? Brennan argues we ought to consider disenfranchising voters who break from the experts for their ignorance. By the same logic, one might say Brennan's unwillingness to defer to the judgment of most scholars in his field should disqualify him from democratic debates. But that would be wrongheaded. While the considered opinions of experts and the incoherence of Brennan's positions do matter, your author believes we might gain from taking even the Jason Brennans of the world seriously and engaging with their perspectives. Overly optimistic, perhaps. But that's the democratic spirit.

★ ★ ★

Beyond the arguments we've already examined about democracy in practice—about whether the people can rule wisely as a practical matter—democracy's modern critics have also raised doubts that it makes sense as a matter of abstract logic. Here, a thought experiment might clarify what they mean.

Imagine that three friends are trying to decide how they should spend their Saturday night together. Friend A would like to see a movie. Friend B wants to go to a rave. And Friend C—the wisest and most admirable of the three, beloved by all—wants them to spend the evening inside, listening to the audiobook of *The Right of the People: Democracy and the Case for a New American Founding* in silence. Taking a simple vote would end in a stalemate—each of the three wants to do a different thing. So the friends get to discussing the available options. It emerges that while Friend A wants to see a particular movie the most, she thinks going to a rave would be the next best option, and doesn't want to sit inside listening to a book at all. Friend B wants to go to the rave the most, but would settle for listening to the book and doesn't want to go to the movies, having already seen the one that A has suggested. Finally, while Friend C, bless her heart, really wants to listen to the book, she would settle for seeing the movie and really doesn't want to go to the rave. Their preferences are laid out below.

	1st Choice	2nd Choice	3rd Choice
Friend A	Movie	Rave	Book
Friend B	Rave	Book	Movie
Friend C	Book	Movie	Rave

How useful is this information? Well, just ranking the options hasn't helped matters very much—every option is a first, second, or third choice as many times as the next. But something interesting happens when the options are directly compared to each other. We can see now that a majority of the three (Friends A and C) would prefer seeing the movie to the rave. But another majority (Friends B and C) would prefer listening to the book rather than seeing the movie. And a third majority (Friends A and B) would prefer going to the rave over the book. They now have a rock-paper-scissors situation on their hands: The movie beats the rave, the book beats the movie, and the rave beats the book. Our hypothetical group of just three people contains three equally legitimate but contradictory majorities.

They're in about as much of a stalemate as they were before the comparisons were made, but this one is more illuminating for our purposes than the simple tie they initially faced. It's an example of what academics call *cycling*—a logical conundrum that has haunted and confounded democratic theorists since the eighteenth century, when it was noted by Nicolas de Condorcet. But it won't confound our group very much longer—two more friends have joined in to plan the night out. Friend D, another sensible fellow, wants to listen to the book the most, would settle for the rave, and doesn't want to see the movie. And an evidently impressionable Friend E agrees fully with Friend A's choices: movie over rave, rave over book. Here's what our group looks like now:

	1st Choice	2nd Choice	3rd Choice
Friend A	Movie	Rave	Book
Friend B	Rave	Book	Movie
Friend C	Book	Movie	Rave
Friend D	Book	Rave	Movie
Friend E	Movie	Rave	Book

With the initial tie broken, the group now tries a simple show of hands based on everyone's first choices. The rave gets one vote out of the five, or 20 percent of the vote, while the movie and the book each get two votes out of the five, tying at 40 percent of the vote. Friend A pulls out a coin to break the new tie—heads they see the movie, tails they listen to the book. It lands heads and the movie wins.

Friend D protests. Because Friend B's first choice—the rave—lost out, why not use her second choice—listening to the book—to break the tie rather than leaving it to chance? If they did, the book would get an additional vote and win, earning three out of five votes (60 percent) to the movie's two out of five (40 percent). Friend C nods in agreement.

At this point, Friend B, not fond of being spoken for, pipes up. The rave wasn't the first choice of most, she points out, but it was still a popular second choice. And overall, most clearly preferred it to sitting inside listening to an audiobook of someone prattling on about the dilemmas of collective decision-making. So why not award each option points based on how it was ranked by everyone in the group? An option might get two points, for instance, for being ranked as someone's first choice, one point for being ranked second, and zero points for being ranked third. Having done the math, Friend B concludes that the rave would wind up with just as many points—five—as the competing options.

Here, Friend C swears, Friend D rolls her eyes, and Friends A and E storm off to the movies together.

What decision should our group of friends (who may no longer be friends) have made? Which procedure and which outcome would have truly reflected the will of our group of five? As you've surely gathered, that question gets no easier to answer when it's five thousand or five million votes that have to be sorted out—and when much more is at stake than a night on the town.

Democratic Dilemmas

At every level—whether it's voters choosing candidates or policies through referenda or duly elected candidates voting on legislation—democratic outcomes are shaped powerfully by the procedures that produced them. There are always many roads to a collective decision. Our hypothetical touched upon just three decision rules commonly discussed by democratic theorists, political scientists, and election reformers: plurality voting (the group's first vote, utilized in most American elections today), "ranked choice" or "instant runoff" voting (Friend D's suggestion), and the Borda count (proposed by Friend B). There are many others, each with advantages and drawbacks of their own.

Decades ago, the Nobel Prize–winning economist Kenneth Arrow made an unsettling observation about *all* decision rules. There are five characteristics, he reasoned, we might intuitively expect any good rule to have:

The first is that the rule can take any set of individual preferences and put all of them into a single ranking of options that reflects the preferences of the group as a whole.

The second is that the ranking should be transitive—that is if a group prefers Option 1 over Option 2 and Option 2 over Option 3, that means the group prefers Option 1 over Option 3.

The third rule is that unanimous opinions should matter. If everyone in a group prefers one available option to another, the resulting outcome should reflect that.

The fourth is that the group's ranking of any given set of two options shouldn't be affected by the availability of some other irrelevant alternative. If a group chooses Option 1 over

Option 2, for instance, adding or taking away some Option 3 can't change that.

Finally, the fifth rule is that the outcome for the group cannot depend solely on a single individual's preferences. No dictator in the group winds up settling everything.

As reasonable as these criteria may seem, what Arrow discovered is that it's logically impossible for any decision rule to meet them all at once when three or more options are on the table. Any given collective decision-making process where choices are ranked, in that case, will be deficient in at least one basic way.

Democratic theorists have quibbled with the relevance of some of the criteria Arrow chose for real-world democratic processes. They note, too, that his theorem doesn't apply if voters are limited to a choice between two options—a solution that also eliminates Condorcet's paradoxical cycles.

But that solution only underscores another set of problems. Beyond the abstract design of decision rules, democratic outcomes are also influenced by the often arbitrary constraints imposed on voters and strategic behavior. Limiting voters to a choice between just two candidates or policies might get around cycling and Arrow's impossibility theorem, but would a process that banned or failed to include more options really reflect "the will of the people"? What if a disqualified or unavailable alternative would have changed the outcome if voters could have chosen it?

Obviously, having the power to determine voting procedures, the choices available to voters, and how those choices are presented can be huge and potentially antidemocratic advantages for someone or a group to hold. But voters themselves can act strategically in ways that distort outcomes too—when those who prefer third-party candidates wind up supporting major-party candidates because the third party can't win, for instance, or when people vote in an opposing party's primary for a candidate they hope their actual party can beat.

With all the potential paradoxes, constraints, and strategic maneuvering that might be at work, can any democratic process reliably give us an accurate picture of what the people want? In his 1982 book *Liberalism Against Populism*, the culmination of years of research, political scientist William Riker answered that question with a hard *No*. The fact that different democratic decision rules can produce different outcomes, he argued, makes it impossible to say that any given outcome truly reflects "the will of the people" or even the will of a given majority. To know for certain what voters really wanted, we'd have to have direct access to their genuine intentions. We don't, obviously, so we make do with democratic processes that are inherently flawed—vulnerable to both manipulation and irrationalities such as Condorcet's cycles, which undermine the idea that there can be a single true majority among voters. "Outcomes of voting cannot, in general, be regarded as accurate amalgamations of voters' values," Riker wrote. "Sometimes they may be accurate, sometimes not; but since we seldom know which situation exists, we cannot, in general, expect accuracy. Hence we cannot expect fairness either."

Democracy, by Riker's lights, was less a reliable tool for translating "the will of the people" into policy than an intrinsically broken instrument of potential chaos—an instrument that nevertheless usually left political elites in control. "The people," he wrote, "cannot rule as a corporate body in the way that populists suppose." Instead, he continued, echoing Schumpeter, "officials rule, and they do not represent some indefinable popular will." The most we can expect from democracy, Riker concluded, is that it might act as a mostly arbitrary check on the power of those officials from time to time—an "intermittent, sometimes random, even perverse popular veto." Crucially, unlike the critics we examined earlier, the problem for Riker was less the voters than the voting: Even if every voter was an expert on the issues, the process of voting would face the very same challenges and paradoxes he emphasized.

It would be difficult to overstate the impact that Arrow, Riker, and their academic followers have had on political science and democratic theory. "At one point," writes the political scientist Gerry Mackie in his 2003 book *Democracy Defended*, "Riker had published more refereed articles in the *American Political Science Review,* the premier journal of the political science profession, than any other figure. Indeed an editor of that journal wrote to Riker that 'there is some danger of turning this journal into the William H. Riker review.' "

By the late 1970s, a consensus had formed that the paradoxes and logical limitations of democratic processes truly mattered. "The theory of democracy can never be the same," economist Paul Samuelson, another Nobel winner, wrote in one paper. "The search of the great minds of recorded history for the perfect democracy, it turns out, is the search for a chimera, for a logical self-contradiction." Few serious works of democratic theory today avoid engaging with, or at least referencing, that general claim.

★ ★ ★

How to answer it? We might start by noting that democracy is not the only system we take for granted that happens to be rife with contradictions. Few of the economists who argue that democracy's paradoxes should diminish our faith in it are as critical of our market economy, for instance, even though the economy is riddled with complicating irrationalities you'll find in no Econ 101 textbook. Some of those irrationalities are directly comparable to the problems that voting systems face. Obviously, strategic behavior and manipulation by companies and consumers can distort economic outcomes, and cycles are even theoretically possible in economic trades. And genuine preferences are just as difficult to glean from consumer behavior as they are from a vote, as the theorist Keith Dowding points out:

> The market does not reveal our preferences for social states any more than do electoral processes. It only reveals our preferences given the constraints under which we buy and sell. If I buy a pint of beer rather than a bottle of champagne, does this reveal that I prefer beer to champagne? No. It shows I prefer beer to champagne, given my budget constraints. It re-

veals my preferences given the products on offer, and given my resources (which are measured relative to others' resources). Similarly, voting reveals my preferences for the alternatives on offer given the constraints under which I vote. These include what candidates are standing for what policies, and the way I think others are going to vote. We operate strategically in markets, just as we do in elections.

It doesn't follow, though, that markets are incapable of telling us anything about what people actually want and need. Economists argue, reasonably, that what consumers want can be at least partially inferred or "revealed" by examining patterns and putting individual decisions and data points into broader context— a mode of economic analysis developed, funnily enough, by Paul Samuelson. As Mackie points out, Riker once argued this himself in a coauthored paper: "People are not invariably disturbed by the inconsistencies and incoherencies of market outcomes—such as the oft-discovered fact that society spends more on liquor than education although surely a majority would wish otherwise," he had written. "Markets have been churning out such inconsistencies for centuries without leading us to reject them as useful tools."

Another reason not to reject democracy is that the contradictions Riker identifies are potentially inescapable in *any* group decision, democratic or not—from a group of friends democratically planning a night out to a group of philosopher-kings *undemocratically* running a city or nation-state. The only way to avoid them is a wholly individual dictatorship, which Riker doesn't have the heart to endorse. He settles instead for democracy cynically understood. But those of us who want to make the most out of democracy instead have an alternative—keeping the paradoxes of collective decision-making in mind, and trying to choose the best decision rules, as flawed as they might be by Arrow's lights, for a given situation.

Mackie makes a helpful analogy here to choosing how we get around. There are no flawless modes of transportation. Still, we have to get from place to place. So we use our heads and make choices:

> We do know that circumstances favoring crawling or rolling are quite rare, and that teleportation always fails. As to whether one wants to walk, run, bike, drive one make or model of car or another, train, bus, plane, and so on, it always depends on purposes and constraints. Does the mere multiplicity of methods mean that when an individual chooses one method over another that her choice is arbitrary? No. Often there are reasons for one choice over another; and often we might be indifferent among some subset of choices, but there's nothing at all wrong with considered indifference. And practically, sometimes a bicycle will have to do when a car would be much better.

Democracy's paradoxes might even be beneficial, in some respects. Some democratic theorists have argued that cycles, contra Riker, might actually *increase* political stability. The fact that different majorities can be formed on a political question could give losers in an election or vote another reason to stick with the system and try again. Again, that kind of "institutionalized uncertainty about the future" is, as said in Chapter 1, what some theorists believe democracy is fundamentally about. But the evidence that cycles happen as often as Riker supposed in the first place is thin. In *Democracy Defended,* Mackie notes that every example of cycles researchers had offered by then had been debunked or seriously challenged. In general, political outcomes do seem far more intelligible than we might expect if cycling and truly paradoxical outcomes were common. That might be because voters are more rational than we assume. Experiments tell us people can change their contradictory positions with thought over time—suggesting, to some democratic theorists, that deliberative democratic practices and institutions might reduce cycling, to the extent that it ever really occurs.

Still, democracy's paradoxes do leave us in a real bind. As defensible, workable, and improvable as democracy might be, we can't say with confidence, given all we've just considered, that any individual democratic decision accurately reflects "the will of the people" or even "the will of the majority" of the people. "The majority," as a single, stable entity, cannot exist. What a particular democratic decision can capture, imperfectly at best, are the preferences of *a* majority—perhaps one among others. You needn't know much about democratic theory to grasp this. We might cheer rhetoric that says otherwise, but when one candidate in an election beats another 51 percent to 49 percent, for instance, we tend to understand it as an election that easily could have gone the other way rather than "the people" making themselves obviously and overwhelmingly heard. Even when candidates win out more decisively, it's often common sense to us that other alternatives might have won or made a difference had they been considered and that the winners of the contest aren't necessarily thinking as one—that they might not fully agree on all the issues at hand. These are the things that make democracy dynamic—a system of contests, none fully decisive on their own, between groups that can try forming different coalitions and attempting different strategies to win rather than a system of rigid dominance by a single majority.

The political scientist Sean Ingham works through all this in a novel way. The idea that democracy embodies the will of *the* majority, he argues, should be abandoned altogether for an understanding of democracy as rule by *multiple* majorities that can exist all at once and overlap within a population. "Each majority will share preferences over some, but not all of the political alternatives under consideration," he writes in *Rule by Multiple Majorities.* "No majority is likely to share a 'will' in any straightforward sense of the term. In a majoritarian democracy that distributes political power equally, one would expect the outcome of the political process to reflect each majority's shared preferences. Recognizing this simple fact is the first step in developing a workable account of popular control."

What Ingham contends, to put that simple fact even more simply, is that democracy isn't about one true majority getting exactly what it wants. Instead, it's about a variety of potential majorities having the power to shape political outcomes if they choose to get involved. Those majorities might not all agree on, say, how exactly to make health care more affordable or how to solve gun violence. But in a well-functioning democratic system, policies should broadly *reflect the range* of solutions and ideas the different majority coalitions within society support. "The members of a majority may disagree about the optimal level of the minimum wage," Ingham writes as an example, "but they may all prefer a wage of seven dollars to any lower wage level, and they may all prefer a wage of twelve dollars to any higher level. Then the wage level will be constrained to lie in the interval between seven dollars and twelve dollars, provided they care enough about the minimum wage relative to other variables."

The concept is new, and there's still some fuzziness to it in the abstract, but its broad outlines do, again, resemble our intuitions about how politics works in practice. There is no single majority a candidate must appeal to in order to win an election. Instead, candidates try to figure out and be mindful of what different majorities of their constituents might think on a variety of issues. If polls show, for instance, that 60 percent of voters want more funding for public education, 57 percent want lower taxes on small businesses, 54 percent back a woman's right to choose, and 53 percent support fracking for natural gas, it should be obvious that those majorities, all of which have to be considered, aren't made up of the exact same people and don't comprise a single unified group, as much as they might overlap.

As helpful as a multi-majoritarian conception of democracy might be, it should still trouble us, at least a bit, that it undermines one of our most basic intuitions about what democracy's for. Can "the will of the people" even exist if there's no single majority to will it? And can the people really rule, in any meaningful sense, without it?

The Right of the People

In the last chapter, it was argued that any true democracy should be egalitarian, responsive to the people, and responsive on a majoritarian basis—it can't really be said that the people rule absent any of those criteria. But nowhere has it been said that the people must "will" as one in an election or when a law is passed—they can't. Unanimity is impossible on most matters. And again, we turn to majoritarianism as the next best thing because it's based upon the equality of each vote cast when making a decision. Unanimity and supermajority requirements, by contrast, give more power to whoever happens to be in the minority and structurally advantage the status quo.

Still, majority decisions are never really "the will of the people" as a whole in any concrete sense. They can't, obviously, be the will of the people who lose an election or a legislative battle. And as we've just seen, there can be no single majority of the people to begin with—a collective-decision rule can only imperfectly capture the preferences of *a* majority that might exist among others.

All of this should lead us to an important and hopefully clarifying conclusion. Democracy isn't about *the will* of the people winning out in a given collective decision. It's about *the right* of the people to govern themselves through collective decision-making in the first place. The rules that determine what collective decisions get made won't be perfect. The decisions made will rarely, if ever, satisfy everyone. And the notion that the decisions made will reflect the wishes of *a definitive* majority is, essentially, a fiction. But to believe in democracy is to believe that the people, nevertheless, should have the right to come together, in equal standing, and make collective decisions in systems designed to respond to majorities.

Democratic governments, in practice, will often fall short of this principle. And it will be argued later that the American political system, in particular, falls so far short that it can't reasonably be called democratic at all. Nevertheless, securing the right of the people to collective, majoritarian decision-making is the ideal to strive for—the form government of the people, by the people, and for the people must necessarily take in concrete terms.

In Chapter 1, the case for democracy was grounded in theory and principle rather than in measured outcomes. But given the centrality of outcomes to the critiques we've looked at, it's worth reminding ourselves, again, that the expansion of democratic rights across the world in the last century has worked out far better than we'd expect if democratic processes were as totally irrational—and if the people were as totally incompetent—as democracy's critics assume. Societies have materially improved even as the power of elites has diminished, as voting rights have been granted to more politically inexperienced groups, and as the outcomes of voting have become more authoritative.

And while group dynamics can skew our political judgments in negative ways, that doesn't justify the idea that individual voters have to spend their evenings poring over data tables and making fully independent judgments for democracy to work. In fact, democratic processes have functioned well enough already to suggest a kind of collective intelligence might be at work in democratic politics—although, again, that intelligence might be a matter of bringing our principles into alignment rather than, as some democratic theorists argue, figuring out an objectively "correct" answer to a given political question.

Moreover, though it's problematic to assume that anything like "the will of the people" can make itself known in an individual election or contest, the possibility of collective intelligence leaves room for the hope that the public can come to reasonable consensuses on the issues *over time*. That hope, wooly as it may seem, is a good deal more levelheaded and historically grounded than the notion that the people are fully hapless and mindless or the notion that we could govern just by picking the smartest people around and letting them run everything. One might even call it democracy for realists.

Needless to say, democracy today faces challengers far more dangerous than the ones we've examined in this chapter—from tech world reactionaries like Peter Thiel and Curtis Yarvin, who dream of a future where engineers and developers, empowered by their wealth and supposed genius, can impose their visions on the rest of us, to leaders like Vladimir Putin and Viktor Orbán, who have given old-fashioned authoritarianism new life. And, of course, no one has done more to undermine democratic values in America today than President Trump, who has supporters and sympathizers in both camps, has attacked the democratic process, and who, at the time of writing, is assuming kinglike authority over federal policy for himself.

This alarming array of enemies, though, makes answering the arguments of democracy's milder critics all the more important. The less faith we have in democracy—the less sure we are that it can work, the more given we are to stubborn doubts about its wisdom and our capacity to govern ourselves—the more vulnerable we'll be to the idea that we should do away with it entirely. Yes, our defenses of democracy should be grounded—informed by all we've learned about its frustrations and complexities. But they should also be unwavering, shaped not only by our understanding of democracy's limitations but by our understanding of its strengths and the fundamental promise of self-governance—life in the world as masters of our own fate rather than mere subjects of the world as it is given to us.

CHAPTER 3

THE SHAPE OF DEMOCRACY

L ET'S TAKE STOCK OF ALL THAT'S BEEN SAID THUS FAR. A DE-
mocracy is a system of governance of, by, and for the people—
one in which the governed collectively govern themselves, in
other words. Democracy offers key tools for governance—the
agency of subjects, dynamism, and stabilizing procedures. And
we can tell a system is democratic if its subjects are equals and
their institutions are responsive to them on a majoritarian basis.
Those systems will differ in their design on the basis of how a set
of democratic values are balanced—participation, representation,
and deliberation. And whatever the design of a particular democratic system might be, we have good reasons to believe that the
people, though imperfectly motivated and informed, can make
good decisions when democratically empowered to do so. Those
decisions, though, should be interpreted carefully—the people cannot really "will" as one and a democratic victory is only ever the
victory of a particular majority or set of majorities among others.

That conception of democracy might seem more limited, at
first blush, than the idea that it's about reflecting "the will of the
people"—a loud, clear collective voice offering simple instructions for elected representatives and policymakers to obey. But
democracy understood instead as a system of governance defined
by "the right of the people" to govern themselves is arguably
even more empowering and egalitarian. The idea of a single, obvious, and dominant majority in society embodying "the will of the
people" flattens and constrains politics. Conceptually, the victory of a particular side in a given election, which might have lost

under different circumstances, becomes a transcendent event when viewed through that lens—an outcome that becomes difficult to protest or argue against, unless one's willing to put oneself in opposition to "the people" and what all of them supposedly want. This is why even dictators who rig elections and other figures with authoritarian tendencies make appeals to "the will of the people" when it suits them. In February 2025, Elon Musk defended Trump's illegal attacks on federal government agencies in exactly these terms. "The president is the elected representative of the people, so he's representing the will of the people," he said. "And if the bureaucracy is fighting the will of the people and preventing the president from implementing what the people want, then what we live in is a bureaucracy and not a democracy." So invoked, the concept of "the will of the people" devalues democratic contestation and helps political actors avoid inconvenient realities—in this case, broad disapproval of Musk and Trump's funding cuts.

The alternative, democracy premised merely on the people's right to collective governance, allows us to see that a single election or a particular law or policy being implemented is never the final word on any matter. Democracy is a never-ending series of contests for governing power. When a majority prevails, it sits alongside others just as legitimate—majorities that might grow or shrink or even dissipate, perhaps before reforming and reviving themselves. All will have to vie against, negotiate, or join together with one another in various combinations to succeed at their goals. Democracy, so understood, carries within it the promise not of a particular majority's dominance or "the will of the people" settling a question, but of a lively and open public arena, where the ability to change things is always up for grabs and won or kept, from one contest to the next, by the constant cultivation of allies and reworking of arguments.

If anything, this is an understanding of democracy that might invite *more* warnings from democracy's critics—as though we needed more—about the dangers of further empowering the fickle, inconstant, and irrational masses. While we've seen that the people aren't as fickle, inconstant, and irrational as their critics fear, this general anxiety should be taken seriously. The people aren't and will never be perfect; democratic politics has been the font of both embarrassing blunders and grand atrocities. But we have ample reason to believe democracy remains preferable to rule by kings and elites, especially when democratic outcomes are bounded by a commitment to human equality and when democratic institutions balance participation, representation, and deliberation appropriately. Because it gives us unparalleled agency to shape the conditions of our lives, allows for dynamic governance, and offers us fair procedures that help us mitigate and mediate conflicts, democracy is the most sensible means imaginable for managing our collective affairs. Given the trial and error, give and take, and exchanges of ideas and information intrinsic to democratic contestation and governance, democracy may even be the best available means for discovering the common good collectively and reaching what is best within us as individuals.

But while we've reached some clarity on what it means to govern ourselves and why we should, we're still far from a detailed picture of what an ideal democratic system might look like. That's partially because there can't be a single ideal. The democratic values we've examined—participation, representation, and deliberation—can be reasonably combined in many ways. And beyond meeting the basic requirements we outlined at the outset—equality, responsiveness, and majoritarianism—we should avoid the presumption that democratic institutions built for one society or community will necessarily suit another.

All that said, our thinking about democracy today should be shaped by principles tailored to broadly shared values and particularly suited to addressing contemporary problems. This chapter will examine four such principles: liberalism, republicanism, agonism, and materialism.

Liberalism

We're far afield now from the kinds of communities where democratic thought began. While the ancient Athenians, for instance, practiced slavery and accepted rigid class, gender, and cultural hi-erarchies, most modern societies with democratic institutions today have been shaped by the premise that all subjects are, at least in principle, intrinsically equal—as well as the guiding aspi-ration that we might finally *see* each other as equals someday, even in our private lives.

We live today, in other words, in a world shaped profoundly by liberalism, which we touched upon briefly in Chapter 1. Lib-eralism and its relationship with democracy could take up an-other book all its own; here a rough sketch of it will have to do.

Liberalism is an ideology built upon the idea that human be-ings have intrinsic value and dignity as individuals. No matter who we happen to be or what our circumstances are, liberals be-lieve, we are all fundamentally equal and entitled by that equality to certain rights—rights that both empower us, within reasonable limits, to live freely and think as we please, and that should pro-tect us from people and institutions that could do us harm. Those include rights of conscience—the freedoms of expression and as-sociation, for example—and property rights. While many liberals argue there are deep spiritual bases for them, both families of rights are, in practice, defined, bounded, and enforced by govern-ment. These concepts have spread across the world over the last few centuries. And democracy's advocates today generally spec-ify that the kind of democracy they'd like to protect and see more of is "*liberal* democracy"—or democracy in keeping with liberal rights. But liberalism isn't inherently democratic—one might imagine a monarch ruling over a relatively free, diverse, and toler-ant liberal society of equal subjects each living as they please within the bounds of basic laws they have no real power to choose or amend. In a telling and classic 1784 essay called "What Is En-lightenment?," for instance, the liberal philosopher Immanuel Kant praised—and deeply exaggerated—the Prussian king Fred-erick the Great's religious tolerance and willingness to support a free press. "Only one ruler in the world," he gushed, "says, 'Argue as much as you want and about what you want, but obey!'"

Unsurprisingly, the tensions between kingly authority and the idea of human equality became more difficult to paper over with time. But even as liberals reasoned, and fought, their way toward democratic principles, they also came to fear the disruptive forces democracy might unleash—as eloquently and profoundly as they spoke about liberalism's ideals, they lived and often prospered in societies marked by slavery, prejudice, and repression.

Today we tend to take human equality more seriously than those who first suggested it. And although this has deepened our commitment to democracy, it has also made us all the more attentive to the risks that democracy can pose to individual rights. The men who founded liberal society were troubled mostly by the possibility that democratic politics would destroy the liberties of elites and others not too dissimilar from themselves. Nowadays we worry more about majorities ganging up on the underprivileged. If we believe in individual rights, the powers of democratic government cannot be unlimited—there's no doubt about that. The difficult question is whether that reality demands that we place liberal values over and above democracy.

As we saw in the first chapter, we have reason to think not—we can find grounds for many of the rights we've come to call liberal rights within democratic principles. Again, as Corey Brettschneider has argued, the democratic idea that we each should be treated equally as governors implies that we cannot treat any democratic subject as lesser than another—when people are abused and mistreated by the state or other groups and individuals for who they are, we're clearly less capable of equally participating in democratic governance. On that basis, dehumanizing, degrading, and disempowering laws could conceptually be struck down by some entity *on democratic grounds,* even if they've been passed democratically or supported by majorities of the public.

One other point made in Chapter 1 is worth repeating here. While it might not make much of a practical difference whether democratically passed laws to, say, repress political dissidents or religious minorities are struck down on liberal or democratic grounds, understanding certain liberal rights instead as liberal *and* democratic rights helps us see that democratic principles and the liberties of the individual can be reconciled.

In fact, many key rights we tend to see as liberal are essential to democracy functioning well. If ordinary people are to rule, they need the rights and privileges we would expect good rulers to have. And some of those rights and privileges relate to the free flow of information—as Brettschneider also argues, we should expect rulers not only to speak freely but to have all that's being done in their name explained and justified to them. We'd also expect rulers to have a broad array of facts and arguments about the conditions of their domain at their disposal. That means the press and others should engage in free discussion and debate for the ruling public's benefit. Otherwise, we'd know too little about the world we'd like to govern to properly govern it:

> The right of free speech, therefore, concerns not merely citizens' capacity as rulers, but also their fundamental status as addressees of law. Specifically, the idea of free speech as a right to "listen" emphasizes the importance of the core values for citizens in this nonprocedural capacity. Like the rule of law, the right to listen fundamentally concerns citizens' entitlement to be given reasons for government coercion. . . .
>
> The rights of addressees, however, extend beyond rights to know facts; they include rights to hear arguments considered "wrong" and "subversive." The Communist Scare cases of the early twentieth century help to demonstrate why the rights of citizens as addressees of law to hear arguments from across the political spectrum are fundamental to what it means to treat citizens as rulers.

"No citizen," Brettschneider concludes, "should be judged less capable of withstanding and evaluating arguments than a Supreme Court justice, an executive administrator, or a censor." All this amounts to a sound democratic basis for the right to free expression, broadly construed—democracy demands the free exchange of ideas and information not only on questions of policy and law but on all kinds of less obviously political matters. If we're to govern the world around us wisely, we need to be attuned to all the realities of human life; we can get the ideas and information we need not only from articles and protest signs but from art and various forms of cultural expression. And inevitably joined to the freedom of expression here is the freedom of association—democracy can't work unless individuals have the right to come together with others to get things done. Political parties, civic and activist organizations, more loosely bound friends, neighbors, and groups of the like-minded working toward a common purpose—associations are the very foundations of political life. It's impossible to imagine democracy without them.

These rights don't come without costs. Defending free expression often means protecting bad ideas and bad information from censorship; freedom of association can be abused by bigots. But free expression and association are vital nonetheless, and the task of a democratic society is to balance, apply, and enforce them in ways that are in keeping with the egalitarian premises that both liberalism and democracy share.

Republicanism

Though they're often conflated in the public mind, particularly when it comes to their influence on Western culture and politics, we've said a lot about ancient Greece and not very much about ancient Rome in our discussions so far. That's for good reason— they were very different societies with different relationships to democracy. Though limited in critical ways that we've already touched upon, Athens's pioneering government did confer an extraordinary amount of direct power upon anyone lucky enough to be a citizen. But while power devolved to the Roman people from the end of the Roman monarchy in 509 B.C. through the rise of Julius Caesar in the first century B.C., we generally refer to Rome in this era not as a democracy but as a "republic"—a word derived from the Latin phrase *res publica,* which roughly translates to "the People's thing." The word itself is at some conceptual remove from the Greeks' *demokratia.* The clarity of "the people" (*demos*) in "power" (*kratos*) has been replaced with something more vague.

That ambiguity suited Rome's political institutions—it's not clear how much power the republic actually gave to most of the Roman people. Rome was governed by a remarkably complex system that relied far more heavily than Athenian government did on elections and appointments. And while there were several assemblies with different functions, they were different from the Athenian assembly in power, purpose, and design. There was, granted, a "Council of the Plebs," representing ordinary Romans, which could pass some laws binding all citizens, from 287 B.C. through the republic's end. But there was also a more powerful Senate, populated by the republic's elites, which controlled foreign policy and public finance and had a significant influence even on the "Tribunes of the Plebs," who were elected to represent ordinary Romans and technically held veto power over legislation.

Republican governments since Rome have taken a wide variety of forms—Italy's wealthy, independent, and city-sized merchant republics, founded in the Middle Ages; the Dutch confederation of provinces founded in the sixteenth century; the short-lived and martial Commonwealth of England, propped up in 1649 during the English Civil War and dominated by Oliver Cromwell; the massive, multicultural Polish-Lithuanian Commonwealth, a constitutional monarchy with a population in the millions from the sixteenth to eighteenth centuries; the United States and the nations that have taken after it; and too many other examples, large and small, to name. That diversity makes it all the more difficult to pin down what a republic really is. But theorists who call themselves republicans today believe republicanism can be best understood through its differences with liberalism.

As ideologies, liberalism and republicanism both focus on the protection of individual freedom. For liberals, as we've seen, a tyrannical government throwing minorities and peaceful dissidents in jail, for instance, would be unjust—under liberalism, people are equally entitled to basic rights like free expression and fair treatment under the law, no matter who they are. Given that, governments shouldn't unduly interfere with our lives or curtail our rights arbitrarily. Republicans agree, but also argue that they see freedom in a different way. Freedom for republicans, as the theorist Philip Pettit has written, means freedom not only from unjust interference but from *domination*—we should oppose not only being abused and treated unfairly but others *having the power* to abuse us and treat us unfairly if they choose, even when those abuses and injustices aren't happening just yet:

> Think, by way of exercising such imagination, of how you would feel as a student if you depended for not failing a course on the whim of an instructor. Or as a wife if you had to rely on the mood of your husband for whether you could enjoy an unmolested day. Or as a worker if you hung on the favour of a manager for whether you retained your job. Or as a debtor if you were dependent on the goodwill of a creditor for whether you had to face public ignominy. Or as someone destitute if you had to cast yourself on the mercy of others just to survive or maintain your family. Or think about how you would feel as the member of a cultural minority if you had to rely on the humour of majority groups for whether you escaped humiliation; or as an elderly person if you depended on escaping the notice of youth gangs for walking safely home; or as a citizen if you were dependent on winning the favour of some insider group for whether you or your kind ever caught the eye of government.

The fundamental injustice of slavery, as the Roman statesman Cicero once said similarly, has less to do with being whipped and tortured, as bad as that is, than with the master's dominion—the realities of life under the total control of someone else. "The most miserable feature of this condition," he argued, "is that, even if the master happens not to be oppressive, he can be so should he wish." Above and beyond any specific abusive act, *the relation-ship itself* is wrong. To be truly free, by contrast, is to live without depending on the goodwill or mercy of others—to make independent decisions with the knowledge and guarantee that your agency will be respected by the people and institutions you interact with. As Cicero put it, "Freedom consists not in having a just master, but in having none." Republicans are thus mainly concerned with identifying where power is located between parties in society and how that power might be balanced. And when it comes to governance, republicans contend that we should fear not only tyrannical acts by government and the powerful, but governments, entities, and individuals that have taken on *potentially* tyrannical powers.

As might already be obvious, there's a substantial amount of overlap between the conditions most liberals and republicans think we should avoid, and many influential liberal thinkers and political figures were also republicans. There's even some debate in philosophical circles as to whether republican freedom as non-domination and liberal freedom, which is often called freedom as noninterference, are all that different to begin with. But, in general, republicans do tend to be committed institutionalists—concerned not only with the assertion of rights and freedoms but the construction of actual infrastructure for their protection. While some liberals see government primarily as a threat to individual freedom, all republicans, though highly attentive to the risks that bad governments pose to the individual, also emphasize the ways that good governing institutions can expand freedom by fighting domination across society—wherever those with an abundance of wealth, resources, or clout have grown dangerously powerful. "The possible modes of subjection are many and diverse," Pettit writes, "but it should be clear that the state is capable of curtailing them in various ways. Without assuming the cast of a Leviathan in their lives, it can assure its people of a level of protection, support and status that frees them from at least the more egregious forms that such dependency can take."

To ensure that states defend freedom rather than threaten it, republicans back the rule of law, constitutions (whether formally written or not), the separation of governing powers, and systems of checks and balances among the people empowered to create, execute, and adjudicate the laws.

Given the familiarity of its institutions and its commitment to protecting and enhancing agency, republicanism might seem like a natural fit with democratic principles. Indeed, political commentators and politicians often say that a republic is nothing more than a representative democracy. But like liberalism, and as Rome's example suggests, republicanism isn't inherently democratic. In general, republicans share with liberals an anxiety about the threats democracy might pose to the individual. In fact, many early republicans believed ordinary people were among the potentially dominating constituencies the state needed to weaken. Still, republicanism and democracy are joined together in the public mind for good reason. There are really two republican traditions: one more hostile to democratic principles and the other—more useful for our purposes—focused on democratically empowering the people through republican governance.

Republican theorist John McCormick calls the first tradition "aristocratic republicanism" and counts among its key thinkers figures like Cicero and French philosopher Montesquieu. Notably, writes McCormick, even aristocratic republicans have historically professed concern that inequality can endanger liberty and the integrity of the state:

> It is fair to say that aristocratic republicans like Cicero, Guicciardini, Harrington, and Montesquieu were sincerely worried that society's richest individuals rather than its "best men" would hold the preponderance of a republic's offices and that extensive economic inequality would corrupt the virtue required of common citizens to maintain their liberty.

However, what actually makes them aristocratic republicans is the fact that they also thought, and were more committed to the notion, that democratic and egalitarian solutions to these problems were potential cures far more deadly than the actual disease. In response to the wealth problem, they were loath to accept appointment of magistrates through anything other than elective means, and, moreover, they were terrified of permitting economic equality to be legislated through majoritarian procedures.

For these men, republicanism was a way to protect themselves and their property. "It is the proper function of a citizenship and a city," Cicero once said, "to ensure for everyone a free and unworried guardianship of his possessions." Wealthy republicans troubled by concentrations of wealth didn't want to *end* inequality. Instead, they wanted a stable sociopolitical order, fair rules for economic competition, and governing institutions that would secure all that they managed to gain through competition from a variety of potential threats: the state, religious authorities, other wealthy and noble rivals, and, most threatening of them all, the needy masses. "Greek oligarchs, Roman nobles, and the grandees of early modern city-states deemed majority tyranny to be the greatest threat to republican liberty," McCormick writes. "Consequently, they advocated the use of indirectly accountable senatorial or judicial bodies to temper the authority of majoritarian assemblies, and they preferred election to lottery as a political appointment device."

Some aristocratic republicans were open to giving the general public a role in governance. In fact, as we've already seen, some republican thinkers, such as Machiavelli, had an extraordinary amount of faith in the public's ability to discern virtue. But giving the people equal political rights and letting them govern themselves was nevertheless out of the question. Instead, aristocratic republicans expected the public to consent to governance by elites. Early on, that meant not only the exclusion of minorities, women, and those without property from political rights, but the creation of institutions that limited the power of even propertied male citizens who could participate in politics. As democratic as certain features of republican constitutions may have seemed, aristocratic republicans took pains to ensure they would never be reliably responsive to majorities of the people.

None of this sits very well with the principle of nondomination. In the name of fairness and stability, aristocratic republicans created institutions that just so happened to empower wealthy men like themselves at the expense of ordinary people, who didn't deserve to be dominated any more than they did. But republicans in the second tradition that McCormick identifies, democratic republicanism, took the right of the people to govern themselves more seriously and worked to limit the power and influence of the wealthy in the interest of the masses:

Historically, democratic republicans deemed the excessive political influence of wealth to be the primary threat to the liberty of popular governments. I am thinking of hoplites and thetes in ancient Greek democracies, the plebeians of ancient Italian republics and lower guildsmen within medieval and early modern Swiss, German, and Italian city-states. As a result of this central concern, they placed at the forefront, not at the sideline, of institutional reforms practices that directly mitigated the excessive political influence of the wealthy; these included, among others, the extensive use of lottery rather than election in the appointment of public officials and the reservation of powerful offices and assemblies for poorer citizens. Of course, they always insisted that large citizen assemblies, governed by majoritarian procedures, should function as the most powerful institutions within republics, even when the latter were understood as "mixed regimes."

For democratic republicans, fighting domination meant truly protecting the freedoms of all, even the masses, through democratic institutions. And thus they believed concentrations of wealth and power should be challenged to the extent that they could lead to dominance—corroding democracy and the liberty of ordinary people.

In his work, Pettit paints a striking picture of what experiencing republican liberty, once built and protected, would be like:

> In the received republican image, free persons can walk tall, and look others in the eye. They do not depend on anyone's grace or favour for being able to choose their mode of life. And they relate to one another in a shared, mutually reinforcing consciousness of enjoying this independence. Thus, in the established terms of republican denigration, they do not have to bow or scrape, toady or kowtow, fawn or flatter; they do not have to placate any others with beguiling smiles or mincing steps. In short, they do not have to live on their wits, whether out of fear or deference. They are their own men and women, and however deeply they bind themselves to one another, as in love or friendship or trust, they do so freely, reaching out to one another from positions of relatively equal strength.

Conceived this way, republicanism not only meshes well with democratic principles but enlarges them. The principle of non-domination encourages us to measure our freedom and ability to govern ourselves not just by how well our *political* institutions are designed but also by whether we hold power elsewhere in our lives.

Agonism

Fundamentally, republicanism is about understanding and managing distributions of power. As democratic republicans contend, democratic institutions and processes can help balance out competing interests in society and guard against domination. One of the intuitions underpinning that idea is that building consensus in societies is hard. Rather than assuming factions will resolve their differences naturally and share power fairly, republicans look to the law for stability and construct constitutions to keep competing interests in balance. But we often talk about politics as though debate and deliberation, done properly, are supposed to pull us toward broad agreement on the issues that divide us. And when deep divisions persist, commentators tend to insist they're inherently destructive and destabilizing.

The trouble is that as much as we might pine for a more harmonious politics, the very rights that allow us to live and think mostly as we please only diversify our thoughts and make it harder for us to agree. As we've seen, democracy is fundamentally about competition—the right of the people to govern themselves through fair contests where majorities win. Given that, we should adopt an understanding of democracy that takes differences and divisions for granted rather than resting on the utopian hope that we'll all find ourselves on the same page someday.

The challenge is figuring out how to embrace competition and the reality of division without letting democratic competition and our divisions break society apart. "We could say that the aim of democratic politics is to transform an 'antagonism' into an 'agonism,'" the theorist Chantal Mouffe has written. "Far from jeopardizing democracy, agonistic confrontation is in fact its very condition of existence."

For agonistic democrats like Mouffe, preserving the rough and tumble of active political competition and debate prevents any one constituency or set of ideas from achieving unchallenged dominance. And those who win out should have to retain their power by continuing to prevail in fair and lively political contests rather than domineering efforts to force political unity—a perspective, clearly, that fits well with what we've said about multiple majorities. "Contestation," as the theorist Marie Paxton writes, "can act as a check and balance on the power of any consensus, status quo, or majority, highlighting the importance of democratic process, whilst leaving behind attempts to unite citizens through a shared outcome."

The challenge of agonistic democracy—and the key to making

it work—lies in finding ways to promote and protect competition without deepening political instability. We don't have to
agree or even like each other all that much, but we do, on some
level, have to get along. And for Mouffe, getting along is a matter
of choosing not to see our opponents as enemies:

> The "other" is no longer seen as an enemy to be destroyed,
> but as an "adversary," i.e., somebody with whose ideas we are
> going to struggle but whose right to defend those ideas we
> will not put into question. This category of the adversary
> does not eliminate antagonism, though, and it should be dis-
> tinguished from the liberal notion of the competitor, with
> which it is sometimes identified. An adversary is a legitimate
> enemy, an enemy with whom we have in common a shared
> adhesion to the ethico-political principles of democracy. But
> our disagreement concerning their meaning and implementa-
> tion is not one that could be resolved through deliberation
> and rational discussion, hence the antagonistic element in the
> relation.

Here, politics isn't about pursuing compromise for its own sake —
while compromises are often politically necessary and substantively good, we shouldn't consider democratic processes or
democracy itself defective when one side simply triumphs over
another. And if we're committed to political equality, we
shouldn't intentionally design our institutions to force compromises through supermajority requirements or to unfairly frustrate political radicals either. Doing so, as Mouffe writes, amounts
to "transform[ing] political problems into administrative and
technical ones." Commentators and academics who suggest, contra Mouffe, that we *should* design our way out of division—those
you'll see on television or in respected papers and magazines be-
moaning extremism and polarization on the regular—forget all
too often that racial equality, gender equality, and other basic
moral premises we now take for granted were once extreme and
subversive doctrines. And the movements for equality eventually

built majorities not only through formal politics but through often-disruptive protests and social action. In doing so, they demonstrated the value of political conflict. It is through conflict, agonistic democrats contend, that we discover, test, and amend our values. And to the extent that it offers fair and peaceable ways for conflict to play out, democracy brings us closer to understanding—at least for ourselves and even if others disagree—who we really are and what we really care about.

Conversely, the pursuit of consensus for its own sake—and designing institutions to shut out or disempower those with radically different perspectives than everyone else—may encourage certain factions to lash out against the political system and others in society. "The concern," Paxton writes, "is that, when democracy fails to adequately mediate such conflict, either side of these disputes can turn to populism, extremism or even violence, as demonstrated by events such as the 2016 murder of Remain campaigner, MP Jo Cox, by a far-right extremist; the 2017 Charlottesville neo-Nazi attack on counterprotesters; and the 2019 Christchurch mosque shootings by a white supremacist. This distinction between nonviolent and violent conflict—and the potential for the former to merge into the latter—is actually part of the case for agonistic institutions."

Democracy can be an extraordinary system for both generating and managing differences. When calls for political unity deny that, they constrain democracy and its possibilities. That said, it is obviously crucial that healthy contestation doesn't devolve into our killing one another. Having democratically fair, well-designed institutions is a key means of preventing that. But our capacity to treat others as legitimate opponents—not to mention our willingness to defend fair democratic institutions in which we might lose out from time to time—will inevitably rest upon the depth of our commitment to political equality. If we don't believe people are equally and fundamentally entitled to basic rights and democratic power, politics really could become a dangerously uncontrolled zero-sum game.

Materialism

The ever-present challenge for equality as an ideal is inequality as a material reality. As republicans understood, we don't enter into politics on level ground. The average citizen will have a much harder time contesting political power than a billionaire will. The poor and very disadvantaged have, by comparison, very little political power to speak of at all. For those who lack political money, organization, voices in the media, and advocates where laws and policies are made, equality is a mere abstraction—one too weak to bear the weight of all we'd like democracy to accomplish.

Our ideas about democracy and how it's working for us, in other words, should be informed by a materialism—a recognition that for all its strengths and justifications and for all its promise, democracy can be fundamentally and even fatally undermined by certain material realities. This is a key missing piece in all that's been said in democracy's favor so far—one large answer to the question of why our democratic aspirations and institutions often fall short. As entitled as we might be in the abstract to govern ourselves, we cannot do it well without understanding how the societies we'd like to govern materially function. In short, we cannot talk meaningfully about democracy without thinking critically about the economy.

In certain respects, the impacts of economic forces and economy inequality on democratic politics are already widely discussed in our political discourse and in academia—well-justified pleas for campaign finance reform and efforts to rein in corporate lobbying are made routinely. But we have good reasons to believe democracy demands more of us than that low-hanging fruit. Even under a seemingly fair, uncorrupted, and democratic political system, the economically disadvantaged and even the average citizen would still face the threat of domination by those wealthier and more powerful than them within their economic lives— the worker who depends on the favor of their manager for their livelihood, for instance, or the debtor dependent on the goodwill of a creditor to return to two of Pettit's examples. And, as will be discussed later in the book, even with more limits on campaign donations and lobbying, the wealthy would still have an easier time broadcasting their political opinions and advocating for the laws and policies they want than ordinary people.

This is why some democratic theorists, such as Thomas Christiano, argue that granting everyone in society a basic minimum of economic resources would be necessary to make meaningful democratic participation possible for all:

> The exact nature of the economic minimum would also by right be decided by the democratic assembly. I do not want to enter here into debates about exactly how much this minimum should be nor do I want to discuss the exact mechanism of transfer that would be required. Basic human needs, such as health care, education, a decent childhood, and others, are needs such that a serious lack in one of these can clearly be compared with someone else's good fortune. Someone who is seriously ill with no access to health care or has had no access to education or has been severely abused as a child is pretty clearly worse off than many others. And such a person is likely to experience serious obstacles to the exercise of their liberal and democratic rights. When there is a serious deficiency with regard to one of these interests, justice requires that some attention be paid to them. And no democratic assembly that ignored such fundamental needs of citizens could be regarded as fully legitimate.

Philip Pettit argues that a basic minimum would also build the agency and protect the republican freedom of ordinary people:

> There are a variety of conditions in which people are going to be unable to exercise some of their basic liberties or are going to be exposed to the domination of others. People will suffer such vulnerabilities if they do not have sure access to shelter

and nourishment; to treatment for medical need or support for disability; or to representation in appearing as plaintiffs or defendants in the courts. It is going to follow straightforwardly, on the republican approach, that they should therefore be publicly insured—or publicly required and enabled to have private insurance—against such possibilities. They should be provided with social security, medical security and judicial security, whether by means of a system of social insurance, national health and legal assistance, or by any of a number of alternatives: say, the provision of a basic income for each citizen.

Having government provide citizens with basic necessities and social programs has been a goal of reformers and activists the world over for some time, of course—usually for reasons that have little to do with republican freedom or bolstering democracy. Some countries have been more successful in achieving that goal than others. But just about everywhere, efforts to have governments give more to ordinary people are often opposed and frustrated by the wealthy, who resent being taxed to bring those programs about. And the wealthy are also often hostile to the basic political reforms aimed at reducing their influence, including campaign finance reforms and limits on lobbying. Clearly, political and economic inequality produce and reinforce one another. Efforts to address economic inequality through politics (or to reduce the impact of economic inequality on politics) are attacked by the economy's winners, who use their resources to win at politics as well.

One other way, beyond a basic minimum, to counter the domination of the wealthy would be to more fundamentally restructure the economy—granting ordinary people more agency by ensuring that economic power and resources accrue to more than a wealthy few in the first place. In the 1980s, Robert Dahl posed a key question often overlooked in both our political reform and economic policy debates: "What about the ownership and control of economic enterprises as a source of political inequality?"

> Ownership and control contribute to the creation of great differences among citizens in wealth, income, status, skills, information, control over information and propaganda, access to political leaders and, on the average, predictable life chances, not only for mature adults but also for the unborn, infants, and children. After all due qualifications have been made, differences like these help in turn to generate significant inequalities among citizens in their capacities and opportunities for participating as political equals in governing the state.

As Dahl observed, the design of our basic economic institutions—including the structure and ownership of companies—clearly matters. It's plain that our efforts to tackle inequality will be incomplete unless we're willing to address how they produce inequality to begin with. And one significant way that they produce inequality is through the remarkable amount of authority that executives and managers have over their workers, who generally are denied a say about how their companies are run. Nor are they given much of the wealth their work produces, beyond wages and salaries that amount to a fraction of what their bosses earn at the top.

In recent years, that reality has been the subject of renewed interest from theorists, including Elizabeth Anderson, who notes in her 2017 book *Private Government* that we've come to accept a level of unaccountable control in our workplaces that we would never accept from a state:

> Imagine a government that assigns almost everyone a superior whom they must obey. Although superiors give most inferiors a routine to follow, there is no rule of law. Orders may be arbitrary and can change at any time, without prior notice or

opportunity to appeal. Superiors are unaccountable to those they order around. They are neither elected nor removable by their inferiors. Inferiors have no right to complain in court about how they are being treated, except in a few narrowly defined cases. They also have no right to be consulted about the orders they are given. There are multiple ranks in the society ruled by this government. The content of the orders people receive varies, depending on their rank. Higher-ranked individuals may be granted considerable freedom in deciding how to carry out their orders, and may issue some orders to some inferiors. The most highly ranked individual takes no orders but issues many. The lowest-ranked may have their bodily movements and speech minutely regulated for most of the day.

This government does not recognize a personal or private sphere of autonomy free from sanction. It may prescribe a dress code and forbid certain hairstyles. Everyone lives under surveillance, to ensure that they are complying with orders. Superiors may snoop into inferiors' e-mail and record their phone conversations. Suspicionless searches of their bodies and personal effects may be routine. They can be ordered to submit to medical testing. The government may dictate the language spoken and forbid communication in any other language. It may forbid certain topics of discussion. People can be sanctioned for their consensual sexual activity or for their choice of spouse or life partner. They can be sanctioned for their political activity and required to engage in political activity they do not agree with.

In short, the modern workplace is a dictatorship, run by intrusive and intimidating bosses who are not easily challenged and, from a republican perspective, stand in a position of dominance over their employees—whether or not, as the theorist Tom O'Shea writes, they actually choose to abuse them at any given moment and despite the basic legal protections that generally exist for workers:

For instance, even when some regulations are in place, the employer often has great latitude to determine work pace, alter job roles, assign and withdraw shifts, commence disciplinary proceedings, and shape the physical and social environment where work takes place. Even in those areas that are supposed to be tightly legally governed, such as wrongful dismissal and minimum wages, the effective ability to enforce the law is often lacking, especially where union representation is low and the threat of employer retaliation is hard to defend against. Furthermore, the social position occupied by managers often allows them to enjoy considerable informal authority, which can enable them to goad staff into working longer, harder, and in worse conditions than the law itself allows. Thus, while legal protections shape aspects of employment relationships, these are not always effective, and inevitably leave unregulated a significant subset of the powers of employers over their workers. When this unregulated power is extensive enough to threaten secure access to the economic capabilities necessary for civic equality, then we can identify economic domination.

Economic domination should deeply trouble us if we believe in all we've said about democracy. If we truly believe that self-governance, in principle and in practice, is better than leaving governance to a lone ruler or a select few, we have to grapple with the reality that we are governed not only through our political institutions but at work, where we spend much of our lives and earn our livelihoods. There, decisions made by unaccountable bosses can affect us even more directly, intimately, and immediately than laws and policies enacted by politicians. And with the economic power and resources that control of firms entitles them to, executives and investors can buy off politicians and prevent democracy from working in the interests of ordinary people.

Political democracy is vital. We cannot do without it. But if we take democracy seriously, we should consider too—and indeed will, later in this book—the possibilities of *economic democracy:*

granting ordinary people more agency and authority within the economy, including within the workplace.

★ ★ ★

As might be obvious by now, this book is best understood less as a narrow work about democratic politics than as a work about what might be called democratic "political economy"—a wonderful, underappreciated phrase that's roaring back into use now, and with good reason. We no longer have the luxury of imagining that the economy is a mere backdrop for the political stage, where the real action unfolds. At the time of writing, there are eighteen centi-billionaires on the planet; it's plausible that we're only a few years away from one of them becoming the world's first trillionaire. The democratic project is threatened by an economy that puts so much wealth and power in the hands of so few. And in the face of material inequality so vast, the *ideal* of equality may not survive long in the hearts of people who see—in politics and at work—that the economic might of the rich tends to make right.

Given that, it shouldn't surprise us in the slightest that deepening inequality has been accompanied not only by deepening political dysfunction but by a collapsing faith in democracy and the spread of antidemocratic ideas. Books like this one often imply that improving things might be a matter of sending the general public, en masse, to remedial civics classes that might revitalize our commitment to democratic ideals. But it's doubtful that we can ideologically bind people to democracy without binding them to it materially. The democratic ideal may not survive unless ordinary people come to understand how they might benefit concretely from political equality and self-governance. Our collective commitment to democratic values, in other words, will be all the stronger if we see them working in real terms, and if we put them into regular practice in more places—not just at the ballot box, but at work in the growth of paychecks and improvement of working conditions.

Not all who shun and spite democracy do so because they think it should work better, of course. Much of the hostility to democratic values at work today is an outgrowth of hostility to social and cultural changes—for reactionaries, shifts such as America gradually becoming a majority-minority society have made the very concept of majoritarianism an existential threat. But we shouldn't give short shrift to the possibility that many are down on democracy because they haven't seen democracy deliver. As parties cycle in and out of government, economic conditions and the drudgery and abuses of working life stay mostly the same. The economic opportunities that politicians promise rarely arrive; whole towns and communities wither away waiting for replies to the messages they dutifully send to their leaders, year after year, through the ballot box. As has been widely reported, budding authoritarians have found such communities particularly welcoming—perversely, voters within them seem to reward figures who resemble the domineering bosses they've come to know. Pining for a CEO who gets things done is a cliché of American politics in particular. Donald Trump crafted much of his political identity around the idea that his business experience would allow him to apply an "ahead of schedule, under budget mentality to the government." Elon Musk was brought into his second administration to carry that vision out—or at least to pretend to. A boss or executive, the thinking they tapped into goes, is someone who can get what they want when they want it—someone granted broad deference and the leeway to bypass systems of accountability and "who gets things" done largely because they can't be told no. Voters who say they want this from their leaders are speaking from both experience and desperation. They hope that in politics, at least, they might luck upon a dictator, unlike their bosses, finally willing to work on their behalf.

They won't. And while it's easy to bemoan the forces pulling portions of the public away from democracy, we should consider, too, whether democracy's advocates are making their cases as fully and as well as they should. Many democratic theorists, for instance, write as though the economy hardly concerns their discipline at all. But democratic thought wasn't always so blinkered. In the late nineteenth and early twentieth centuries in particular, the project of bringing democratic values into the economy was a live subject. John Stuart Mill was among the theorists who considered it inevitable. "The form of association, however, which if mankind continue to improve, must be expected in the end to predominate," he wrote, "is not that which can exist between a capitalist as chief, and work-people without a voice in the management, but the association of the labourers themselves on terms of equality, collectively owning the capital with which they carry on their operations, and working under managers elected and removable by themselves."

None of that panned out, of course, and no single book can do justice to the reasons why. But part of the answer may be that, as we've come to take it for granted, we've come to expect less from democracy than we should. "As it gains practical extension in the affairs of society, [democracy] is getting lower theoretical appreciation," John Dewey wrote in *The Ethics of Democracy*. "While it has never had such an actual hold on life as at present, no observer can deny, I believe, that its defenders have never been so apologetic; its detractors so aggressive and pessimistic."

The same could be said today. Donald Trump's victory in the 2024 election has undermined faith in democracy both as a system and as an ideal that might galvanize and inspire the public; the disdain for democratic principles and the voting public is growing louder, even among Trump's critics, as attacks on the democratic process are growing more brazen. Through it all, though, democracy remains one of our best ideas. In America, as we will see, it remains a project unfinished.

PART II

A NEW FOUNDING

CHAPTER 4

A REPUBLIC KEPT

As we draw close to marking the 250th anniversary of our Founding, optimism about America is in short supply. By the end of 2024 according to Gallup, a mere 19 percent of Americans were satisfied with the country's direction, the bottom of a national malaise that has deepened greatly since the turn of this century. That isn't especially surprising given the problems that have beset us over the last twenty-five years. An unprecedented terrorist attack that brought us to two futile, destructive, and expensive wars. The greatest financial collapse since the Great Depression. A pandemic that killed more than a million Americans and brought about yet another economic crisis. The highest levels of inequality in a century. The impacts of climate change. America, in the eyes of most Americans, stands today a humbled, bruised, and battered country. And most of us think things are bound to get worse. In 2023, a survey by Pew found that more than 60 percent of Americans believed the economy would be weaker in 2050. More than 70 percent believed America would be less important in the world and more politically divided by then. And more than 80 percent believed the gap between the rich and the poor would be wider.

Clearly we've entered a season of profound self-doubt—we're set to begin our 250th year as a nation profoundly skeptical of our capacity to address our deepest challenges and perhaps of the American project itself. The man who will be our national master of ceremonies for that milestone obviously bears some of the blame. President Trump has waged an extraordinary campaign against American norms and institutions. His second administration, somehow even worse than his first, has been reckless, lawless, and vile beyond description. And the protests his governance has inspired this time around—thick with chants and slogans implying that, against the spirit and concerns that founded this country, he has taken on quasi-monarchical powers for himself—have only bemused him and his supporters. "LONG LIVE THE KING," the White House wrote in a social media post about a month after his second inauguration. This captioned an image of the president in a crown. Just over a month later, it was reported that he was considering an unconstitutional third term in office.

But as central as Donald Trump might be to perhaps most diagnoses of what ails America today, we'd do well to remember that many Americans were drawn to him in the first place as a radical solution to the problems the country faces—a wrecking ball many believed and continue to believe our institutions needed. As said in the introduction, faith in "our democracy" has been dwindling—weakened by a belief that our system is far more responsive to the interests of the wealthy and powerful than the needs of ordinary Americans and the urgency of the challenges this new century has brought us. Demagogues like Trump and those sure to follow him will continue to exploit our pessimism unless the American people are offered real answers as to why "our democracy" so often falls short of their expectations and given compelling ideas for improving it. And we'll stand little chance of soundly evaluating what ails "our democracy"—or understanding what democracy ought to be doing for us in the first place—without a sound understanding of what democracy really means and how democracy really works.

This book has worked through fundamental questions about democracy to that end. Though we've come to take certain ideas about democracy for granted, and our leaders make rhetorical appeals to democratic values with ease, democracy, as we've seen, is much more complex than politicians and pundits tend to imply. Obviously, there's much more to democratic theory than could be said within the space of this book. But the preceding chapters have presented ideas that will be especially key to the analysis of "our democracy" that follows.

Democracy, again, is a system in which the governed govern. It is desirable because it offers us especially useful tools for governance in our own interests. Systems are democratic to the extent that they respond to the governed, who should be equal in standing, on a majoritarian basis. Democracies cannot reflect some stable and transcendent "will of the people" or even the "will" of a single cohesive majority. Instead, they give the people they govern the right to govern themselves through fair, majoritarian contests for power. And as imperfect as we may be individually and collectively, we have good reasons to believe that democratic decision-making can work well for us. Given this, we should embrace democracy with confidence, evaluating and improving our democratic systems in keeping with certain principles advanced in the last chapter: a liberalism that secures certain basic rights; a republicanism that gives us the means to ward off domination; an agonism that recognizes the inevitability of division and conflict; and a materialism that recognizes how economic conditions—and the reality that we are both politically and economically governed—shape our democratic agency.

Here, we turn from an exploration of democracy in the abstract to an assessment of how "our democracy" works in practice. And given all we've said and learned about democracy so far, the chapters ahead will lead us through a set of sobering conclusions.

America is not, in fact, a democracy. It was not founded as one. And though the work of generations has brought more political rights to many more Americans than our Founders could have imagined (or would have wanted), those efforts still have not brought democracy to America. The American people are not equal as political subjects. When majorities successfully compete for power, our political system is often unresponsive to them. Even when the system responds, the victories won through political contestation can be overturned by the machinations of the wealthy, major corporations, and their allies within our political institutions. And those victories are undermined, too, by the power corporations and the wealthy wield over us within the economy, including at work. It might be argued that the same can be said of most putatively democratic societies in the world today—that thus far in the text, we've occupied ourselves with a democratic ideal that can never be fully met. That may well be true. Still, as we will see, "our democracy" falls far further from the ideal than the governments of our peers do in many respects; in calling them democracies, one doesn't subject the concept to quite as much abuse. To call America a democracy is to strain the word beyond meaning—in doing so, we occlude basic and remediable defects in our political and economic systems.

The remainder of this book will examine those defects, their origins, and potential solutions to them in the interest, as we mark the 250th anniversary of our first Founding, of inspiring us to another. Again, our Declaration of Independence affirms that it is the right of the people to "alter and abolish" governments when they are no longer capable of securing our rights to life, liberty, and the pursuit of happiness or achieving our just ends. Like the Founders, we should conceive of that right as a constructive one. "The right to revolution," Sheldon Wolin once wrote, "is not solely a right to overturn and destroy institutions but to fashion new ones because those who rule have perverted the old ones. The right to revolution is the right to create new forms."

As most Americans correctly perceive, the institutions of "our democracy" have failed us. In fact, in elevating Donald Trump and securing him in power, our institutions—and the economic conditions shaping them and American life more broadly—have come close to replicating the kind of unaccountable rule that motivated the Founding of our country to begin with. Our Founders won the chance to forge this republic through violence. The new republic this book urges us toward—one that might finally fulfill the promise of American democracy as envisioned by Dewey, Whitman, and others—can be founded peaceably and less radically through a program of deep reform and democratic experimentation.

We'll be best positioned to craft that program—to embark on the project of creating "new forms"—with an understanding of how the "old forms" we've inherited came about. Before setting our sights on a new Founding, we should come to terms with our first.

★ ★ ★

At the close of the Constitutional Convention, a prominent Philadelphia woman, one Elizabeth Willing Powel, famously confronted Benjamin Franklin with a question.

"Well, Doctor, what have we got?" she asked. "A republic or a monarchy?" It's likely you already know Franklin's reply.

"A republic," he said. "If you can keep it."

The power of that line, immortalized in countless books and speeches since it was first recounted by Maryland delegate James McHenry, is undiminished by the fact it may never have been said. Years later, Powel told a friend she had "no recollection of any such conversations," though she acknowledged the possibility she might have forgotten it.

We haven't, though. Franklin's directive—and warning—is another one of those bottled messages, floating in the brackish water between history and myth, that's been picked up and passed down to us over generations. As soon as we're old enough to contemplate politics—and, in truth, perhaps earlier—we are told, solemnly, that the American political order is fragile—a precious thing that might crack and shatter under pressure. The document that Franklin, McHenry, and fifty-three other men began composing that spring in Philadelphia, our leaders and teachers insist, established institutions we should consider our primary defense—and perhaps our sole defense—against despotism on one hand and lawlessness on the other.

That document has been tested and tattered. Less than a century after the convention, the country was torn in two by a Civil War that remains our bloodiest conflict; short of war, grand social upheavals and economic crises have fractured our country repeatedly. The work of activists and visionary leaders has improved it. But despite all that's changed—the major additions grafted on, all that's been blotted out or excised, all that's been stressed and strained—the basic structure of the government the Founders designed for us remains intact. Today, more than 230 years after the Constitution's ratification, America remains a republic of states united under a sovereign federal government. Per the Founders' instructions, we've held on to a unitary president who approves and executes the laws, a bicameral legislature containing a House with population-apportioned seats and a Senate with seats equally apportioned to each state, and a Supreme Court at the top of a federal judiciary.

The Founders' republic, in other words, has been kept. "Our democracy" still closely resembles their original design. And the longevity of their basic framework, in the eyes of many Americans and many of our leaders, is proof that the Founders designed a system that works miraculously well. Yet the Constitution hasn't been sustained by law and procedure alone. Even when we do subject it to interpretation and amendment—the rare moments where deep revisions are possible—we're encouraged to respect the Constitution's text or, more grandly, the spirit of the document. Throughout our history, even radically new policies and constitutional arrangements the Founders never would have conceived have been framed, by earnest reformers and conniving politicians alike, as ends the Founders clearly would have desired.

To change the Constitution, in other words, we tend to convince ourselves we're leaving it well enough alone. And as far as its most fundamental elements are concerned, we usually do. But the Constitution has always had deeper critics—those, throughout our history, who've argued the Founders' republic falls well short of democracy and that the project of American democracy remains unfinished. This book belongs to that critical tradition.

Some readers have surely picked it up with a particular critique of the Constitution and the Founding already in mind. Franklin made his perhaps-apocryphal entreaty to keep our republic to a woman—one who, though politically and socially influential, would die nearly a century before the Nineteenth Amendment guaranteed women the right to cast votes about how the republic should be kept. There were no women deliberating in that hall in Philadelphia. There were no African Americans, no Native Americans. Instead, the Constitution was written by fifty-five white men who had a hand in subjugating all of them. On slavery in particular, even those who might have opposed it in the abstract agreed to compromises within the Constitution that protected it.

What's more, even if the Founders had been morally perfect—and as intelligent as they genuinely were—the fact remains that the Constitution has us working to address the problems of the twenty-first century through institutions designed by men of the eighteenth—people who would have been dazzled by a lightbulb. America is a much larger and more complex society than they ever dreamed it would be; the American people have needs and expectations that would have staggered them. Given all this, some say, there's no particular reason we should consider ourselves morally or ideologically bound to the Constitution or the intent of the Founders in any way.

These are compelling arguments. But they won't be central to this particular chapter—nor to the book as a whole—for four reasons.

The first is that they would produce a text much shorter than the book that has been promised to Random House. The case is too simple and straightforward; it's just been made in full.

The second is that those arguments are already familiar to many readers. Few who haven't already been swayed by them are likely to be convinced by restatements of them.

The third reason is that taking the time to examine the Constitution's specific flaws and their origins—to explain to ourselves, whether one respects the Founders and Founding or not, exactly why the document itself is defective—can help us understand why many of the country's problems have proven difficult to solve.

And the fourth, relatedly, is that examining those flaws might also guide us in the design of better, more democratic institutions in the event that we finally replace the Constitution, as we should.

One of the main obstacles to doing so is our reverence for the Founders and their handiwork, which the Founders themselves worked to build within the American mind as soon as the ink on the Constitution was dry. The debates of the ratification process were peppered with arguments that the compromises reached by delegates in Philadelphia were not only sensible but literally divine. Benjamin Rush, a famed surgeon who had served the Continental Army during the Revolutionary War and signed the Declaration, reportedly told Pennsylvania's ratifying convention, for instance, that the Constitution had been delivered to the American people "from heaven"—and that, according to a transcript, "he as much believed the hand of God was employed in this work as that God had divided the Red Sea to give a passage to the children of Israel, or had fulminated the Ten Commandments at Mount Sinai." In Federalist 37, James Madison would similarly write that deliberations at the convention had been guided by the "finger of that Almighty hand" that had brought Americans to an improbable victory over the British.

The idea that the Constitution had been handed down as holy writ was pushed by the Founders to win an intense nine-month messaging war against a diverse, intelligent, and passionate array of opponents whom most Americans have largely forgotten, though they may have been more numerous than the Constitution's supporters. History, the saying goes, is written by the victors. That's true enough, but it's often the case that the eventual winners, if they're prudent, set about writing history before they've even won. And so it was with the Founders. "Indeed," Harvard's Michael Klarman writes in *The Framers' Coup*, "even while the convention was still completing its work in Philadelphia, one advocate for a more powerful national government observed that 'such a body of enlightened and honest men perhaps never before met for political purposes in any country upon the face of the earth.' Such men were 'entitled to the universal confidence of the people of America.' "

In a democracy, of course, no class of leaders, however "enlightened and honest" they might be, is "entitled" to the public's confidence. Instead, the faith and support of the masses must be earned and re-earned through political contestation. This is what it means for the people at large to be both fully empowered and equal—what it means for the governed to govern.

After many tense and tumultuous months, the Founders did win the ratification contest. But the political system that prevailed—the system we've inherited—reflects their deep hostility toward mass politics. As eloquently as the Founders made references and appeals to the people—in their speeches and writing, within the text of the Constitution itself—they were brought to Philadelphia by a sense that the people had been up to no good in the years following the American revolution. An economic crisis, they believed, had pushed the young country dangerously toward democracy.

The Founders' Crisis

Although quill pens, powdered wigs, and pamphlets have mostly survived in the American public's imagination, we won our independence through a major war as chaotic, bloody, and brutal as most others—a protracted, nearly decade-long international conflict that killed an estimated 25,000 Americans and violently upended colonial life. "Roaming armies and frontier raiders uprooted thousands of people by destroying their farms, plantations, and towns," historian Alan Taylor writes in *American Revolutions*. "As a percentage of the population, the mortality exceeded every American conflict but the Civil War of the 1860s." The revolution also triggered the greatest economic collapse the nation would see until the Great Depression. In our first fifteen years of existence, America's gross national product per capita fell by nearly 50 percent—a crash caused not only by ravaged land and lost assets, including thousands of slaves who had escaped to freedom, but the sudden collapse of military spending as well as retaliatory British trade restrictions.

These and other early challenges overwhelmed a federal government that was, almost by design, barely functional. The Articles of Confederation, ratified in 1781, had established a Congress, elected by state legislatures, with very few powers beyond those key to fighting a war that had been caused, after all, by the perceived legislative overreaches of Parliament. Even the major responsibilities Congress had explicitly been given—the appropriation and borrowing of money, the approval of treaties, new declarations of war—required supermajorities of at least nine states, a tall bar to clear that was made especially onerous by frequent delegate absences. And even when it did act, Congress lacked real authority over the states—the Articles had given Congress no real way to enforce its mandates.

Congress likewise lacked the power to directly collect taxes. It came to rely instead on requisitions—firmly requested but often denied or delayed payments from the states. Compliance with requisitions only declined as the war wore on and finally drew to a close, making it difficult for Congress to meet its expenses and pay down the nation's rapidly ballooning debts. And by 1783, the government's fiscal situation was so dire that George Washington was forced to personally intervene against a threatened mutiny by officers owed back pay. Even in victory, Washington and others worried that an inability to stably finance and field an army left American territory vulnerable to incursions by major powers—and attacks from Native Americans whom settlers on the Western frontier were trying to uproot.

Meanwhile, state governments under the Articles were both powerful and active. While Americans had jointly declared independence as one nation, the country remained, in practice, a coalition of thirteen largely separate and rivalrous societies—a coalition shaped by deep regional divides. When Spain closed the Mississippi River to Americans in 1784, for instance, enraged

Southerners and Western settlers who depended upon it for trade threatened war. But Northerners were willing to give up access to the river in order to reach a commercial treaty with Spain for their own benefit—so willing, in fact, that some Northerners floated the possibility of seceding from the just-formed United States and starting a new country.

In the absence of a national trade strategy set and enforced by Congress, states also crafted their own tangle of individual trade policies to counter British trade restrictions—and impose fees on each other. And, like Congress, the states found themselves deeply indebted at war's end. Unlike Congress though, state governments had the power to collect and raise the taxes they needed to pay creditors and meet their other obligations—including the occasional congressional requisition. And raise them they did—so much, in fact, that taxes in most states were three to four times higher than the colonial taxes that had driven many to war against the British. Against the backdrop of a nationwide economic depression, many ordinary Americans—including growing numbers thrown, like their states and the country as a whole, ever deeper into debt—found those taxes increasingly difficult to bear.

Yet as far as many elites and political leaders were concerned, the mounting financial troubles of those struggling were their own fault. New Jersey Governor William Livingston, for instance, dismissed the critics of rising taxes as "lazy, lounging, [and] lubberly," while legislators in Maryland claimed individual debtors had been wasting their money on "the exorbitant importation of foreign luxuries" and "gambling contracts." The supposed spending habits of women in particular drew blame. "One author reminded American women that 'feathers and other frippery of the head, are badges of prostitutes in Europe,'" the historian Woody Holton writes in *Unruly Americans*, while another scold in New Jersey, "urged women to forgo an article that had become fashionable on both sides of the Atlantic: 'artificial rumps.'"

One woman who happened to agree that economically frustrated Americans were being unreasonable was future First Lady

Abigail Adams—if the struggling were "harder-prest by publick burdens than formerly," she wrote in one letter, "they should consider it as the price of their freedom." But as more and more Americans were pointing out, much of the tax money being collected as the "publick's burden" to pay down government debts was building the private wealth of speculators, including Adams herself, who had been buying up that debt on the cheap.

By the mid-1780s, the frustrations of hard-bitten farmers in particular had boiled over into organized protests, rowdy revolts, and campaigns to win economic relief from state legislatures, including personal-debt deferrals and laws that allowed the debts to be paid in installments or in goods and property. Most consequentially, populist farmers and their sympathizers also pushed state governments to issue paper money as an alternative to hard currency which made it easier to pay down both personal debts and growing tax bills. These campaigns succeeded across the country thanks largely to relatively broad suffrage, at least for white men—it's thought that 60 percent or more of them could vote at the beginning of the 1780s.

But while most states had issued paper money in response to growing economic discontent by 1786, leaders in Massachusetts refused to budge. Though it had been the crucible of the revolution, Massachusetts was ironically governed by America's most conservative state constitution, which featured the nation's only executive veto. And in the legislature, relief policies were on tough political ground—property qualifications for voters and political candidates were high, and the apportionment scheme of the Massachusetts legislature disadvantaged rural communities. So the petitions and protests of the state's populists went mostly ignored. Indeed, in the winter of 1786, Massachusetts lawmakers openly defied them with a tax *increase.*

By then, out in the state's countryside, irate farmers had already begun taking up arms. Thousands mobilized to protect debtors, frustrate tax collection, and stop foreclosures by shutting down local courthouses. Although the Massachussetts legislature responded to the unrest with some modest and belated relief measures, it also inflamed the situation by passing a Riot Act and allowing the governor to summarily imprison demonstrators. In January 1787, Daniel Shays, a farmer and a veteran of the Revolutionary War, led a raid on the federal arsenal in Springfield and was repelled after a skirmish. Local militias called up by the governor to put down the uprising refused, forcing private financiers—including many wealthy holders of government debt—to raise the money for their own private army instead. By February, Shays' forces were surrounded and outnumbered, essentially bringing the rebellion to an end.

While Shays' Rebellion was defeated in the field, it won a major victory at the polls just months later. Massachusetts Governor James Bowdoin was replaced by his rival, the former Governor John Hancock, who won a whopping 75 percent of the vote and went on to pardon Shays and free most of the imprisoned rebels. The state's old guard also suffered major losses in the state legislature. And while paper money remained off the table after the elections, lawmakers began slashing taxes almost immediately.

All this sent shock waves through elite circles across the country. It would be difficult to overstate the impact that Shays' Rebellion had on the Founders in particular—most were apoplectic. Already dismayed by the defects of the *federal government* under the Articles, men such as James Madison—who wrongly suspected most rebels supported, in his words, "an abolition of debts public and private, and a new division of property"—grew intensely alarmed that populist fervor was ruining *state* economic policies, even in conservative Massachusetts.

The rise of paper money had been particularly disturbing. In Virginia's legislature, Madison, born into a wealthy planter family, had reflected the views of most elites in denouncing paper money as "unjust, impolitic, destructive of public and private confidence, and of that virtue which is the basis of republican governments." More concretely, the wealthy tended to believe that paper money encouraged sloth and irresponsibility by easing the burdens of financial obligations. They also believed it threatened property rights by undermining the stability of contracts and investments—and, perhaps, by paving the way for the direct abolition of debt, as Madison feared. One fellow Virginian, for instance, warned George Washington in a letter that unless state legislatures could be reconstructed to make them "more powerful and independent of the people, the public debts and even private debts will in my opinion be extinguished." In the fall of 1786, Washington himself worried that the popular movements in Massachusetts and elsewhere had "exhibit[ed] a melancholy proof" of what the British had predicted about the United States—"that mankind left to themselves are unfit for their own government."

In sum, by early 1787, most of the Founders believed their new country was already falling apart. The defects of the Articles of Confederation left America unable to meet its basic financial obligations, and militarily vulnerable on a continent still dominated by Britain and Spain. In lieu of a national trade policy, the states were doing as they pleased and were tied up in spats shaped by regional economic divisions. And thanks in part to the need for unanimity among the states, efforts to address these problems by amending the Articles had foundered for years.

As dysfunctional as the federal government had become, few were optimistic about the prospects for major reform. But the mass movements for paper money and other economic relief measures in the states, particularly Shays' Rebellion, finally pushed many elites from mere frustration with the status quo to a panic that inspired calls for drastic and perhaps even authoritarian action. In August 1786, Washington relayed rumors to foreign affairs secretary John Jay "that even respectable characters speak of a monarchical form of government without horror." In a February 1787 letter, Madison similarly wrote that the "turbulent scenes" in New England had "done inexpressible injury to the republican character in that part of the United States," adding that "a propensity towards monarchy is said to have been produced by it in some leading minds."

Most of the Founders, though, hoped to find a medium between bringing the American experiment to an early end with a

return to monarchy on one hand and sticking with the unworkable Articles on the other. In September 1786, a convention was
held in Annapolis, Maryland, to consider reforming the nation's
trade policies. When representatives from only five of the nine
states slated to show up arrived, the convention adjourned early—
but not before the delegates in attendance, including Madison
and Alexander Hamilton, drafted a report recommending another convention in Philadelphia the following May to consider
broad amendments to the Articles.

Initially, leaders in several states—especially the New England
states, which had been absent from Annapolis—were deeply am-
bivalent about a second gathering. But Shays' Rebellion in January quickly changed minds. And in late February 1787, Congress
voted to approve a resolution endorsing a convention in Philadelphia for "the sole and express purpose of revising the Articles of
Confederation."

The Constitutional Convention

The fifty-five men who gathered in Philadelphia and wound up
writing an entirely new Constitution disagreed sharply on many
key issues they would consider; at times, debates grew strained to
the point that some delegates worried they would adjourn, once
again, in defeat. But their deliberations did eventually succeed,
partially because they had much in common in spite of their
differences—collectively, they represented the highest and most
comfortable echelons of American society. All were at least mod-
erately affluent. Most owned sizable amounts of land. Most were
either lawyers or legally trained. Most had gone to college. Most
had been congressmen. Nearly all were Protestants. Nearly half
owned slaves.

Obviously, and as noted before, there were no women, no African Americans, and no Native Americans at the convention.
Nor were there any struggling back-country farmers—the class
of white men whose protests had done so much to bring the con-

vention about. In fact, Rhode Island, which had been infamously friendly to economic relief measures, refused to send any delegates at all to the convention out of a suspicion that the other delegates would be deeply hostile to paper money.

That suspicion was well-founded. As wealthy men generally opposed to paper money and other relief measures, the convention's delegates were also several degrees of separation from direct democratic influence and the populist movements that had successfully influenced lawmakers in the years leading up to the convention. Every delegate had been appointed to the convention either by a state legislature or, in South Carolina's case, a governor. Additionally, many who might have offered more strident defenses of paper money and relief policies at the convention (had they attended it) doubted that fundamental changes to the political status quo were truly on the table. Congress's resolution, after all, had endorsed only amendments to the Articles, and past efforts at major revisions had failed.

Yet unbeknownst to those outside the convention's halls, most delegates backed a true break from the Articles early on. Debate would focus not on whether a new federal government was needed, but on what form that government might take.

★ ★ ★

In the very first speech of the convention, Virginia delegate Edmund Randolph named the form it surely wouldn't. "Our chief danger," he told those assembled, "arises from the democratic parts of our [state] constitutions. It is a maxim which I hold incontrovertible, that the powers of government exercised by the people swallows [sic] up the other branches. None of the constitutions have provided sufficient checks against the democracy." On this, there was broad agreement. Alexander Hamilton, the most ostentatiously conservative of the convention delegates, affirmed that many Americans—not just himself—were growing "tired of an excess of democracy," Holton writes. "Others identified the problem as 'a headstrong democracy,' a 'prevailing rage of excessive democracy,' . . . 'democratical tyranny,' and 'democratic licentiousness.'"

The terms of the convention's debates over what to do about "democratic licentiousness" were set substantially by James Madison, who, at thirty-six, was a true child of the Enlightenment. Madison had been highly educated—technically, for a span of about half a year in 1771, he'd been Princeton's first-ever graduate student—and had put his studies in political philosophy to good use eleven years prior to the convention as one of the drafters of Virginia's constitution and Declaration of Rights. And he was also an experienced legislator who had grown intimately familiar with the defects of the Articles as a delegate in Congress. In the months before the convention, he'd talk at length about those defects to peers and friends including George Washington, Thomas Jefferson, and Randolph.

The Virginia Plan introduced by Randolph at the convention was the product of Madison's deliberations and conversations. In it, the Congress of the Confederation was replaced with a government that would have three distinct branches. There would be a legislative branch containing a new Congress with broad powers "to legislate in all cases . . . in which the harmony of the United States may be interrupted by the exercise of individual legislation" and to veto unconstitutional state laws. This Congress would consist of two houses: a lower house elected by the people of the states, and an upper house elected by the lower house from nominees selected by state legislatures. And in both houses, the number of representatives per state would be based on "quotas of [financial] contribution" or "the number of free inhabitants, as the one or the other rule may seem best in different cases." There would also be a distinct judicial branch, responsible for carrying out impeachments within the federal government, resolving interstate disputes, and adjudicating all other cases involving "the national peace and harmony."

Finally, there would be an executive branch, elected by Congress, responsible for implementing Congress's laws. Together with federal judges in a "council of revision," the executive would also have the power to veto any unconstitutional laws or acts by Congress. No explicit guidelines were offered for amending the Constitution. Instead, the Virginia Plan stipulated only that amendments would not require congressional approval, and that they would be considered "whensoever it shall seem necessary."

All of this was a radical break from the Articles—a blueprint for shifting America from a loose coalition of mostly independent states to a tighter union under a sovereign and mighty federal government, empowered not only to make its own national laws but to invalidate the laws of state legislatures and directly resolve interstate disputes. And as Madison had designed it, that government would essentially act directly upon the public, rather than through state governments—which, under the Articles, had been able to ignore laws and acts of Congress.

Madison had also pushed for major revisions to how Congress worked. In the Articles' unicameral Congress, states had been represented equally, regardless of population. By contrast, neither house of the Virginia Plan's new, bicameral Congress would have equal representation. Instead, Madison favored apportionment by population, or by contributions to the federal government. And while all members of the Congress of the Confederation had been appointed by state legislatures, Congress as Madison envisioned it would substantially diminish the influence of the state legislatures given that representatives of the lower house would be popularly elected. The Virginia Plan also implied the new Constitution would be much easier to amend than the Articles—reformers would be able to bypass Congress entirely, though Madison was light on details about how that process would work.

★ ★ ★

Most delegates to the convention, exasperated by the weakness of Congress under the Articles, were receptive to Madison's vision of an expanded, more complex, and more powerful federal government. And in keeping with that vision, the finished Const tution, unlike the Articles, would allow Congress, without super-majorities, to regulate commerce, collect taxes, and—vaguely and consequentially—make any laws "necessary and proper" to executing those and other responsibilities designated in the text.

The convention also agreed with Madison's vision for a true executive branch, which the Articles had lacked, and decided to vest the branch's powers within a single president—over the objections of delegates who argued the presidency too closely resembled the British monarchy. In keeping with that impression, some delegates floated having the president serve as long as ten to twenty years—or even for life, assuming "good behavior"—as opposed to the four-year terms the convention would settle upon.

Even with those shorter terms, the president would be quite powerful. Unlike the governors of most states, the president would work without an executive council. With the advice and consent of the Senate, he would have the power to make major appointments most state constitutions and the Articles of Confederation had left to legislators. And after some debate, the convention traded Madison's proposal for an executive council of revision for the president's individual veto of federal laws—enjoyed by almost no governors at the time—which would be subject to overrides only by congressional supermajorities. Such a veto, Madison told the convention, would be "useful to the community at large, as an additional check against a pursuit of those unwise and unjust measures which constituted so great a portion of our calamities," including paper money and debt relief measures.

For the same reason, delegates to the convention also initially supported Madison's federal veto for unconstitutional state laws. In fact, a proposal was made to expand the federal veto even to *constitutional* state laws that Congress simply disapproved of—a notion Madison had backed in his preconvention writings as necessary to prevent state governments from "oppressing the minority within themselves by paper money and other unrighteous measures which favor the interest of the majority." Once that more expansive veto was brought up again in Philadelphia, Madison seconded it. But most delegates eventually changed their minds about instituting a federal veto at all, agreeing it would be both unworkable—"Is no road nor bridge to be established without the sanction of the general legislature?" Virginia's George Mason asked—and unpopular.

In the end the federal veto was dropped, to Madison's bitter disappointment, in favor of the Supremacy Clause, which establishes the Constitution and federal laws as the highest laws of the land. And the clause would be cited as one of the principal justifications for 1803's landmark *Marbury v. Madison* decision establishing judicial review, the ability to declare an act or law unconstitutional, at the Supreme Court—performing the role Madison had envisioned for an executive branch "council of revision." Specific concerns about paper money and debt relief in the states, which a federal veto might have overturned, were also addressed by Article I, Section 10 of the final document, which bars states from issuing their own money and passing laws "impairing the obligation of contracts."

Beyond ditching the federal veto, the convention would also dramatically alter Madison's legislative scheme after intense and protracted debate. Though he had been deeply troubled by mass politics in the states, Madison firmly believed popular elections were necessary *somewhere* in government to sustain popular legitimacy. As he described himself in his transcript of the convention's proceedings, Madison had been "an advocate for the policy of refining the popular appointments by successive filtrations, but thought it might be pushed too far." Indirect election, he went on to argue, was best used "only in the appointment of the second branch of the Legislature, and in the Executive & judiciary branches of the Government"—in other words, in every other part of the federal government but the house of Congress that would become the House of Representatives.

Yet as Michael Klarman notes, the concept of popular elections even on that limited scale proved too democratic for some delegates:

The proposal for direct popular election of members of the lower house elicited some of the most vigorous denunciations of democracy heard at the convention. Invoking Shays's Rebellion, [Elbridge] Gerry opposed direct election of representatives on the grounds that the people were "the dupes of pretended patriots" and were "daily misled into the most baneful measures and opinions by the false reports circulated by designing men." [Roger] Sherman preferred that state legislatures choose members of the lower house because he considered the people unqualified to do so . . . Charles Cotesworth Pinckney defended state legislative selection of members of the House on the grounds that a majority of his state's citizens had been "notoriously for paper money as a legal tender," while the state legislature, from "some sense of character," had refused to comply with that demand.

These detractors aside, most delegates generally agreed with Madison on popular election to the lower House—both out of principle and out of a sense that incorporating popular elections into the Constitution's design would help build public support for it. But the final text of the Constitution would also make elections to the House harder for populists to influence and win than elections to the state legislatures. The chamber's small size—sixty-five members at the outset, tiny compared to lower houses in the states—would create districts so large that few candidates but the already well-known and well-regarded would be able to compete. Madison had reasoned that larger districts would also be more diverse, making the formation of popular—and populist—majorities more difficult. "The election may safely be made by the People if you enlarge the Sphere of Election," delegate Rufus King noted him saying. "If bad elections have taken place from the people, it will generally be found to have happened in small Districts."

Even so, Madison also supported doubling the House's initial size, fearing that the resulting districts had been made *too* large.

The convention rejected that proposal, but approved provisions allowing Congress to expand the House in the future, based on a census every ten years. The convention also rejected having the lower house elect members of the upper house in favor of having the upper house elected by state legislatures—both to maintain, in Connecticut delegate Roger Sherman's words, "a due harmony" between the states and the federal government and to ease the Constitution's ratification by the states.

Consensus on how to apportion representation in Congress would prove far more difficult to reach. A few weeks into the convention, small-state delegates introduced what came to be called the New Jersey Plan, which was similar to the Virginia Plan in most respects with the major exception of Congress's design. In essence, the New Jersey Plan preserved the Congress of the Confederacy—a unicameral body, elected by the state legislature, with equal representation for each state, regardless of population. It was never likely that most delegates to the convention would back another unicameral Congress—at the time, all but two states had bicameral legislatures similar to the Congress of Madison's Virginia Plan, which was itself influenced by the bicameral British Parliament. But the New Jersey Plan was less a sincere proposal than a negotiating maneuver—a line drawn in the sand by the small states against apportionment in Congress based on population or taxes, as Madison had proposed, and in defense of equal state representation, which had bolstered their influence under the Articles. Delaware, for example, would get the same number of representatives under the principle as Madison's Virginia despite having a population that was about twelve times smaller.

Naturally, Madison and many other larger-state delegates loudly and persistently opposed equal state representation as grievously unfair. "It is not in human nature that Virginia and the large States should consent to it, or if they did that they should, long abide by it," Madison notes Hamilton saying. "It shocks too much the ideas of Justice, and every human feeling." In mid-July,

Madison himself expanded on the implications of using equal representation in Congress's upper house:

1. The minority could negative the will of the majority of the people.
2. They could extort measures, by making them a condition of their assent to other necessary measures.
3. They could obtrude measures on the majority, by virtue of the peculiar powers which would be vested in the Senate.
4. The evil, instead of being cured by time, would increase with every new State that should be admitted, as they must all be admitted on the principle of equality.
5. The perpetuity it would give to the preponderance of the Northern against the Southern scale was a serious consideration.

Opponents of equal state representation also argued that the convention had been convened in the first place out of a shared sense that states had been too powerful as entities under the Articles. In fact, some delegates at the convention, most notably Hamilton, were open to essentially dissolving them. "Even with corporate rights," New York delegate Robert Yates notes him saying, "the states will be dangerous to the national government, and ought to be extinguished, new modified, or reduced to a smaller scale."

Most, including Madison, weren't willing to go that far. But the larger state delegates did insist that the new federal government would have to govern the American people more directly, rather than relying upon the compliance of often-stubborn state governments, as it had under the Articles.

To that point, Massachusetts delegate and future vice president Elbridge Gerry contended that the states had grown "intoxicated with the idea of their sovereignty," and that equal representation had been a mistake of the Articles. "He was a member of Congress at the time the federal articles were formed,"

Madison notes him saying. "The injustice of allowing each State an equal vote was long insisted on. He voted for it, but it was against his Judgment, and under the pressure of public danger, and the obstinacy of the lesser States."

James Wilson put the central question to the convention with palpable frustration: "Can we forget for whom we are forming a Government?" he asked. "Is it for men, or for the imaginary beings called States?" Madison himself argued that "too much stress was laid on the rank of the States as political societies" and characterized equal representation as a defect that would threaten the stability of the Constitution and the country—"a principle," he warned, "which was confessedly unjust, which could, never be admitted, & if admitted must infuse mortality into a Constitution which we wished to last forever."

In response, the small states insisted repeatedly, to Madison's exasperation, that the larger states and smaller states were coherent factions with distinct interests. Larger states such as Madison's Virginia, for example, had opposed ceding their western lands to Congress, which would have been able to sell them off to pay down the nation's debts—proving that the larger states could and would collude to shape the country's policies to their benefit at the expense of the smaller states. As such, "the power of self-defence was essential to the small States," Madison notes Connecticut delegate Oliver Ellsworth saying. "Nature had given it to the smallest insect of the creation." New Jersey's William Paterson, chief author of the New Jersey Plan, claimed that his state "would be swallowed up" by a system deviating from equal representation and even declared that he would "rather submit to a monarch, to a despot, than to such a fate."

As Paterson's comments suggest, the debates over equal representation heightened tensions at the convention dramatically—thanks, in part, to delegates from Delaware. On June 30, Delaware delegate Gunning Bedford Jr. delivered a stem-winder of a speech, excerpted here from Yates's notes, denouncing the delegates of the large states as a cabal:

I do not, gentlemen, trust you. If you possess the power, the abuse of it could not be checked; and what then would prevent you from exercising it to our destruction? You gravely allege that there is no danger of combination, and triumphantly ask, how could combinations be effected? "The larger States," you say, "all differ in productions and commerce; and experience shows, that instead of combinations, they would be rivals, and counteract the views of one another." This, I repeat, is language calculated only to amuse us. Yes, sir, the larger States will be rivals, but not against each other—they will be rivals against the rest of the States.

For the small states, Bedford concluded, protecting equal representation was a matter of simple self-interest. Madison's notes record him making reference to the infamous "rotten boroughs" of British Parliament—depopulated districts with very few voters that nonetheless retained seats in the House of Commons. "Can it be expected that the small States will act from pure disinterestedness?" he asked. "Have not the boroughs however held fast their constitutional rights? And are we to act with greater purity than the rest of mankind?" Moreover, he warned, in abandoning equal representation, the convention, led by the large states, would be violating a principle that had been at the very heart of the Confederation. He ended his speech by threatening secession:

The Large States dare not dissolve the Confederation. If they do, the small ones will find some foreign ally of more honor and good faith, who will take them by the hand and do them justice. He did not mean by this to intimidate or alarm. It was a natural consequence; which ought to be avoided by enlarging the federal powers not annihilating the federal system.

Bedford wasn't the first to suggest the question of equal representation might bring about the country's dissolution. Earlier in the day's proceedings, for instance, James Wilson—the same

Pennsylvania delegate who had called states "imaginary beings," had all but welcomed the threat Bedford would make. "He hoped the alarms exceeded their cause, and that [the small states] would not abandon a Country to which they were bound by so many strong and endearing ties," Madison notes him saying. "But should the deplored event happen, it would neither stagger his sentiments nor his duty. If the minority of the people of America refuse to coalesce with the majority on just and proper principles, if a separation must take place, it could never happen on better grounds."

At the outset of deliberations, a majority of delegates supported population-based representation in both houses of the proposed Congress. But winning that fight at the convention may well have meant losing the new Constitution to the opposition of the small states during ratification—or even the country's breakup, as Bedford and Wilson alike suggested. Ominously, Delaware, for its part, had instructed its delegates to walk out of the hall if equal representation was defeated. Deliberations grew so protracted and tense that Benjamin Franklin suggested that delegates try "imploring the assistance of Heaven" on the matter with prayer. They didn't—and ultimately didn't have to: The large states were forced to a painful compromise once Georgia delegates who had backed population-based representation left the convention to attend Congress, bringing the remaining delegates to a tie on representation in the upper house.

That tie was broken once a committee appointed to resolve the debate backed a solution that had been proposed earlier by Roger Sherman: Representation in the lower house, the House of Representatives, would be population-based, while representation in the upper house, the Senate, would be equal for every state. The committee also proposed having revenue and spending bills originate in the House of Representatives, though this provision was revised later in the convention to apply only to revenue bills.

After protests from Madison and other large-state delegates and the floating of more alternatives, the convention narrowly voted to approve the compromise, five states to four. Separately and infamously, after another protracted debate between the Northern and Southern states, convention delegates would also agree to count a slave as three-fifths of a person for the purposes of allocating seats in the House and apportioning direct taxes among the states. As far as the Senate was concerned, the small states won their victory largely because the states, which voted as blocs, were represented equally at the convention in the first place, just as they would be in the Senate—the delegates who backed equal representation were representing only about a quarter of the American population at the time.

The equally apportioned Senate would be given important and exclusive powers approving treaties and confirming executive officers and federal judges nominated by the president. Beyond those critical tasks, the centrality of the Senate to the federal scheme would be underscored by the length of Senate terms—the convention eventually decided upon six years to the House's two. In a speech to the convention about the upper chamber's function, Madison—who had backed first a seven- and then a nine-year term—defended long tenures in the Senate with a prediction about the country's future. The Senate and its wise representatives, he argued, would keep America stable by resisting the demands of the masses and making the redistribution of wealth more difficult:

> In framing a system which we wish to last for ages, we shd. not lose sight of the changes which ages will produce. An increase of population will of necessity increase the proportion of those who will labour under all the hardships of life, & secretly sigh for a more equal distribution of its blessings . . . symtoms, of a leveling spirit, as we have understood, have sufficiently appeared in a certain quarters to give notice of the future danger. How is this danger to be guarded agst. on republican principles? How is the danger in all cases of interested coalitions to oppress the minority to be guarded agst.? Among other means by the establishment of a body in the

Govt. sufficiently respectable for its wisdom & virtue, to aid
on such emergences, the preponderance of justice by throwing its weight into that scale.

These remarks echoed a speech on the Senate Madison had
made two weeks earlier: "Mr. Madison," Yates recorded in his
notes on those remarks, "considers this branch as a check on the
democracy. It cannot therefore be made too strong."

★ ★ ★

Delegates at the convention also extensively debated the selection
of the president. The Virginia Plan had followed the example of
most state constitutions in having the executive elected by the
legislature for a single term. But Madison and most other delegates came to decide that the executive branch would need more
independence from Congress, whose powers they hoped to
check. One alternative considered was the election of the president by popular vote. There was some precedent for this—voters
in Massachusetts and New York directly chose their governors.
And Madison made his own case for the popular vote: "The people at large," he told the convention in mid-July, would likely be
"the fittest in itself" to choose the nation's executive.

But his support for the popular vote was rooted less in a deep
trust of the masses that had been responsible for paper money
and debt relief in the states than in the assumption, made with the
same reasoning he'd applied to the relatively large size of House
districts, that the size of the country would hobble the candidacies of all but the most prominent and respectable of the country's elites. "The people," he said, "generally could only know &
vote for some Citizen whose merits had rendered him an object
of general attention & esteem." He did, though, note one critical
drawback to a popular vote—that Southern states such as Virginia would be at a relative disadvantage, given that their slaves
couldn't vote and wouldn't count.

Most delegates disagreed with Madison that a popular vote
would be wise even in principle. "It would be as unnatural to

refer the choice of a proper character for chief magistrate to the people," Mason declared, "as it would be to refer a trial of colors to a blind man." Mason argued, too, that voters would favor candidates from their own states.

As with the question of apportionment in Congress, the convention spent a good deal of time grasping around in frustration for a solution to presidential selection that would be agreeable to all sides. And eventually they settled upon a proposal, first advanced by Wilson, to have the president chosen by a college of electors, who themselves would be selected in ways specified by state legislatures every election. As the delegates envisioned it, the Electoral College was a solution that preserved the advantages of election by the public—a healthy independence from any other standing branch of government, the likelihood of an esteemed and prominent candidate being chosen—without directly *involving* the public.

The Electoral College also had the added benefit, as far as Southerners were concerned, of bolstering the influence of slave states. Each state's electoral votes would be a total of their senators plus their seats in the House, which would reflect slave populations thanks to the Three-Fifths Compromise.

★ ★ ★

The presidency and the Electoral College, the design of the House and the Senate, the creation of the Supreme Court and the federal judiciary, the establishment of the Constitution as the highest law of the land—the delegates would debate many other issues at the convention, but these were the basic components of the final document as it was signed that September in 1787. With some major and minor revisions, they remain the basic components of the federal government today.

As we've seen, delegates designed these institutions with their particular political and economic moment in mind. As a whole, the Constitution was crafted by a set of the nation's political elites to address perceived crises that governance under the Articles had either caused or ineffectively responded to. And to the Founders, the worst of those crises was an "excess of democracy" in the states. Economic conditions and tax policies had driven ordinary people across the country to push state governments—by conventional politics and more radical means—into adopting populist policies that most wealthy Americans found dangerous and destructive. The success of those efforts encouraged the Founders to make a full break from the Articles. Under the Constitution, a confederation of states would be upended and replaced with a consolidated union under a powerful federal government. That government would wield its authority not only over the state governments but directly over the American people—though the people, for their part, would have no direct voice in federal governance outside the House of Representatives, whose districts had been made large to frustrate democratic action.

The Founders fully understood that the ratification of the new Constitution would be an extraordinary undertaking, and that the scale of the changes it heralded for the American political order would pit much, if not most, of the enfranchised public against them. But they did make one bold move to tilt the odds in their favor. The Articles had required the unanimous support of the states for amendments, a hurdle that had made even basic revisions impossible. Having drafted *an entirely new document,* delegates at the convention decided to try a novel strategy— simply ignoring the requirement. The Constitution would be approved through a flagrantly unconstitutional process. Only nine states would be required to ratify it. Why? Because Article VII of that Constitution, which had yet to be ratified, said so. What's more, the Constitution would be ratified by state conventions rather than by the state legislatures the Articles had mandated for amendments—the very legislatures the new Constitution would disempower. Unsurprisingly, the brazen and total usurpation of the Articles was a major reason the Constitution was met with furious opposition once the ratification process began.

"It is an undisputed fact," the playwright and poet Mercy Otis Warren wrote in a 1788 pamphlet:

that not one legislature in the United States had the most distant idea when they first appointed members for a convention, entirely commercial, or when they afterwards authorized them to consider on some amendments of the Federal union, that they would without any warrant from their constituents, presume on so bold and daring a stride, as ultimately to destroy the state governments, and offer a consolidated system, irreversible but on conditions that the smallest degree of penetration must discover to be impracticable.

The Constitution's Federalist supporters countered that particular objection with an insistence that government under the Articles had been totally dysfunctional, and that the country was teetering on the edge of collapse. They emphasized, too, the nobility of those who had gathered at the convention in Philadelphia—again, Madison and others even suggested that their proceedings had been guided by divine providence. But the Federalists also rooted their claims about the legitimacy of the new system in the idea that the Constitution would be ratified by the American people, who elected the members of the state ratifying conventions.

In practice, the composition of the ratifying conventions would be skewed in all sorts of ways, including the overrepresentation of—and the staging of several key conventions within— urban areas where very few Americans lived at the time relative to the rural communities that had backed debt relief and paper money. Nevertheless, the Founders framed the ratification process they devised as an instantiation of popular rule. "The people," Madison had said during the convention, "were in fact the fountain of all power and by resorting to them, all difficulties were got over. They could alter constitutions as they pleased."

But the Anti-Federalists didn't buy it—the ratification process aside, "the dangerous power and structure of the Government," Madison notes George Mason saying, "would end either in monarchy, or a tyrannical aristocracy; which, he was in doubt.

But one or other, he was sure." At Virginia's ratifying convention, Mason, one of three delegates who had refused to sign the
Constitution, placed particular emphasis on the deficiencies of
popular representation under the Constitution relative to state
governments under the Articles of Confederation:

> Is this general representation to be compared with the real,
> actual, substantial representation of the state legislatures? It
> cannot bear a comparison. To make representation real and
> actual, the number of representatives should be adequate;
> they should mix with the people, think as they think, feel as
> they feel,—should be perfectly amenable to them, and thor-
> oughly acquainted with their interest and condition. Now,
> these great ingredients are either not at all, or in a small de-
> gree, to be found in our federal representatives; so that we
> have no real, actual, substantial representation: but I acknowl-
> edge it results from the nature of the government.

Virginia's Patrick Henry agreed, calling the Constitution's design "pernicious, impolitic, and dangerous." He argued too, contra Madison, that the Constitution would be difficult to amend
thanks to supermajority requirements—two-thirds in each house
of Congress or the state legislatures for passing amendments,
three-fourths of the states, in their legislatures or conventions,
for ratification—that might empower a "trifling minority," in
contravention of democratic principles:

> What, sir, is the genius of democracy? Let me read that clause
> of the bill of rights of Virginia which relates to this: 3rd
> clause:—that government is, or should be, instituted for the
> common benefit, protection, and security of the people, na-
> tion, or community. Of all the various modes and forms of
> government, that is best, which is capable of producing the
> greatest degree of happiness and safety, and is most effectu-
> ally secured against the danger of mal-administration; and
> that whenever any government shall be found inadequate, or

contrary to those purposes, a majority of the community hath an indubitable, unalienable, and indefeasible right to reform, alter, or abolish it, in such manner as shall be judged most conducive to the public weal.

This, sir, is the language of democracy—that a majority of the community have a right to alter government when found to be oppressive. But how different is the genius of your new Constitution from this! How different from the sentiments of freemen, that a contemptible minority can prevent the good of the majority! If, then, gentlemen, standing on this ground, are come to that point, that they are willing to bind themselves and their posterity to be oppressed, I am amazed and inexpressibly astonished.

In the end, of course, the Federalists won out, thanks in large part to shrewd politicking and an important concession—a Bill of Rights that many Anti-Federalists had demanded as a condition for ratifying the Constitution, and which Madison and most of the Founders had initially seen as superfluous. Even so, the Constitution prevailed only narrowly at several conventions. And after New Hampshire became the decisive ninth state to ratify it, the states that remained faced serious political and economic pressure to join the new union—Rhode Island, for instance, which had refused to send delegates to the convention, became the last state to ratify the Constitution not long after the first Senate, already in session, voted to ban trade with the state.

Republic or Democracy?

As Franklin related to Powel, the compact finally ratified by all thirteen states in 1790 established a republic—of that there can be no doubt. Whether it also established a democracy, on the other hand, remains a live question today. A common refrain from many contemporary conservatives is that the republic the Founders created is emphatically *not* a democracy. Calls for democratic reforms to the federal system, they argue, therefore betray the Founders' intentions. "The contemporary efforts to weaken our republican customs and institutions in the name of greater equality," a 2020 report from the conservative think tank the Heritage Foundation reads, "run against the efforts by America's Founders to defend our country from the potential excesses of democratic majorities."

Liberals, meanwhile, tend to find this line of argument obtuse, misleading, and even dangerous. All the Founders meant by republican government, they insist, was representative democracy—they envisioned and intended majoritarian government through leaders elected by the people, as opposed to the more direct democracy of the Athenian assembly, which they considered unstable and impractical. The conservative interpretation of the Founding, *Vox*'s Zack Beauchamp wrote in 2020, "originated as arguments for curbing democracy in the ordinary sense of the word—the ability of majorities to enact popular policies (that conservatives disapproved of)." "What we call 'representative democracy,'" he continued, "is what the founders called a 'republic.' Their attacks on 'democracy' in the Athenian sense do not mean that America is not a democracy in the contemporary sense."

But the question of whether America is a democracy today—in the sense defended by this book or by any other "contemporary sense" one might choose—isn't solely or even primarily a matter of the Founders' intent. Even if the Founders had intended to create a democracy, they might have simply failed to do so, leaving us with a Constitution more defective than they perceived. And even if the Founders *hadn't* intended to create a democracy, one could argue that changes to the Constitution since the Founding have transformed the undemocratic republic the Founders might have desired into a genuinely democratic republic today. As it happens, this book argues both these views are wrong. But the point is that connections between what the Founders intended and our government today must be drawn carefully—with reference not only to what the Founders *may have wanted* but to what they actually *did* within the Constitution, and the extent to which their handiwork endures.

Moreover, neither what the Founders *intended* for America nor what America *is* at present can determine for us what America *should be.* The origins of the Constitution are of interest here not because the Founders' intentions should bind us in the present, but because the historical record helps us understand why the institutions we've inherited from them function as they do.

One thing the historical record tells us, though, is that "the Founders' intent" is no straightforward thing to divine. As we've seen, delegates in Philadelphia who largely agreed about the problems the country faced in 1787 still differed sharply on the solutions. Again, three delegates, each of whom had been major participants in the convention's debates—Elbridge Gerry, George Mason, and Edmund Randolph—refused to sign the finished Constitution altogether. And even many of those who did had strong reservations about the compromises the convention had been forced to strike. That included Madison and Hamilton, who swallowed their criticisms of the final document and made the best case they could muster for it in the Federalist Papers.

Even there, the two could hardly conceal their disappointment with some of the Constitution's features. In Federalist 22, for instance, Hamilton noted that the equal representation of states had been an "exceptionable part" of the Articles of Confederation:

> Every idea of proportion and every rule of fair representation conspire to condemn a principle, which gives to Rhode Island an equal weight in the scale of power with Massachusetts, or Connecticut, or New York; and to Deleware an equal voice in the national deliberations with Pennsylvania, or Virginia, or North Carolina. Its operation contradicts the fundamental maxim of republican government, which requires that the sense of the majority should prevail. Sophistry may reply, that sovereigns are equal, and that a majority of the votes of the States will be a majority of confederated America. But this kind of logical legerdemain will never counteract the plain

suggestions of justice and common-sense. It may happen that this majority of States is a small minority of the people of America; and two thirds of the people of America could not long be persuaded, upon the credit of artificial distinctions and syllogistic subtleties, to submit their interests to the management and disposal of one third.

Nevertheless, small states at the convention had forced the adoption of equal state representation in the Senate. And while that chamber would be paired with the population-based House in Congress, bicameralism meant that the Senate, sharing the defects Hamilton had denounced in Congress under the Articles of Confederation, would functionally hold veto power over all federal legislation—in addition to its exclusive power to approve treaties and executive and judicial appointments.

The power given to the small states by that arrangement, Madison wrote in Federalist 62, was born of a compromise motivated less by political principle than political necessity:

> It is superfluous to try, by the standard of theory, a part of the Constitution which is allowed on all hands to be the result, not of theory, but "of a spirit of amity, and that mutual deference and concession which the peculiarity of our political situation rendered indispensable." . . . A government founded on principles more consonant to the wishes of the larger States, is not likely to be obtained from the smaller States. The only option, then, for the former, lies between the proposed government and a government still more objectionable. Under this alternative, the advice of prudence must be to embrace the lesser evil; and, instead of indulging a fruitless anticipation of the possible mischiefs which may ensue, to contemplate rather the advantageous consequences which may qualify the sacrifice.

Those and other misgivings notwithstanding, the project of drafting and ratifying a new Constitution was undertaken by the

Founders with a broadly shared sense of purpose—the government of the Articles would be replaced with a new and improved system, built upon republican principles as the Founders understood them. And, as liberals argue, there is *some* textual support for the idea that they took republican government to mean what *we* might call *representative democracy*. "In a democracy," Madison wrote in Federalist 14, for instance, "the people meet and exercise the government in person; in a republic, they assemble and administer it by their representatives and agents." As a practical matter, he continued, republican government was best suited for a country as large as the United States. While a democracy would be "confined to a small spot," a republic "may be extended over a large region." Still, as Madison explains in Federalist 39, both republics and democracies derive their authority and legitimacy from the masses:

> We may define a republic to be, or at least may bestow that name on, a government which derives all its powers directly or indirectly from the great body of the people, and is administered by persons holding their offices during pleasure, for a limited period, or during good behavior. It is ESSENTIAL to such a government that it be derived from the great body of the society, not from an inconsiderable proportion, or a favored class of it; otherwise a handful of tyrannical nobles, exercising their oppressions by a delegation of their powers, might aspire to the rank of republicans, and claim for their government the honorable title of republic.

But in Federalist 10, he also describes the Constitution as a republican compact that would put the country at some distance from democracy's perils:

> A pure democracy, by which I mean a society consisting of a small number of citizens, who assemble and administer the government in person, can admit of no cure for the mischiefs of faction. A common passion or interest will, in almost every

case, be felt by a majority of the whole; a communication and concert result from the form of government itself; and there is nothing to check the inducements to sacrifice the weaker party or an obnoxious individual. Hence it is that such democracies have ever been spectacles of turbulence and contention; have ever been found incompatible with personal security or the rights of property; and have in general been as short in their lives as they have been violent in their deaths. Theoretic politicians, who have patronized this species of government, have erroneously supposed that by reducing mankind to a perfect equality in their political rights, they would, at the same time, be perfectly equalized and assimilated in their possessions, their opinions, and their passions.

A republic, by which I mean a government in which the scheme of representation takes place, opens a different prospect, and promises the cure for which we are seeking.

A key benefit of representation, Madison continues—beyond its practical advantages over direct or "pure" democracy in large societies—is that it can act as a filter, working "to refine and enlarge the public views, by passing them through the medium of a chosen body of citizens, whose wisdom may best discern the true interest of their country."

★ ★ ★

For liberals, this is where discussions of Madison's views on representation often end. Madison believed America should be a republic, by which he meant a government "in which the scheme of representation takes place." And republican government would be more suited to governing a large society like the United States than direct or "pure" democracy not only as a practical matter but also because it would establish a class of leaders who could process raw public opinion into more considered and useful ideas—thus avoiding the "turbulence and contention" Madison believed "pure" democracies were susceptible to. And though he was dismayed by the equal representation of states, Madison suggests in Federalist 63 that the Senate in particular would embody the representative ideal:

> As the cool and deliberate sense of the community ought in all governments, and actually will in all free governments ultimately prevail over the views of its rulers; so there are particular moments in public affairs, when the people stimulated by some irregular passion, or some illicit advantage, or misled by the artful misrepresentations of interested men, may call for measures which they themselves will afterwards be the most ready to lament and condemn. In these critical moments, how salutary will be the interference of some temperate and respectable body of citizens, in order to check the misguided career, and to suspend the blow meditated by the people against themselves, until reason, justice and truth, can regain their authority over the public mind? What bitter anguish would not the people of Athens have often escaped, if their government had contained so provident a safeguard against the tyranny of their own passions?

Madison, one might come away believing from all we've read above, did believe America should be a democracy—just a representative one, with institutions designed to check the public's passions.

But, importantly, Madison didn't believe representation was a panacea for the problems the country had faced under the Articles of Confederation. While representation *could* offer key advantages over "pure" democracy, he writes in Federalist 10, representative government could clearly still be captured by the same "interests" and "passions" that were so dangerous in "pure" democracies:

> Under [representation], it may well happen that the public voice, pronounced by the representatives of the people, will be more consonant to the public good than if pronounced by the people themselves, convened for the purpose. On the

other hand, the effect may be inverted. Men of factious tempers, of local prejudices, or of sinister designs, may, by intrigue, by corruption, or by other means, first obtain the suffrages, and then betray the interests, of the people.

All told, the Federalist Papers establish fuzzy but critical distinctions between republican government and democracy. Madison did believe, as liberals insist, that "republican" government, understood as representative government, was more feasible and sensible, in theory, than the Athenian assembly. But Madison distinguished between *good* republics and *bad* republics. While "*it may well happen*" that representation leaves the people better off than directly following public opinion "pronounced by the people themselves"—as would be the case in a "pure" democracy— representation in a republic could still fail at the hands of "men of factious tempers, of local prejudices, or of sinister designs."

In short, Madison believed a republic could be nearly as bad as a direct democracy. And the same might be said of the Founders as a whole, who had been pushed to draft the Constitution, after all, not by the failures of direct or "pure" democracy but by the perceived failures *of representative democracy* under the Articles of Confederation. This is the key defect in the liberal interpretation of the Founding. While Madison and the other Founders made illustrative historical references to ancient Greece, resurrecting the Athenian assembly was not on the table in America in 1787. The choice facing the country at the Founding wasn't between representation under a new Constitution and democracy as practiced in Greece more than two thousand years prior. It was between representation under a new Constitution and representation under the Articles of Confederation—which most Founders believed had given too much power to state governments too easily captured by mass democratic action. It was a choice between whether America would become *a good republic less democratically responsive* to the American people or remain, from the Founders' perspective, *a bad, dangerously democratic one.*

The Constitution, as the Federalist Papers argued, would keep representation and a republican structure while establishing a government less susceptible to the "factious tempers" that Madison feared, which he saw as existential threats to the stability of both "pure" democracies and republics. And in Federalist 10, Madison is crystal clear about the "factious tempers" he finds most worrisome:

> The most common and durable source of factions, has been the various and unequal distribution of property. Those who hold, and those who are without property, have ever formed distinct interests in society. Those who are creditors, and those who are debtors, fall under a like discrimination. A landed interest, a manufacturing interest, a mercantile interest, a monied interest, with many lesser interests, grow up of necessity in civilized nations, and divide them into different classes, actuated by different sentiments and views. The regulation of these various and interfering interests, forms the principal task of modern legislation, and involves the spirit of party and faction in the necessary and ordinary operations of government.

Everything Madison says here is consonant with republican thought as explored in Chapter 3—a variety of interests compete in society, and the business of government, Madison says, is to prevent them from dominating each other. But as we've seen, there are two republican traditions. Democratic republicanism hopes to reduce domination by disempowering the wealthy and addressing economic inequality. In aristocratic republicanism, on the other hand, reducing domination often means defending the wealthy from others, including the masses.

The distinction between these kinds of republicanism was understood in the Founders' time. The lexicographer and writer Noah Webster, for instance, explained in a 1790 essay that "the basis of a democratic and a republican form of government is, a fundamental law, favoring an equal or rather a general distribution of property." And in 1790, at least, property (or *landed* property) was distributed more equally in America than it was in Europe—where, Webster wrote, "many of the governments might, with propriety, be called *aristocratic republics.*" But Webster went on to predict the very same future for the country that Madison had in his speech to the Constitutional Convention defending long terms in the Senate. With time, Webster speculated, the growth of America's population would lead to more conflicts between the haves and the have-nots:

> The tracts of land first taken up by the settlers, were not very considerable; and these having been repeatedly divided among a number of heirs, have left the present proprietors almost without subsistence for their families. Vast numbers of men do not possess more than thirty or forty acres each, and many not half the quantity. It is with difficulty that such men can support families and pay taxes. Indeed most of them are unable to do it; they involve themselves in debt; the creditors take the little land they possess, and the people are driven, poor and helpless, into an uncultivated wilderness. Such are the effects of an equal division of lands among heirs; and such the causes of emigration to the western territories.

Webster concludes with a warning that "the vast inequality of fortunes" and the power imbalances they produced had toppled Rome. He and Madison would surely agree that conflicts between the classes threaten the stability of republican governments. But Madison's conception of republican government, as described in the Federalist Papers, wasn't rooted in the equal distribution of property. Instead, Madison's position and the position of most of the Founders—as defended in Federalist 10 and elsewhere—was that inequality and the tensions it produced should be *institutionally managed* rather than directly reduced or eliminated. Although Madison and most Founders genuinely worried about the impact the odd wealthy scoundrel with "sinister designs" might have on politics, they were less troubled by *their own wealth and property*—which, in Madison's words, arose naturally from "the diversity in the faculties of men." "The protection of these faculties," he writes in Federalist 10, "is the first object of government."

Again, fears that the mass movements for paper money and debt relief had also demanded "a new division of property" had fueled elite support for a new governing compact in the first place; the hope of most Founders was that it would *protect* the wealthy, as Hamilton wrote in a 1787 essay on the Constitution, from "the depredations which the democratic spirit is apt to make on property." Where *democratic* republicans might have embraced egalitarian economic policies in response to the nation's post-Revolution economic crises, the Founders wrote a Constitution that would make enacting them more difficult instead.

The agitations of democratic republicans—those, as Madison had said at the convention, who possessed "a leveling spirit" and pined "for a more equal distribution"—were precisely what the new Constitution had been set up to oppose. And, again, that objective would rely upon more than mere representation, which had been turned to populist ends in the state legislatures. "It is in vain to say that enlightened statesmen will be able to adjust these clashing interests, and render them all subservient to the public good," Madison writes in Federalist 10. "The inference to which we are brought is, that the CAUSES of faction cannot be removed, and that relief is only to be sought in the means of controlling its EFFECTS." The Constitution would attempt to control those effects by limiting the democratic influence of the masses everywhere the Founders thought possible; to do so, it divided the federal government into a complex set of interlocking parts that would make policymaking difficult even for elected majorities.

Madison also hoped that America's already large and growing size would mitigate the effects of "faction." In a departure from the French philosopher Montesquieu, who had influentially argued that republics were best suited to small territories, Madison argued—with the same reasoning used in his argument for large House districts and his discussion of a popular vote for the president—that larger societies were difficult for factions to overtake. Mass democratic politics of the kind that had swept the state legislatures, he seemed to believe, were impossible on a national scale—a reality he hoped, as he writes in Federalist 10, would frustrate the ambitions not only of self-interested minorities but of those who might hope to form democratic majorities to fight inequality:

> Extend the sphere, and you take in a greater variety of parties and interests; you make it less probable that a majority of the whole will have a common motive to invade the rights of other citizens; or if such a common motive exists, it will be more difficult for all who feel it to discover their own strength, and to act in unison with each other.
>
> . . . The influence of factious leaders may kindle a flame within their particular States, but will be unable to spread a general conflagration through the other States. A religious sect may degenerate into a political faction in a part of the Confederacy; but the variety of sects dispersed over the entire face of it must secure the national councils against any danger from that source. A rage for paper money, for an abolition of debts, for an equal division of property, or for any other improper or wicked project, will be less apt to pervade the whole body of the Union than a particular member of it; in the same proportion as such a malady is more likely to taint a particular county or district, than an entire State.

In other words, the very aim of Madison's republicanism—an aim shared by most of the Founders—was to make democratic politics much harder. Beyond being a more convenient means than direct democracy of governing a society as large as the United States, representation, as the theorist Hannah Pitkin wrote of Madison's thinking, was "a way of stalemating action in the legislature, and thus in society, until wisdom prevails among the people." And those stalemates were to be forced not only by representatives filtering public opinion and the Constitution's system of checks and balances, but by the practical challenges of trying to conduct democracy in a large country—which, Madison hoped, would frustrate the kind of organizing and campaigns that had pushed state legislatures to back paper money and debt relief in the years after the Revolution.

This, plainly, is the sketch of an *aristocratic* republicanism. The Founders, of course, would have furiously rejected the label, though not merely because it's an unflattering one. Against charges from the Constitution's Anti-Federalist opponents that the new compact would empower the aristocracy, the Founders often replied that there were no real aristocrats in America to begin with—at least not titled nobles with hereditary privileges, as there were in Britain. Instead, they argued, all power in the Constitution's new government would flow directly from ordinary Americans—most directly, as Madison explains in Federalist 57, in the House of Representatives:

> Who are to be the electors of the federal representatives? Not the rich, more than the poor; not the learned, more than the ignorant; not the haughty heirs of distinguished names, more than the humble sons of obscurity and unpropitious fortune. The electors are to be the great body of the people of the United States. They are to be the same who exercise the right in every State of electing the corresponding branch of the legislature of the State. Who are to be the objects of popular choice? Every citizen whose merit may recommend him to the esteem and confidence of his country. No qualification of wealth, of birth, of religious faith, or of civil profession is permitted to fetter the judgement or disappoint the inclination of the people.

But Madison's defense was disingenuous on several counts. Though the Constitution had imposed no requirements for voting or holding office beyond age and citizenship restrictions, it was simply not true that those rights would be shared equally, even among white men—states had property qualifications that would remain in place under the Constitution. And at the convention, the Founders had generally supported the idea of putting new property qualifications directly into the Constitution. They hadn't only because they feared it would complicate ratification further.

Madison also didn't mention that the convention had featured laments over the absence of a true American nobility—which, in the eyes of some delegates, would have made designing the Senate much easier. "I revere the theory of the Brit. Govt. but we can't adopt it," Rufus King noted Wilson saying. "We have no laws in favor of primogeniture—no distinction of families—the partition of Estates destroys the influence of the Few." There had also been discussions about apportioning representation in Congress based on wealth. And while that didn't come to pass, there was an expectation, as King notes Madison saying, that the Senate would come to "represent the wealth of the nation."

Though most of that wealth had been produced by commerce in America, critics of the Constitution like the young future president John Quincy Adams suspected it had been drafted "to increase the influence, power and wealth of those who have any already"—influence, power, and wealth that they feared would be passed down from narrow generation to narrow generation, just as it would be under a traditional hereditary aristocracy. "If the Constitution be adopted it will be a grand point gained in favor of the aristocratic party," Adams wrote in his diaries. "There are to be no titles of nobility, but there will be great distinctions, and those distinctions will soon be hereditary, and we shall consequently have nobles, but no titles."

To critics like Adams, arguments that republics derived their power "directly or indirectly from the great body of the people" had to be regarded with suspicion—the Constitution made clear that the Founders wanted power to flow as indirectly from the people as possible. As Madison wrote in Federalist 63, this was the chief advantage that governance in America held over ancient societies such as Athens. "The principle of representation was neither unknown to the ancients nor wholly overlooked in their political constitutions," he wrote. "The true distinction between these and the American governments, lies IN THE TOTAL EX-CLUSION OF THE PEOPLE, IN THEIR COLLECTIVE CAPACITY, from any share in the LATTER, and not in the TOTAL EXCLUSION OF THE REPRESENTATIVES OF THE PEOPLE from the administration of the FORMER."

The exclusion of the people meant not only the absence of direct democracy but the absence of any true responsibility, on the part of the people's representatives, to democratically reflect the public's views. It should be remembered here that in 1787 the first modern public-opinion surveys with random sampling were still more than a century away. As Madison pointed out, not unfairly, at the convention, political leaders had no reliable means of gauging what the broad public thought or wanted beyond election results even if they had wanted to. "If the opinions of the people were to be our guide, it would be difficult to say what course we should take," he said. "No member of the Convention could say what the opinions of his constituents were at this time; much less could he say what they would think, if possessed of the information and lights possessed by the members here; and still less, what would be their way of thinking six or twelve months hence."

But even at the ballot box and the point of election, the Founders worked to establish more distance between representatives and the opinions of their constituents than there had previously been. Unlike some state constitutions, the Constitution would deny voters the power to issue binding instructions to their representatives in Congress. While term limits had been included in the Virginia Plan, the finished Constitution would similarly depart from the state governments in omitting them—which would have forced elected officials to rejoin the public after some time—and do away, too, with the states' right to recall their representatives. And again, even successful legislation in Congress could be subject to the veto of an indirectly elected president acting alone.

All in all, the kind of republicanism the Constitution embodied reflected a principle that Benjamin Rush expressed in his 1787

"Address to the People of the United States." "It is often said, that 'the sovereign and all other power is seated in the people,'" he said. "This idea is unhappily expressed. It should be—'all the power is derived from the people.' They possess it only on the days of their elections. After this, it is the property of their rulers, nor can they exercise or resume it, unless it is abused."

★ ★ ★

It would have been helpful for us all if the Elizabeth Willing Powel of legend had pestered Ben Franklin with a follow-up question: "You've given us a republic, yes. But what kind?" We remain confused on this point, preoccupied with a question—*Is America a republic or a democracy?*—that amounts to a false choice. A republic can be a democracy. And this is precisely what the Founders hoped to avoid. While they established a republican government and considered representation integral to both the Constitution's design and republican thought more broadly, the Founders did not believe that representatives should be the democratic agents of their constituents. Although power under the Constitution would be derived from the people, the Founders did all they could to ensure the people themselves would not be in power. And it was Madison's hope in particular that the size of the United States would frustrate democratic attempts to gain power by forming majorities.

The Founders did argue against minority rule in the abstract; a good number, like Madison and Hamilton, were genuinely troubled by the minoritarian implications of equal state representation in the Senate in particular. But they also feared, even more strongly, democratic majorities animated by the kind of "passion and interest" that had taken hold of state politics in the wake of the American Revolution. The final impetus for the drafting of the Constitution was the fear that democratic action had posed a dire threat to property rights and a minority group that merited special protections—wealthy elites.

As stated at the outset, there is something admittedly strange—silly, even—about investigating the democratic commitments of men who excluded women, African Americans, and Native Americans from the polity they constructed. Though respectable figures throughout American history have labored heroically to pretend otherwise, no governing compact crafted with provisions to protect slavery can be considered meaningfully democratic at all. But what the historical record also demonstrates is that the Founders doubted white men—even propertied white men such as themselves—could be entrusted with democratic power. They designed our governing institutions accordingly.

In the decades immediately following the Constitution's ratification, however, the political power of ordinary white men would continue to grow. Thanks to state-level action, suffrage grew more expansive. And that expanded electorate would be mobilized and guided through the system the Founders had erected by the emergence of political parties, which the Founders had failed to anticipate. Some of the Founders themselves—including Madison, who had condemned factions so forcefully—would helm those parties and find themselves swept into the early stirrings of national mass politics.

The emergence of partisanship also changed one aspect of the Constitution relatively quickly. The Electoral College had not been designed with partisan presidential tickets in mind, and it had been expected that the second-place vote-getters in the College would be awarded the vice presidency. But in 1800, Democratic-Republican electors cast an equal number of votes for Thomas Jefferson and Aaron Burr, their party's candidates for president and vice president; the result was a first-place tie for the presidency that threw the election to the Federalist-controlled House of Representatives, which sent Jefferson to the White House after thirty-six ballots. The Twelfth Amendment, requiring separate ballots for the presidency and vice presidency, fixed that glitch as a technical matter.

But the episode demonstrated something significant. The Electoral College would never be the august and factionless deliberative body the Founders had envisioned. Instead, it would be a mere vehicle for partisan politics. And the public would also come to have a greater role in the election of the president than the Founders knew. While electors were initially chosen with a variety of methods, nearly every state would eventually award all of its electoral votes to the winners of its statewide popular vote—a system that remains in place today in all states except Maine and Nebraska, which award some of their votes by congressional district.

With time, even the Senate would be fundamentally altered—in 1913, the Seventeenth Amendment finally mandated the direct election of senators. And the powers of those elected to the White House and Congress would also undergo gradual but dramatic shifts from Founding intent. Today, thanks substantially to the "Necessary and Proper" and Commerce clauses and the federal government's authority to tax, a political order created in large part to keep politics out of economic policy governs and guides the American economy in ways the Founders scarcely could have dreamed.

It is the contention of this book that political contests over the direction of our economy, and much else besides, are not resolved democratically. That said, many more Americans can consider themselves parties to those contests today than could a hundred years ago. On paper, full political rights are now afforded to Americans irrespective of race and gender; the Elizabeth Willing Powels of the country—and those she might have employed as slaves—can vote and hold office.

All of this is to the good. None of it is enough. Democracy demands much more from us than we've been able to accomplish. And certainly much more from us than the Founders intended.

CHAPTER 5

TOWARD A DEMOCRATIC POLITICS

IT WOULD TAKE AT LEAST ANOTHER BOOK, AND LIKELY SEVERAL, to give a full account of how woefully the American political system falls short of democratic ideals even today, more than two centuries after the Founding. It's true, as many might protest, that the Founders wouldn't recognize much of what's cropped up atop the basic framework they put in place; again, the United States today is a far more egalitarian society than they would have thought possible or desired. But the basic foundation they laid down remains remarkably strong—to our detriment. We find our political system frustrating largely because it was designed to frustrate us. Many Americans have come to suspect our institutions do more to protect the wealthy than they do to represent ordinary people. This is precisely what the Founders wanted and what the Constitution was written to achieve. And atop our system's antidemocratic design, newer challenges have corroded our democratic agency even further.

This chapter's catalog of our system's defects and potential fixes for them is necessarily incomplete. Much of what *is* here can be credited to the work of scholars and reformers who've labored over the last few years on tremendous pieces of legislation like the For the People Act, a 2021 package of voting rights, campaign finance, and ethics reforms that was blocked by Republicans using the Senate filibuster—a procedure this chapter will spend quite a bit of time examining. The fact that the For the People Act and other pushes for democratic reform have stalled in recent years, though, is no reason to give up on the project of making American democracy real. In fact, the intensifying war President Trump and the Republican Party are waging against democratic principles gives us all the more reason to think ambitiously about the cause of reform and fundamentally transforming our political order. Consider this chapter an invitation to do so.

The House of Representatives

If democracy means that the governed should govern through fair competition, politicians who compete shouldn't get to fix the results in their favor by fiddling with rules and procedures. This commonsense principle is why ballot stuffing, real and imagined, angers us so. But in America, elections can be legally rigged in one significant way.

As laid out in the Constitution, congressional districts are re-drawn and reapportioned every ten years after the Census. The goal of this "redistricting" process, which is controlled by state governments, is to capture shifts in the country's population and adjust the seats in the population-based House of Representatives accordingly. But our parties have worked out a variety of ways to exploit the process and give themselves the voters that they want—an ignoble tradition that stretches back to the early days of the republic. In 1812, Elbridge Gerry—the Constitutional Convention delegate, now governor of Massachusetts—signed off on an infamously contorted district drawn to benefit his own Democratic-Republican Party. His opponents sneered that it looked something like a salamander—or a *Gerry*-mander. Not an especially good joke, truth be told, but the name stuck.

The methods for gerrymandering have gotten quite sophisticated since Governor Gerry's time. But there are two basic strategies the parties that control the redistricting process in each state use. There's *packing*, where parties try to pool voters of a certain kind into districts, and there's *cracking*, where voters of a certain kind are divided up between districts. Political operatives have both down to a science now; consequently, gerrymanders are thought to account for as much as one-third of the decline in competitive congressional districts in the United States since the early 1980s.

The Republican Party showed a real gift for the practice in the 2010s. After the 2010 Census, the GOP launched a campaign called REDMAP (for Redistricting Majority Project) that was aimed at winning enough state legislatures to control the redistricting process. That effort largely succeeded. Republicans brought in veteran mapmakers such as Thomas Hofeller—who had once accurately called redistricting "a legalized form of vote-stealing"—to draw new districts. Democrats and reformers fought back in the courts. But by 2017, one analysis of the twenty-six states accounting for 85 percent of the country's congressional districts found that Republicans had engineered themselves a sixteen- to seventeen-seat advantage in the House with gerrymandered maps.

To be fair, both parties gerrymander, and the whole business is routine. It has been allowed, in fact, by the Supreme Court, which has never struck down a partisan gerrymander and has even ruled that partisan gerrymanders *cannot* be struck down on constitutional grounds. "Federal judges," Chief Justice John Roberts wrote in that 2019 decision, "have no license to reallocate political power between the two major political parties, with no plausible grant of authority in the Constitution, and no legal standards to limit and direct their decisions."

The gerrymandering of House districts has attracted a tremendous amount of attention in the political press and in academia for many years for good reason—it is among the most obvious and galling of our political problems. But it should also trouble us that House maps are often undemocratically skewed even when they aren't gerrymandered. Populations are never evenly distributed across space—people tend to cluster in and around urban areas, while rural populations are more spread out. If rural and urban voters, as groups, tend to prefer distinct parties or policies, elections in rural and urban districts won't be particularly competitive whether they've been gerrymandered or not.

One of the issues arising from that dynamic is that urban voters with certain political views might naturally be packed into *one or a few* highly populous districts that they dominate, while rural voters with a different set of views might naturally dominate *many* more sparsely populated districts outside cities. Consequently, it's often said that urban votes can be "wasted"—because they're so tightly clustered into a few districts, urban voters might have far less impact on control of the House than voters who live elsewhere. Conversely, rural voters who might heavily support a certain party in rural districts "waste" those votes relative to how valuable they might have been for their party in more competitive and perhaps *suburban* districts. In both cases, votes that should count equally, democratically speaking, actually count more or less in House elections simply as a function of where voters happen to live.

Together, that reality and gerrymandering create gaps between the votes a political party wins in House elections and the proportion of House seats it winds up with. In 2012, for instance, Republicans managed to keep the chamber with a 54 percent majority of seats, despite having won more than a million *fewer* votes than Democrats nationwide. In 2022, on the other hand, Republicans won three million more votes than Democrats nationally but managed to gain only an underwhelming nine seats.

There's another problem with House districts, one that at least partially reflects Madison's intentions for the chamber. As discussed in Chapter 4, Madison argued that large district sizes would tame democracy by making elections more difficult for rabble-rousers to win. Obviously, technological advances that Madison couldn't have imagined have made mass politics easier. But, almost as if to compensate, House districts have also gotten considerably more populous.

That's largely a product of population increases, of course. But it hasn't helped that the number of House districts has been frozen for decades, preventing the chamber from growing with the country. As a result, the average House district contained 760,000 people in 2020, over three times more than the average population of a district in 1910, when the number of seats in the House was expanded to the current 435. That's the highest ratio of people to lower house seats in the developed world. By comparison, the peer country with the next-highest ratio, Japan, had an average district size of just over 272,000 people in 2018. In the United Kingdom and Germany, the average district contains around 100,000 people.

Behind the average, the size of districts varies considerably from one state to the next, thanks to two requirements—that each state have at least one representative, and that districts be equally sized *within* states rather than between them. "Wyoming, with just under 578,000 people, winds up overrepresented because it's guaranteed a seat despite falling well short of that 760,000 national average," explains *FiveThirtyEight*'s Geoffrey Skelley. "Conversely, Delaware has nearly 991,000 people, which leaves it underrepresented because it isn't quite large enough to earn a second seat."

These structural factors shape outcomes in the House before anyone even goes to the polls. And after elections, of course, the preferences of the majorities that prevail can be thwarted in a number of ways. Money in politics and the game of influence in Washington will be addressed later. Beyond those notorious means of legal corruption, however, even basic features of how the House goes about its business make it difficult for members to do the jobs that voters expect and elect them to do. The entire chamber is up for reelection every two years, meaning that much of the time legislators should be spending on legislation is actually spent campaigning—or preparing to do so.

The chamber's rules also hobble the work of legislating in the first place. Through a variety of rules and procedures, leaders of whatever party holds the majority have gotten very good at limiting the independence of House members and blocking the formation of interparty majorities. These measures range from informal provisions such as the GOP's Hastert Rule (which prevents bills from being brought to the floor unless a majority of Republicans support them, even if a majority of House members overall do) to formal provisions such as the "closed rule" (which bars amendments to proposed legislation). Both sit atop a complex committee system that allows party leaders to kill bills they dislike before most members of the chamber have a chance to consider them. All told, the House of Representatives, designed to be the most democratically responsive part of the federal government, is strikingly unresponsive and ineffectual in significant ways.

What could be done? For starters, the House's rules could be changed, and easily so as a technical matter. A party in control of the chamber can simply decide to run it on a majoritarian basis—ensuring that bills with broad support in the House overall get votes in committees and on the House floor even if they might lack the support of most party members. The party in control can also decide to keep legislation open to amendment rather than restricting bills to the amendments they prefer—while retaining the right, of course, to refuse amendments not made in earnest or that would contravene the spirit of the bills in question. Actually convincing Democrats or Republicans to conduct things this way when they hold the House will be far easier said than done, of course—though far easier even in the doing than fixing redistricting.

The most obvious remedy for partisan gerrymandering is deceptively simple. Drawing congressional districts specifically to benefit or disadvantage a party should, of course, be banned. But reformers have had some trouble settling on a standard for determining when a district has been gerrymandered in the first place—the political scientist Lee Drutman notes that at least eighteen different measures of partisan fairness have been proposed. Twenty states have tried to address biased maps by using independent redistricting commissions, with equal numbers of Democrats, Republicans, and unaffiliated or minor-party members such as Greens and Libertarians. But the results of those commissions have been mixed. Disagreements between the parties can lead to impasses on maps, and some commissions have had their maps simply overruled by state legislators.

And as we've seen, gerrymandering isn't the only problem we face on the redistricting front. Because populations are naturally clustered in certain urban areas, it can be genuinely hard to draw a large number of competitive districts, where every vote meaningfully counts, if the urban and more rural populations tend to differ in the parties they support.

Electoral reformers have proposed many remedies for all this, but one of the more commonly proposed alternatives to representation as we know it is the "single transferable vote system" (STV), or multiple-winner ranked-choice voting. All that's a mouthful, so let's take it bit by bit.

We tried out ranked choice or "instant runoff" voting in Chapter 2. In most American elections, each voter chooses one candidate and the candidate who receives a plurality of the vote—that is, more votes than any other individual candidate—wins, even if a majority of voters opposed them and preferred other candidates. In a ranked-choice election, by contrast, voters can rank multiple candidates on the ballot. If no candidate wins a true majority of the first-choice votes, the count goes to an instant runoff. The candidate receiving the fewest votes is eliminated, and those who ranked that candidate first have their second-choice votes given to the remaining candidates. This continues until one candidate wins a majority.

Ranked-choice voting makes elections a bit harder to win. But it also makes them more democratic. No one gets elected without a true majority—and that's accomplished without asking voters to go to the polls again in new runoff elections, as is now the case in some states.

Additionally, ranked-choice voting gives voters who support minor parties and independent candidates much more influence. In most of our elections, run by plurality, voters whose first choices aren't candidates from the parties most likely to win can either suck it up and vote for them anyway or cast essentially worthless votes for the minor party or independent candidates they prefer. But under ranked-choice voting, they can support their first-choice candidates while also having their second-choice and other votes count for the major-party candidates—who would thus have more reason to listen to minor-party and independent voters than they do now.

After decades of activism and advocacy from groups such as FairVote and Common Cause, ranked-choice voting is now used for public elections in fifty-two jurisdictions across the country containing nearly 14 million voters. That includes Maine, where ranked-choice voting is used for all federal elections and state primaries, and Alaska, where ranked-choice voting is used for all state and federal general elections. It's a more complex system than most American voters are used to, but research and surveys from places where ranked-choice voting has been implemented show that voters find it rather simple and satisfying once they get used to it.

Still, while ranked-choice voting would be a clear democratic improvement over the status quo in most American elections, it doesn't solve the redistricting problem on its own. Most districts would still be dominated by one party, and the few voters who happened to live in more competitive districts would still have much more of an impact than other voters on the House. The losing voters in uncompetitive districts would have their votes count more, but still not for much.

The key issue here is that whether an election is close and competitive or not, only one candidate can win—the voters who lose can't send one-third or one-fourth of a congressperson to Washington to represent their share of the vote. But what if they could, in a sense—without resorting to butchery?

This is where having "multiple members" comes in. Today, if Party A wins 70 percent of the vote in a House district, Party B wins 20 percent, and some third Party C wins 10 percent, only Party A's candidate goes to Congress. Party B and Party C don't get representation. But imagine if each House district had multiple seats—a number determined by population—and voters voted for parties, which would appoint representatives themselves, rather than for individual candidates. In that case, parties could win a share of each district's seats proportional to their share of the vote, provided they meet some threshold level of support—say, at least 10 percent of the vote. Now voters from Party A, Party B, and Party C could *all* send representatives to Washington—if the district in question was allocated ten seats, for example, they would send seven, two, and one, respectively. Party A's voters would get a large majority of seats, but voters from Parties B and C would get some too, giving them much more influence on the House's composition—three seats rather than zero—than they have under the present system, even though Party A clearly dominates their district.

Multi-winner elections, or "proportional representation," would utterly transform American politics. It would, yes, be incredibly difficult to map opposing parties into irrelevance within a district, either naturally or by gerrymandering. But proportional representation is also more democratically representative than the status quo in general. More votes and voters would truly matter, and minor parties would get more seats at the table—so many more, in fact, that proportional representation would likely encourage the formation of new and competitive parties, ending our two-party duopoly, which most Americans dislike.

Additionally, proportional representation can be combined with instant-runoff voting—allowing voters to choose specific candidates, as we're used to in this country, rather than parties—with a simple tweak to how the runoff votes are counted. In single-member districts, as stated earlier, the candidates with the fewest votes are eliminated and the second-and-beyond–choice votes of their supporters are given to the remaining candidates until one candidate receives a clear majority. But in a system of proportional representation, candidates are eliminated if they don't receive a minimum quota of votes—the second-and-beyond–choice votes of their supporters are given to the remaining candidates until all the district's seats are filled. This is STV.

There are many, many different ways to go about elections, and our peers around the world use a variety of designs that would improve our status quo if adopted here. But the single transferable vote system would likely suit us best, especially given our tradition of going to the polls to choose specific candidates rather than parties. As such, in 2022 more than two hundred American political scientists wrote an open letter to Congress urging lawmakers to adopt proportional representation. "Proportional, multi-member districts are not only constitutional, they are broadly consistent with American history and political norms," they wrote. "In fact, multi-member House districts were common across the country for over 150 years—albeit without proportional representation, which proved a fatal flaw, as at-large districts were used to effectively disenfranchise minority groups and grossly over-represent narrow majorities. Congress must now improve upon, not ignore, this history."

True proportional representation, combined with rank choice voting, would prevent the feared disenfranchisement that led to the 1967 ban on multi-member districts. That ban should be repealed. The Fair Representation Act—a bill first introduced by Virginia Congressman Don Beyer that would implement STV—should be passed in its stead.

And we should also enlarge the House, while we're at it. More and smaller districts represented by more people would reduce the disparities between district sizes in different states and could make elections easier to contest for the nonwealthy. Lee Drutman, for one, recommends a House with perhaps 700 members. And if that number seems preposterously large when compared with our current 435, consider that France, the United Kingdom, and Germany—all much smaller countries—have lower houses with over 500, over 600, and over 700 members, respectively.

The Senate

In one important way, our upper house, the modern Senate, is *more* democratic than the legislative upper houses of some peer nations. In France and Germany, members of the upper house are still selected by other elected officials rather than by the people—just as American senators were before the Seventeenth Amendment in 1913. Still, in almost every other democratic respect, our Senate is one of the world's worst deliberative bodies.

The Senate's most egregious flaws are actually aspects of its basic design but, as with the House, the rules and procedures the chamber has adopted for itself also matter. One particularly important rule has attracted renewed attention in recent years. While the Senate ostensibly runs by majority rule, it takes the support of a supermajority—since 1975, three-fifths of the chamber, or sixty senators—to bring debates to a close, or *cloture.* Functionally, that means that a bill can be held in limbo unless sixty senators support it enough to end debate and bring it to a vote. Without that supermajority, the minority in opposition to a bill can keep debates going in an attempt to wear down its supporters—a tactic known as the *filibuster.*

Historically, filibusters often took the form of epically long speeches and were used to especially great effect in blocking civil rights legislation. "This minority veto power," Steven Levitsky and Daniel Ziblatt note, "was used to block antilynching legislation in 1922, 1937, and 1940 (despite more than 70 percent public support), as well as bills to abolish the poll tax in 1942, 1944, and 1946 (despite more than 60 percent public support)." In 1957, Strom Thurmond infamously spoke for over twenty-four hours in opposition to that year's Civil Rights Act, which passed not long after he finally left the floor. But senators today don't have to pull the same stunt. The mere threat of a filibuster is enough to torpedo legislation without sixty votes—a situation that means most bills can't pass Congress without a Senate supermajority. Majorities in the Senate can change the chamber's rules if they want to; out of desperation in the 2010s, Democratic and Republican majorities decided to eliminate the filibuster for judicial- and executive-branch appointments. But the parties have yet to back eliminating the filibuster for ordinary bills. There, the chamber's minorities can still rule.

In recent years, legislators have leaned on a workaround. Spending and revenue bills can be passed with simple majorities through a process called *budget reconciliation,* provided they meet certain rules. In brief, policies in reconciliation bills must have a substantial impact on the federal budget but cannot increase the budget deficit for a period of more than ten years. But reconciliation bills—which can be passed only once per fiscal year and are integrated with the budgeting process for the federal government as a whole—tend to be massive and unwieldy; policies must often be shrunken and reshaped to conform to the rules restricting each bill's overall budgetary impact. Thanks to the filibuster, absolutely everything else that can't be passed under reconciliation has to win the support of at least sixty senators— a hurdle that has killed proposed bills on a broad array of issues, despite the support of majorities of the American people and simple majorities of our senators.

Though the filibuster has been around for a long time, its use has exploded over the past few decades. Between the introduction of the first cloture rule in 1917 (which originally required a two-thirds majority to end debate) and 1970, the Senate attempted a total of just forty-nine votes to break filibusters—an average of less than one per year. But from 2010 to 2020, the Senate was holding an average of more than eighty votes to break a filibuster *every single year,* an increase that has made the chamber much more dysfunctional. "The cloture process consumes more than 30 hours of floor time," Ezra Klein writes, "which is one reason a strategy of constant filibustering is so appealing to minority parties: The simple act of breaking constant filibusters paralyzes the Senate majority, ensuring they have less time to legislate, and thus can get less done. That's why filibusters are routinely launched against nominations or bills that ultimately pass unanimously."

Defenders of the filibuster in both parties often suggest that the rule is as old as the Senate itself, or that the Founders intended its creation. In 2018, for example, Democratic senator Dick Durbin argued that eliminating the filibuster "would be the end of the Senate as it was originally devised and created going back to our Founding Fathers." Similarly, in 2019, Republican Senate Majority Leader Mitch McConnell—who had backed eliminating the filibuster for Supreme Court justices in 2017 in order to put a Republican nominee on the bench—argued that while it appears nowhere in the Constitution, the filibuster is nonetheless "central to the order the Constitution sets forth." These are lies. As political scientist Sarah Binder has noted, the filibuster was essentially created by mistake. In 1806, an effort to simplify the Senate's rules led to the deletion of a motion that had allowed majorities to end debates, a loophole first successfully exploited to block legislation in 1837, half a century after the Founding.

As we've seen, the Founders were no friends of democracy. They greatly feared the influence of mass majorities on governance—a fact that defenders of the filibuster have deployed in its defense. But the Founders also believed, quite strongly, that *within the bodies they designed,* simple majorities *of elected or appointed officials* should prevail on most matters. Even they were capable of recognizing that legislative supermajority requirements—of the kind that had hobbled governance under the Articles of Confederation, which the Constitution was written to replace—could make it too difficult to craft and enact policies. Alexander Hamilton is crystal clear about this in Federalist 22. "To give a minority a negative upon the majority (which is always the case where more than a majority is requisite to a decision)," he wrote, "is, in its tendency, to subject the sense of the greater number to that of the lesser." And minorities so empowered, Hamilton warned, could undermine governance with "tedious delays; continual negotiation and intrigue; [and] contemptible compromises of the public good."

Although the Founders did back supermajority requirements on a few things—specifically amendments to the Constitution, overriding vetoes, ratifying treaties, and convicting impeached officials—they rejected them for the passage of ordinary legislation. James Madison addresses this explicitly in Federalist 58: "In all cases where justice or the general good might require new laws to be passed, or active measures to be pursued," he writes of requiring more than a majority of a quorum for a decision, "the fundamental principle of free government would be reversed. It would be no longer the majority that would rule: the power would be transferred to the minority." So empowered, Madison adds, a minority might "screen themselves from equitable sacrifices to the general weal" or "extort unreasonable indulgences" from the majority in exchange for its support.

That line of thought cuts against another oft-heard argument in favor of the filibuster—that allowing minorities to kill legislation supported by majorities pushes lawmakers toward moderation and consensus, making politics more sensible. Even if one wants to believe moderation and consensus are intrinsically sensible and desirable—they are not—moderation and consensus in the Senate and our politics as a whole have *decreased,* if anything, as the filibuster's use has expanded. That might have at least a little to do with the fact that even bipartisan bills that win solid fifty-plus vote majorities in the Senate still can't pass unless they receive at least sixty votes. In 2013, for instance—a few months after twenty-six people, including twenty children, were killed by a gunman at a Connecticut elementary school—a bipartisan bill to implement universal background checks for gun purchases failed in the Senate despite winning a fifty-four-vote majority of senators from both parties.

The Senate's equal representation of the states has compounded the antidemocratic impact of the filibuster. As we saw in Chapter 4, many Founders only grudgingly agreed to this feature of the Senate's design, and the disparities that made equal representation such a bitter pill for them to swallow have only deepened since the Constitution was written. In theory, states that account for less than 20 percent of the country's population can hold a Senate majority, while states representing as little as 11 percent of the population can block legislation through the filibuster. Back in 1787, Virginia, then the largest state, had a population twelve or thirteen times larger than Delaware, the smallest state, which had done so much to push equal representation through at the convention. But our largest state today, California—which, on its own, would be among the forty largest countries in the world—has a population more than *sixty-seven* times larger than our smallest state today, Wyoming. Mathematically, because both have an equal two seats in the Senate, each resident of Wyoming thus has sixty-seven times more representation in the chamber than each resident of California.

In a democracy, as we've seen, all members of a polity should be politically equal—all are equally entitled to representation, and all votes should count roughly the same. While practicalities of institutional design make the ideal difficult to squarely achieve, some representative bodies come closer to achieving it than others. And the Senate is inarguably one of the world's most unequally apportioned upper houses. In fact, one 2014 analysis of thirteen major countries organized as federations of states found that only Argentina and Brazil had upper houses that are more inequitable.

It's often said in the Senate's defense that its system of equal representation is balanced out in some way by population-based apportionment in the House of Representatives. Both chambers, after all, are needed to pass ordinary legislation, and the House enjoys special powers—the exclusive rights to introduce revenue bills, begin the impeachment process, and break Electoral College ties. This is nonsense. While it's true that the Senate can't pass bills without the House, it's plainly antidemocratic that the Senate also holds veto power over the House—that legislation desired by majorities of the American public and passed by the House may be torpedoed by small states in a body that favors them.

And the filibuster only makes all this worse. While they can and have been used in majoritarian ways—by senators who represent majorities of the population but make up minorities of the

Senate—most filibusters tend to advantage small states and minorities of the population. An analysis of filibusters from 1991 to 2010, for instance, found that 66 percent of them had been used to block bills supported by senators representing majorities of the population. Nearly a third of the filibusters launched during that span, in fact, had been used to block bills supported by senators representing *60 percent or more* of the American people.

Moreover, the special powers of the House don't hold a candle to the powers of the Senate, which can convict the impeached, approve international treaties, and—crucially—approve all judicial- and executive-branch appointments. These responsibilities make the Senate one of the few upper houses among peer nations with more power than the lower house.

Given this, small-state voters get an especially privileged say in some of the most important decisions our representatives have to make. In 2020, for instance, Supreme Court justice Amy Coney Barrett was confirmed to the bench—for life—despite the opposition of senators representing over thirteen million more Americans than her supporters. Her confirmation came two years after Justice Brett Kavanaugh was confirmed in the same way—despite the opposition of senators representing about *thirty-eight million* more Americans than his supporters. Similarly, in 2021, President Trump was acquitted in his second impeachment trial even though fifty-seven senators, a simple majority, had voted to convict him of inciting insurrection. Yet per the Constitution, a full conviction would have required the support of a two-thirds *supermajority* of the chamber, or sixty-seven votes. Trump's defenders prevailed, even though senators representing nearly *seventy-seven million* more Americans backed removing him from office.

If current population trends continue—with the large states getting larger and the small states either shrinking or staying roughly the same size—the inequities in the Senate will only increase as time goes on, with a smaller and smaller share of the American population electing a larger and larger proportion of the chamber's seats. And those inequities will have a bearing not only on the amount of representation Americans receive but on the quality of their representation—scholars have noted differences in the behavior of senators from small and large states. Small-state senators, for instance, tend to have closer relationships with both constituents and lobbyists than senators from larger states, who must meet and cater to more interests and groups. Small-state senators also tend to need less money for reelection, and they tend to spend less time raising it than large-state senators—who might focus on national issues at the expense of state and local issues to draw attention and donors.

In sum, the Senate makes the accident of where voters happen to live much more significant than it would be in a democratic system premised on the political equality of all. None of these disparities and differences are a secret; like the filibuster, the basic design of the Senate has been the subject of increased debate in recent years. Those debates typically feature a few standard defenses of the Senate that are worth addressing here. The first is the very same argument that was made for the Senate's design at the Constitutional Convention—equal representation, it's been said, is simply a good way to defend the interests of the small states, which might otherwise be dominated in the system by the larger ones. But states don't share many interests simply by virtue of being small. It's an argument that invites us to imagine that Delaware and Alaska, for instance, with their relatively tiny populations, have a lot in common—enough so that we should have a legislative chamber designed to defend them both from conniving New Yorkers. This is ridiculous. Delaware is a largely urban state that has much more in common sociopolitically and economically with its larger Northeastern neighbors than it does with Alaska and more rural states elsewhere in the country.

That brings us to another defense of the Senate's design—that equal state representation protects the interest of rural (and more conservative) voters, who predominantly live in smaller states, from urban (and more liberal) voters who, Delaware notwithstanding, tend to live in larger states. "Why should Los Angeles and San Francisco have an outsized role in governing distant, rural parts of the country," *National Review* editor Rich Lowry asked in a 2018 column on the Senate, "with which they have no sympathy?" But given the actual math of representation in the Senate, one might ask more soundly why distant rural parts of the country should have an outsize role in governing Los Angeles. As we've seen, equal state representation ensures that voters in states like Wyoming have many times more power in the Senate than Californians—a disparity that amounts to dominance in the chamber rather than a mere tilt in the defense of their interests. Moreover, equal state representation actually overrepresents urban voters who live in small states and underrepresents rural voters who live in large states. Residents of Oklahoma City, for instance—one of the twenty-five largest cities in America— have five times more representation in the chamber than the twenty-five residents of Morehouse, New York, and other tiny rural upstate towns like it.

Nothing here is written to suggest that rural interests don't demand consideration or even protection, in certain instances, when policies are being made. But that's also true of urban interests and the interests of the many other nongeographic constituencies of ordinary people that make up our country. Making democracy work means ensuring all have a seat at a very large table and being attentive to the concerns of those distant and different from ourselves. Given that, we should think about ways to ensure that the typically unheard, from all corners of the country, are afforded more of a voice within our institutions. Still, in a democracy, every vote and every voter must count as equally as practically feasible—no group of people should be considered more special or worthy of representation than others. The idea that equal state apportionment should be tolerated in defense of small-state or rural interests violates that principle.

So too does the idea that equal state apportionment makes the Senate a more deliberative body, an argument that has the added demerit of not making sense even on its own terms. Even if one supposes, antidemocratically, that America needs a chamber smaller, more deliberative, and less responsive to the public than the House of Representatives, it doesn't follow at all that equal state representation—or that representing states in any fashion—is a particularly good way for the Senate to do that. One might imagine, for instance, a chamber of one hundred, fifty, or even five esteemed, chin-stroking luminaries—each collectively chosen by governors or state legislatures to represent the country as a whole—performing the very same function and with less bias to particular states and their interests. Alternatively, one might take inspiration from the governments of the states themselves. State senates have relationships with state lower houses similar to the relationship the U.S. Senate has with the House of Representatives; they perform similar roles in the legislative process. But unlike U.S. senators, our state senators don't represent subunits such as counties or towns. Instead they represent roughly equal shares of each state's population, thanks to the Supreme Court's ruling in the 1964 case *Reynolds v. Sims*—which held that other schemes violated the principle of an equal entitlement to representation. Similarly, one might imagine a U.S. Senate with senators each representing blocs of, say, 10 or 20 million Americans.

But if one agrees with the arguments this book has put forward about democracy thus far, the idea that democratic legislatures need special chambers to check or complicate democratic action should seem dubious, even if such chambers are equally apportioned—facilitating deliberation as a matter of institutional design doesn't have to mean frustrating the mass public or boxing it out. As we've seen, though, the Founders disagreed.

That brings us to the last commonplace argument in defense of the Senate we'll examine, one that really isn't much of an argument at all: Equal state representation in the chamber, it's often said, is simply what the Founders intended—an intentional and integral part of our constitutional order.

Obviously, the Founders having intended something doesn't make the thing intended right or sensible. Moreover, we've already substantially done away with the Founders' intentions in the Senate with the direct election of senators. That change, together with the filibuster, has already produced a chamber significantly different from the Senate the Constitution initially established. And, again, while the equal representation of the states is indeed the central feature of the Senate's original design, many of the Founders, including Madison and Hamilton, *strongly opposed it,* as we've seen. While they wanted a deliberative Senate that would check the power of popular majorities, they also argued at the convention that equal state representation would amount to minority rule over the large states and their voters. "There can be no truer principle than this—that every individual of the community at large has an equal right to the protection of government," New York delegate Robert Yates notes Hamilton saying. "If therefore three States contain a majority of the inhabitants of America, ought they to be governed by a minority? Would the inhabitants of the great States ever submit to this?"

Of course, the larger states and their defenders eventually *did* submit, thanks to the compromise the small states forced at the convention. More than two centuries later, that bargain, only grudgingly struck, profoundly deforms and distorts our politics.

As with the House, the easiest reforms to pull off in the Senate would be changes to the chamber's rules—which, here again, are not set in stone. The majority party can vote to fundamentally change the way things are done, provided they can get themselves to agree on those changes. In recent years, Democrats have come to something like a consensus on the legislative filibuster, which, again, has already been eliminated for executive- and judicial-branch appointments; anyone the president nominates to fill a post can be approved with a simple majority of the chamber. But the filibuster remains in place for all legislation that can't be crammed through the budget-reconciliation process, which was designed for budgetary matters.

One suggestion, endorsed by former president Joe Biden and cautious reformers, is a return to the talking filibuster—forcing those who hope to block legislation to stand on the Senate floor and speak for hours on end, as they once did. But this wouldn't be a democratic reform—it would leave the filibuster intact and, in fact, only deepen its absurdity. Rather than introducing tests of physical stamina into the policymaking process, other reformers have more soundly suggested making the filibuster more majoritarian, somehow—by stipulating that bills supported by a supermajority of the House can be passed by simple majorities in the Senate, for instance, or that only senators representing a majority of the population can utilize the filibuster. The latter idea, in particular, would be a clear democratic improvement over the status quo. Of course, so would simply abolishing the filibuster altogether.

Still, reforming or eliminating the filibuster won't fix the Senate's fundamental inequities—the equal apportionment of senators to all states, irrespective of population, is democratically untenable. Equal apportionment in the Senate, unfortunately, happens to be one of the few parts of the Constitution that are essentially unamendable—per Article V, altering that aspect of the chamber's basic design seemingly requires the unanimous consent of all states. Some reformers argue that this prohibition can be ignored, or somehow circumvented—perhaps we could pass an amendment eliminating the clause stipulating that the Senate can't be amended, then amend the Senate with another amendment.

What alternative designs for the Senate might we consider, assuming changes could be made possible? The most obvious tweak, of course, would be allocating senators proportionally to each state's population. But some reformers, arguing we've outgrown the need for an empowered upper house, have suggested the Senate could be transformed by amendment into a mostly ceremonial body like the U.K.'s House of Lords, which itself was gradually disempowered in favor of the House of Commons. In 2018, Michigan Congressman John Dingell, the longest-serving member of Congress in American history, backed a much simpler idea—the Senate, he argued, should simply be abolished.

It's not obvious, after all, that we need a bicameral legislature in the first place. About two-thirds of the world's countries have only one legislative house—not counting technically bicameral countries such as the United Kingdom, where one house holds nearly all real legislative power. Federalism—the idea that the interests of states as entities should be represented in the legislature as though they were themselves people—is not a very compelling democratic defense, especially in a country like ours, where states already have so much independent power that state governments often frustrate the federal government's objectives. And again, we should disabuse ourselves of the notion that popularly elected representatives in a large, population-based chamber like the House of Representatives should have their decisions checked by a smaller, slower body of more elite politicians. In fact, if we're absolutely set on having two houses, we might consider making one of them even more directly representative of the public than the House is—perhaps, as theorists such as Tom Malleson argue, by making it a deliberative assembly of ordinary people chosen by lot:

> Imagine a People's House composed of, say, one thousand people chosen at random (and stratified to ensure accurate representation along gender, race, class, and other important lines). These members could serve four-year terms. The first two years they'd lack legislative power, during which time they'd receive substantial training in issues of budgets, taxation, and distributive justice; be exposed to the various fields of government; take classes in how to deliberate rationally, empathetically, and with a sense of the common good; and "intern" in a specific policy department, such as Health or Energy or the Environment. In the second half of their term, members would have legislative power, perhaps divided into ten departments with one hundred members each. Each department would deliberate on issues within its purview (in a similar manner to the Citizens' Assemblies), before submitting legislative proposals to be voted on by the entire body to become law.

Deliberative experiments in Canada, the U.K., France, Spain, Belgium, the Netherlands, and even here in America have shown that ordinary citizens are wholly capable of productively debating the issues among themselves and consulting with experts on policy issues in assembly-like settings. The difficulty with such schemes has less to do with the competence of the citizenry than with how few participate in them—there's something democratically problematic, if we take decision-making agency seriously as a democratic concern, about having a randomly selected subset of the public, and even a demographically representative one, make decisions for the public instead of having the whole public decide for itself. Given all the factors that can influence how groups come to decisions—individual personalities, temperaments, and moods; differences in writing and speaking ability, and so on—it doesn't make all that much sense to assume that a randomly selected assembly of individuals would deliberate or act just as any other randomly selected group of people or the public at large would have. But something like a People's House might do some good as a kind of advisory body—a way of bringing our representatives and policymakers into regular contact with a cross section of America and a pool that might be informatively polled and consulted by the press on matters before the legislature.

Whether we settle on an idea like this or not, we should think ambitiously about what a more democratic legislature might look like. Whatever form our next one might take, it certainly shouldn't resemble Congress as we know it.

The Presidency

Of all the undemocratic features of our government, few have attracted as much sustained criticism and attention as the way we elect our presidents. On five occasions in our history, the presidential candidate with more votes than the others has lost the election; this has happened twice within the last twenty-five years alone. In 2000, Al Gore lost to George W. Bush despite winning more than half a million more votes. And in 2016, Hillary Clinton lost to Donald Trump despite winning *nearly three million* more votes.

Both outcomes were products of the Electoral College, a system the Founders, again, initially designed to ensure that presidents would be chosen by a group of sober and independent elites rather than self-interested state governments, Congress, or the public at large. But the College has gradually evolved into a bizarre device for indirect popular election. The states and the District of Columbia are entitled to a share of electors equal to their number of representatives in Congress. When we vote in a presidential election, we're actually voting to have electors who support our candidates become our state's electors. The candidates who win the popular vote in each state get all of the state's electors (except, again, in Nebraska and Maine, where electors are partially awarded by congressional district). The candidate who wins the vote of the majority of the country's electors—at least 270 out of the 538 up for grabs—then wins the election, though not officially until the electors meet to cast their votes on the first Monday after the second Wednesday in December (yes, really) and the results are certified by Congress. The meetings of the electors are a formality—again, they're awarded and pledged to candidates based on state election results, though occasionally one or a few "faithless electors" break their pledges and back other candidates.

As a matter of basic design, this is all quite stupid—even if one happens to like state-by-state indirect election in principle. Why bother having *actual human electors* in the first place if they just represent the results in each state without exercising their own judgment? But the Electoral College should seem especially hideous to anyone with basic democratic commitments. For starters, the system is influenced by the inequities we've already examined in Congress. Because every state gets at least three representatives in Congress regardless of population—two senators and at least one House member—every state likewise gets at least three electoral votes. Consequently, while California's representatives in Congress give it a massive fifty-five electoral votes (the most in the country), each resident of tiny Wyoming still has nearly four times the impact on presidential election results than a Californian does when electoral votes are divided by each state's population. And in 2017, an analysis by University of Washington professor Dale Durran, a mathematician, found that votes cast by Wyoming residents had counted about three times as much as the votes cast by the average American in deciding the 2016 election.

But the main problem with the Electoral College is a little more complicated than that math suggests. None of the places where votes were *mathematically* worth the most per Durran's analysis—Wyoming, D.C., Vermont, Alaska, and Hawaii—get much attention during presidential campaigns, while the state where votes counted the least, Florida, has been a critical battleground for years. That's because the Electoral College's real bias, in practical terms, is less toward small states than *swing* states. Because the winner of the popular vote in nearly every state takes all of that state's available electoral votes, campaigns tend to focus on states where both parties have a good shot at winning and a good number of electoral votes are up for grabs. Consequently, voters in a handful of competitive and decently sized states such as Florida or Michigan get visits, ads, and attention to the issues particularly important to them each cycle, while voters everywhere else hardly see much of the campaign at all. Ninety-six percent of the in-person campaign events held by the major-party candidates during the general election campaign in 2020 took place in just twelve battleground states. Twenty-two percent of them took place in Pennsylvania alone. But the campaigns didn't bother visiting thirty-three less-important states or D.C. even once. What's more, nearly 90 percent of the ad dollars spent in the general election through October of that year were spent in just six states.

While it's doubtful that voters in the other forty-four states were keen to be bombarded with presidential campaign mailers and commercials, those figures are democratically troubling. Ideally, presidential candidates would have to actively compete for the support of all Americans, no matter where they happen to live. Instead, voters in battleground states get the vast majority of their interest and attention, while the rest of the states are written off as though they already belong wholly to the Democratic or Republican parties.

Yet the notion that there are solidly "blue" and "red" states or regions oversimplifies and distorts our understanding of the political landscape. As loudly as Republicans might denigrate large states and their cities as impenetrable bastions of Democratic politics, the fact remains that more people voted for Donald Trump in New York City alone in 2016, 2020, and 2024 than in both of the Dakotas combined. And while Kamala Harris never stood a chance at winning the Dakotas, more than a quarter of a million voters in those largely rural states—or nearly one out of every three who went to the polls—turned out to back her in 2024 anyway. In both cases, the losing voters might as well have stayed home: Thanks to the Electoral College and the winner-take-all system of allocating most states' electoral votes, their ballots counted for practically nothing.

Again, the upshot of all this is that the candidate who wins more votes might wind up losing the Electoral College and thus the election. Among peer nations with elected presidents, the United States is the only country where this can happen. In the aftermath of Donald Trump's victory in the 2016 election, the Pew Research Center noted that the United States was one of only a half-handful of countries in the world—alongside Botswana, the Marshall Islands, Micronesia, Nauru, South Africa, and Suriname—to indirectly elect a leader with the roles and duties our presidents perform. Eighty percent of countries with presidents like ours, by contrast, elect theirs by a simple popular vote. In fact, most countries with presidents like ours require the winning candidate to win a true 50-plus percent *majority* of the popular vote rather than a mere plurality. Really, one needn't look abroad to understand how strange the Electoral College is as a system. The president is the only major official in America elected this way; the equivalent would be electing our senators or governors by county.

The arguments usually offered in the College's defense are flimsy. It's often said, as with the Senate, that the Electoral College protects the interests of rural- and small-state voters. As we've seen, however, it does no such thing for any voters outside a handful of competitive states. Those voters merit no more interest and attention than Americans living anywhere else; it's democratically untenable to hold that their votes should count more than others. The broader idea—that the masses cannot be trusted to popularly elect a national leader—likewise doesn't wash if we take the arguments for democracy we've already examined seriously. And again, electing presidents by popular vote also happens to be the international norm.

Obviously, the Electoral College should be abolished. And while other democratic reforms might take some convincing, the College's flaws have long been clear to most Americans. Surveys suggest that majorities of the public have backed moving to a popular vote for the presidency for many decades; in a 2024 Gallup survey, 58 percent of Americans favored a constitutional amendment to do so. That's the most obvious fix, but it's not an especially likely one, at least in the near to medium term.

Fortunately, reformers and state lawmakers have spent the last twenty years working on an ingenious alternative. The Constitution doesn't stipulate exactly *how* electors are to be selected. That's left up to the states, which gradually settled upon the system we have now everywhere but Nebraska and Maine—all of a state's electors and their votes are awarded to the popular-vote winner in each state. But states could also decide to award their electors some other way—for instance, to the winners of the national popular vote. And if states with a majority of the electoral votes in the College did this, the winner of the national popular vote would also automatically win the Electoral College—essentially nullifying the College as we know it without a constitutional amendment. All this plan requires, instead, is a compact among participating states that would go into effect once they amass the 270 needed electoral votes—and perhaps, some scholars argue, Congress's approval of their agreement.

Getting enough states on board with this plan might sound like a heavy lift, but seventeen states, plus the District of Columbia, with 209 of the needed 270 electoral votes have already done so. At the time of writing, we are only sixty-one electoral votes shy of seeing the National Popular Vote Interstate Compact (NPVIC), as it's been dubbed, go into effect. At that point, the scheme would likely face a constitutional challenge from Republicans, but the compact is the best shot we have, short of an amendment, of finally doing away with the College. The remaining votes on the table will be harder to win over than the ones garnered from the liberal states that were first to sign on, but we need only a handful of moderate states—perhaps Arizona, Michigan, Nevada, Pennsylvania, and Virginia—to get it done. This is well within the realm of the possible. And someday, once a popular vote is established, we may even consider electing our presidents by ranked-choice vote.

★ ★ ★

The Electoral College is the most glaring of the presidency's democratic defects, but other aspects of the office merit scrutiny. The Constitution requires a two-thirds majority in each house of Congress to overturn a presidential veto. Like all other legislative-supermajority requirements, this is democratically unacceptable and has had predictable results—as of 2025, only about 7 percent of all regular vetoes had ever been overridden. Presidential vetoes and signing statements—pronouncements about signed bills that might affect how they're implemented also raise broader questions about which branch, legislative or executive, truly represents the public. Those questions would remain even if the president and Congress were elected more democratically, and even if vetoes could be overturned by a simple majority. Is it right for a single person—even one who has been justly elected—to overturn the decision of a justly elected legislature of hundreds? To unilaterally substitute their individual judgment for a consensus built by negotiation, deliberation, and argument among multiple parties? The democratic tensions here become even more acute when elections are staggered. If a justly elected president's party were to lose the support of voters and a legislative majority in the middle of a term, would the president be democratically justified in vetoing the new legislature's bills?

Given these quandaries, one may well wonder whether we should have an executive independent of the legislature in the first place; parliamentary systems get along just fine with legislatures and prime-ministerial cabinets performing the functions we place under the purview of the executive branch. While we've grown accustomed to the presidential system, it has clear democratic downsides, beginning with the fact that it adds an extra hurdle to the policymaking process that government by legislature would not face. And presidential systems also tend to be more unstable, thanks in some part to the tensions between the executive and legislative branches—the attack on Congress as it worked to certify Donald Trump's loss in the 2020 election being a case study in what can go wrong.

As the Constitution was being drafted and defended, many of its critics argued that the Founders had made the president something like an elected king. And since the Founding, the presidency's powers have only grown—from launching military interventions without the authorization of Congress to effectively legislating through the agencies via actions, rules, and regulations the public knows and is asked little about.

Again, at time of writing, President Trump is remaking executive power in extraordinary and alarming ways—from unilaterally repealing regulations without notice or public comment to abusing emergency powers for the unilateral imposition of tariffs that have shaken the global economy. The experience of his second administration thus far is reason enough to revisit criticisms of the American presidency past and present, and to give serious thought to turning the White House into a museum someday—a relic from a benighted time when we thought it wise to put so much authority in the hands of just one politician.

The Supreme Court

As argued in previous chapters, democratic principles imply an entitlement to certain democratic rights and equal treatment under the law. Courts, obviously, can be important venues for the protection of our rights and ourselves. Beyond that, fair systems to interpret laws and impartially resolve disputes between parties are part of the essential infrastructure of any complex society. To perform those roles effectively, even when doing so might be unpopular, courts should be as distant from politics as possible. Ideally, courts in this country would also make their decisions in accordance with a constitutional framework far more democratic than the one we have. But as it stands, our federal judiciary, tasked with upholding our antidemocratic Constitution, is among the most politicized in the developed world. While peer countries strive to choose many of their judges through neutral processes closed to elected officials, most of our federal judges are simply chosen, for life, by senators and the president.

As one might expect, our courts are thus coveted prizes that our political parties compete for in order to further their respective agendas, rather than venues for neutrally interpreting the Constitution and resolving disputes. The highest prize of all, of course, is the Supreme Court, which—thanks to the Court's own ruling in *Marbury v. Madison*—can overturn or substantially alter laws and government actions on constitutional grounds through judicial review. While justices swear up and down upon nomination that their opinions will be guided wholly by the Constitution, past legal precedents, and historical sources, it's plain to legal scholars that they carry their personal politics with them to the Court—conservative justices tend to issue conservative rulings and liberal justices tend to issue liberal rulings. As such, there is nothing truly impartial about the Supreme Court as an institution, its decisions reflect the preferences of whoever the parties have managed to shove onto the bench rather than neutral analyses of the Constitution and the law. The ambiguities and contradictions we've seen in the Court's rulings and opinions over time illustrate this, as Michael Klarman has written:

> Justices love referenda, except when they distrust them. Justices celebrate the Court's role in defending the rights of unpopular minorities, except when they celebrate the virtues of democratic decisionmaking, in which case the opposing Justices suddenly become "black-robed rulers overriding citizens' choices." Precedents are not to be lightly overruled, except when "there are strong grounds for doing so," which is not the most determinate of legal standards. Legislative departures from tradition are frowned upon in constitutional law, except when they are not. Justices instruct us to interpret the past at a low level of generality when defining constitutional rights, except when that approach will not get them the result they favor, in which case they read the past at a higher level of generality. Justices insist they should not second guess the cost benefit calculus of legislatures, except when they know better. The primary responsibility of the Court is to declare what the law is, except when Justices determine that the judiciary has no business involving itself in a certain sphere. In some doctrinal areas, government motive is everything, but in others it is irrelevant, and no attempt to reconcile the inconsistencies is offered. Judicial intervention in a particular sphere requires administrable standards, except when it does not. The Court will not decide more than is necessary to resolve the matter before it, except when it does; and the Court will not decide issues unless properly presented, unless it feels like doing so.

The Supreme Court thus functions less like a court narrowly interpreting the law and the Constitution and more like another highly politicized but indirectly elected legislature—one with the power to invalidate laws or even past rulings that justices on the Court dislike without any direct input from the public. In 2022, the court's dominant conservative majority—including three justices appointed by Donald Trump, a president who had lost the popular vote—did just that when it overturned *Roe v. Wade*, gutting abortion rights against the wishes of some two-thirds of the American public.

That decision was no outlier in the Court's history—while civil rights cases like *Brown v. Board of Education* and *Obergefell v. Hodges* (which ended segregation in public schools and legalized gay marriage respectively) loom large in the public mind, justices on the Supreme Court haven't reliably used that power to defend or expand basic rights. The Court protected slavery and racial segregation for much of its history, and its record also includes ignoble rulings on matters such as eugenics and the internment of Japanese Americans during World War II. The Court has also been a fairly reliable ally of domineering economic elites, most especially during the early twentieth century, when an infamous train of rulings struck down a variety of state and federal laws that had been passed to regulate businesses, fight monopolies, and protect workers. And in recent years, conservatives on the bench have moved the Court against democratic principles. The 1965 Voting Rights Act, for instance, has been functionally overturned over the course of multiple rulings, giving lawmakers more freedom to try disenfranchising voters who oppose them.

While judicial review, the locus of the Court's power, isn't uncommon among our international peers, some countries do place limits on what kinds of measures their courts can review. And the Netherlands, for its part, actually bans judicial review outright— laws passed by the legislature cannot be overturned by the courts under any circumstances. Again, courts, through judicial review and other means, can theoretically play an important role protecting democratic rights and ensuring equal treatment under the law. But in practice, legal fights in our federal judiciary and at the Supreme Court can be lengthy, complex, and costly, advantaging those who can afford good lawyers.

It also doesn't help that our judiciary is positively medieval in design. Unlike virtually all of our peers, federal judges in the United States, from the Supreme Court on down, serve for life.

There are no age or term limits whatsoever, meaning judges can shape legal outcomes for generations after the temporary majorities that chose them have collapsed. And the fate of major policies and programs can turn on the physical health of elderly justices, who strain to stay alive and working long enough to influence as many rulings as possible. As such, the press keeps a vigilant watch over the hospitalizations and coughing fits of the justices most likely to kick the bucket; the moment a justice dies, legal strategists from the president's party spring into action to seize the awaited opportunity and put another trusted nominee on the bench.

The last years of liberal justice Ruth Bader Ginsburg's life underscored the absurdity of all this. During the Obama administration, some commentators called on Ginsburg to retire, which would have allowed Democrats to appoint another—and younger— liberal justice, eliminating the risk that a future Republican administration might appoint a conservative justice upon Ginsburg's death. But Ginsburg stayed on and, as feared, Republicans came to control Congress and the White House by 2016. In 2018, after she broke three ribs in a fall, Democrats on social media, perhaps only half-jokingly, offered to donate their organs to her.

Two years later, Justice Ginsburg died of pancreatic cancer at the age of eighty-seven and was replaced by conservative justice Amy Coney Barrett—an outcome made particularly galling by the already-discussed defects of the Senate and Electoral College. Trump, elected to the presidency despite losing the popular vote, nominated three justices to the Supreme Court over the course of his term. All of them—*and more than two hundred other federal judges*—were confirmed by a Republican Senate representing a minority of the American people, one that had blocked President Obama's attempt to fill another vacancy during his term in anticipation of winning the presidency themselves. It's likely now that the Court will be controlled by conservatives for many, many years to come. But even if that weren't the case, the basic features of the Court and our federal judiciary would still be cause for democratic concern.

No one in government should serve for life. But, beyond impeachment, there are no means for removing or reappointing federal judges until they (or their bodies) decide their time is up—perhaps generations after their initial appointment. Terms of ten to fifteen years are common in courts with constitutional jurisdiction abroad; Joe Biden and California congressman Ro Khanna have recently proposed limiting service on the Supreme Court to eighteen years and allowing presidents to appoint only two justices per term. In theory, that routinization of Supreme Court vacancies could somewhat lessen the partisan shenanigans and intrigues involved in seating judges on the bench, though political parties in the Senate could still try blocking a president's nominees.

The same might be said about a proposal from scholars Daniel Epps and Ganesh Sitaraman transforming the Court into a fully bipartisan body with five Democratic justices, five Republican justices, and five additional justices chosen unanimously by the first ten. That arrangement, moreover, would not only privilege the two major parties—at the expense of political independents and minor parties—but bias the court toward ideologically centrist outcomes.

Epps and Sitaraman have also proposed turning the Supreme Court into a panel of judges selected at random from the appeals courts. That would end the partisan battles over court appointments—though it would raise the political stakes of appeals-court nominations—and would not consistently bias the Court in a particular direction as much as a fixed, bipartisan bench would. But the proposal should still leave us feeling democratically uneasy.

In all of these proposed reforms, the Court remains a body of unelected judges granted the unilateral power to overturn legislation crafted by our elected representatives. As said before, independent courts at some remove from direct electoral pressures can be important venues for the defense of basic rights. But democratically speaking, judicial review as we know it has granted the courts too broad a mandate. From the bench, judges can invalidate or even create law on putatively constitutional grounds even when basic rights are not at issue.

As such, some reformers have recommended "jurisdiction stripping" as a means of reining in the courts' authority. In Article III, Section 2 of the Constitution, which outlines the jurisdiction of the federal judiciary, the Supreme Court is granted appellate jurisdiction in federal cases "with such Exceptions, and under such Regulations as the Congress shall make." *Technically* this gives Congress the authority to determine which legislation is reviewable by the judiciary in the first place—meaning, reformers argue, that Congress can "strip" the courts of the right to review specific bills, or even all bills pertaining to a particular subject (climate change, say, or new taxes on the wealthy). But that really amounts to granting Congress the license to pass whatever nonsense it wants. Imagine that a bill infringing some minority's right to vote gets passed, leaving no recourse to the courts or any hope of reversal—beyond that minority trying to participate in the next election. Other reformers have advocated, more conservatively, subjecting the Court to a supermajority requirement—perhaps two-thirds of the judges on the bench might be needed to overturn a law.

The issues at hand in the judiciary are especially complex. Just about all the reforms mentioned here raise democratic and constitutional questions. But one unambiguously constitutional idea could offer a temporary corrective to the Supreme Court's current conservative skew—Democrats should expand the Court's size and add more liberal justices to the bench.

A tremendous hue and cry arose over President Franklin Delano Roosevelt's own failed "court-packing" scheme, but the idea was perfectly constitutional—the Constitution says nothing whatsoever about the Supreme Court's size, which has changed seven times since the Founding. Some have objected that Republicans would simply pack the Court again at the next opportunity, and that the Court would grow and ping-pong between the two parties with each new governing majority. But that's fine. While the Court would be something like a third, elected legislature for a while, the experience would probably build support for thoroughly depoliticizing the judiciary with time—moving us closer to our peers who take professional, nonpartisan judges for granted.

The District and the Territories

As far as our political system is concerned, America truly is, in many respects, an exceptional nation. Compared with most of our peers, the presidency and the design of our legislature make it exceptionally hard for us to pass legislation. When the role and design of our courts and the power of the states are taken into account, there simply aren't very many other nations like ours at all. That's a curious thing, given that we've had a hand in designing political institutions in so many other countries. Japan and the European nations ravaged by World War II, for instance, didn't really take after us at all, even though we helped craft their new constitutions. "It's striking that even though the U.S. Constitution is treated as a sacred text in America's political culture," the writer Matt Yglesias has noted, "we did not push any of these countries to adopt our basic framework of government."

That might be because the outcomes our political system produces don't offer much for our peers to envy or emulate. Even Americans who don't know much about the structural defects we've explored complain about gridlock and dysfunction in Washington, which is often attributable to divided government: Unless both houses of Congress and the president back a policy, it goes nowhere. And even when a law *is* passed, its opponents might appeal to the courts in the hopes of getting it struck down or fundamentally altered. With all this as a backdrop, politicians routinely promise voters that they have what it takes to unstick the gears of governance and "get things done."

Those promises generally fall flat—and it's often not obvious that they should be kept to begin with. Good governance should be measured in the quality of the laws that make it through our system rather than their quantity. As a matter of democratic principle, the chief problem with our system isn't that too few things are getting done. It's that American voters, being unequally represented, don't have a roughly equal say in *what* gets done.

In fact, there are more than four million Americans with very nearly no say in federal governance at all. America's inhabited territories—American Samoa, Guam, the Northern Mariana Islands, Puerto Rico, and the U.S. Virgin Islands—and our special capital district, the District of Columbia, have been denied full voting representation in Congress. Among them, only the District has a say in our presidential general elections. The residents of American Samoa, for their part, are not even full American citizens by birth; Samoan "nationals" who don't go through the naturalization process are barred from voting in federal elections or running for office. The majority of these Americans lacking full political rights live in Puerto Rico—at a population of over three million, it is larger than twenty-one states entitled by the Constitution to two senators and at least one voting representative in the House. Instead, like D.C. and the other territories, Puerto Rico sends but a single member to the House—one who cannot vote on the final passage of legislation.

This is despite the fact that these parts of the country are subject to federal authority. In 2016, for instance, Congress created an unelected board to manage and reduce Puerto Rico's debt without any say from the territory's residents. Policymakers in the territory have their hands tied by federal rules when it comes to crafting economic policy, and the island has faced hurdles in the receipt of federal funding and relief in the wake of natural disasters that the fifty states have not. And in the District of Columbia, policies passed by city officials on issues from gun control to drugs have been overridden or impeded by the federal government—members of Congress from other parts of the country and the president can block the city's laws or impose new ones without the approval of residents. This is especially galling, as the city's TAXATION WITHOUT REPRESENTATION license plates famously attest, given that the District is also the only nonstate entity whose residents must pay federal income taxes. Although D.C. boasts a larger population than Vermont and Wyoming, its residents are denied full representation in Congress—and have only a minimal say as to where their federal tax money goes.

All this can and should change. With simple acts of Congress, we could grant statehood, and all the rights and representation that statehood confers, to some or all of our territories and D.C.—provided, of course, that residents of the territories actually want them to be states.

In the District's case, residents of the city and their elected officials have made themselves perfectly clear on the matter for decades now, and in 2016, a referendum asking the city council to petition Congress for admission as a state passed with nearly 86 percent of the vote. There's one constitutional hitch, though, as Republicans doggedly opposed to D.C. statehood routinely point out. Because the Constitution mandated D.C.'s creation as a wholly independent federal capital district, simply admitting the District as a state in its own right would obviously be unconstitutional. But statehood advocates have devised a solution—Congress can shrink the constitutionally mandated district from the entirety of the city to the largely uninhabited portions of it where the federal government resides. The rest of the city could then be admitted as a state. And while opponents of statehood correctly note that this would leave the shrunken District with three of the Electoral College votes that D.C. was granted by the Twenty-third Amendment, that amendment also grants Congress the authority to decide how the District's electors are selected. Congress could simply end presidential elections in the uninhabited District, or award the District's electoral votes to the winner of the electoral or popular vote in other states. Dozens of scholars agree this approach to the statehood question is constitutional. Conservatives in our judiciary, of course, might disagree.

The admission of other territories as states would be much more straightforward as a constitutional matter. But it's less clear that their residents strongly support joining the union. The territories haven't all conducted recent referendums on their status;

the ones that have, such as Puerto Rico, have had participation and ballot-wording issues. To resolve the matter, a round of well-worded and well-attended referendums should be conducted in order to establish whether statehood is the clear preference of territorial voters over alternatives like independence or other, more representative arrangements than our colonial status quo.

Elections and Voting Rights

Our democratic failings have been belied by the liveliness of our politics. By outward appearances, at least, democracy is our constant business. Americans are asked to participate in as many as six elections within every four years when party primaries are taken into account—not including special elections, referendums, and recalls. And beyond the frequency of elections, we elect an unusually vast number of officials in this country. At the state and local levels, many of us even elect judges, a practice almost unheard of in the rest of the world. "Most American voters," a team of researchers noted in 2014, "elect officials for four to six, or even more, levels of government: national, state, county, municipal, and frequently special-function authorities, such as school boards, that may not coincide with other local jurisdictions. In 2007, there were 50,432 county and municipal governments, 13,051 school districts, and 37,381 special districts responsible for various local administrative functions. All of these entities have elected officials who run them."

But while we have many more elections than our peers, we also have far fewer constant voters. Though turnout has increased in recent years, thanks in part to accommodations made for voters during the coronavirus pandemic, only about 63 percent of Americans of voting age voted in the 2020 presidential election, making the United States thirty-first in turnout among comparable peers. And turnout for nonpresidential elections in off years has predictably been much worse. From 2004 to 2014, about 40 percent of eligible Americans voted in midterms, ranking us

113th in an analysis of turnout in 114 countries. In the recent 2018 and 2022 midterms, turnout among voting-age Americans bounced up to a still-underwhelming average of about 48 percent. In primary and state and local elections, we've averaged an anemic turnout rate of about 20 percent.

Those figures probably have at least a little to do with the daunting number of elections American voters have to keep up with, along with hurdles that make voting inordinately difficult. Nothing about the American way of doing elections suggests we want large numbers of people voting in the first place. While most countries have either automatic or mandatory voter registration, we let large numbers of potentially eligible voters fall through the cracks of the registration process. And while recent years have seen significant expansions in voting by mail and other policies that make it easier to cast a ballot, many of those who show up at the polls in person still face long lines and other inconveniences made worse by the fact that we ask Americans to vote during the workweek. Many other countries hold their elections during special national holidays, or over weekends.

We're also unusual in the number and kind of voters we go out of our way to exclude. In 2022, 4.6 million Americans were barred from voting on account of felony convictions; thanks to state-level policies, America is one of the rare countries in the world where even those who have served their time and been released from prison may be permanently disenfranchised. The poor and racial minorities, disproportionately likely to face incarceration and already less likely to vote, are disproportionately burdened by these laws. The same can be said of voter ID laws—poor and minority voters are less likely to have valid ID on hand partially because they're likelier to get around on public transit, which requires no driver's license.

While proponents of these laws argue they're a simple way to prevent voter fraud, research has repeatedly demonstrated beyond doubt that voter fraud is not a problem in the United States. A representative study of elections from 2000 to 2014, in which more than *one billion* ballots were cast, found *no more than thirty-one* potential instances of voter impersonation. The rarity of fraud, in fact, goes some way toward explaining why no states bothered requiring photo ID to vote until 2005.

Thanks to the spread of scurrilous propaganda about voter fraud, things have changed dramatically since then. Ten states now strictly require photo ID to vote in person and millions of Americans have been subject to new ID requirements since 2020, thanks to a campaign by Republicans, aided by the Supreme Court's neutering of the Voting Rights Act, to tighten voting restrictions by any means available. These have ranged from purging hundreds of thousands of registered voters from voter rolls just for not having voted recently to imposing limitations on early, absentee, and mail-in voting.

Though they're discussed less often than restrictions on voting rights, we also impose undemocratic restrictions on running for office. As far as federal elections are concerned, every American adult under the age of thirty-five is a second-class citizen without full political rights. Before then, your ability to run in federal elections is limited by the Constitution's arbitrary age requirements. Candidates must be at least twenty-five, thirty, and thirty-five years old for the House, Senate, and presidency respectively.

The states have their own hodgepodge of contradictory and nonsensical age-of-candidacy laws as well. As things stand now, an eighteen-year-old in California might be elected governor, while Utah residents of the same age cannot even run for the state House. A thirty-year-old can represent Oklahoma on matters of war and peace in the United States Senate, but no one a day under thirty-one can legally serve as Oklahoma's state treasurer.

Similarly, though a bit more straightforwardly, we discriminate against naturalized citizens. Per the Constitution, they are barred from the presidency and aren't eligible for Congress until they've spent several years as full citizens—seven years for the House, nine years for the Senate. These and other restrictions on candidacies flout the principle of political equality, denying voters the opportunity to evaluate disqualified candidates and their proposals on their own merits.

As far as basic voting rights are concerned, a top priority should be the restoration and updating of the 1965 Voting Rights Act (VRA), which has been functionally dismantled by a set of conservative Supreme Court rulings over the last decade. In the original bill, states and jurisdictions with a history of infringing upon voting rights were required to "preclear" changes to election law and redistricting plans with federal authorities before they went into effect. But in 2013's *Shelby County v. Holder,* the Supreme Court ruled that the formulas used to determine which states and jurisdictions should be subject to preclearance were outdated. This was followed by 2018's *Abbot v. Perez* ruling, which upheld redistricted maps in Texas that a lower court had found to be racially gerrymandered, as well as by 2021's ruling in *Brnovich v. Democratic National Committee,* which made it much harder to challenge election laws on racial-discrimination grounds.

The John Lewis Voting Rights Advancement Act, first introduced in 2021, would have fully addressed the Court's putative concerns by updating the VRA's preclearance formulas and strengthening the VRA's other protections against racial discrimination. It should be passed. The For the People Act, for its part, would have fought specific suppression strategies the right has employed in recent years. Voter purges, for instance, would be curbed with new regulations on the updating of voter rolls and a ban on purging voters merely for not having voted recently. And states with voter ID laws would be required to let those lacking ID cast a regular ballot upon signing a sworn statement attesting to their identity. The For the People Act also would have bolstered federal funding for election administration and gone some way toward standardizing election processes across states, further insulating voting rights from the schemes and caprices of state and local election officials and administrators.

The For the People Act also contained a slew of reforms that would have made it much easier to vote. Same-day voter registration and automatic voter registration—signing up voters when they come into contact with social services such as motor-vehicle departments or agencies dispensing public benefits—would have been made available in all federal elections, and all states would have been required to conduct at least two weeks of early voting. Mail-in voting, which grew substantially over the course of the pandemic, also would have been made universal for all federal elections. These ideas would functionally turn Election Day as we know it into a period of Election Days, obviating the idea of turning Election Day into a public holiday, which many reformers are fond of. While giving people days off for voting seems to measurably increase turnout in other countries, the American experience with public holidays suggests that turnout might be skewed—white-collar workers are more likely to be able to take time off than less-affluent blue-collar and service workers, who might work even longer, harder hours to cater to those on holiday. A similar reform, weekend voting, hasn't produced turnout rates appreciably higher than ours in other countries.

Some reforms, like those making registration easier, clearly work. But the factors that boost or reduce voter turnout can be complex, and there are trade-offs for policymakers to consider. While early voting, for instance, makes access to the ballot easier, research suggests that it actually *lowers* turnout—perhaps because it encourages voters to procrastinate, some of whom wind up missing Election Day. And busy schedules aren't the only difficulties voters have to navigate. Illness, disability, and transportation issues are among the challenges that can depress turnout among lower-income voters in particular—and are all the more reason why policymakers should work to make polling places and drop boxes as accessible as possible. And all voters, of course, would appreciate efforts to make Election Day lines much shorter.

Beyond making it easier to vote and protecting voting rights, we should also set about expanding them. One idea for this, popular among many reformers and already famously in place in Australia, is *mandatory* voting. Clearly, obligating everyone to vote would raise turnout considerably. Provided that it's turning in a ballot—even a blank one—that's necessary, mandatory voting seems democratically sound, as it would be an unjust denial of

agency to force voters to choose between options they're unde-
cided about or might ethically object to. But most countries
haven't needed mandatory voting to achieve their high turnout
rates. And this isn't a reform worth exploring until we've done all
we can to make casting a ballot easy and equitable—otherwise,
any penalties imposed could fall disproportionately upon low-
income and minority Americans, who find it most difficult to
vote.

A reform that would help on that front would be restoring
voting rights to felons. As we've seen, some of our states are the
only places in the developed world where one can be denied the
right to vote after serving their sentence, a status quo made especially problematic by our justice system's clear racial inequities.
At a minimum, voting rights for those released from prison
should be federally restored, and we should consider, too, granting the still imprisoned voting rights on good behavior. Few are
more informed than the incarcerated about life at the margins of
American society, the problems that ail our most broken communities, and the inequities that shape the justice system. Allowing them to vote and engage with politics would be an easy way
of acculturating them to the responsibilities of good citizenship
and preparing them for reentry into civic life.

For similar reasons, we should consider extending the vote to
noncitizen residents committed to earning citizenship, as well as
young voters aged sixteen and up. And we should ditch candi-
dacy rules, establishing that all those eligible to vote should be
eligible to run for office without restriction.

We might consider, too, ways to expand democracy beyond
elections. We've already explored the idea of replacing the Senate
with a body of randomly selected citizens; those who find that
idea too quixotic might see a role for similar bodies at least at the
state and local levels, where direct and participatory democratic
institutions are already common, from the referendum to venues
for community input. As putatively democratic as those mechanisms are, they do tend to mask important inequities as presently
designed. The wealthy and well-organized will always have a leg

up in amassing the support needed to place a referendum on the ballot. And as mentioned in Chapter 1, forums and other processes set up to gather input from communities on matters such as infrastructure and housing can be dominated by fairly affluent and change-resistant people with time and resources that busier, poorer folks simply lack.

Electing and replacing empowered representatives, of course, should be a good way—perhaps the primary way—of gathering community input on what should be done. And once in office, our elected officials would ideally get feedback on specific proposals from forums more representative than community forums today tend to be. Again, as mentioned in the section on the Senate, political scientists have been experimenting with small deliberative assemblies of ordinary people here and around the world. In James Fishkin's deliberative polls, for instance, random, demographically representative samples of the public discuss and debate policy issues with subject-matter experts and one another before having their opinions gauged. That would certainly be an improvement over public comment as we know it.

Amending the Constitution

Many of the reforms we've considered thus far could or must be implemented through constitutional amendments. But the process of amending the Constitution is itself democratically defective. Of the twelve thousand amendments proposed since the Founding, only twenty-seven have been ratified—the first ten of which constitute the Bill of Rights, ratified in 1791. The last of the seventeen to be ratified in the more than two hundred years since was ratified in 1992—an amendment regulating congressional pay increases, which was originally sent to the states for ratification alongside the Bill of Rights and resurrected in the 1980s by a nineteen-year-old sophomore at the University of Texas.

Of course, there have been amendments of much greater consequence, including the Nineteenth Amendment, which granted women the right to vote, and the post–Civil War Reconstruction Amendments—the Thirteenth, Fourteenth, and Fifteenth—which, among other things, ended slavery, defined American citizenship and established equal protection under the law, and secured, at least on paper, the right of racial minorities to vote. But with the potential exceptions of the previously discussed Twelfth Amendment on the Electoral College, the Fourteenth Amendment's reworking of congressional apportionment, the Seventeenth Amendment, which established the direct election of senators, and three amendments on presidential terms and succession, amendments since the Bill of Rights have not fundamentally altered the architecture of the federal system as crafted at the Founding. In fact, one of the major defects of the system that we've examined, equal apportionment in the Senate, may not even be amendable: Article V of the Constitution, which establishes the rules for constitutional amendments, specifies that "no state, without its consent, shall be deprived of its equal suffrage in the Senate."

As the crowded graveyard of proposed amendments suggests, it would be extraordinarily difficult to fundamentally reform any aspects of the federal system through amendments anyway—the process is particularly onerous. First, a proposed amendment needs to either pass the House and the Senate with two-thirds supermajorities, or it needs to be backed by a national convention called by two-thirds of the states. Then, to be ratified, the proposed amendment must win the support of three-fourths of the states—either through their state legislatures or in state ratifying conventions.

These rules make our Constitution the hardest in the world to amend as a practical matter; as a matter of democratic principle, the amendment process is simply abominable. As we've seen with the Senate, counting the states equally at different stages of the ratification process means that some Americans will have much more of a say on amendments than others; supermajority requirements, again, grant a tremendous amount of power to partisan or ideological minorities. Given all this—and taking political polaization into account—some scholars have speculated that the Constitution may never be amended again. At the very least, the high level of political consensus required by the process makes major new amendments unlikely in the near future.

Our peers, meanwhile, have replaced their entire constitutions with some frequency. The French, for instance, are on their fifteenth constitution; written constitutions tend to last about seventeen years on average or a higher thirty-two years in the developed world. Political tumults we shouldn't envy partially account for that, but from time to time some countries—Sweden in 1974 or Finland in 1999, for example—fundamentally rework or replace their governing documents absent strife.

Our Constitution is 238 years old. In 1789, Thomas Jefferson famously reasoned to James Madison that a just constitution would ideally last no more than nineteen years. "If it be enforced longer," he warned, "it is an act of force, & not of right." Jefferson arrived at his number on the basis of dated and rather arbitrary assumptions about life expectancy, but we'd do well to remember his larger point:

> No society can make a perpetual constitution, or even a perpetual law. The earth belongs always to the living generation. They may manage it then, & what proceeds from it, as they please, during their usufruct. They are masters too of their own persons, & consequently may govern them as they please.

The States

The path to deep constitutional reform lies unavoidably through building a large amount of geographically well-distributed support from the American people. Again, it would take the support of two-thirds of the states to bring about a convention at which multiple amendments—or even a wholly new constitution— might be proposed and three-fourths of the states to ratify whatever the convention came up with. It should be said though that if we ever reached a point where, say, at least 60 or 70 percent of the public backed a slew of democracy-building amendments or a new democratic Constitution, we'd have good reason to consider circumventing the Constitution entirely and setting up an extra-constitutional convention—just as the Founders did when they set aside the Articles of Confederation's rules to draw up our present Constitution.

As will be discussed at the end of this book, we're a long way away from any of that. But making American democracy real will require a deeply revised or new constitution sooner or later—a new Founding, again, best conceived less as a single revolutionary moment than a grueling, perhaps century-long project of expanding democracy step-by-step. We should start with the states and territories. It's worth remembering that the American people live under not one but fifty-seven constitutions and charters. The federal Constitution may be the supreme law of the land, but the lower constitutions also shape policy in profound ways, and we can put them to use as instruments for democratic experimentation. "It would be easier from a procedural perspective to turn at least one state into a pure parliamentary government with proportional representation than it would be to simply change the method by which we select the president," *Liberal Currents* editor Adam Gurri has written. "This does not mean that the former is politically feasible. But politics is the art of the possible, and quite drastic constitutional reform is much more possible at the state level than minor constitutional reform is at the federal level."

As we've seen, the Constitution was written in large part to create a national government powerful enough to keep the states in check. Ever since, the states have guarded the power and independence they managed to retain jealously and even violently; in recent decades, conservative hostility toward the federal government has fueled efforts to devolve federal power, freeing states from federal mandates in the name of "states' rights"—a mantra historically deployed in defense of slavery and racial segregation. Despite their often-unflattering history, state governments are broadly popular. A 2018 survey, for instance, found that 63 percent of Americans trusted their state government while only 30 percent trusted the federal government. That's thanks in part to conservative efforts and rhetoric, but even non-conservatives have historically lauded the role the states play in our system. The progressive Supreme Court justice Louis Brandeis, for instance, famously called states the "laboratories of democracy," arguing that the states and the country as a whole might learn from the successes and failures of states taking different approaches to solving problems.

The powers and responsibilities of the federal government have grown substantially over the last century in particular. But state governments still have a more consistent and direct impact on our day-to-day lives. For better or for worse, the problems with our roads or our schools, for instance, fall more under the purview of our state legislators than our members of Congress. And even federal government initiatives—such as anti-poverty programs or federal investments in infrastructure—are often shaped and administered by the states.

Despite the promise of "laboratories of democracy" as a concept, what this decentralization means in practice is that there are often vast inequities between states—not just in how their economies fare, but in how democratically their governments function. This was perhaps most obvious during the Jim Crow era, when Southern states did all they could to protect racial segregation and bar African Americans from voting—and as we've seen, states controlled by the Republican Party have renewed efforts to restrict voting rights for African Americans and other groups. But even when basic rights aren't in question, state governments today, more than two centuries on from the populist campaigns that led the Founders to distrust them, can be perhaps surprisingly undemocratic.

State legislatures, for starters, share some of the basic structural defects we've examined with Congress, including the gerrymandering of state legislative districts and the distortionary effects of geographic clustering—as in Congress, there are often serious gaps between the preferences and votes of majorities and electoral and legislative outcomes in our statehouses. "Roughly half the time, opinion majorities lose—even large supermajorities prevail less than 60% of the time," political scientists Jeffrey Lax and Justin Phillips wrote in a 2012 study of state-policy outcomes. "In other words, state governments are on average no more effective in translating opinion majorities into public policy than a simple coin flip."

What's more, the fact that voters are often less engaged with state politics than with federal politics means that voters and donors in state elections can be even more unrepresentative of the public than voters and donors in federal politics. And once elected, state politicians are now subject to much less scrutiny than their federal counterparts, thanks largely to the collapse of local newspapers. Democratically troubling too is the fact that state governors and legislators have spent a nontrivial portion of their time in recent years upending or subverting laws and ordinances democratically passed by local governments, as Emily Badger of *The New York Times* reported in 2017:

> States have banned local ordinances on minimum wage increases, paid sick days and lesbian, gay, bisexual and transgender rights. They've banned "sanctuary cities." They've even banned a number of bans (it's now illegal for Michigan cities to ban plastic bags, for Texas towns to ban fracking). A law passed in Arizona last year threatens to withhold shared state revenue from local governments that adopt ordinances in conflict with state policy. Texas' new sanctuary city law imposes civil fines as high as $25,500 a day on local governments and officials who block cooperation with federal immigration requests. And it threatens officials who flout the law with removal from office and misdemeanor charges.

These are among the reasons why the states at present, in the words of political scientist Jacob Grumbach, might best be considered "laboratories against democracy."

Still, the states abound with opportunities for democratic reform. It helps, as Gurri notes, that state constitutions are obviously much easier to amend than the federal constitution. And most also happen to include elements of direct democracy, such as referendums and the solicitation of constitutional amendments from the public. One-third of our state constitutions even allow the public to directly instruct their representatives on legislation, and several actually mandate asking citizens about the need for a constitutional convention every so often. All of this creates opportunities to test some of the aforementioned reforms on a small scale; state-level successes could inform and inspire federal changes, helping to secure a steady place for the cause of democratic reform in our political discourse.

The Republican Party

Again, there is no singular and stable majority of the American people whose preferences the government is obligated to respect. But a tremendous amount of survey research suggests consistent majorities of the American electorate support policies the federal government has failed to enact. These include much higher taxes on the rich, a higher minimum wage, a reformed immigration system, a federal paid-leave standard, and a federal job-guarantee program, just to name a few. Despite this, the Republican Party, which is steadfastly opposed to these policies has run or dominated the federal government for much of the century thus far.

This, readers, is the grand old elephant in the room. Our political institutions obviously weren't designed at the Founding to help specific contemporary political parties; as we've seen, voters of all stripes, whether they know it or not, can be functionally discounted in national politics as a consequence of where they happen to live. All of that said, it is inescapably true that our system has substantially advantaged Republicans, whose conservatism has been deeply appealing to Americans in rural and less populous parts of the country whose votes functionally count far more than the votes of Americans elsewhere.

Much of the discourse about those advantages often centers around the Electoral College, where the Republican Party has had an edge in recent years. (Twice so far this century, Republicans have won the presidency by winning the College despite losing the popular vote.) In fact, as data journalist G. Elliot Morris has written, given the statistical relationship between the national popular vote and Electoral College results, Republicans might have won the presidential election in 2020 even had they lost the popular vote by six to seven million votes; Joe Biden wound up winning just over seven million more votes than Trump. But, as previously discussed, outcomes in the Electoral College are shaped less by the kind of small and rural states that the Republican Party has been able to win easily than they are by a shifting set of swing states. For that reason, advantages in the Electoral College can change over time—it's thought that the system actually benefited Democrats from 2004 to 2012.

The Republican Party's more durable advantages are in Congress. The House of Representatives has had a Republican tilt for more than half a century. And Republicans in the Senate have not represented a majority of the American public since 1996—despite that, they have controlled the chamber for more than ten years total since then. The 2020 election, in which Democrats and Republicans split the Senate fifty-fifty, illustrated the GOP's advantage in the chamber well—the Republican half of the Senate represented 41.5 million fewer Americans than the Democratic half. Obviously, Democrats have to work much harder than Republicans do to win an equivalent number of seats. What's more, the filibuster allows Republicans to blockade policy even when they're in the minority any time the Democrats lack a sixty-vote supermajority to move forward on legislation.

The specific policies favored by the parties matter here. Republicans tend to favor hacking away at taxes and government programs—which, under the rules of budget reconciliation, can generally be done with a simple fifty-one-vote majority. But Democrats tend to favor the creation of new programs, the drafing of new regulations, and social and political reforms that generally aren't permissible under reconciliation, meaning most of the party's goals do have to reach that sixty-vote threshold in order to make it through the Senate. And again, even legislation that Democrats manage to pass and sign into law faces potential challenges within a judiciary and before a Supreme Court that conservatives now dominate—thanks, again, to Republican power in the Senate. As if that weren't enough, Republicans have also been working against the democratic process to bolster their structural power in the states. Such efforts have ranged from attempted gerrymandering, as previously discussed, to bids in the wake of lost elections to preemptively strip power from incoming Democratic governors and state officials in states such as North Carolina, Michigan, and Wisconsin.

None of this is to say that the Republican Party is incapable of genuinely winning popular majorities or pluralities. The party won the national popular vote in the 2004 and 2024 elections, and it wins it with some frequency in House elections. But much of Republican politics is animated by the conviction that Republicans are truer Americans—and thus worthier voters—than Democrats and the more liberal portions of the electorate. And, as discussed earlier, many conservatives are deeply hostile to democracy itself. "The idea of democracy and majority rule," Republican senator Rand Paul argued to *The New York Times* in 2021, "really is what goes against our history and what the country stands for."

That perspective goes some way toward explaining why Republicans oppose, for instance, granting statehood to D.C. and the territories. Even the party's previous support for Puerto Rican statehood has been reversed in recent years out of a fear that it, like statehood for the others, would undermine the Republican advantage in the Senate—it's widely expected that the new states on the table would be Democrat-leaning.

Really, the admission of new states has always been a messy, politicized business. Then-Democratic Alaska and then-Republican

Hawaii were admitted as a balanced pair after negotiations between the two parties in 1959; within the space of two years in 1889 and 1890, Republican majorities in Washington admitted four sparsely populated but GOP-dominated territories as states— Idaho, Montana, Washington, and Wyoming—a move immediately preceded by Democrats shrewdly dividing the Dakota territory into two new states of their own. Given the Senate's skew, the lack of democratic representation for the territories discussed earlier, and the Republican Party's demonstrated hostility to democratic values, Democrats would be well within their rights to bolster their standing in the chamber by similarly admitting the territories as states— a partisan move that would likely require the filibuster's elimination if Democrats can't win sixty seats in the chamber—provided, again, that the territories actually can and want to be states.

There are other sources for new states. Some reformers have rather quixotically suggested California could be broken up; not to be outdone, the *Harvard Law Review* argued in 2020 that D.C. could be split up into 127 neighborhood-size states, each with two senators and a representative, that would then constitute a majority large enough to amend the Constitution with other democratic reforms. These will not happen, but the proposals do help illustrate the absurdity of equal state representation.

Republican indifference to the inequities of equal state representation is part of the same general disposition that lies behind Republican efforts to limit the right to vote—both reflect the party's investment in defending the inequities in political representation that benefit them. As we've seen, while voter fraud is exceptionally rare in the United States, Republicans over the last decade have doggedly pushed for new voter-identification laws that disproportionately burden minority voters likely to vote Democratic. And while both parties engage in gerrymandering, Republican mapmakers and strategists such as Thomas Hofeller have done their level best to disempower communities specifically on the basis of race.

Republican losses in recent elections suggest that these and other antidemocratic efforts have had only mixed success thus far. But the Republican Party, as an institution, remains an obvious and growing threat to our political rights. Upon losing both the Electoral College and the popular vote to Joe Biden in his bid for reelection in 2020, Donald Trump claimed that the election had been stolen. He then attempted a coup to overturn Biden's victory and remain in office. Though Trump failed, his lies fueled campaigns to threaten and replace state election officials on his behalf, drove calls for more voting restrictions, and culminated in an attack by his supporters on the U.S. Capitol on January 6, 2021—the day Congress certified the election result over the objections of 147 Republicans who voted to overturn it. In the year after the attack, polls suggested that about 70 percent of Republicans continued to believe the election had been stolen.

As dramatic as the events surrounding the 2020 election were, they merely underscored what the previous decade of Republican politics should have made plain: that the Republican Party simply does not believe, as a matter of principle, that the votes and voices of the American people should count equally. If they did, Republicans have increasingly come to fear, liberal city dwellers, African Americans, immigrants, and other constituencies they consider likely ideological opponents would gain more political power. Given this, Republican policymakers can be counted upon to doggedly defend our undemocratic institutions, which generally advantage them—though they obviously lose from time to time—and make rule by Republican minorities feasible. "Minority rule is not just a fact of life for the GOP—it is a strategy, encouraged by Republican politicians who fear ceding power to a more and more diverse majority," *FiveThirtyEight*'s Laura Bronner and Nathaniel Rakich wrote in 2021. "And because political institutions interact to shape the rules of our democracy, they have created a vicious cycle where minority rule can perpetuate itself."

★ ★ ★

The Republican Party's crusade against democracy and for minority rule has been financed substantially by major corporations and the wealthy. The party's gerrymandering campaign in 2010, for instance, was run through the Republican State Leadership Committee (RSLC), a group founded in 2002 that has received tens of millions of dollars from wealthy donors and companies such as AT&T, Bank of America, Coca-Cola, ExxonMobil, Facebook, FedEx, Google, and Walmart. Since 2010, the RSLC has supported a number of antidemocratic projects above and beyond gerrymandering, including backing state legislators supportive of new voting restrictions—restrictions generally justified, again, by lies about the supposed prevalence of voter fraud.

As discussed in the introduction, hundreds of companies announced that they would stop donating to candidates who had backed lies about fraud in the 2020 election specifically after conspiracy theories prompted the January 6, 2021, attack on the Capitol, including members of Congress who had voted to overturn Joe Biden's election on that day. But, again, many firms simply resumed giving once the public outcry over the attack had subsided. In January 2023, an analysis by *Politico* found that seventy companies that had suspended giving after January 6 had quietly restarted their donations in the time since then, collectively donating more than $10 million to members of Congress who had voted to overturn Biden's election. *Politico* also mentioned a similar analysis by the group Accountable.US, which had focused on major corporations within the Fortune 100:

> The organization found that out of the 50 companies that pledged to pause or reconsider political donations after the Jan. 6 attack—either specifically to those who voted against certification, or political contributions entirely—34 went on to give at least $5.6 million to members who voted against certification over the last two years.
>
> In total, fifteen of those Fortune 100 companies identified by Accountable.US gave at least $100,000 to those objectors through their corporate PACs: AT&T, Boeing, Cigna, Comcast, General Motors, Home Depot, Lockheed Martin, Marathon Petroleum, Pfizer, Raytheon, UPS, UnitedHealth, Valero, Verizon and Walmart.

The health-insurance company Cigna, *Politico* noted, had been among the first to resume giving. Despite having assured employees that it would "discontinue support of any elected official who encouraged or supported violence, or otherwise hindered the peaceful transition of power," just two months after the Capitol assault Cigna gave more than $11,000 to five Republicans who had voted to overturn Biden's election. By November 2022, the company had spent more than $200,000 breaking its promise.

Clearly, the Republican Party's economic agenda—lower taxes, fewer labor rights, deregulation, and the like—has earned it broad and frighteningly durable support from the corporate world. Executives at Cigna and the other companies named above are willing to countenance plenty of nonsense—even violence—in the name of backing candidates they believe will be good for their bottom line.

Money in Politics

This is illustrative of the democratic defect within our system that already troubles Americans the most—the role that money plays in politics. Money, voters fear, too often determines who wins or loses on the campaign trail, or what policies win out in the halls of government. We have failed to adequately address many of our most pressing socioeconomic challenges, many Americans suspect, because those who are already doing well have bought themselves some key advantages.

As far as campaign spending is concerned, donors try to purchase influence in the system by exploiting gaps in a regulatory framework that's been in place for about fifty years now—one that has been gradually weakened by a series of major Supreme Court decisions, including 1976's *Buckley v. Valeo* (which held that limits on campaign spending are unconstitutional), 2010's *Citizens United v. Federal Election Commission* (which ruled that corporations, unions, and other groups can make unlimited "independent expenditures" for or against candidates, provided those expenses aren't coordinated with the candidates or their parties), and 2014's *McCutcheon v. FEC* (which struck down a previous two-year cap on the amount an individual can contribute to federal campaigns).

Those rulings and recent developments in the finance landscape—including the internet-facilitated explosion of small-dollar donations and the rise, abetted substantially by *Citizens United*, of anonymous "dark money" donations—have helped increase campaign expenditures dramatically. Adjusted for inflation, the federal elections in 2020 were the most expensive of all time. Over $15 billion was spent across all races—more than double the amount spent just four years earlier in 2016. Beyond the routinely pricey race for the White House, the 2020 cycle also happened to include what were then five of the ten most expensive House races of all time, as well as nine of the ten most expensive Senate races. The top two of those latter races took place in Georgia, which proved key to determining Senate control. In the special election between incumbent Republican senator David Perdue and Democrat John Ossoff alone, both candidates and their supporters spent more than $500 million. For perspective, the first Senate race ever to cost at least $100 million occurred in 2014—just six years earlier.

While small-dollar donations have transformed political fundraising in many ways, candidates lean heavily on the richest people in the country for their funds. According to one study, donors from the wealthiest 0.01 percent of the population made more than 40 percent of federal campaign contributions in 2012. In the midterm elections of 2014, the one hundred largest donors collectively contributed slightly less ($323 million) than all donors who had given less than $200 ($356 million). And in 2016, half the money backing Democratic and Republican presidential candidates in the early months of their campaigns came from just 158 wealthy families, most of whom supported such conservative policies as tax cuts, government-spending cuts, and deregulation. Altogether, the more than $3 billion in contributions made by the country's top twelve donors from 2009 to 2020 accounted for more than 7 percent of all federal political spending in that period.

Given the cost of contemporary campaigns, it should come as little surprise that the task of raising funds isn't over once a candidate is elected. In 2016, Congressman Rick Nolan told *60 Minutes* that leaders of both parties had recommended their members in the House of Representatives spend at least thirty hours a week—that's six hours per workday—calling donors for money. A leaked PowerPoint slide from 2013 suggested Nolan was in the right ballpark. That year, Democratic leaders had told new members to spend four hours each workday calling donors—twice the amount of time they recommended spending on the House floor and working in their committees.

Indeed, fundraising is so central to the day-to-day schedules of House members that call centers have been created near the Capitol for that very purpose. According to the *60 Minutes* report, the Republican center at the time featured about a dozen phone booths and a fundraising scoreboard for members. "It is a cult-like boiler room on Capitol Hill where sitting members of Congress, frankly I believe, are compromising the dignity of the office they hold by sitting in these sweatshop phone booths calling people asking them for money," Congressman David Jolly told the program. "And their only goal is to get $500 or $1,000 or $2,000 out of the person on the other end of the line. It's shameful. It's beneath the dignity of the office that our voters in our communities entrust us to serve."

It should be said that raising more money than a rival candidate—whether on the clock in Congress or out on the campaign trail—is no assurance of victory. In 2016, for instance, Hillary Clinton's presidential campaign raised hundreds of millions more in campaign funds than the Trump campaign, only to lose. And research strongly suggests the link between fundraising and victory is more complex than often imagined, even in less exceptional races. Though it's true in general that winning candidates tend to have raised more money, that may be because candidates likelier to win in the first place tend to attract more donations.

Still, having a large war chest is key to mounting a viable campaign, even if winning one's race is not a matter of spending the most.

The question of what exactly donors receive in exchange for their money has been one of the most intensively studied matters in political science. Surprisingly, as best as researchers can tell, campaign donations, with few exceptions, don't really buy votes from legislators. In an influential 2003 paper, political scientists Stephen Ansolabehere, John de Figueiredo, and James Snyder found that donations likely had very little independent impact on votes taken in the House from 1978 to 1994 when more influential factors (such as a House member's party, their own views, and the views of their constituents) were taken into account.

Intuitively, this makes some sense. Pro-life donors and groups, for instance, aren't exactly in the habit of giving money to pro-choice politicians in the hopes of changing their minds. And vice versa—it would probably be a waste of money for a wealthy environmentalist to give money to politicians from coal and oil country in the hopes that they might back bills ending fossil-fuel production. As donors understand, politicians face pressures, incentives, and constraints that money alone can't free them from. "Members of Congress care foremost about winning re-election," wrote Ansolabehere and his colleagues. "They must attend to the constituency that elects them, voters in a district or state and the constituency that nominates them, the party."

Nevertheless, political money matters a lot—campaign donations bedevil us in the details of the legislative process. While they might not regularly buy final votes, contributions do buy access— donors get more meetings with legislators than nondonors. And through those meetings and other avenues of communication, as researchers Benjamin Page and Martin Gilens have written, donors influence policies well before they come up for a vote—and in ways well beyond whether a legislator votes yes or no:

If the official already shares a donor's worldview, access can turn into active collaboration about what policies to support and what the details of rules or legislation might be. Excellent access can even lead officials to introduce bills drafted by donors or occasionally to take still stronger personal actions. For example, a filibuster-empowered senator might promise a donor to kill any effort to take away a favorite subsidy or tax break by threatening to talk it to death. This practice has been described as billionaires' "get a senator" strategy. Even if a donor and an official have serious partisan or ideological disagreements, campaign money can help defuse opposition. So can friendly socializing—giving the official a couple of bottles of whiskey for the holidays (big gifts are now outlawed), sharing a meal, sponsoring an "information-gathering tour" or vacation abroad, inviting (and paying) the official to give a speech, and the like.

Money also influences which issues wind up on the table for discussion in the first place. One 2021 study found that rising economic inequality is mentioned less on the floor of Congress than issues of narrow concern to corporations, and that corporate money encourages individual legislators to discuss those issues more. Money from unions similarly encourages legislators to talk about issues that matter to ordinary working Americans (such as inequality and wage and salary growth), but labor spends only a fraction of the amount that corporate and industry entities do on political campaigns.

Beyond campaign donations, labor unions and other groups representing the interests of American workers lose out in another sphere of influence in Washington: lobbying. In 2011, nearly half of the lobbying groups in Washington represented corporations and particular industries, while only 0.7 percent represented unions and 1.1 percent represented social-welfare organizations and the poor. Together, those business groups account for roughly three-quarters of the money spent to lobby in Washington.

As with campaign donations, those who lobby our legislators are seeking more than just an up or down vote on a bill. Like donors, they craft relationships that shape the details of policies on often complex, technical issues that neither politicians nor their constituents know much about. "The prevalence of low-visibility lobbying concerning narrow issues is apparent in a 2009 study of ninety-eight issues that lobbyists themselves identified as the most recent ones on which they had spent time," Page and Gilens write. "Those issues touched on some rather broad, important matters affecting many people (a 'patients' bill of rights'; repealing the estate tax; banning late-term abortions). But they included many more 'small' (but multimillion-dollar) issues of interest only to a few corporations: patent extension for pipeline drugs; increasing funding for the CH-47 Chinook helicopter; easing credit union membership; requiring that airline ticket fees be used only for aviation; supporting Securities and Exchange Commission (SEC) regulation of over-the-counter derivatives; and so forth." And infamously, those who represent the interests of certain industries can pass through the ever-revolving door between government and the private sector, leaving political office for lucrative jobs at companies they helped with the policies they worked on.

Lobbying and campaign donations deservedly attract the public's ire, but they are far from the only or even the most significant ways that corporations and the wealthy influence our politics. It should be remembered that roughly half to a majority of those in Congress have been millionaires for some time now; while most Americans do manual labor, service work, or clerical work for a living, just 2 percent of those in Congress and 3 percent of those in state legislatures did the same before their election. Outside the Capitol and our statehouses, many if not most of our politicians mill around the same institutions and social functions as other wealthy and powerful people in the private sector; they live in the same neighborhoods and send their children to the same schools. It's true, as the saying goes, that "money talks." But the insidious thing about wealth is that money itself doesn't have to do the talking: Even without checks being signed, and without lobbyists as intermediaries, business leaders and the wealthy have greater access to our politicians than the rest of us simply because they occupy, more often than not, the same stratum of American society.

Businesses and the wealthy can also have an extraordinary amount of influence on what ordinary voters think. Many of our international peers have strong, publicly funded media and news outlets—about 30 percent of television viewers in the U.K. and France and nearly half of viewers in Germany tune in to public television. But only 2 percent of the American television audience does the same. Instead, the vast majority of Americans get nearly all of the news that shapes their political views from for-profit companies that depend on the advertising dollars and goodwill of other for-profit companies. That's particularly worrying given that the line between advertising and news content has gotten considerably blurrier over the airwaves and online in recent years, according to media scholars. And beyond advertising, the wealthy people who run major media outlets—among them the Murdoch family, which controls Fox News and *The Wall Street Journal,* or the similarly conservative Smith family, which controls the Sinclair Broadcast Group and its nearly two hundred local news stations across the country—can simply spread their own views to millions of viewers, along with whatever propaganda they see fit.

But the views and concerns of the wealthy are usually introduced into coverage in more subtle ways—through on-air commentary from experts at think tanks funded by major corporations, for instance, or in economic reporting that measures the health of the economy through economic data that reflects how well the rich and major corporations are doing more than the economic well-being of ordinary Americans. On the latter point, a recent paper analyzing forty years of American newspaper coverage found that reporting on the economy is more positive when the rich get richer, but isn't especially affected by the economic conditions facing the rest of the country. Rising stock prices and good corporate earnings reports are routinely presented as good news for the economy as a whole, even if most working Amer-cans don't benefit from them.

That kind of coverage is animated by a sincere belief held by many politicians, journalists, and voters alike—that most of us do well when the wealthiest among us do well. And that belief, contradicted as it is by decades of data on rising inequality, leaves us in a state of deference that corporations and the wealthy routine y exploit. Companies often influence policy, news coverage, ard the attitudes of voters with nothing more than veiled threats—to hold back on investment, say, or to leave a region (or even the country as a whole) unless lawmakers pass the tax or regulatory policies they prefer.

Upon his election in 2008 during the global financial crisis, for instance, President Obama faced skepticism and hostility from the business community over his policy agenda, which had to be allayed through constant, time-consuming engagements with corporate leaders and their Republican allies in Congress. As the 2012 election drew nearer, economic analysts and commentators observed that major corporations were sitting on trillions in funds that might have been used for new investments in the recovering economy. Instead, as a 2018 paper on the period by researchers Kevin A. Young, Tarun Banerjee, and Michael Schwartz recounts, these firms were demanding policy concessions from Congress and the administration first:

> In November 2010, Emerson Electric CEO David Farr told [*The Wall Street Journal*] that "he would expand more in the U.S. only 'if I felt the government was going to get out of the way'" by overhauling the tax code and streamlining "environmental and hiring rules." Taxes and regulation—not the lack of demand—were also key themes in a meeting between CEOs and Obama later that month. Barclays CEO Robert Diamond said that U.S. corporations "don't have the confidence to hire in the United States of America until we can believe that the government, the private sector and financial

institutions are working together and connected again." Bausch & Lomb CEO Brent Saunders warned that "we're being a little more tentative on whether or not you [sic] want to move a plant, or invest," because of disagreements with the administration over rules governing profit repatriation. A few months later Joseph Czyzyk, the chairman of the Los Angeles Chamber of Commerce, said that "the thing that bothers us the most is regulatory reform." To unlock the $2 trillion stockpile of investment capital, Czyzyk said that the administration would have to get serious about dismantling regulations: "It can't be lip service. . . . it's got to be sacred cows."

In a September 2011 speech, Republican House Speaker John Boehner explained the nation's economic situation with a fair amount of candor. "Job creators in America," he said, "are essentially on strike."

"There is little doubt that corporations utilized the hoarded cash to extract pro-business policy changes, including many, like corporate tax cuts, that would not directly facilitate new investments," Young, Banerjee, and Schwartz explain. "Corporate leaders were instead offering a quid pro quo of domestic investment in exchange for pro-business reforms. Thus, whether or not business amassed trillions in cash reserves as part of a conscious political strategy, the reserves gave them a political bargaining chip that they deployed strategically." That strategy at least partially worked. As the researchers note, Obama went on to propose reducing the corporate tax rate, to pursue new trade agreements, and to appoint figures connected to the corporate world to official posts, including General Electric CEO Jeffrey Immelt, who was "named the chief of Obama's 'President's Council on Jobs and Competitiveness,' the body 'charged with finding ways to foster private-sector job growth.'"

These are the people and interests the American political system responds best to. While the votes of ordinary Americans might not be worth especially much, the wealthy, the well-connected, and corporations wield a tremendous amount of political influence inside and outside the halls of government—even when checks aren't being written and the services of lobbyists aren't being employed. Scholars and commentators who appreciate these problems often present them as evidence that our system isn't working—that American governance is "broken" in some critical sense. But the history of our political institutions invites an obvious question: Who was our system intended to work for in the first place? While the Founders hadn't an inkling of what the American polity and economy would become, they held views on democracy that plainly shape policy outcomes today. More than two centuries after Shays' Rebellion, the institutions crafted at the Founding and the wider system they have shaped make it extraordinarily difficult for majorities of the mass public to make economic policy and curb inequality—just as the Founders intended.

★ ★ ★

Some of the solutions worth considering here are simple. On the lobbying front, regulations could be tightened by expanding the definition of activities that might be considered *lobbying* to include consulting and advisory work. And federal agencies and institutions such as the Congressional Research Service (CRS) could be granted more resources to inform lawmakers, diminishing their reliance on lobbyists and industry-funded groups and think tanks for analysis and information. Some reformers have also suggested forming "people's lobbies"—employing public lobbyists who, much like public defenders, would represent underrepresented constituencies such as the poor or the uninsured on the Hill. All of that would improve the policymaking process.

Serious campaign finance reforms are also long overdue. On dark money, the For the People Act would have required the disclosure of nearly all large donors to politically active groups and organizations that spend more than $10,000 per election cycle It also would have bolstered regulations against coordination between candidates and putatively independent outside groups, such as super PACs. Even more ambitiously, the For the People Act would have required corporations to consult their shareholders before making political contributions, and it would have given the Securities and Exchange Commission (SEC) the authority to further regulate corporate political contributions.

One other way to better align our campaign finance system with the interests of the public would be to incorporate more money from the public. Then-senator Obama's decision to decline taking public funds for his primary campaign in 2008 functionally killed our already paltry public-financing system at the presidential level; no nominee has taken public funds since. Cities and states, however, have developed their own public-financing systems, and the For the People Act would have established a public fund to help finance congressional elections by matching small donations. One drawback with matching, though, is that it tends to amplify the influence of middle-class voters over poorer voters, who are less likely to contribute. Public vouchers—granting all voters a set sum, perhaps fifty or one hundred dollars, to spend on candidates as they choose—skirts this problem. Like matching, vouchers could conceivably be used to shape or limit the other private fundraising that candidates do, as receipt of public money could be made conditional on following certain campaign finance rules. But it seems doubtful that we'd put enough money toward public fundraising to meaningfully compete with the billions candidates now raise by conventional means. Ultimately, these reforms have been proposed to rein in political money on the campaign finance landscape as we know it today, which has been utterly reshaped by the *Citizens United* ruling. And in the long view, we should work toward overturning the *Citizens United* ruling by a constitutional amendment, one that might also place hard limits not only on political contributions but on the amounts political campaigns can spend.

Still, as our analysis of how diffusely money comes to influence politics should have suggested, limits on political spending can only do so much to ensure ordinary Americans truly govern themselves. The ideas offered here would do much to renovate our political institutions. But our economic institutions are the piece of the reform puzzle that analysts often miss. It is obvious that corporations and the wealthy will do their utmost to maintain their dominance over our politics; it should be equally obvious that growing economic inequality enhances their capacity to do so. Moreover, as we've seen, the economic sphere raises democratic concerns of its own—at work, just as in politics, ordinary Americans have their agency constrained by elites that govern them.

Despite all this, well-meaning reformers have long proceeded as though protecting and expanding democracy is a political project alone—as though the promise of democracy might be fulfilled before or without addressing the material inequities structuring American life. The constant frustration of their agendas suggests otherwise. It's time to correct their mistake.

CHAPTER 6

TOWARD A
DEMOCRATIC ECONOMY

WHILE WE TEND TO FRET ABOUT THE STATE OF OUR POLITI-
cal institutions and the state of our economy separately, it
was argued earlier in the book that our ideas about democracy
should be informed by a materialism—an understanding that
economic conditions and alignments of economic power determine the extent to which the governed can govern. The last two
chapters have illustrated why materialism is important. As we saw
in Chapter 4, the major features of our Constitution were profoundly influenced by economic conditions at the time it was
written. Troubled by the demands struggling Americans were making of government after the American Revolution, our Founders
designed a federal system that frustrates our ability to democratically address our economic concerns and other matters to this day.
And as we saw in Chapter 5, money in politics has made matters
worse—on top of our federal system's anti-democratic design,
corporations and the wealthy shape policy in ways visible and
invisible to ordinary Americans on the outside looking in.

Curbing the political power of our economic elites would take
more than imposing new limits on how they can directly engage
in politics, as important as that goal remains. Again, corporations
and the wealthy exert their political influence through a variety of
indirect channels, from the media to their social circles. As such,
an ordinary American would still wield far less political power—
and be far more subject to political domination—than a million-
aire or billionaire even with major campaign finance and lobbying

reforms. And while the basic economic minimum that democratic theorists noted in Chapter 3 have endorsed would help the poor and disadvantaged engage in democratic politics—it's much harder to be a good democratic citizen if you haven't had a good education or don't have a stable place to live—it would hardly level the political playing field. What's more, as we've seen, some democratic theorists have convincingly argued that the wealthy and corporations also wield a democratically troubling amount of power over us within the economy itself. At work especially, we are subject to the unaccountable authority of superiors in ways that we would never accept from our political institutions.

And as Elizabeth Anderson has written, many workers have come to accept or endure levels of control and coercion at work that should deeply trouble all who believe workers are entitled to dignity and respect:

> Consider some facts about how employers today control their workers. Walmart prohibits employees from exchanging casual remarks while on duty, calling this "time theft." Apple inspects the personal belongings of their retail workers, who lose up to a half-hour of unpaid time every day as they wait in line to be searched. Tyson prevents its poultry workers from using the bathroom. Some have been forced to urinate on themselves, while their supervisors mock them. About half of U.S. employees have been subject to suspicionless drug screening by their employers. Millions are pressured by their employers to support particular political causes or candidates. If the U.S. government imposed such regulations on us, we would rightly protest that our constitutional rights were being violated. But American workers have no such rights against their bosses. Even speaking out against such constraints can get them fired. So most keep silent.

As said in Chapter 3, these are good reasons for us to consider the possibilities of *economic democracy*. The power that the rich, corporate executives, and investors have accrued in our politics, as Robert Dahl observed, is the product of the wealth and power they've been able to structurally accrue within our economy to begin with. There, through the control and ownership of firms, they also shape the conditions of our lives as or more directly than politicians do. On these grounds, our sense of what it would mean to fulfill the promise of American democracy should be enlarged. If we take all we've said about democracy thus far seriously, we should work toward ensuring that ordinary Americans are democratically empowered not just within our political institutions, but within the economy.

The Case for Economic Democracy

Presidents and other prominent American leaders used to invoke the idea of a democratic economy with some frequency. "If we allow great industrial organizations to exercise unregulated control of the means of production and the necessaries of life," Theodore Roosevelt said in a 1909 message to Congress, "we deprive the Americans of today and of the future of industrial liberty, a right no less precious and vital than political freedom. Industrial liberty was a fruit of political liberty, and in turn has become one of its chief supports, and exactly as we stand for political democracy so we must stand for industrial democracy."

In 1919, Woodrow Wilson would echo Roosevelt in an address where he named economic discontent as one of the major causes of World War I. "It is a conviction all over the world that there is no use talking about political democracy unless you have also industrial democracy," Wilson said. "With the control of the few, of whatever kind or class, there can be no democracy of any sort. The world is finding that out in some portions of it in blood and terror."

Franklin Roosevelt and his allies invoked "economic democracy" as they made the case for the programs of the New Deal. "All American workers, brain workers and manual workers alike, and all the rest of us whose well-being depends on theirs," Roosevelt said in a 1936 fireside chat, "know that our needs are one in building an orderly economic democracy in which all can profit and in which all can be secure from the kind of faulty economic direction which brought us to the brink of common ruin seven years ago." And John F. Kennedy would use the phrase in reference to unions. "The fact that public, labor and management representatives are in unanimous agreement that collective bargaining is an essential element of economic democracy," said Kennedy in 1962, "is a mark of our progress as a nation when contrasted with the disagreements on this subject in the not too distant past." In a 1961 address to the AFL-CIO, Martin Luther King Jr. had done the very same, celebrating how unions had grown in the decades prior. "[Labor] was warned to go slow, to be moderate, not to stir up strife," he said. "But labor knew it was always the right time to do right, and it spread its organization over the nation and achieved equality organizationally with capital. The day of economic democracy was born."

Economic democracy is a phrase and a concept that can be put to many ends. But some democratic theorists have taken a particular interest in the question of democratizing work specifically — giving workers a say in the governance of the companies they work for.

While most Americans believe, as they should, that cooks and cashiers and warehouse workers are democratically entitled to having their voices heard on the full range of policy issues that come up for discussion within our politics—from local zoning laws to our relations with Russia or Iran—it's taken entirely for granted that workers should be mostly excluded from decision-making on how their own workplaces are run. "In places, circumstances, and settings they know best in which they are arguably the most qualified to assess situations and make decisions," the sociologist Isabelle Ferreras writes, "workers become subordinates." What's more, if it really is the case, as explored previously, that there are epistemic benefits to people coming together to solve problems democratically rather than delegating decision-making to one or a few, it stands to reason that those benefits could apply to decision-making in both governments and companies alike.

It should be said that democratic theorists are far from unanimous on these points—the grounds for economic democracy have been debated for some time. Much of that debate has revolved around the logic of the analogy that the supporters of economic democracy tend to draw between the firm and the state: The two are different enough, opponents argue, that democracy isn't necessarily justified in both places. One difference between states and firms, opponents of economic democracy argue, is that workers consent to the authority of their employers when they apply and are chosen for a job. "Territorial associations are qualitatively different from economic organizations in terms of voluntariness of subjection, and that is why the entitlements of their respective members differ," the theorist Robert Mayer writes. "Adult residents have an inalienable right to democratic power in territorial associations but employees lack this moral right in the firm. The latter are only entitled to what they can negotiate, and this usually means alienating the claim to power in exchange for something deemed more valuable—remuneration." Workers don't have the right to democracy in firms, in other words, because they've knowingly made the choice to work for firms that aren't democratically run and are being compensated for their lack of agency with pay. In the state, by contrast, it's not up to residents at all whether they consent to the state's authority or not; as such, we might think they're entitled to a democratic say as to how the state uses its authority.

Opponents of economic democracy often relatedly point out that workers who don't like their working conditions can, at least theoretically, leave their jobs. It's harder, by comparison, to leave one's country for a better place.

Proponents of economic democracy tend to counter all this with two basic arguments. The first is that consent to undemocratic employment is essentially coerced. People need to work—to earn a stable living and to meet sociocultural expectations—and they don't have many choices as to the type of firm they might work for. "Most workers are compelled to join hierarchical workplaces because of two conditions: (i) pressure to get a job, and (ii) the absence of alternative democratic options," the theorist Tom Malleson writes. "The precise degree of material pressure that individuals face varies from country to country and depends on a number of factors—most importantly, the level of unemployment, one's bargaining power in the labor market, and the extent of social security."

Defenders of the firm-state analogy also argue that leaving one's job can be more difficult than their opponents assume. It's also worth saying here that it's unclear that the ease of exit is philosophically relevant in any context. Are people who live near national borders less entitled to democratic rights than people who live closer to their country's interior? Should there be fewer democratic rights in countries with less land area than others because they would be easier to traverse and escape? Are people who live in landlocked countries less entitled to democracy than people who live in island nations? And consider local government. Imagine an elected mayor of a small town assuming dictatorial control over the community and, when challenged, insisting that those opposed to his rule can simply leave for a democratic town a fifteen-minute drive away. Would that really be justified?

These are compelling responses. But even proponents of the firm-state analogy tend to concede that firms and states are different in meaningful ways. In *Private Government,* for example, Anderson acknowledges that firms, as a practical necessity, need to have intensive control over what their employees do in order to function. While states obviously subject us to rules, they generally don't actively direct our basic activities. But firms absolutely must direct their workers with specific objectives in mind:

Efficient production nearly always requires close coordination of activities according to centralized objectives, directed by managers exercising discretionary authority. This frequently entails that the authority of managers over workers be both intensive (limiting workers to highly particular movements and words, not allowing them to pursue their own personal objectives at work or even to select their own means to a prescribed end) and incompletely specified. The state imposes traffic laws that leave people free to choose their own destinations, routes, and purposes. Walmart tells its drivers what they have to pick up, when and where they have to deliver it, and what route they have to take. In addition, managers need incompletely specified authority to rapidly reassign different tasks to different workers to address new circumstances.

Additionally, the state and the firm sit at two different levels of structural hierarchy. The state is an overarching entity—what the theorist Roberto Frega calls a "second-order institution"— that governs many smaller institutions and individuals, while the individual firm, a "first-order institution," sits alongside many other firms within the larger economy and is subject to the rules of the state. To compare the two, Frega argues, is to conceptually misalign them. Firms have specific objectives to fulfill within the societies that states govern and should utilize the most effective means of fulfilling them, which may or may not be workplace democracy. But the state or "political community," he contends, has no guiding purpose or function as clear as the firm's. Instead, "it defines the social framework which creates the demands for functions to be fulfilled." As such, it can't be assumed that the state and the firm must conform to the exact same ethical requirements.

But thinking about the state as a second-order entity only partially clarifies the underlying trouble with the analogy: It is not clear, even at that level, what the state really is or means. Although the phrase tends to call government at the scale of the nation-state to mind, political regimes obviously include subnational and local governments as well. Critically, the different levels of government often operate at cross-purposes, competing with and contradicting one another. And even within national governments, different branches and institutions can clash, especially when they're controlled by different political factions with different goals. As convenient as it might be as philosophical short-hand, it makes little sense, given all this, to suggest that the laws, policies, and people that govern a populace constitute a single stable and coherent entity. We're better off thinking about the political world as a polity—a complex tangle of people, structures, and institutions that underpins a messy political order.

And for the purposes of democratic theory, the appropriate analogy to consider isn't one between the polity and the firm, but between the polity and the wider economy. Like a polity, an economy is a complex order made up of smaller units—firms and companies of all kinds and sizes in tension and competition with one another. Neither the polity nor the economy has a singular coherent purpose; nevertheless, both of them structure society. And unlike the firm and the state, polities and economies are similar enough that consent and exit happen to work in mostly the same ways within each. Most of us don't consent to membership in the political orders we find ourselves within; they are often difficult to leave. But neither do we consent to membership in the economic systems we find ourselves within. And the latter can be even more difficult to exit than our polities are, especially in our age of globalization and broadly free international trade. It is far easier to escape the reach of American laws than it is to escape the reach of the American economy.

If consent and exit matter as much as the opponents of the firm-state analogy insist they do, the polity-state analogy would seem to offer us a solid case for economic democracy. The only hitch—and it's a significant one—is that levels of hierarchy still matter. While all of the above suggests we might be entitled to democratic agency and more control over conditions within the overall economy, that doesn't fundamentally entitle us to democracy at the level of the individual firm. It could be argued, in fact, that achieving economic democracy might be a matter of regulating and improving the economy in the public's interest through ordinary politics and policymaking.

The challenge there, however, as we've already seen, is that the economically powerful hobble and corrupt the political process. And even if the right to economic democracy exists at the level of the broad economy, it can be instantiated at least in part, as a practical matter, by democratizing work.

And while many readers might remain unconvinced, for one reason or another, that a real right to economic democracy exists in the first place, it should be emphasized here that democracy at work is desirable whether we're fundamentally entitled to it or not.

Democracy, as we've established, is the most sensible way to govern in the interest of the governed. And domination, as we've likewise seen, is a bad thing at any level. "The rationale for employee participation in enterprise decision-making processes is not that managers have power analogous in scope and magnitude to state agents," the theorist Keith Breen writes. "Rather, it is simply that they have dominating power, and this power frequently has intolerable consequences for people and should be curtailed regardless of any resemblances it may share with governmental power."

In their subordinate position, America's workers are not only governed but dominated. A more democratic economy would empower them. Just as in politics, economic democracy need not and, in fact, cannot mean granting everyone an up or down vote on all things—like governments, businesses cannot run without delegation, representation, and the work of experts.

Nonetheless, just as in politics, that fact offers no grounds for wholly excluding the people from economic decision-making, including in the workplace. John Dewey made just this argument in the aftermath of World War II. "It is so common to point out the absurdity of conducting a war for political democracy which leaves industrial and economic autocracy practically untouched," he wrote, "that I think we are absolutely bound to see, after the war, either a period of very great unrest . . . or a movement to install the principle of self-government within industries."

That didn't happen. But for a time the postwar economy did

deliver Americans a measure of economic democracy—thanks, as Kennedy and King said, to the growth of the American labor movement.

The Rise and Fall of the American Union

America left the Great Depression and World War II on top of the world economy—thanks partially to the fact that the economies of its major rivals had been reduced to rubble. Beyond that, the public investments of the New Deal and wartime production created millions of new jobs and a massive amount of productive infrastructure; in 1956, the project of improving our infrastructure was continued with the Federal-Aid Highway Act, which created the interstate highway system as we know it. Our policymakers were also investing directly in the American people. The GI Bill funded education and job training for nearly eight million returning veterans and had granted more than four million low-interest, no-down-payment home loans by 1955. The Social Security Act of 1935 created our Social Security program, an economic lifeline for American seniors, as well as our unemployment insurance system. It was followed thirty years later by the creation of Medicare and Medicaid under Lyndon Johnson, whose Great Society agenda also included food stamps and the Head Start early childhood development program, along with new federal investments in housing and education. The fights for civil rights and gender equality—and the policies they motivated— also strengthened the American economy: Reductions in discrimination and the entry of minorities and women into higher-wage work produced more than 40 percent of our economic growth per worker after 1960. These were the achievements of a federal government much bigger and bolder than ours is today. The growth that America experienced between World War II and the 1970s simply would not have been possible without government help. But always and everywhere, economies are built upon the backs of workers. The drivers and the miners, the clerks and the cooks, those who build and fix and clean and carry, those who staff the factories and the shops—whatever politicians and their donors say about the wealthy "job creators" at the top of companies, it's the job doers to whom we owe everything. And for generations, job doers seeking a greater share of the prosperity they produce have turned to labor unions. In 1935, the National Labor Relations Act, better known as the Wagner Act, guaranteed most private-sector workers the right to organize and to bargain for better pay and working conditions. As a result, union membership spiked—in the twelve years after its enactment, nearly eleven million Americans joined up.

In 1935, about 13 percent of the country's workforce had been unionized. By 1955, that proportion jumped to roughly one-third of American workers. Beyond getting the American people a better deal at work, unions used that newfound strength to push the New Deal and Great Society agendas forward. By politically organizing and mobilizing their workers, unions helped win the fights for Medicare and other major programs. And though the labor movement was not uniformly supportive of civil or women's rights, unions whose members were predominantly women and people of color had been critical in agitating for both since the turn of the century. After 1935, organizers with the Congress of Industrial Organizations (CIO) and other progressive labor groups continued the push for equality in the workplace and worked to elect policymakers who would champion equal rights.

In both ways, unions—which are democratically formed by majority rule either in elections administered by the National Labor Relations Board (NLRB) or by an employer's voluntary recognition—have played a significant role in ensuring that the gains from our economic growth flowed to workers and not just the already wealthy. According to one 2021 paper, increasing union membership alone likely explains nearly a quarter of the decline in American inequality from 1936 to 1968. And while union families earned 10 to 20 percent more in income than nonunion families between the 1940s and the 2010s, unions also made nonunion workers better off than they otherwise would have been;

to compete with union workplaces for new hires and to keep their employees content, even nonunion workplaces wound up offering better pay and working conditions.

It should come as no surprise that the wealthy and their backers in Washington fought back hard against the expansion of the labor movement. In 1947, over a veto by President Harry Truman, Congress passed the Taft-Hartley Act, which imposed a laundry list of restrictions on union activity—including a ban on secondary boycotts aimed at getting companies to stop doing business with other companies involved in labor disputes—and included other measures to limit their growth. Among the most significant of them was giving states the ability to pass right-to-work laws, which are often framed as granting workers the right not to join a union. But American workers never have to join unions if they wish not to: Workers who don't want to belong to a union at their workplace can pay fees that cover the costs of the union's bargaining activity on their behalf rather than actual union dues. What right-to-work laws actually do is starve unions of resources, ensuring that workers in unionized workplaces needn't pay unions anything at all.

Here an analogy to political democracy might be helpful. Imagine if, after your preferred party or candidate lost an election, you no longer had to pay taxes. That would be absurd. While we might not like much of what those who disagree with us do in government, the government nevertheless keeps us safe and provides all of us with many services we benefit from. These things are possible only if everyone pays in—even those who might oppose a particular set of people in power or the government as we know it in general. Similarly, unions—formed, again, by majority rule—typically bargain on behalf of all workers in a given bargaining unit, whether those employees support the union or not. Given this, the right to work might be better understood as the right not to accept the results of a democratic election and to refuse contributing to democratic institutions that deliver collective benefits.

The proliferation of right-to-work laws and the other limitations on labor organizing imposed by Taft-Hartley nonetheless put the brakes on the growth of the labor movement. And disempowering unions became one of the cornerstones of the economic agenda that took root after an economic downturn in the early 1970s—an all-out assault on the policies of the New Deal and the Great Society. The labor movement was tamed, taxes were slashed, government programs were gutted, government functions were privatized, industries were deregulated, jobs were enthusiastically sent overseas, and finance took up a greater share of our economic activity.

Policymakers assured voters that these changes would eventually deliver economic freedom and prosperity to all Americans. But on the whole, this agenda made the wealthy wealthier and more powerful while ordinary working Americans struggled to adjust, deepening inequality. Though the productivity of our economy has grown by 111 percent since the mid-1970s, the hourly pay of the median American worker has increased by only 50 percent during that time, after roughly a quarter-century of tracking productivity closely. Meanwhile, Americans at the top of the income distribution have seen their earnings skyrocket. From 1979 to 2022, according to analysts at the Economic Policy Institute, annual earnings for the top 1 percent of Americans grew by nearly 172 percent. Earnings for the top 0.1 percent of Americans, meanwhile, grew more than 344 percent. And the nation's top executives, naturally, have done the best of all: In the same period, pay for the CEOs of the 350 largest companies on the stock market grew by over 1,200 percent. The average CEO now makes 344 times more than the average worker, compared to just 21 times more back in 1965.

These are among the reasons why the Organisation for Economic Co-operation and Development (OECD) now ranks the United States among the worst of the countries it studies on income inequality—we're thirty-fourth, between Bulgaria and Turkey. And our inequalities in overall wealth are even starker. The top 10 percent of American households—those with an average net worth of about $6.9 million—now own about 67 percent of household wealth in this country. Meanwhile, the bottom 50 percent of American households, worth about $51,000 on average, have less than 3 percent of our household wealth. Between 2007 and 2016 alone, which included the Great Recession and its immediate aftermath, the wealth of the median American family fell by more than $40,000, as one might expect. But the wealth of the top 1 percent of Americans actually grew — by nearly $5 million, on average. That owed largely to increases in the value of stock — while most Americans own some securities, nearly 93 percent of them are owned by the top 10 percent of Americans. When the financial markets do well, so do Americans rich enough to play the markets in the first place. Off of Wall Street, Americans who truly work for a living — the vast majority who depend on a wage or a salary, whose most valuable assets might be the roofs over their heads, if they happen to own them — have had a much harder time building and maintaining wealth, especially racial minorities.

That's substantially a product of how the American economy was remade, beginning in the 1970s. And few changes were as dramatic or consequential as the fall of the labor movement. From its peak at roughly one-third of the American workforce in the 1940s and 1950s, union membership has declined to about 10 percent of the workforce today, including just 6 percent of the private-sector workforce. According to one estimate, the decline in union membership since 1968 accounts for about 10 percent of the increase in income inequality America has seen since then. According to another, when the impact on the hourly wages of nonunion members is factored in, the decline of unions likely explains as much as one-fifth of the rise in wage inequality among American women and one-third of the rise among American men working in the private sector from 1973 to 2007.

While the average American might have more money and a higher standard of living today than they would have fifty or a hundred years ago, rising inequality and the collapse of worker power have nonetheless had dire socioeconomic consequences. In 2020, the World Economic Forum (WEF) released its latest report on global social mobility—the extent to which countries, based on factors including access to good jobs, education, and health care—offer their citizens "a fair chance to fulfill their potential, regardless of their socio-economic background, the origin of their parents, or the place where they were born." In it, the United States ranked twenty-seventh, just behind Lithuania. By the WEF's estimates, it takes five generations for the poorest of American families to reach middle income. And of the thirty-eight industrialized or rising economies assessed by the OECD in 2022, the United States had the second-highest poverty rate, just ahead of Costa Rica's. We also rank twenty-fourth in life expectancy, twenty-ninth in infant mortality, and thirtieth in what the OECD calls "potential years of life lost," a measure of premature and preventable deaths.

Among many Americans, there's a growing sense that we used to do better than this—a feeling that the American people used to be more secure, and that American prosperity used to be more broadly shared. Politicians in both major parties speak nostalgically about the days when a single middle-income job might have secured a family's place in the middle class. In the last half of the twentieth century, films and television shows depicting the United States as a land of affordable homes in prosperous, stable communities enchanted and inspired people the world over. And while that America was never fully real for many, our longing for a return to our economic past is rooted in our collective memory of the economy unions built by democratically empowering the American worker.

The State of the American Worker

As unions collapsed, so too did the bargaining power that workers had gained with their growth in the first decades after the passage of the Wagner Act. And companies are working hard to cripple unions even further. Although the Wagner Act prohibits them from explicitly firing or punishing workers for trying to unionize, U.S. employers spend more than $400 million a year on consultants who specialize in discouraging or thwarting unionization efforts with a variety of tactics that skirt the edges of legality. And even when companies engage in flagrantly illegal activity—firing unionizing workers, say, or spying on employees who are organizing—the National Labor Relations Board (NLRB) cannot directly impose monetary penalties on them for breaking the law.

That weakness has made employers brazen. In recent years, major firms such as Starbucks, Chipotle, Walmart, and Trader Joe's have not just fired workers trying to organize but shut down entire stores with ongoing union activity, supposedly for unrelated reasons. And as union organizers know well, even when a union is formed, negotiating a labor contract can be a long, drawn-out process, thanks in substantial part to the company's stalling tactics. In 2018, a study found that 63 percent of new unions were unable to do so within a year, while 43 percent could not within two years—delays that allow time for union-supporting employees to get frustrated or leave.

This landscape and the difficulty of organizing have taken power away from workers and given an increasing share of it to executives and wealthy investors on Wall Street. "Workers often have no say in pay equity . . . in executive hiring, or in their organization's adjustments to health or financial crises," Harvard Business School professor Julie Battilana has written. "Instead, especially in non-unionized workplaces, control over these decisions is concentrated in the hands of top executives and board members who represent the interests of shareholders. Since power derives from control over access to valued resources, this disparity in control over strategic decisions results in a great power imbalance among workers, top executives, and capital investors, placing workers in a heavily disadvantaged position."

The decline of American unions has left workers with not only stalled wage growth but fewer means to address and improve their working conditions. Some of those conditions are an abject embarrassment by international standards. The United

States, for instance, is one of only six countries in the entire world—and the sole wealthy nation—that lacks a national paid-leave policy. On average, countries around the world guarantee twenty-five weeks of paid maternity leave for new mothers and sixteen weeks of paid paternity leave for new fathers. The United States guarantees zero. Seventy-one percent of the world's countries require employers to provide at least twelve weeks of paid sick leave. The United States requires none. Instead, federal law guarantees up to twelve weeks of unpaid family or medical leave—a policy that, due to exclusions based on business size and certain eligibility requirements, does not cover a staggering 44 percent of American workers.

Certain states and localities have passed a patchwork of paid-leave laws on their own: Thirteen states have paid family- and medical-leave policies, and fifteen have paid sick time. But most Americans are left with the paid time to care for themselves or their families that their employers choose to offer. Consequently, 73 percent of American workers in the private sector don't have paid family leave, and nearly one-fourth of them lack even paid sick time.

While surveys show few Americans actively hate their jobs, they deserve better than what employers have been willing to offer. In one 2019 survey, Gallup asked workers to rate their jobs across ten dimensions—not just pay but hours, job security, benefits, their sense of purpose at work, and their capacity to change aspects of their jobs they disliked. After using those results to form a measure of job quality, the survey company found that 60 percent of Americans are working in mediocre or bad jobs based on their own reported satisfaction and job priorities.

Workers who speak out about their conditions can be easily fired largely because in the vast majority of workplaces not covered by a union contract—and in every state save Montana—workers are hired "at will." That means their employers can legally fire them for nearly any reason not explicitly prohibited by labor law—or, indeed, for no reason at all. The United States is virtually the only country in the world where this is the case.

Just about everywhere else, employers have to demonstrate cause for firings—that the employee being dismissed has either done something wrong or must be let go for financial reasons or other difficult circumstances. In the U.S., by contrast, you can be fired simply because your boss is having a bad day.

And even workers fired for an illegal reason—racial or gender discrimination, for example, or trying to organize a union—may be unable to take their employers to court. More than sixty million workers (including 56 percent of the nonunion private-sector workforce and 65 percent of workers making less than $13 an hour) are bound by so-called mandatory-arbitration clauses, often tucked into the documents signed when one takes a job, that surrender their right to bring a legal dispute about their work. Instead they must settle with their employer through a private arbitrator, a process where they're less likely to succeed— and, even if they do prevail, likely to win less in damages than they would in court. That makes it easier for employers to get away with the kind of abuses and poor working conditions that Anderson and others have examined. It also facilitates outright income theft: Wages stolen by employers, it's been estimated, may cost minimum-wage workers in America as much as $15 billion a year.

Companies and their defenders justify much of all this with an argument we've touched on: A firm can fire its workers for nearly any reason, yes, but workers can also generally leave their job for a better one whenever they like and for whatever reason they care to. That freedom to leave is supposed to keep employers in check. They might have a tremendous amount of power to abuse or exploit their workers in theory, employers claim, but won't do so in practice if they know employees can walk away if they get fed up.

But as Anderson and others have documented, egregious abuses are common—partially because workers across the economy have lost so much power to set wages and working conditions. There might not be better jobs to walk away to, especially when economic conditions are tough and especially in economically disadvantaged communities. And as working Americans know, looking for a new job can be difficult, costing those in the hunt more time and money than they can easily afford.

Making matters worse, many employers have actually tried to ban their employees from seeking similar jobs through "noncompete agreements"—provisions that might prevent a worker from immediately taking the same job at another company. According to the Federal Trade Commission (FTC), which tried to ban noncompetes in a 2024 rule that was blocked in court, roughly one in five Americans have been subject to such agreements.

As much as companies try to maximize the leverage and power they hold over their employees, it's often most profitable for them to outsource labor to workers who aren't actually theirs at all—temporary and contract hires who can be employed more cheaply, and as needed. This "fissuring" of the workforce, as labor experts call it, has swept the American economy over the last few decades. "Indeed, from hotels to corporations, hospitals and universities," researchers Ruth Dukes and Wolfgang Streeck wrote in 2023, "it has become standard practice to contract out for cleaning and janitorial services, for gardening, landscaping and security, sometimes even for human resource, payroll and IT services. Franchising agreements have spread from hospitality and fast food into many and varied sectors of the economy."

Fissuring can make it difficult for workers to understand who they're working for and who they should approach about a job issue. One might go to work at a particular workplace for a company while actually being employed, technically, by another company hired by the first. Fully independent contractors, employed directly as individuals by companies, don't necessarily fare any better—they can be paid less than employees for the same amount of work, aren't entitled to the same benefits, and lack the right to unionize. That goes a long way toward explaining why, according to one study, as many as 30 percent of employers in America misclassify their employees as contractors—some intentionally and illegally.

Companies of the "gig economy" such as Uber, Instacart, and TaskRabbit represent fissuring at its most extreme. Though work-

ers at these companies often believe they're working for themselves (because so they've been told), the algorithms and reward
systems that shape how they work can saddle them with hours
and expectations that make them indistinguishable from employees. "For Uber, TaskRabbit, and the like to function as intended,"
Dukes and Streeck write, "they require at a minimum that a sufficient number of drivers, couriers or taskers make themselves
available for work at the right times of day and, secondly, that
those workers readily agree to undertake whatever gigs are as-
signed to them. In some cases, platforms also require that the gigs
be completed in a particular way—for example, with a particular
level of customer service."

In the gig economy, decades of eroding labor rights—the collapsing power of the American employee—have culminated in an
attack on the very concept of being an employee. Fissuring more
generally is a product of the basic economic incentives that have
always driven businesses seeking a profit. Absent regulation,
companies are inclined to wring as much as they can out of those
who work for them for as little as they can get away with—without
discouraging employees and potential hires from working there.
Conceptually, again, labor arrangements in the U.S. proceed
from the presumption that workers who don't like the pay and
conditions at a particular company can simply leave for a better
one. That freedom is supposed to dissuade employers from un-
derpaying, overworking, and otherwise abusing them.

But in practice, as we've seen, jobs are hard to leave and getting harder, thanks not only to the actions of particular employers but to the bare fact that there might not be many better jobs
available. The decline of unions and the democratic agency they
offered has left workers with less power, across the economy, to
demand and negotiate for better pay and working conditions.
That explains a substantial proportion of the rise in inequality
America's seen over the past several decades. Larger and larger
shares of the economic gains that workers produce have gone to
executives and investors; as explored in the previous chapter, the
influence over politics and policy outcomes their growing wealth

buys them is an obstacle to fully realizing political democracy in America.

While the weakening of worker power has taken place throughout the economy and shaped conditions at companies in every sector and industry, the problems described here are especially well-illustrated by Amazon, a truly twenty-first-century firm that has single-handedly reshaped American commerce and American life.

Amazon: A Case Study

In July 2021, having reached the summit of American commerce, Jeff Bezos—the founder of Amazon, with about $200 billion to his name—finally ascended into the heavens. Twenty years after launching the private space company Blue Origin, Bezos volunteered himself for the launch of its manned rocket, the *New Shepard,* bound for the point where our skies touch the edge of space. He was accompanied by three other lucky passengers, including one in a seat that had been auctioned off for $28 million. The winner couldn't make it—a scheduling conflict, these things happen—so it went to the runner-up, a private-equity CEO who gifted the seat to his eighteen-year-old son.

That $28 million wasn't a bad price for a ticket off-planet; at the time, a trip to the International Space Station was going for about $55 million. On the other hand, a short jaunt aboard Virgin Galactic's *SpaceShipTwo* could be taken for a mere $450,000—a bargain. Virgin Galactic also had the distinction of being founded by a man who had narrowly beaten Bezos skyward—Virgin's Richard Branson had flown aboard *SpaceShipTwo* nine days before the *New Shepard*'s launch, making Bezos, surely to his regret, only the second billionaire that month to reach space. Still, he enthused to a crowd upon returning to Earth, "It was the best day ever."

As one might expect of a man in the running to become the world's first trillionaire, Jeff Bezos has interesting hobbies. He's also been working on a clock, for instance—it's five hundred feet tall and being built inside a West Texas mountain, where, if the $42 million he's put into the project has been invested well, it will keep time for the next ten thousand years. And if it hasn't, he's got plenty more untaxed millions to burn. According to a ProPublica report published the month before the *New Shepard*'s launch, Bezos paid a rate of 0.98 percent on the $99 billion of wealth he gained from 2014 to 2018.

In a press conference after his flight aboard the *New Shepard*, Bezos was surprisingly candid about where that wealth came from. "I want to thank every Amazon employee and every Amazon customer, because you guys paid for all of this," he said. "So seriously, for every Amazon customer out there and every Amazon employee, thank you from the bottom of my heart very much."

Bezos was right about who paid, and who pays. It is ordinary Americans, as consumers and as workers, who generate the wealth that our economy produces, and that men like Bezos—founders, executives, or investors as distant as the stars from the hard work most Americans do—hoover up. But how much, beyond thanks, are Amazon's workers getting in return?

At a market capitalization of nearly $2 trillion, Amazon is now one of the most valuable companies in the world; with 1.5 million Americans on its payroll, it is also the second-largest private employer in this country. And though Amazon has moved from its core business into a remarkable range of new domains—web infrastructure, artificial intelligence, consumer electronics, satellites, grocery stores, films, television, and music—it still derives most of its revenue from online shopping and the extraordinary logistical operation it has built to sell and deliver nearly everything to everyone. In sprawling warehouses across America and through a fleet of delivery trucks that is second only to the United States Postal Service in the number of parcels it handles, Amazon's workers and contractors toil to process, ship, and deliver millions to our doorsteps each and every day.

While Amazon touts the fact that it raised the minimum wage

for those workers to $15 an hour in 2018—after a tremendous amount of public pressure—Amazon's warehouse employees still tend to make less than other warehouse workers, and the company tends to pull down wages for all warehouse workers in the places where it opens shop. According to reporting from Bloomberg in 2020, pay for warehouse workers in counties where Amazon opens its largest facilities falls by roughly 6 percent in the first two years. "Wages often tick higher in subsequent years, but don't reach their pre-Amazon level till five years after a new facility opens," Bloomberg's Matt Day and Spencer Soper wrote, "meaning that industry workers, on average, find themselves no better off half a decade after Amazon's arrival."

In 2023, a survey of nearly 1,500 Amazon warehouse workers at 451 facilities around the country found that nearly half had experienced housing insecurity, 56 percent had been unable to pay all their bills, and 53 percent had experienced food insecurity in the previous three months. That helps explain why a 2020 Government Accountability Office (GAO) report found that in six of nine states studied, Amazon was one of the top twenty-five employers in terms of the number of its employees on food stamps.

Those warehouse workers are being underpaid for their labor—including highly physical labor—under difficult conditions, as described in a 2024 report by Oxfam:

> Imagine an enormous building the size of 10 football fields with seas of boxes and storage units. The warehouse floor is littered with robotic devices—that workers describe as a "dresser with a Roomba underneath"—that roll over to your workstation and tell you what to pick up and scan. As a worker you can be standing for long stretches of time, sometimes up to 12 hours, engaging in the same repetitive, grueling, and physically taxing motion for hours on end. During the holidays, all employees are forced to work mandatory overtime, sometimes resulting in an almost 60-hour workweek. Even during the year, employees report grueling shift schedules—what the company once called "megacycles" but

now euphemistically calls "single cycles"—in which workers are made to work overnight from 1:20 a.m. to 11:50 a.m. These shifts can be punishing on the body, and they also isolate workers from friends and family.

Long shifts are the product of Amazon's constant drive to deliver more things to more people more quickly; the expectation that their workers strive to do more faster is enforced by methods of electronic surveillance designed to ensure no spare second is wasted completing tasks. In the 2023 survey of Amazon warehouse workers, 53 percent of them reported finding it difficult, at least sometimes, to take bathroom breaks. Unsurprisingly, given the pace and demands of their work, Amazon workers in warehousing and delivery have experienced higher rates of injury than non-Amazon workers in recent years, according to the Strategic Organizing Center. In 2021 for instance, the rate of serious injury for workers at Amazon warehouses was more than double the rate at non-Amazon warehouses. The 2023 survey of Amazon workers additionally found that 51 percent of those who had been at the company for more than three years had been injured on the job, and nearly 70 percent had taken unpaid time off within the previous month to deal with pain or exhaustion at work. Another 52 percent reported being burned out by their employment at Amazon more generally.

Though Amazon dismisses the claims of its critics and frustrated workers as exaggerations, the company occasionally admits more than it intended to about its working conditions. In a pamphlet from an Oklahoma warehouse that came to light in 2021, for instance, Amazon workers were encouraged to think of themselves as "industrial athletes" and to make changes to their diet and sleep habits in order to prepare themselves for work and avoid injuries, "just like an athlete who trains for an event." "All of Amazon's tips for avoiding injuries on the job," *Vice*'s Edward Ongweso Jr. wrote, "also ignore the simplest fix: reducing the pace of work."

Amazon would likely treat its workers better if it faced pressure from unions. But whereas there's been a recent surge in labor organizing at the company, those efforts have been an uphill battle. At the time of writing, New York's Amazon Labor Union is the only certified union of Amazon warehouse workers in America. In 2022 alone, Amazon spent more than $14 million on anti-union consultants, who offered the company strategies and tactics to persuade its workers not to start or join a union. And sometimes the company takes a blunter approach: Organizing workers have been fired and disciplined, which has drawn the scrutiny of the NLRB. All told, though, Amazon's hostility to unions has successfully weakened labor within the warehousing industry. From 2009 to 2019, as Amazon grew, union membership in transportation and warehousing fell from 21 percent to 16 percent.

Amazon has also taken full advantage of fissuring. Many of its warehouse workers are technically employed by outside agencies. And Amazon's "delivery service partners," who carry out the last bit of transportation that brings orders to homes, are in fact independent businesses with Amazon contracts. That makes it easier for Amazon to shirk accountability for working conditions and evade giving injured workers what they might be owed in compensation claims, benefits, and time off—even though those workers are, for all intents and purposes, working for Amazon.

"These drivers may wear Amazon-branded clothing, drive Amazon-branded vehicles, and in all meaningful senses of the term be laboring under Amazon's edicts," labor reporter Alex Press wrote in 2023, "but rather than taking workplace grievances to Amazon itself, those workers deal with DSP management. Amazon, in turn, gets millions of packages delivered, without the liability and responsibility that accompanies employer status." It also gets a key advantage over unionization efforts—if workers at the companies Amazon contracts with start unions, Amazon can drop those companies and sign new contracts with others.

Even without unions, Amazon workers are finding ways to fight back. In June 2024, for instance, more than fifteen thousand drivers in California, Illinois, and Massachusetts filed arbitration claims—thanks to contracts that barred them from filing a class-action lawsuit—alleging that Amazon had misclassified them as independent contractors and demanding compensation for unpaid wages. The NLRB determines how independent contractors are defined under the Wagner Act, and as such the board has a major role to play in advocating for workers of all kinds: employees and contractors, union members and nonmembers.

It should thus come as little surprise that Amazon has made an enemy of the NLRB. Indeed, the company has gone so far as to argue, in court, that the NLRB is unconstitutional—and that the board should be abolished on "separation of powers" and other dubious grounds. If it prevails, Amazon's argument will destroy vital labor protections not only for its workers, but for every worker in America.

While the Amazon case is dubious, it reflects the firm's understanding of a fundamental truth: Our political institutions, structured federally by the Constitution to which Amazon is appealing, are deeply intertwined with our economy. Again, as we saw in Chapter 5, money from corporations and the wealthy influences the policymaking process at multiple levels of government, making our already-undemocratic political system even more undemocratic. But political contributions and lobbying are only part of the story. Amazon's announcement of its plan to build a second headquarters in 2017, for instance, drew more than 238 bids from cities around the country, offering the company billions of dollars' worth of tax breaks and land for development, among other perks. One town in Georgia even promised to rename itself Amazon.

That public stunt was an exception. In the vast majority of cases, the officials responsible for assembling a city's bid tried to keep the incentives they offered Amazon a secret from voters—and even from other officials. "The only time the public may become aware if the city has promised Amazon incentives," Indianapolis City-County Council member Jared Evans told *The New York Times,* "is if we win and then we need to get those incentives passed."

The cities making the bids cozied up to Amazon by putting off democratic input and the possibility of public scrutiny, a trade-off the cities justified by talking up the jobs Amazon would surely bring in. But those jobs are arriving behind schedule in Arlington, Virginia, the city where Amazon finally decided to place half of its new headquarters in 2018. (Plans to locate the other half in New York City were scrapped in the wake of opposition from activists and hostile officials.) Virginia had offered Amazon $750 million of subsidies in exchange for bringing 25,000 jobs to the city by 2030. But by spring 2024, six years later, Amazon employed barely 8,000 in Arlington—and its employees in the city had actually decreased slightly from the year before.

Whether or not Amazon manages to get back on track and hit its target, the episode illustrates the extent to which major companies can distort, subvert, or thwart the democratic process even without political contributions or active lobbying. Vague promises to create or eliminate jobs can shape policy directly and dramatically.

★ ★ ★

Making American democracy real will mean making policymakers less vulnerable to the political influence companies like Amazon and billionaires like Bezos can wield. The reforms aimed at getting money out of politics discussed in Chapter 5 are, again, worth pursuing to that end. But, as we've seen, our democratic commitments also demand that we build democratic agency for workers within the economy, including at work. The proposals that follow do this in three ways—reviving unions and labor power, reforming corporate governance, and promoting worker ownership.

Reviving Unions and Labor Power

In recent years, unions and their advocates have united in support of the Protecting the Right to Organize (PRO) Act—the most significant piece of proposed legislation for organized labor since the Wagner Act. An override of state right-to-work laws; a ban on forced anti-union meetings at work; a ban on permanently replacing striking workers; a ban on forcing employees to waive their right to class-action lawsuits; civil penalties for violations of the Wagner Act; and a presumption in law that workers are employees rather than independent contractors unless employers can prove otherwise—these and the PRO Act's other provisions would be utterly transformative, making it easier to organize unions, bolstering their power, and extending new protections to all workers, both union and nonunion.

Still more could be done. Federal labor law could be changed so that a union is automatically formed and recognized by the NLRB once a majority of employees in a given unit sign cards authorizing one—without the need for a separate election if employers protest. And workers should have the right to bargain over more in union contracts than "wages, hours and other terms and conditions of employment," as the Wagner Act currently allows. As Harvard Law's Sharon Block and Benjamin Sachs have written, internal protests have been mounted at a variety of firms over a broad range of issues recently:

> Health-care workers are making demands about patient safety. Google employees protested the firm's creation of a censored search engine for the Chinese market, Accenture workers asked their employer to cancel a contract to help the Trump Administration recruit border patrol agents, and Wayfair employees wanted a say in their firm's decision to supply furniture to ICE. More and more workers want a role in addressing how their employers are contributing to—and how they might stop contributing to—the climate crisis. The democratic principles that give workers a claim to voice over wages and hours similarly demand that workers have voice in these other decisions that their firms make and that have profound impacts on the workers and their communities.

What's more, the Wagner Act has never covered public employees or agricultural and domestic workers. Federal law should grant them the same labor rights as all other workers. It should also end at-will employment by establishing that workers can be fired only for just cause—a reform that would not only grant American workers a basic protection afforded to nearly all other workers in the world, but also facilitate the formation of unions by making it more difficult for employers to invent reasons for firing union organizers and supportive employees. It should also be established that federal labor law, once reworked, should be the floor for labor protections in this country rather than the ceiling. States and localities should be allowed to pass labor laws of their own, provided they are at least as protective of unions and workers.

While these policies would surely rejuvenate and expand unions, it must be remembered that even at peak membership, the vast majority of American workers have never been represented by a union—thanks, in part, to a system that forces workers to organize themselves piecemeal, individual workplace by individual workplace. To broadly unionize the workforce of a large company such as Walmart, for instance, organizers would have to win the fight for representation and negotiate contracts at thousands of stores and facilities across the country—a daunting and likely impossible task, especially given the resources that Walmart commits to anti-union efforts. And to broadly unionize retail workers as a whole, the same would have to be done at many companies across the retail sector.

Expanding the reach of union contracts could help here. Historically, unions have at times been able to negotiate master contracts that cover workers at multiple companies. And labor law could be changed to help make those agreements more common—once workers at a few workplaces reach similar contracts, for instance, the law could have those contracts automatically cover other newly organized workers in the same region and sector, without each workplace having to negotiate separate agreements.

Policymakers could also more fundamentally transform labor law by instituting sectoral bargaining—a system, common in Europe, in which representatives of employers and unions come together to negotiate over and set basic pay and conditions for workers across entire sectors of the economy all at once. On bargaining panels, those representatives might craft and vote on agreements that (for example) set a minimum wage-and-benefits package for all retail workers in a given state or region, rather than waiting for workers to organize unions and negotiate contracts store by store. New unions at each workplace could then focus on negotiating issues specific to each workplace, or try to push for even better pay and conditions than the minimums established by the bargaining panels.

Sectoral bargaining has a number of advantages beyond being a quicker and easier way to improve things for workers than depending solely on traditional union organizing. For one thing, companies might be less resistant to improving pay and conditions for workers if all of their competitors were made to do the same in a sectoral agreement. (As matters stand now, one reason companies fight hard against unions is that they fear spending more on their workers will put them at a competitive disadvantage against their rivals.) For another thing, sectoral agreements could address fissuring by protecting all workers doing the same kind of work. "It matters not whether someone is employed directly, is employed by a subcontractor or by a franchisee, or is an independent contractor," Block and Sachs explain. "If they work in the sector, they are covered by the sectoral collective bargaining agreement."

But perhaps most important of all, sectoral bargaining panels—each a kind of legislature governing work in a particular sector—would be a remarkable instantiation and expansion of economic democracy. And that would be especially so if all the workers in a sector could elect the union members who represent them on each panel.

As dramatically different as sectoral bargaining would be from the status quo, the seeds for it have already been sown. At various points over the last century, the federal government established boards and committees with business and labor representatives to set or advise on wage standards. And in recent years, policymakers in states and cities across the country have set up similar "wage" and "workers' boards" to set or advise on wages and working conditions in particular sectors. In 2015, a wage board in New York approved raising the minimum wage for fast-food workers to $15 an hour. Likewise in California, a "Fast Food Council" was established in 2022 to set wages and conditions for fast-food workers in that state. Colorado and Nevada have created boards (which also include patients) to offer recommendations on the home- and direct-care industries, while Philadelphia and Seattle set up boards to improve conditions for domestic workers. Efforts like these should be expanded and made more fully democratic—allowing for the election of worker representatives by workers themselves—on the way to true sectoral bargaining in America.

While giving workers more power to negotiate over pay and conditions by expanding and transforming labor law would go some way toward building their democratic agency, bargaining isn't governing. Beyond the basic conditions set by law or union contracts, most workers have little to no voice over a great many decisions that could upend their lives or dramatically affect the way they work. Factories and shops and offices get shuttered, layoffs get handed down, business strategies are fundamentally changed, and projects get pushed along that pose far more risks for workers if they fail than they do for wealthy bosses. For the most part in America, workers (who make possible everything that companies do) get no say on most of these matters—and likely would not even if unions were strengthened and we additionally moved toward sectoral bargaining.

As we've established, whether or not one believes workers may be entitled, in the abstract, to the same kind of democratic voice in workplaces that they might be entitled to as citizens of a state, they are plainly entitled to agency over the general economic conditions they face. As we saw with unions, democracy in the workplace gives them that agency: When unions were stronger, the power that workers wielded played a significant role in reducing inequality and keeping the power of executives and investors in check. But unions and bargaining are far from the only ways that we might build democratic agency for workers.

Reforming Corporate Governance

Here again, policymakers should take a page from Europe—this time with reforms that would give workers a direct say in business decisions. One such reform would be to have businesses institute work councils—bodies of representatives, elected by workers, that are consulted on working conditions, firings and layoffs, and other matters directly affecting employees' lives at work. While councils in most countries are merely informed of certain impending decisions, a few countries have given their councils a degree of real authority. In Sweden, for instance, work councils actively influence decisions on working conditions and have set up educational programs for workers. And in Germany, councils can even overturn dismissals of workers they deem unjust.

Contrary to what skeptics might assume about the business sense of granting worker representatives that much power, research has shown that work councils have no impact on a firm's profitability. If anything, they may increase productivity—perhaps by offering workers forums in which they can discuss and solve problems. That makes them a good supplement for traditional unions: Work councils can address new or specific issues in the workplace atop the contracts that unions have already negotiated. They can offer workers a voice in workplaces where a union has yet to be organized.

The fear that work councils could be used to manipulate workers—through representatives undermined, selected, or controlled by managers—led to the adoption of provisions in the Wagner Act that essentially banned them in the United States.

But those concerns should be allayed by new laws mandating that companies put councils in place when workers themselves demand them, and protecting such assemblies from the interference of bosses (much like the Wagner Act protections for those trying to organize unions).

Workers should also be given democratic power at much higher echelons of corporate governance. In some countries, companies are required, under an arrangement known as codetermination, to reserve for their workers a portion of the seats on their governing board, ensuring that ordinary employees get at least some say in decisions that might otherwise be left wholly to executives and investors. Germany's system is perhaps the most well-known and widely studied. There, most companies with five hundred to two thousand employees are required to have their workers elect one-third of the supervisory board that chooses and manages the executives running the company. Most companies with at least two thousand employees are required to have their workers elect one-half of that board. And, as with work councils, research suggests that firms with codetermination are as or more productive than others.

While codetermination is often discussed as a European model for corporate governance, the world's oldest still-operative law allowing it (a bill covering Massachusetts manufacturers) was passed in the United States in 1919. And in the 1970s, American unions briefly pushed to put workers on the boards of major corporations. In recent years, a few new proposals inspired by European codetermination schemes have been proposed by major politicians here. In 2018, Wisconsin senator Tammy Baldwin introduced a bill that would have required all corporations on the stock market to let workers elect at least one-third of their board of directors. This was followed by presidential-campaign proposals from Senators Elizabeth Warren and Bernie Sanders. Warren would have required companies collecting at least $1 billion in revenue to let workers elect 40 percent of their boards. Sanders would have had all companies on the stock market, as well as companies with at least $100 million in assets or revenue, let their workers elect 45 percent of their boards. Either way, the Warren and Sanders proposals would have applied to companies employing roughly thirty million workers.

Under the Baldwin, Warren, and Sanders plans, employee power would obviously be limited. As is just about universal in all codetermination schemes, worker representatives would have only a minority of seats on each board. Even in most large German companies where worker representatives make up half of supervisory boards, deadlocks are resolved by the representatives of shareholders.

Still, granting workers elected seats at the table where corporate decisions are made would significantly empower them. Even with a minority of seats, worker representatives could deeply influence corporate governance by casting key votes on issues where other board members might be split and ensuring that matters important to workers are raised for discussion. And they could use that influence to help bolster the democratic power of workers elsewhere—by pushing back against company efforts to discourage or frustrate union organizing, for instance, or by trying to rein in political contributions to anti-union candidates and groups.

But even if workers were on their boards, companies would still fundamentally be accountable to those who own them—founders, executives, and anyone else owning company shares. For public companies, that includes Wall Street investors who buy and profit from stock sold in the markets without contributing anything whatsoever to a company's operations and success. As shareholders, all are entitled to vote on corporate matters—including selecting company board members—and the dividends that boards decide to pay out. A company's actual employees, on the other hand, are generally entitled to none of this. Unless their employers are generous, they earn nothing more from the wealth their work produces than their pay and benefits—no shares or income as their companies do well, no votes as shareholders. Even with all the reforms explored above, those wealthy or well-placed enough in the company to own stock would still be calling the shots. Given all that, there's one more fairly straightforward idea we should consider here.

Promoting Worker Ownership

Workers should also be owners, entitled to an ownership stake in the companies they work for. Some already are. According to Rutgers professor Joseph Blasi, about 10 to 20 percent of companies on the New York Stock Exchange and NASDAQ have substantial programs where some stock is either granted to employees or offered to them at a discount. That includes corporations such as Alphabet (Google), Apple, ExxonMobil, Ford, Goldman Sachs, and Microsoft. And at some private companies, employees can come to own a substantial proportion of shares. The supermarket chain Publix, for instance—one of the top-ten largest private U.S. companies—is fully owned by its 250,000 employees and the company's founding family. Other notable private companies owned in large part by their workers include King Arthur Flour (100 percent owned), the manufacturer W. L. Gore (majority owned), and Wawa (one-third owned).

For years now, the primary vehicle for achieving worker ownership at that scale in the United States has been the employee stock-ownership plan (ESOP). In an ESOP, a company's stock is gathered from various sources and placed in a trust for employees, who receive an allocation of shares that the company can buy back from them for cash once they retire. About 6,500 companies employing some fourteen million workers—about 10 percent of the private-sector workforce—have ESOPs today. Roughly 2,000 of them are wholly owned by their employees. And research suggests that employee ownership is both good for workers and good for business. Companies with ESOPs tend to grow faster and are more productive after starting such plans than they would have been otherwise. Privately held ESOPs are also less likely to go bankrupt, and ESOP workers are less likely to be laid off. While some might assume that companies with ESOPs would compensate for the stock given to employees by reducing wages, evidence shows that their wages may, if anything, be higher. Moreover, companies with ESOPs tend to invest deeply in their employees with training and educational programs, among other benefits.

From a democratic perspective, most ESOPs have one key limitation: Workers usually don't have much of a voice in corporate governance as shareholders. Instead, ESOPs are run by trustees, who vote for employees on most matters (except major changes such as a company's sale or merger).

Yet they can be structured differently. Employees could be allowed to vote directly on more matters, for example, or they could be given the right to control the votes cast by trustees. And the tax and other government incentives and supports that ESOPs are offered could be amended specifically to encourage the formation of ESOPs of this kind.

In 2019, Bernie Sanders proposed another democratically promising and ambitious model for worker ownership, inspired by an idea floated by the U.K.'s Labour Party. Under his plan, the federal government would pass a law requiring all companies on the stock market and all companies with at least one hundred dollars in revenue or on their balance sheets to establish what he called Democratic Employee Ownership Funds (DEOFs), controlled by worker-elected trustees. Each company would then gradually place 20 percent of its stock into its DEOF over ten years. And workers at each company would have the right to vote through their portions of stock in the fund, just like typical shareholders.

The Sanders DEOFs would also hold a couple of key material advantages over ESOPs: Shares in an ESOP cannot be sold, meaning that workers don't earn anything from an ESOP, for the most part, unless they leave their companies or retire. But whereas shares in a Sanders fund, though similarly held in a trust, likewise could not be sold, they would pay out stock dividends to workers during their actual employment. At the same time, Sanders's

DEOF's would avoid a major pitfall of ESOPs, which is that they leave employee retirement plans in jeopardy if their companies go under. This is what happened at Enron in the early 2000s, when workers there who'd been encouraged to directly invest much of their retirement savings in the company's stock saw them wiped out as Enron was bankrupted by the discovery it had been engaging in fraud. Keeping employee shares in a DEOF trust that pays out dividends, by contrast, provides a layer of insulation that allows workers to hold investments in their companies without becoming too ensnared in their financial woes.

In plainer terms, the Sanders plan would have given workers ownership and control over 20 percent of every major company in the country—every big corporation you've heard of and thousands more besides, employing some 56 million Americans. And their ownership stakes would entitle workers to both full voting rights as shareholders and additional income from dividends worth, according to one analysis, an average of at least $2,622 per worker per year at publicly traded companies. As far-reaching and transformative as Sanders's own proposal is, evidence suggests there may be public support for taking it even further. In 2019, a survey found that a majority of Americans would support companies with more than 250 employees transferring as much as 50 percent of their stock to worker funds, making them halfway worker-owned and worker-controlled.

Beyond ESOPs and the funds envisioned by Sanders, there are fully fledged worker cooperatives—companies directly owned and controlled by their workers. In a cooperative, the divisions between workers and managers are eroded or erased to establish self-government. Collectively, it's up to the workers in a cooperative to decide what the business should do, and then to do it. The profits, like the employees' responsibilities, are divvied up among themselves.

The worker-cooperative sector in most countries is small. In the United States it is positively tiny—by one estimate there are perhaps one thousand such enterprises in America, employing some ten thousand workers. But cooperatives are nonetheless instructive, illustrating how much workers are capable of when left to their own devices—and how well democracy at work can function as a practical matter. Consider Spain's Mondragon Corporation, perhaps the best-known collection of cooperatives in the world, which employs tens of thousands of workers across some ninety-five firms in a variety of industries. Here's how Nick Romeo described them in a 2022 feature for *The New Yorker*:

> One makes bicycles at an industrial scale; others make elevators or produce huge industrial machines used in the production of jet engines, rockets, and wind turbines. Mondragon's businesses include schools, a large grocery chain, a catering company, fourteen technology R. & D. centers, and a McKinsey-like consulting firm. In 2021, the network brought in more than eleven billion euros in revenue. The collective enforces five hundred and five types of patents and employs about twenty-four hundred full-time researchers. It also owns subsidiaries in countries including China, Germany, and Mexico, and competes effectively in international markets, winning contracts from firms such as General Electric and Blue Origin. The odds are good that key elements of something within a hundred feet of you—an espresso maker, a gas grill, a car—were made at Mondragon.

In general, cooperatives—as large as Mondragon or much smaller—tend to be about as profitable and grow about as much as traditional companies while offering their workers more job security. They do come with their own unique challenges—worker congresses, like all congresses, do not always work well, and full participation in cooperative governance can demand a lot from workers. But they're a viable and democratically empowering business model, and we could do more to foster them. States can pass statutes laying out how cooperatives should be incorporated to help them comply with state laws built around more traditional businesses and secure funding from banks. Tax breaks and loans can be offered to help start cooperatives or convert existing businesses into them. And more worker-ownership centers, like those in Sanders's Vermont, could be founded with government support to offer them resources and technical assistance.

Pursuing the agenda described here would remake the American economy once again, this time to the benefit of America's workers—reducing inequality, improving the conditions of their working lives, and dramatically expanding their democratic agency in ways that will pay off not only at work but within our politics. We've explored some of the political benefits already: Empowering workers and the unions advocating on their behalf could hamper the anti-worker political activities of their employers, and putting more money in workers' pockets could facilitate democratic participation.

But economic democracy would bolster political democracy in another way. Democracy, as should be plain by now, is a vastly complicated thing; like all complicated things, engaging in it well takes practice. Habits and skills such as learning how to present and debate one's ideas, when and how to compromise, and how to critically assess and synthesize different sources of information before coming to a decision are critical for democratic life. Ideally, we'd be better at them than we seem to be today; we might improve if we gave ourselves the chance to work on such skills more often, between and beyond elections. Economic democracy—whether through participating in unions, electing work councils, voting as shareholding workers, or working in full-fledged cooperatives—gives us the opportunity to hone those skills at work, where we come together with people often very different from ourselves to achieve things big and small. Through work, democracy could be made more concrete to those who've come to doubt it—understood, materially, as the means by which raises can be won and problems in our daily working lives that trouble us can be solved, rather than as abstractions bandied about by politicians who always seem to promise more than they accomplish.

★ ★ ★

All told, the democratic agency of the American people has been fundamentally constrained by our undemocratic political system. But it has also been constrained by an economy in which American workers have much less power than they did half a century ago. And the inequality the decline of the labor movement has contributed to has filled the coffers of the wealthy, executives, and investors with money they use, as explored in the previous chapter, to further game our political system and our economy — partially by electing politicians willing to subvert the democratic process by extraordinary means. "As business interests in the U.S. consistently back extremist Republicans who legitimize the January 2021 attack on the U.S. Capitol, drive gerrymandering, limit the franchise, or lie that the November 2020 presidential election was stolen," the legal scholar Ewan McGaughey writes, "it is doubtful that politics can remain stable and democratic while the economy is not."

Beyond the aftermath of the 2020 election, our billionaire president Donald Trump and his "special government employee" Elon Musk — the richest man in the world — have illustrated McGaughey's broader point with an alarming clarity. The federal regulatory state and federal agencies disliked by conservatives have been illegally dismantled. The rights of immigrants and transgender Americans have been flagrantly violated and curtailed. And America's civil institutions, including our universities, have been bullied by our government into accepting right-wing views.

The political power Trump and Musk have used to dominate and abuse us was purchased. American inequality has, plainly, become a threat not only to our democratic aspirations but free society writ large. Some of the policies critical to fighting it will be familiar to readers. Raising taxes on the wealthy and closing corporate loopholes would help disempower the richest Americans and put some of their wealth to public use. Stronger antitrust enforcement would prevent the formation of domineering monopolies and break up firms that have grown too powerful. And expanding the social safety net by making more public investments in health care, housing, education, and other areas would improve our standard of living, make full democratic citizenship less daunting for struggling Americans, and give workers more security in their bargaining for better wages and conditions by easing the disruptions and financial risks of being fired or laid off.

These ideas are fortunately under wide and active discussion in American politics today. But the same can't be said for policy ideas that would newly and directly empower American workers. The democratic agency that workers exercised when American unions were strong helped slash inequality; the power they wielded helped make the New Deal and Great Society agendas possible. Without that agency and power, however, American workers have lost ground. They are dominated at work; in Washington and around the country, politicians favored by corporations and the wealthy have not only failed to govern effectively in the interest of the many but have pulled the country toward authoritarianism.

As deeply and undemocratically flawed as our republic has long been, we've moved onto perilous new ground. It's unclear what the years just ahead of us have in store. This much, though, *is* clear: If all we've said about democracy holds true and our economic history is any guide, the project of American democracy cannot be fully realized without building economic power for the American worker and democratizing work.

CONCLUSION

I have written, and then thrown away, several endings to this book. Over all of them there hung that fatality of last chapters, in which every idea seems to find its place, and all the mysteries, that the writer has not forgotten, are unravelled. In politics the hero does not live happily ever after, or end his life perfectly. There is no concluding chapter, because the hero in politics has more future before him than there is recorded history behind him. The last chapter is merely a place where the writer imagines that the polite reader has begun to look furtively at his watch.

Walter Lippmann, *Public Opinion* (1922)

MANY YEARS AGO, MAHATMA GANDHI WAS ASKED BY ONE OF the reporters buzzing around him those days for his thoughts on "Western civilization." Famously, Gandhi furrowed his brow, thought for a moment, and turned back to the reporter with a broad smile. "I think it would be a good idea," he replied.

This oft-told story bears a superficial similarity to the one about Benjamin Franklin and Elizabeth Willing Powel, beyond the fact they probably never happened. They each bear within them a challenge—to preserve the American republic, to make good on the promise and pretensions of Western civilization—though the Gandhi tale has an edge to it that I prefer. It is, after all, an inducement to change, rather than an invitation to self-satisfaction. As such, it has proven harder to flatten into a lesson for schoolchildren.

In the spirit of pseudo-Gandhi, this book has argued that "American democracy" is an idea whose time has come. The well-meaning calls to defend "our democracy" elide the reality that for all the progress we've made since the Founding in the granting and expansion of political rights, democracy, soundly understood, remains a goal unachieved. There are no perfect democracies abroad to envy, no societies that have brought about unalloyed mass rule. The tensions and complexities of democratic thought, as we've seen, give us ample reason to doubt that such a thing is even possible. But our country sits much further afield from the democratic ideal than our peers and our own self-perceptions; our frustrations with our false democracy have corroded faith in the ideal to the benefit of antidemocratic figures on the right and the interests they serve.

Beyond being worthwhile on their own merits, the political and economic reforms we've examined constitute a democratic agenda that stands a better chance of defeating the right than the flimsy and predictable rhetoric their opponents have offered up so far. It contains remedies for institutional problems that have undermined confidence in democracy's efficacy and bolstered a radicalized right. It also contains a set of proposals that would bring democracy into our economy—expanding worker power by means that would counter the political and economic dominance of corporations and the wealthy and executives—and build a material interest in the defense of democratic principles among American workers, who will come to see democracy work directly to their benefit within their own lives in new ways.

The major changes proposed sum up to the blueprint for a "new founding" because, pursuing them, we'd find ourselves in a new country, one in which it could be said with more honesty that the American people—not a favored subset of them, not just the wealthy and the powerful—truly govern themselves. That misty-sounding aspiration is no idle dream. It is a project, one that can be advanced by public policy. There are bills to be written and passed, workers and workplaces to be organized. It would be a fool's errand to try laying out how precisely we should go about it all. I am but one very tired writer; there are details here that political professionals and organizers are going to have to work out. I do, though, have a few closing thoughts on the way forward.

The immediate task for those committed to the project of American democracy is mounting an effective resistance to the forces of the right. And while the authoritarianism of the Trump administration has deservedly garnered much more attention, we should be attentive to the moves the right is making on the Constitution elsewhere. One of the ironies of the well-justified calls for new democratic amendments (or even a whole new Constitution) is that conservatives—who, as we've seen, are significantly advantaged by the document as is—are far ahead of liberals and progressives in organizing for a new constitutional convention. To that end, the group Convention of States raised an estimated $38 million in dark-money donations from 2016 to 2021; its aim, according to a document for sponsors published by *Business Insider* in 2022, is to get state legislatures to back a convention that would propose amendments to "impose limits on federal spending and/or taxation," significantly limit the federal government's capacity to regulate businesses and other entities, and "get the federal government out of" health care and education. What's more, a new constitutional convention, much like our first, could easily exceed the mandate given to it by the states and pass conservative amendments on guns, abortion, immigration, and other matters.

Some commentators have suggested that an Article V convention in the near future, even if called by conservatives, might present a real opportunity to propose democratic reforms or a new, more democratic Constitution. It will not. A constitutional convention called by conservative activists—backed by conservative donors and malapportioned for the dominance of conservative states, as it surely would be—will be a convention where conservatives win out, passing amendments for ratification that would make our Constitution worse democratically than it already is. Of this, there can be no doubt whatsoever.

Again, it takes the support of two-thirds of states to call an Article V convention. If all outstanding, historical requests for a convention are counted, we are already at or above that threshold; an act of Congress certifying the count may be all the right needs to get a convention underway. Needless to say, congressional action on this should be opposed, as should the efforts of the right's convention activists in our state legislatures; wisely, Democrats in a few states have moved to rescind requests for a convention already on the books. Make no mistake—our Constitution must be substantially amended or replaced for all the reasons previously explored. But the prospect of a grand revision or replacement in one fell swoop by an Article V convention or other means should be rejected until large majorities can be built for the democratic reforms the country needs most, and until such time as advocates for democracy have gained enough power in the state legislatures to design and control the process for proposing amendments or an entirely new document. Getting to that point—and getting ratification through a large and broad enough set of states that the country won't be ripped apart by the process— will take decades of political persuasion and organization.

The goal of a wholly new constitutional system should be considered an end point—the capstone to a process of democratization that should, in its success, gradually build both support for a democratic Constitution and the power its advocates will need to craft and enact it. To an extent that reformers rarely appreciate, economic reforms will be absolutely critical. As we've seen, our first convention would have gone very differently if everyday Americans had been represented among the delegates; absent them, the Founders wrote a Constitution that reflected and protected the interests of their class. Preventing the same from happening again will require more than ensuring that working-class Americans are heard by policymakers as we consider amendments or a new document in the future. It will require more than limits on how much the wealthy and corporations can spend to influence outcomes. Only through worker power can a constitutional system that works democratically in the interests of everyday Americans be brought about—strengthening and organizing workers to the point where they wield enough leverage to make democratic demands of their political leaders and bring the economy to a halt if they aren't met. That threshold surely lies somewhere well north of 10 percent union density.

If all this seems daunting, it should. We are still perhaps generations away from a truly democratic Constitution. But the work toward it—and the work to build a more democratic country—must begin now. Federally, pro-democracy majorities should pass the economic proposals described in Chapter 6 and the political reforms, previously discussed, that can be enacted without constitutional amendments: These include the elimination of the Senate filibuster, the expansion of voting rights, the admission of the District of Columbia and willing territories as states, Supreme Court reform, the implementation of proportional representation in the House of Representatives, and the authorization of the National Popular Vote Interstate Compact. We should also pursue pro-democracy constitutional amendments through the nonconvention process that brought us the twenty-seven we have already got—a process that itself, again, needs amending.

Building democratic agency in the here and now will also mean winning battles closer to ground in state and local politics. Over the last decade, states and cities have taken action both to expand and to limit access to the vote; obviously democracy's advocates should be attentive to those fights and try, additionally, to get policymakers to implement and experiment with novel democratic mechanisms and institutions including ranked-choice voting and deliberative assemblies. Amending state constitutions might be a promising avenue for both political and economic reform, but as far as enacting labor policy at a subnational level is concerned, it will be crucial for federal policymakers to guarantee that states and localities can pass labor laws of their own atop federal standards.

★ ★ ★

The proposals outlined in this book, as improbable as many of them might outwardly seem, are in fact quite modest relative to changes our country has seen within living memory. How much of American life as we know it today would have seemed plausible in 1925? The strides that women and minorities have made since then would have seemed a ludicrous fantasy to the average American of the 1920s; a population dazzled beyond comprehension by radio, flight, and the automobile would have had no capacity whatsoever to imagine the scale of the changes our economy and culture have undergone in just the last thirty to forty years. In the last hundred, our politics and society have transformed several times over. To doubt that another hundred years could bring us more-democratic working arrangements and governing institutions constitutes not only a failure of imagination but a failure of reason.

Nothing proposed here is assured. All of it is possible, and obviously so. That includes the eventual replacement of our Constitution, whose most-committed defenders often seem as though they expect it to endure for all eternity. If that characterization is unfair, I invite those who take offense to it to tell us when, if not this century, replacing our 1787 charter should be put up for serious discussion: in two hundred years? three hundred? five hundred? a thousand?

Thomas Paine, a man who did nearly as much to write America into existence as Thomas Jefferson, shared his disdain for perpetual constitutions. "There never did, there never will, and there never can, exist a Parliament, or any description of men, or any generation of men, in any country, possessed of the right or the power of binding and controlling posterity to the 'end of time,' or of commanding forever how the world shall be governed, or who shall govern it," wrote Paine in *Rights of Man*. "Every age and generation must be as free to act for itself in all cases as the age and generations which preceded it."

And even as they defended a Constitution that they hoped

would endure for some time, the Founders appealed to our right and capacity to reason new institutions into existence. "It seems to have been reserved to the people of this country," Hamilton wrote in Federalist 1, "to decide the important question, whether societies of men are really capable or not of establishing good government from reflection and choice, or whether they are forever destined to depend for their political constitutions on accident and force."

The years since have given us much to reflect upon. We have more than two centuries of experience with the Founders' Constitution. We've seen governments across the world rise and fall, peer constitutions drafted, amended, and replaced. Political science—a field that was still new in the Founders' day—has developed to maturity; regularly, it tackles questions that vexed them with tools they did not have and a rigor they were not capable of. Human equality, a principle they gestured at but were unwilling to accept and act upon themselves, has come to underpin our society. So too, despite everything their institutions have done to undermine it, has a faith in democracy that the Founders never shared. We know more than the Founders did. We are more practiced at governance. We are more moral, more just. What privileges their intentions for this country over our own?

"The earth," Jefferson wrote, "belongs to the living and not to the dead." As so many have labored to remind us over the last decade, the United States has much to atone for, the sins of Jefferson among them. But his words here—an intuition that can be read in the Declaration of Independence and the act of the Founding itself—are unassailable. Our present is shaped by all America has done and all America has been, yes. But our future will be shaped in large part by our own aspirations—what we decide this country can and must be. America is ours. Not Jefferson's. Not Washington's. Not Hamilton's. Not Madison's. Ours. Our identity is ours to establish and define. Our purpose is ours to determine.

For political journalists, cynicism is often a professional obligation. Even so, I scarcely could have imagined, when I began this book, how thoroughly our leaders would allow faith in democracy and its possibilities to collapse. "Giving the world back to its inhabitants is too big a job for the merely practical," the director Orson Welles once said. "Only the devout deserve the trust of government, for only the devout can face the unimaginable vistas of man's destiny." A characteristically grand statement, yes. But as Welles understood, this is a country that runs on grand visions. The cultivation of them is a core political competency. And the absence of them is an opportunity—not just for those who'd like to pull America forward, unfortunately, but for those who'd like to set America back. It should be plain by now that defending ourselves from the depredations of men like the president—those who would trade our future away for personal profit and the indulgence of their prejudices—will take more than the defense of American institutions as we've known them. The American project will be saved only by a return to the spirit that first inspired it. Each day, the darkness that shrouds this republic as I write these words makes new claims on our freedoms and our livelihoods. But we have known darkness—we have seen it thicker, deeper, and more suffocating than the pall over us now. Through it all, these words set down by Paine in *Common Sense* more than two centuries ago—his benediction for this country—have remained true: "We have it in our power to begin the world over again."

ACKNOWLEDGMENTS

I'S OFTEN SAID THAT WRITING A BOOK IS A LONELY PROCESS. As true as that might feel when one's hunched in front of a computer in the dead of night, a book is always a collective effort. I've had many collaborators on this project, most of whom I have never met and will never know. And given the concerns of this particular text, I'd be remiss if I didn't begin these acknowledgments with a word of thanks to all of the workers whose labor put this book into your hands or onto your screen—from all the publishing-side employees at Random House who have touched this project in some way, however small, to all who pressed and programmed and sold this book into the world as a finished product.

Of the collaborators I do know, my first direct thanks are due to my agent, Gary Morris at the David Black Agency, and my editor, Marie Pantojan. I am more grateful to both than I know how to express. I'd also like to thank Random House editorial assistant Azraf Khan, and Marni Folkman and Michael Hoak of Random House's publicity team, who were indispensable in the final stages of production.

Many, many thanks are also owed to the scholars, experts, and fellow journalists who generously reviewed this text or offered me their thoughts as it was being written and edited: Joseph Blasi, Matthew Bodie, Keith Breen, Michael Brennan, Corey Brettschneider, Ed Burmila, Josh Chafetz, Ryan Doerfler, Lee Drutman, Ruth Dukes, Kevin J. Elliott, Peter Enns, David Estlund, Benjamin Fong, Anthony Fowler, Josh Grant, Chris Griswold, Jake Grumbach, Hahrie Han, Jeff Hauser, Grant Hayden, Alexander Hertel-Fernandez, Sean Ingham, Nathan J. Kelly, Michael Klarman, Ilyana Kuziemko, Sanford Levinson, David Madland, Tom Malleson, Dylan Matthews, Dillon Mayhew, John McCormick, Matthew McManus, Ian Millhiser, Jana Morgan, Samuel Moyn, Suresh Naidu, Tom O'Shea, Josiah Ober, Philip Pettit, K. Sabeel Rahman, Aziz Rana, Rebecca Riddell, Corey Robin, Daniel Schlozman, Marie Staniforth, Jeff Stein, Leo Strine, Todd Tucker, Elizabeth Wilkins, James Lindley Wilson, and Christopher Witko.

I have also relied on the support of many friends, none more so than Kiara Nerenberg, without whose love, patience, and encouragement this book simply would not have been possible. I also owe thanks to Hilary Adams, Nana Kwame Adjei-Brenyah, Mana Afsari, Emefa Agawu, Maximillian Alvarez, Lindsay Ballant, Hamid Bendaas, Max Berger, Valdete Berisha, Jag Bhalla, Lauren Cerand, Kelly Chapman, Brian Charles, Tommy Craggs, Elias Crim, Jared Crum, Joshua Clark Davis, Pete Davis, Safy-Hallan Farah, Sami Gold, Saoirse Gowan, Alex Han, Malcolm Harris, Charlie Hope-D'Anieri, Ankit Jain, Samuel Kimbriel, Talia Lavin, Chris Lehmann, Alec MacGillis, Celeste Marcus, Chris McCaffery, Wes McEnany, Mikra Namani, Gabrielle Newell, Noa Nir, Dharna Noor, Jaisal Noor, Lewis Page, Lucia Petty, Natalie Purser, Hannah Rosenthal, Becca Rothfeld, Lyle Jeremy Rubin, Kristina Saccone, Stuart Schrader, Colette Shade, Steph Stirling, Quinn Thakur, Udit Thakur, Christy Thornton, Michael Tomasky, Griffin Voltmann, Michael Wear, Zach Wehrwein, Lia Weintraub, Adam Willis, Emily Wilson, and Baynard Woods.

Finally and above all, I'd like to thank my immediate family, to whom this book, and my heart, are dedicated—my father John Nwanevu, my mother Charity Nwanevu, and my brother Kelechi Nwanevu.

BIBLIOGRAPHY

"ABA Survey of Civic Literacy 2022." American Bar Association, April 29, 2022. americanbar.org/content/dam/aba/administrative/news/2022/04/survey -of-civic-literacy-2022.pdf.

Abramowitz, Alan. *The Great Alignment: Race, Party Transformation, and the Rise of Donald Trump.* Yale University Press, 2018.

Achen, Christopher H., and Larry M. Bartels. *Democracy for Realists: Why Elections Do Not Produce Responsive Government.* Rev. ed. Princeton University Press, 2017.

———. "Government for the People: A Reply to the Symposium." *Critical Review* 30, no. 1–2 (April 3, 2018): 139–62. doi.org/10.1080/08913811.2018 .1510084.

Adams, John. "Discourses on Davila." In *The Works of John Adams, Second President of the United States,* edited by Charles Francis Adams. Little, Brown, 1851.

"AFL-CIO Labor Commission on Racial and Economic Justice Report." AFL-CIO, 2017. s3.amazonaws.com/dev.unionhall.files/img/RaceReport.pdf.

Agiesta, Jennifer. "CNN Poll: A Growing Number of People Lack Confidence in American Elections." CNN, February 10, 2022. cnn.com/2022/02/10/ politics/cnn-poll-democracy/index.html.

Agiesta, Jennifer, and Ariel Edwards-Levy. "CNN Poll: Percentage of Republicans Who Think Biden's 2020 Win Was Illegitimate Ticks Back up near 70%." CNN, August 3, 2023. cnn.com/2023/08/03/politics/cnn-poll -republicans-think-2020-election-illegitimate/index.html.

Ahlstrom-Vij, Kristoffer. "Is Democracy an Option for the Realist?" *Critical Review* 30, no. 1–2 (April 3, 2018): 1–12. doi.org/10.1080/08913811.2018 .1448510.

Alberta, Tim. "Why Mike Lee Folded." *The Atlantic,* September 10, 2024. theatlantic.com/magazine/archive/2024/10/senator-mike-lee-trump -support/679565/.

Aleem, Zeesham. "Amazon Workers Deserve More than Jeff Bezos' Trite Post-Space 'Thank You.'" MSNBC, July 21, 2021. msnbc.com/opinion/amazon -workers-deserve-more-jeff-bezos-trite-post-space-thank-n1274639.

"All the Ways Trump Tried to Overturn the Election—and How It Could Happen Again—Washington Post." Accessed February 8, 2023. washingtonpost .com/politics/interactive/2022/election-overturn-plans/.

Allmen, Esther Eriksson von. "Corporations Have Given over $100 Million to the Sedition Caucus." Citizens for Responsibility and Ethics in Washington, August 22, 2024. citizensforethics.org/reports-investigations/crew-reports/corporations-have-given-over-100-million-to-the-sedition-caucus/.

Alperovitz, Gar. *What Then Must We Do? Straight Talk About the Next American Revolution.* Chelsea Green Publ, 2013.

"America's Knowledge Crisis: A Survey of Civic Literacy." American Council of Trustees and Alumni, September 6, 2019. goacta.org/wp-content/uploads/ee/download/ACTA-Civic-Survey-2019.pdf.

Anderson, Elizabeth. *Private Government: How Employers Rule Our Lives (and Why We Don't Talk About It).* University Center for Human Values Series. Princeton University Press, 2017.

——. "What Is the Point of Equality?" *Ethics* 109, no. 2 (1999).

Anderson, Jack, and Les Whitten. "Pessimism Is the Mood of the Nation: The Washington Merry-Go-Round." *The Washington Post,* November 6, 1975.

Andrias, Kate, and Alexander Hertel-Fernandez. "Ending At-Will Employment: A Guide for Just Cause Reform." Roosevelt Institute, January 19, 2021. rooseveltinstitute.org/wp-content/uploads/2021/01/RI_AtWill_Report_202101.pdf.

Andrias, Kate, David Madland, and Malkie Wall. "A How-To Guide for State and Local Workers' Boards." Center for American Progress, December 11, 2019. americanprogress.org/article/guide-state-local-workers-boards/.

——. "Workers' Boards: A Brief Overview." Center for American Progress, December 11, 2019. americanprogress.org/article/workers-boards-brief-overview/.

——. "Workers' Boards: Frequently Asked Questions." Center for American Progress, December 11, 2019. americanprogress.org/article/workers-boards-frequently-asked-questions/.

Ansolabehere, Stephen, John M. de Figueiredo, and James M. Snyder Jr. "Why Is There so Little Money in U.S. Politics?" *Journal of Economic Perspectives* 17, no. 1 (Winter 2003): 105–30.

Aristotle. *Politics.* Translated by Benjamin Jowett. Dover Thrift Editions. Dover Publications, 2000.

Armus, Teo. "Amazon HQ2 Was Supposed to Add Jobs Last Year. It Shed Them Instead." April 16, 2024. washingtonpost.com/dc-md-va/2024/04/16/amazon-hq2-jobs-arlington-virginia/.

Arneson, Richard. "Democratic Rights at National and Workplace Levels." In *The Idea of Democracy,* edited by David Copp, Jean Hampton, and John E. Roemer, 1st pbk. ed. Cambridge University Press, 1993.

Associated Press. "Donald Trump and Hillary Clinton's Final Campaign Spending Revealed." *The Guardian,* December 9, 2016, sec. US news. theguardian.com/us-news/2016/dec/09/trump-and-clintons-final-campaign-spending-revealed.

Badger, Emily. "Blue Cities Want to Make Their Own Rules. Red States Won't Let Them." *The New York Times,* July 6, 2017, sec. The Upshot. nytimes.com/2017/07/06/upshot/blue-cities-want-to-make-their-own-rules-red-states-wont-let-them.html.

Bannon, Alicia. "Choosing State Judges: A Plan for Reform." Brennan Center for Justice, October 10, 2018.

———. "The Supreme Court Is Retrenching. States Don't Have To." *Politico,* June 29, 2022. politico.com/news/magazine/2022/06/29/supreme-court -rights-00042928.

Bass, Gary. "The Athenian Plague, a Cautionary Tale of Democracy's Fragility." *The New Yorker,* June 10, 2020. newyorker.com/culture/culture-desk/the -athenian-plague-a-cautionary-tale-of-democracys-fragility.

Battilana, Julie. "Introduction: For a Fairer, More Democratic, Greener Society." In *Democratize Work: The Case for Reorganizing the Economy,* edited by Isabelle Ferreras, Julie Battilana, and Dominique Méda, translated by Miranda Richmond Mouillot. The University of Chicago Press, 2022. doi.org/ 10.7208/chicago/9780226819631.001.0001.

Beam, Christopher. "The 'Democracy' Gap." *The Atlantic,* November 19, 2024. theatlantic.com/politics/archive/2024/11/democracy-meaning-democrats -republicans/680704/.

Beattie, Peter. "Theory, Media, and Democracy for Realists." *Critical Review* 30, no. 1–2 (April 3, 2018): 13–35. doi.org/10.1080/08913811.2018.1466809.

Beauchamp, Zack. "Sen. Mike Lee's Tweets Against 'Democracy,' Explained." *Vox,* October 8, 2020. vox.com/policy-and-politics/21507713/mike-lee -democracy-republic-trump-2020.

Beaumont, Elizabeth. "Philip Pettit, Republicanism: A Theory of Freedom and Government." In *The Oxford Handbook of Classics in Contemporary Political Theory,* by Elizabeth Beaumont, edited by Jacob T. Levy. Oxford University Press, 2017. doi.org/10.1093/oxfordhb/9780198717133.013.60.

Berman, Ari. *Minority Rule.* First edition. Farrar, Straus and Giroux, 2024.

Bernal, Rafael. "Poll: 70 Percent of Americans Support a Path to Citizenship." *The Hill,* February 16, 2022. thehill.com/latino/594625-poll-70-percent-of -americans-support-a-path-to-citizenship.

"The Best Books of 2016." *Bloomberg,* December 8, 2016. bloomberg.com/ features/2016-bloomberg-book-list.

Biden, Joseph. "Remarks by President Biden in Statement to the American People." The White House, July 25, 2024. whitehouse.gov/briefing-room/ speeches-remarks/2024/07/24/remarks-by-president-biden-in-statement -to-the-american-people.

Binder, Sarah A. "Statement of Sarah A. Binder, Department of Political Science, George Washington University." Presented at the Examining the Filibuster: History of the Filibuster 1789–2008, U.S. Senate Committee on Rules and Administration, April 22, 2010. govinfo.gov/content/pkg/CHRG -111shrg62210/pdf/CHRG-111shrg62210.pdf.

Bivens, Josh, Celine McNicholas, Kyle K. Moore, and Margaret Poydock. "Unions Promote Racial Equity." Economic Policy Institute, July 31, 2023. epi.org/publication/unions-promote-racial-equity/.

Blanco, Adrian, and Artur Galocha. "Can Computer Simulations Help Fix Democracy?" *Washington Post.* Accessed March 4, 2023. washingtonpost .com/politics/interactive/2022/algorithmic-redistricting/.

Blasi, Joseph, Douglas Kruse, and Richard B. Freeman. "Broad-Based Employee

Stock Ownership and Profit Sharing: History, Evidence, and Policy Implications." *Journal of Participation and Employee Ownership* 1, no. 1 (August 7, 2018): 38–60. doi.org/10.1108/JPEO-02-2018-0001.

Blasi, Joseph Raphael, Richard Barry Freeman, and Douglas Kruse. *The Citizen's
Share: Putting Ownership Back into Democracy.* Yale University Press, 2013.

Block, Sharon, and Benjamin Sachs. "Clean Slate for Worker Power: Building a
Just Economy and Democracy." Labor and Worklife Program. Harvard
Law School, n.d.

Blumenthal, Paul. "Only One President Had the Guts to Say the State of the
Union Is 'Not Good.'" *The Huffington Post,* January 30, 2018. huffpost.com/
entry/state-of-the-union-not-good-gerald-ford_n_5a70d62ae4b0be822
ba12644.

Bodie, Matthew, and Grant Hayden. "Codetermination: The Missing Alternative
in Corporate Governance." LPE Blog (blog), n.d. lpeproject.org/blog/
codetermination-the-missing-alternative-in-corporate-governance/.

Bollyky, Thomas J., Tara Templin, Matthew Cohen, Diana Schoder, Joseph L.
Dieleman, and Simon Wigley. "The Relationships Between Democratic
Experience, Adult Health, and Cause-Specific Mortality in 170 Countries
between 1980 and 2016: An Observational Analysis." *The Lancet* 393,
no. 10181 (April 2019). doi.org/10.1016/S0140-6736(19)30235-1.

Bonica, Adam, and Jacob M. Grumbach. "Old Money: Campaign Finance and
Gerontocracy in the United States," November 4, 2022. dx.doi.org/10.2139/
ssrn.4892936.

Boris, Eileen, and Annelise Orleck. "Feminism and the Labor Movement: A Century of Collaboration and Conflict." *New Labor Forum* 20, no. 1 (Winter
2011). jstor.org/stable/27920539.

Bouie, Jamelle. "Opinion | Alexandria Ocasio-Cortez Understands Democracy
Better Than Republicans Do." *The New York Times,* August 27, 2019,
sec. Opinion. nytimes.com/2019/08/27/opinion/aoc-crenshaw-republicans
-democracy.html.

Bouk, Dan. "House Arrest: How an Automated Algorithm Has Constrained
Congress for a Century." Data & Society, April 2021. datasociety.net/wp
-content/uploads/2021/04/House-Arrest-Dan-Bouk.pdf.

Bowie, Nikolas. "Antidemocracy." *Harvard Law Review* 135, no. 1 (November
2021). harvardlawreview.org/2021/11/antidemocracy/.

"Breaking Down the NLRB Decision in Atlanta Opera and Its Potential Impact
on App-Based Ridehail and Delivery Workers." National Employment
Law Project, October 10, 2023. nelp.org/insights-research/breaking-down
-the-nlrb-decision-in-atlanta-opera-and-its-potential-impact-on-app
-based-ridehail-and-delivery-workers/.

Breen, Keith. "Freedom, Republicanism, and Workplace Democracy." *Critical
Review of International Social and Political Philosophy* 18, no. 4 (July 4,
2015): 470–85. doi.org/10.1080/13698230.2015.1033857.

Brenan, Megan. "61% of Americans Support Abolishing Electoral College." Gal-
lup.com, September 24, 2020. news.gallup.com/poll/320744/americans
-support-abolishing-electoral-college.aspx.

Brennan Center for Justice. "Annotated Guide to the For the People Act of 2021." Accessed March 7, 2023. brennancenter.org/our-work/policy-solutions/annotated-guide-people-act-2021.

———. "Key Differences Between the For the People Act and the Freedom to Vote Act." Accessed March 13, 2023. brennancenter.org/our-work/research-reports/key-differences-between-people-act-and-freedom-vote-act.

———. "The John Lewis Voting Rights Advancement Act." Accessed March 13, 2023. brennancenter.org/our-work/research-reports/john-lewis-voting-rights-advancement-act.

Brennan, Jason. *Against Democracy.* Rev. ed. Princeton University Press, 2017.

Brennan, Jason, and Hélène Landemore. *Debating Democracy: Do We Need More or Less?* Oxford University Press, 2021.

Brettschneider, Corey. *Democratic Rights: The Substance of Self-Government.* Princeton University Press, 2007.

Bronner, Laura, and Nathaniel Rakich. "Advantage, GOP." *FiveThirtyEight,* April 29, 2021. fivethirtyeight.com/features/advantage-gop/.

Brookings, Robert S. *Economic Democracy: America's Answer to Socialism and Communism.* The Macmillan Company, 1929.

Brown, H. Claire. "Despite Now Offering $15 Minimum Wage, Amazon Still a Top Employer of SNAP Recipients in Many States." *The Counter,* n.d. thecounter.org/15-minimum-wage-amazon-top-employer-snap-recipients-walmart-mcdonalds/.

Brown, Hayley. "The PRO Act Is Critically Important. But We Should See It as Just a Good Start." *Jacobin,* October 5, 2023. jacobin.com/2023/10/the-pro-act-canada-us-labor-law-union-worker-rights.

Bruenig, Matt. "Social Wealth Fund for America." People's Policy Project, August 28, 2018. peoplespolicyproject.org/projects/social-wealth-fund/.

Bryan, Alexander. "The Material Conditions of Non-Domination: Property, Independence, and the Means of Production." *European Journal of Political Theory,* October 14, 2021, 147488512110506. doi.org/10.1177/14748851211050620.

Bump, Philip. "In About 20 Years, Half the Population Will Live in Eight States." *The Washington Post,* July 12, 2018. washingtonpost.com/news/politics/wp/2018/07/12/in-about-20-years-half-the-population-will-live-in-eight-states.

Business Insider. "Unleashing the Power of AI to Democratize Creativity for Everyone." November 15, 2024. businessinsider.com/sc/how-ai-can-empower-and-enhance-creative-tasks-for-everyone.

Business Jet Traveler. "Wheels Up." Accessed December 25, 2024. bjtonline.com/company/wheels-up.

Calabresi, Steven G., and Zephyr Teachout. "Interpretation: The Twenty-Seventh Amendment." National Constitution Center. Accessed February 4, 2023. constitutioncenter.org/the-constitution/amendments/amendment-xxvii/interpretations/165.

Campbell, Jason S. "Charlie Kirk: 'Democracy Is a Bad Idea.'" October 31, 2022. x.com/JasonSCampbell/status/1587147151301394433.

Canovan, Margaret. "The People." In *The Oxford Handbook of Political Theory*, edited by John S. Dryzek, Bonnie Honig, and Anne Phillips. Oxford University Press, 2009.

Cartledge, Paul. *Democracy: A Life*. Oxford University Press, 2016.

Casarino, Marc S., and Karine Sarkisian. "The FTC's Effort for a Non-Compete Ban Has Been Judicially Struck Down, However, Its Fate Still Hangs in the Balance." *Kennedys* (blog), September 6, 2024. kennedyslaw.com/en/thought-leadership/article/2024/the-ftc-s-effort-for-a-non-compete-ban-has-been-judicially-struck-down-however-its-fate-still-hangs-in-the-balance.

Case, John, and Michael Quarrey. "Turning Employees into Owners: An Analysis of Policy Initiatives for Rebuilding the American Dream." *Journal of Participation and Employee Ownership* 2, no. 3 (December 9, 2019): 202–11. doi.org/10.1108/JPEO-09-2019-0022.

Cavallar, Georg. "Kant's Judgment on Frederick's Enlightened Absolutism." *History of Political Thought* 14, no. 1 (1993): 103–32.

CBS News. "Are Members of Congress Becoming Telemarketers?," April 24, 2016. cbsnews.com/news/60-minutes-are-members-of-congress-becoming-telemarketers.

Census Reporter. "Census Profile: Morehouse Town, Hamilton County, NY." Accessed January 24, 2023. censusreporter.org/profiles/06000US3604148340-morehouse-town-hamilton-county-ny.

Cervas, Jonathan, and Bernard Grofman. "Legal, Political Science and Economics Approaches to Measuring Malapportionment: The U.S. House, the Senate and the Electoral College 1790–2010." *SSRN Electronic Journal*, January 1, 2020. doi.org/10.2139/ssrn.3558660.

Cetty, Chetan. "Talking About Private Government: A Review of the Economic Claims Made to Rebut Anderson's Analysis." *Journal of Law and Political Economy* 3, no. 1 (September 28, 2022). doi.org/10.5070/LP63159031.

"Challenges to Democracy: The 2024 Election in Focus." Public Religion Research Institute, October 11, 2024. prri.org/research/challenges-to-democracy-the-2024-election-in-focus-findings-from-the-2024-american-values-survey/.

Chambers, Simone. "Against Democracy." *Perspectives on Politics* 16, no. 2 (June 2018): 503–5. doi.org/10.1017/S153759271800066X.

Chang, Alvin. "The Man Who Rigged America's Election Maps." *Vox*, October 17, 2019. vox.com/videos/2019/10/17/20917852/gerrymander-hofeler-election-map.

Chapman, Michelle, and Haleluya Hadero. "Amazon Labor Union Members Vote Overwhelmingly in Favor of an Affiliation with the Teamsters." Associated Press, June 18, 2024. apnews.com/article/amazon-union-teamsters-labor-warehouse-0d0d751d6800495ed0296e33b4f5835e.

Cheatham, Amelia, and Diana Roy. "Puerto Rico: A U.S. Territory in Crisis." Council on Foreign Relations, September 29, 2022. cfr.org/backgrounder/puerto-rico-us-territory-crisis.

Chemerinsky, Erwin. *No Democracy Lasts Forever: How the Constitution Threatens the United States.* Liveright Publishing Corp., 2025.

Christiano, Thomas. *The Constitution of Equality: Democratic Authority and Its Limits.* Oxford University Press, 2008.

——. "Rule by Multiple Majorities: A New Theory of Popular Control, Sean Ingham." *Economics and Philosophy* 36, no. 1 (March 2020): 186–91. doi .org/10.1017/S026626711900021X.

Cohen, Joshua. *Philosophy, Politics, Democracy: Selected Essays.* Harvard University Press, 2009.

Cohn, Nate. "2022 Review: How Republicans Lost Despite Winning the Popular Vote." *The New York Times,* December 13, 2022, sec. The Upshot. nytimes.com/2022/12/13/upshot/2022-republicans-midterms-analysis .html.

Cohn, Scott. "Amazon Reveals the Truth on Why It Nixed New York and Chose Virginia for Its HQ2." CNBC, July 10, 2019. cnbc.com/2019/07/10/ amazon-reveals-the-truth-on-why-it-nixed-ny-and-chose-virginia-for -hq2.html.

Coleman, Jules, and John Ferejohn. "Democracy and Social Choice." *Ethics* 97, no. 1 (1986): 6–25.

Collinson, Stephen. "Obama Issues a Dire Warning About American Democracy in Stunning Rebuke of Trump." CNN, August 20, 2020. cnn.com/2020/08/ 20/politics/barack-obama-dnc-speech-donald-trump-joe-biden/index .html.

Colvin, Alexander J. S. "The Growing Use of Mandatory Arbitration." Economic Policy Institute, September 27, 2017. epi.org/publication/the-growing-use -of-mandatory-arbitration/.

Common Cause. "Stopping a Dangerous Article V Convention," March 4, 2024. commoncause.org/work/stopping-a-dangerous-article-v-convention/.

Conklin, Carli. "The Origins of the Pursuit of Happiness." *Washington University Jurisprudence Review* 7, no. 2 (2015). openscholarship.wustl.edu/law _jurisprudence/vol7/iss2/6/.

Corasaniti, Nick. "Voting Rights and the Battle Over Elections: What to Know." *The New York Times,* December 29, 2021, sec. U.S. nytimes.com/article/ voting-rights-tracker.html.

Corasaniti, Nick, and Reid J. Epstein. "Map by Map, G.O.P. Chips Away at Black Democrats' Power." *The New York Times,* December 18, 2021, sec. U.S. nytimes.com/2021/12/18/us/politics/gop-gerrymandering-black -democrats.html.

Corasaniti, Nick, Ruth Igielnik, and Camille Baker. "Voters Are Deeply Skeptical About the Health of American Democracy." *The New York Times,* October 27, 2024. nytimes.com/2024/10/27/us/politics/american-democracy -poll.html.

Corasaniti, Nick, Karen Yourish, and Keith Collins. "How Trump's 2020 Election Lies Have Gripped State Legislatures." *The New York Times,* May 22, 2022, sec. U.S. nytimes.com/interactive/2022/05/22/us/politics/ state-legislators-election-denial.html.

"Corporate Accountability and Democracy." Friends of Bernie Sanders, n.d. berniesanders.com/issues/corporate-accountability-and-democracy/.

Courtney, Will Sabel. "A Brief History of Ferrari Supercars, from the 288 GTO to the F80." *Robb Report,* December 11, 2024. robbreport.com/motors/cars/gallery/ferrari-hypercars-supercars-history-1236115676/.

Creswell, Julie. "Cities' Offers for Amazon Base Are Secrets Even to Many City Leaders." *The New York Times,* August 5, 2018. nytimes.com/2018/08/05/technology/amazon-headquarters-hq2.html.

Dahl, Robert. *A Preface to Economic Democracy.* University of California Press, 1985.

———. *Democracy and Its Critics.* Yale University Press, 1989.

———. *How Democratic Is the American Constitution?* 2nd ed. The Castle Lectures in Ethics, Politics and Economics. Yale University Press, 2003.

———. "What Political Institutions Does Large-Scale Democracy Require?" *Political Science Quarterly* 120, no. 2 (2005).

Dahms, Thomas. "Diligent Bureaucrats and the Expulsion of Jews from West Prussia, 1772–1786." *German History* 39, no. 3 (October 15, 2021): 335–57. doi.org/10.1093/gerhis/ghab027.

Daley, David. "The House the GOP Built: How Republicans Used Soft Money, Big Data, and High-Tech Mapping to Take Control of Congress and Increase Partisanship." Intelligencer, April 24, 2016. nymag.com/intelligencer/2016/04/gops-house-seats-are-safe-heres-why.html.

———. "The Secret Files of the Master of Modern Republican Gerrymandering." *The New Yorker,* September 6, 2019. newyorker.com/news/news-desk/the-secret-files-of-the-master-of-modern-republican-gerrymandering.

Daly, Lyle. "The Largest Companies by Market Cap in 2024." *The Motley Fool,* June 3, 2024. fool.com/research/largest-companies-by-market-cap/.

Dammann, Jens, and Horst G. M. Eidenmueller. "Codetermination: A Poor Fit for U.S. Corporations." *SSRN Electronic Journal,* 2020. doi.org/10.2139/ssrn.3565955.

———. "Taming the Corporate Leviathan: Codetermination and the Democratic State." *SSRN Electronic Journal,* 2020. doi.org/10.2139/ssrn.3680769.

Darity, William, Jr., and Dawn Milam. "Memo: The Case for a Federal Job Guarantee Program." Data for Progress, July 30, 2020. dataforprogress.org/memos/case-for-a-federal-job-guarantee-program.

Davis, Susan. "Senate Pulls 'Nuclear' Trigger to Ease Gorsuch Confirmation." NPR, April 6, 2017. npr.org/2017/04/06/522847700/senate-pulls-nuclear-trigger-to-ease-gorsuch-confirmation.

Day, Matt, and Spencer Soper. "Amazon Has Turned a Middle-Class Warehouse Career Into a McJob." *Bloomberg,* December 17, 2020. bloomberg.com/news/features/2020-12-17/amazon-amzn-job-pay-rate-leaves-some-warehouse-employees-homeless?embedded-checkout=true.

De Pinto, Jennifer. "Most Americans Favor a Higher Federal Minimum Wage—CBS News Poll." CBS News, September 5, 2021. cbsnews.com/news/minimum-wage-opinion-poll-09-05-2021.

"Debunking the Voter Fraud Myth | Brennan Center for Justice." Accessed Feb-

ruary 11, 2023. brennancenter.org/our-work/research-reports/debunking
-voter-fraud-myth.

Delgadillo, Natalie, Rachel Kurzius, and Rachel Sadon. "The Past, Present, and (Potential) Future of D.C. Statehood, Explained." *DCist* (blog). Accessed February 7, 2023. dcist.com/story/19/09/18/the-past-present-and -potential-future-of-d-c-statehood-explained/.

"Democracy: An Election Agenda for Candidates, Activists, and Legislators." Brennan Center for Justice, May 4, 2018. brennancenter.org/our-work/policy -solutions/democracy-election-agenda-candidates-activists-and-legislators.

"Democracy Index 2021: The China Challenge." The Economist Intelligence Unit, 2022. eiu.com/n/campaigns/democracy-index-2021/.

"Democracy Index 2023: Age of Conflict." The Economist Intelligence Unit, 2024. eiu.com/n/campaigns/democracy-index-2023/.

"Democracy Index 2024: What's Wrong with Representative Democracy?" The Economist Intelligence Unit, 2025. eiu.com/n/campaigns/democracy-index -2024/.

Demsas, Jerusalem. "Community Input Is Bad, Actually." *The Atlantic,* April 22, 2022. theatlantic.com/ideas/archive/2022/04/local-government -community-input-housing-public-transportation/629625/.

DeSilver, Drew. "Among Democracies, U.S. Stands out in How It Chooses Its Head of State." *Pew Research Center* (blog). Accessed January 26, 2023. pewresearch.org/fact-tank/2016/11/22/among-democracies-u-s-stands -out-in-how-it-chooses-its-head-of-state/.

——. "Turnout in U.S. Has Soared in Recent Elections but by Some Measures Still Trails That of Many Other Countries." *Pew Research Center* (blog). Accessed February 11, 2023. pewresearch.org/fact-tank/2022/11/ 01/turnout-in-u-s-has-soared-in-recent-elections-but-by-some-measures -still-trails-that-of-many-other-countries/.

——. "U.S. Population Keeps Growing, but House of Representatives Is Same Size as in Taft Era." *Pew Research Center* (blog), May 31, 2018. pewresearch .org/fact-tank/2018/05/31/u-s-population-keeps-growing-but-house-of -representatives-is-same-size-as-in-taft-era/.

——. "Weekday Elections Set the U.S. Apart from Many Other Advanced Democracies." *Pew Research Center* (blog). Accessed February 12, 2023. pewresearch.org/fact-tank/2018/11/06/weekday-elections-set-the-u-s -apart-from-many-other-advanced-democracies/.

Detrow, Scott. "Biden: Democracy 'Under Unprecedented Assault' As Pro-Trump Extremists Occupy Capitol." NPR, January 6, 2021, sec. Capitol Insurrection Updates. npr.org/sections/congress-electoral-college-tally-live -updates/2021/01/06/954063529/watch-live-joe-biden-speaks-as -protesters-force-u-s-capitol-into-lockdown.

Dewey, John. *The Ethics of Democracy.* Andrews, 1888.

——. *The Public and Its Problems.* Swallow Press/Ohio University Press, 1927.

DGB. "German Codetermination ('Mitbestimmung')," n.d. en.dgb.de/fields-of -work/german-codetermination.

Di Pizio, Anthony. "People Think Amazon Is an E-Commerce Company, but 74% of Its Profit Comes from This Instead." *The Motley Fool,* January 10,

2024. fool.com/investing/2024/01/10/amazon-e-commerce-company-74 -profit-this-instead/.

Diamond, Larry. "Saving Democracy—Realistically." *Democracy Journal,* no. 65 (2022). democracyjournal.org/magazine/65/saving-democracy-realistically/.

Dingell, John D. "I Served in Congress Longer Than Anyone. Here's How to Fix It." *The Atlantic,* December 4, 2018. theatlantic.com/ideas/archive/2018/ 12/john-dingell-how-restore-faith-government/577222/.

Disch, Lisa. "Toward a Mobilization Conception of Democratic Representation." In *Reclaiming Representation: Contemporary Advances in the Theory of Political Representation,* edited by Mónica Brito Vieira. Routledge, 2017.

Dobski, Bernard. "America Is a Republic, Not a Democracy." The Heritage Foundation, June 19, 2020. heritage.org/american-founders/report/america -republic-not-democracy.

Doerfler, Ryan D., and Samuel Moyn. "Democratizing the Supreme Court." *California Law Review* 109, no. 5 (October 2021). californialawreview.org/ print/democratizing-the-supreme-court/.

Dowding, Keith. "Can Populism Be Defended? William Riker, Gerry Mackie and the Interpretation of Democracy." *Government and Opposition* 41, no. 3 (2006): 327–46. doi.org/10.1111/j.1477-7053.2006.00182.x.

Drutman, Lee. *Breaking the Two-Party Doom Loop: The Case for Multiparty Democracy in America.* New York: Oxford University Press, 2020.

———. "Elections, Political Parties, and Multiracial, Multiethnic Democracy: How the United States Gets It Wrong." *New York University Law Review* 96, no. 4 (October 2021).

———. "What We Know About Redistricting and Redistricting Reform." *New America,* September 19, 2022. newamerica.org/political-reform/reports/what -we-know-about-redistricting-and-redistricting-reform/.

Dukes, Ruth, and Wolfgang Streeck. *Democracy at Work: Contract, Status and Post-Industrial Justice.* Polity Press, 2023.

Dunn, Amina. "Most Americans Support a $15 Federal Minimum Wage." *Pew Research Center* (blog). Accessed February 8, 2023. pewresearch.org/ fact-tank/2021/04/22/most-americans-support-a-15-federal-minimum -wage/.

Durran, Dale R. "Whose Votes Count the Least in the Electoral College?" *The Conversation,* March 14, 2017. theconversation.com/whose-votes-count -the-least-in-the-electoral-college-74280.

Eidelson, Benjamin. "The Majoritarian Filibuster." *The Yale Law Journal* 122, no. 4 (January 2013).

Elkins, Zachary, Tom Ginsburg, and James Melton. *The Endurance of National Constitutions.* 1st ed. Cambridge University Press, 2009. doi.org/10.1017/ CBO9780511817595.

Ellerman, David. "Fallacies About Corporations: Comments on 'Democratizing the Corporation.'" In *Democratizing the Corporation: The Bicameral Firm and Beyond,* edited by Isabelle Ferreras, Tom Malleson, and Joel Rogers. The Real Utopias Project. Verso, 2024.

Ellerman, David, and Tej Gonza. "Less-Known Supporters of Workplace Democracy." *Journal of Participation and Employee Ownership* 4, no. 1 (June 23, 2021): 63–85. doi.org/10.1108/JPEO-06-2021-029.

Ellerman, David P. *The Democratic Worker-Owned Firm: A New Model for the East and West.* Routledge Revivals, 2015.

Elliot, Jonathan, ed. "The Debates in the Convention of the Commonwealth of Virginia, on the Adoption of the Federal Constitution." In *The Debates in the Several State Conventions on the Adoption of the Federal Constitution, as Recommended by the General Convention at Philadelphia in 1787*, 2nd ed. Vol. 3, 1827. oll.libertyfund.org/title/elliot-the-debates-in-the-several-state-conventions-vol-3.

Elliott, Kevin J. *Democracy for Busy People.* The University of Chicago Press, 2023.

English, Jonathan. "How U.S. Infrastructure Plans Shrank in Ambition." *Bloomberg*, January 11, 2022. bloomberg.com/news/articles/2022-01-11/today-s-american-infrastructure-spending-is-no-new-deal?embedded-checkout=true.

Epps, Daniel, and Ganesh Sitaraman. "How to Save the Supreme Court." *Vox*, September 6, 2018. vox.com/the-big-idea/2018/9/6/17827786/kavanaugh-vote-supreme-court-packing.

Epstein, Reid J. "Liberal Wins Wisconsin Court Race, Despite Musk's Millions." *The New York Times*, April 1, 2025. nytimes.com/2025/04/01/us/politics/wisconsin-supreme-court-crawford-schimel.html.

Epstein, Reid J., and Nick Corasaniti. "Republicans Push Crackdown on Crime Wave That Doesn't Exist: Voter Fraud." *The New York Times*, March 17, 2022, sec. U.S. nytimes.com/2022/03/17/us/politics/republican-voter-fraud.html.

Eren, Selcuk, Allan Schweyer, Malala Lin, and Allen Li. "Job Satisfaction 2023." The Conference Board, May 10, 2023. conference-board.org/pdfdownload.cfm?masterProductID=46114.

Erickson, Ryan, and Karla Walter. "Right to Work Would Harm All Americans." Center for American Progress Action, May 18, 2017. americanprogressaction.org/article/right-work-harm-americans/.

Estlund, Cynthia. "Rethinking Autocracy at Work." *Harvard Law Review* 131, no. 3 (January 2018): 795–826.

Estlund, David M. *Democratic Authority: A Philosophical Framework.* Princeton University Press, 2009.

"Evaluating the Effects of Ranked-Choice Voting." New America, March 30, 2022. newamerica.org/political-reform/reports/evaluating-the-effects-of-ranked-choice-voting/.

Evers-Hillstrom, Karl. "Majority of Lawmakers in 116th Congress Are Millionaires." OpenSecrets News, April 23, 2020. opensecrets.org/news/2020/04/majority-of-lawmakers-millionaires/.

———. "Most Expensive Ever: 2020 Election Cost $14.4 Billion." OpenSecrets, February 11, 2021. opensecrets.org/news/2021/02/2020-cycle-cost-14p4-billion-doubling-16/.

FairVote. "Ranked Choice Voting Information." Accessed March 8, 2023. fairvcte
.org/our-reforms/ranked-choice-voting-information/.

Farber, Henry S, Daniel Herbst, Ilyana Kuziemko, and Suresh Naidu. "Unions
and Inequality over the Twentieth Century: New Evidence from Survey
Data." *The Quarterly Journal of Economics* 136, no. 3 (June 30, 202):
1325–85. doi.org/10.1093/qje/qjab012.

"FEDERAL ELECTIONS 2004: Election Results for the U.S. President, the
U.S. Senate and the U.S. House of Representatives." Federal Election Commission, May 2005.

"FEDERAL ELECTIONS 2016: Election Results for the U.S. President, the
U.S. Senate and the U.S. House of Representatives." Federal Election Commission, December 2017.

Feldman, Noah. *The Three Lives of James Madison: Genius, Partisan, President.*
First edition. Random House, 2017.

Ferreras, Isabelle. "A Response to My Readers." In *Democratizing the Corporation: The Bicameral Firm and Beyond,* edited by Isabelle Ferreras, Tom
Malleson, and Joel Rogers. The Real Utopias Project. Verso, 2024.

———. "Democratizing the Corporation: The Proposal of the Bicameral Firm." In
Democratizing the Corporation: The Bicameral Firm and Beyond, edited
by Isabelle Ferreras, Tom Malleson, and Joel Rogers. The Real Utopias
Project. Verso, 2024.

———. "From the Politically Possible to the Politically Inevitable: Taking Action." In *Democratize Work: The Case for Reorganizing the Economy,*
edited by Isabelle Ferreras, Julie Battilana, and Dominique Méda, translated by Miranda Richmond Mouillot. The University of Chicago Press,
2022. doi.org/10.7208/chicago/9780226819631.001.0001.

Ferreras, Isabelle, Julie Battilana, and Dominique Méda, eds. "Manifesto: Work.
Democratize. Decommodify. Decarbonize." In *Democratize Work: The
Case for Reorganizing the Economy.* The University of Chicago Press,
2022. doi.org/10.7208/chicago/9780226819631.001.0001.

Ferretti, Thomas, and Axel Gosseries. "Are Bicameral Firms Preferable to Codetermination or Worker Cooperatives?" In *Democratizing the Corporation:
The Bicameral Firm and Beyond,* edited by Isabelle Ferreras, Tom Malleson, and Joel Rogers. The Real Utopias Project. Verso, 2024.

Fetterolf, Janell, and Sofia Hernandez Ramones. "72% of Americans Say the U.S.
Used to Be a Good Example of Democracy, but Isn't Anymore." Pew Research Center, July 10, 2024. pewresearch.org/short-reads/2024/07/10/72
-of-americans-say-the-us-used-to-be-a-good-example-of-democracy-but
-isnt-anymore.

"Field Listing—Legislative Branch." The World Factbook. CIA, n.d. cia.gov/the
-world-factbook/field/legislative-branch.

Fields, Gary, and Linley Sanders. "Democracy Was a Motivating Factor for
Both Harris and Trump Voters, but for Very Different Reasons." *AP News,*
November 9, 2024. apnews.com/article/democracy-harris-trump-threats
-authoritarianism-election-2024-56b4eb981f34f3e60aec1e45a67fc8a2.

Fishkin, James S. *Democracy When the People Are Thinking: Revitalizing Our*

Politics Through Public Deliberation. First editon. Oxford University Press, 2018.

Fishkin, Joseph, and William E. Forbath. *The Anti-Oligarchy Constitution: Reconstructing the Economic Foundations of American Democracy.* Harvard University Press, 2022.

Fishman, Charles. "The Future of Zero-Gravity Living Is Here." *Smithsonian Magazine,* June 2017. smithsonianmag.com/science-nature/future-zero-gravity-living-is-here-180963243/.

Foa, Roberto Stefan, and Yascha Mounk. "When Democracy Is No Longer the Only Path to Prosperity." *The Wall Street Journal,* March 1, 2019. wsj.com/articles/when-democracy-is-no-longer-the-only-path-to-prosperity-11551457761.

Foner, Eric. *The Second Founding.* First edition. W. W. Norton & Company, 2019.

Forbes. "The World's Real-Time Billionaires." n.d. forbes.com/real-time-billionaires/#9563533d788b.

Fowler, Anthony. "Partisan Intoxication or Policy Voting?" *Quarterly Journal of Political Science* 15, no. 2 (April 9, 2020): 141–79. doi.org/10.1561/100.00018027a.

Fowler, Anthony, and Andrew B. Hall. "Do Shark Attacks Influence Presidential Elections? Reassessing a Prominent Finding on Voter Competence." *The Journal of Politics* 80, no. 4 (October 2018): 1423–37. doi.org/10.1086/699244.

Fowler, Anthony, and B. Pablo Montagnes. "Distinguishing between False Positives and Genuine Results: The Case of Irrelevant Events and Elections." *The Journal of Politics,* March 7, 2022, 719636. doi.org/10.1086/719636.

Franco, Álvaro, Carlos Álvarez-Dardet, and Maria Teresa Ruiz. "Effect of Democracy on Health: Ecological Study." *BMJ* 329, no. 7480 (December 18, 2004). doi.org/10.1136/bmj.329.7480.1421.

Freeland, Robert F. "Prospects for Democratizing the Corporation in US Law." *Politics & Society* 51, no. 2 (June 2023): 278–92. doi.org/10.1177/00323292231164281.

Frega, Roberto. "Against Analogy: Why Analogical Arguments in Support of Workplace Democracy Must Necessarily Fail." *Democratic Theory* 7, no. 1 (2020): 1–26. doi.org/10.3167/dt.2020.070102.

Frega, Roberto, Lisa Herzog, and Christian Neuhäuser. "Workplace Democracy — The Recent Debate." *Philosophy Compass* 14, no. 4 (April 2019): e12574. doi.org/10.1111/phc3.12574.

Frost, Natasha. "The Only U.S. Territory Without U.S. Birthright Citizenship." *The New York Times,* November 25, 2022, sec. World. nytimes.com/2022/11/25/world/australia/american-samoa-birthright-citizenship.html.

Frum, David. "Trump Won. Now What?" *The Atlantic,* November 6, 2024. theatlantic.com/politics/archive/2024/11/trump-wins-second-term-presidency/680546/.

Gallagher, Brian. "Leigh Perkins, Who Built Orvis Into a Lifestyle Brand, Dies at 93." *The New York Times,* May 15, 2021. nytimes.com/2021/05/15/business/leigh-h-perkins-dead.html.

Gallup. "Party Affiliation." Accessed May 11, 2025. news.gallup.com/poll/15370/Party-Affiliation.aspx.

Galvin, Daniel J. "From Labor Law to Employment Law: The Changing Politics of Workers' Rights." *Studies in American Political Development* 33, no 1 (April 2019): 50–86. doi.org/10.1017/S0898588X19000038.

Gerstein, Teri. "How Corporations Keep Their Own Workers in Debt." *Politico,* October 21, 2021. politico.com/news/agenda/2021/10/21/workers-scammed-biden-help-516324.

Gerwin, Marcin. *Citizens' Assemblies: Guide to Democracy That Works.* Open Plan Foundation, 2018.

Glass, Andrew. "Congress Passes Civil Rights Act Aug. 29, 1957." *Politico.* Accessed January 19, 2023. politico.com/story/2007/08/congress-passes-civil-rights-act-aug-29-1957-005470.

Glass, Aurelia, and David Madland. "Momentum for Worker Standards Boards Continues to Grow." Center for American Progress, September 7, 2023. americanprogress.org/article/momentum-for-worker-standards-boards-continues-to-grow/.

Glusac, Elaine. "The Democratization of Airport Lounges." *The New York Times,* July 27, 2022. nytimes.com/2022/07/27/travel/airport-lounges.html?searchResultPosition=6.

Goldberg, Harmony, and Erica Smiley. "Three Paths for Labor after Amazon." *Boston Review,* June 6, 2022. bostonreview.net/articles/three-paths-forward-for-labor-after-amazon.

Goldberg, Jonah. "Literacy Tests." *National Review,* August 12, 2004. nationalreview.com/corner/literacy-tests-jonah-goldberg/.

Goldman, Joe, Lee Drutman, and Oscar Pocasangre. "Democracy Hypocrisy: Examining America's Fragile Democratic Convictions." Democracy Fund, January 4, 2024. democracyfund.org/idea/democracy-hypocrisy/.

Goldstein, Luke. "How Amazon's Outsourcing Facilitates Union Busting." *The American Prospect,* December 22, 2023. prospect.org/labor/2023-12-22-amazons-outsourcing-facilitates-union-busting/.

Gollan, Doug. "Is Democratization of Private Jets Dead?" *Forbes,* October 19, 2024. forbes.com/sites/douggollan/2024/10/19/is-democratization-of-private-jets-dead/.

Golshan, Tara. "Bernie Sanders's Plan to Reshape Corporate America, Explained." *Vox,* October 14, 2019. vox.com/2019/10/14/20912221/bernie-sanders-corporate-accountability-ftc-merger-tax.

Gómez, Vianney, and Carroll Doherty. "Wide Partisan Divide on Whether Voting Is a Fundamental Right or a Privilege with Responsibilities." *Pew Research Center* (blog). Accessed April 29, 2022. pewresearch.org/fact-tank/2021/07/22/wide-partisan-divide-on-whether-voting-is-a-fundamental-right-or-a-privilege-with-responsibilities/.

Goodman, J. David. "Amazon Pulls Out of Planned New York City Headquarters." *The New York Times,* February 14, 2019, sec. New York. nytimes.com/2019/02/14/nyregion/amazon-hq2-queens.html.

Goodwin, Grace Eliza. "Elon Musk's DOGE Has Worked Quickly to Cut Federal Agencies. Here's a List of What's Been Targeted So Far." *Business Insider,* April 3, 2025. businessinsider.com/federal-agencies-musk-doge -targeted-list-2025-2.

Gould, Carol C. *Rethinking Democracy: Freedom and Social Cooperation in Politics, Economy, and Society.* Cambridge University Press, 1990.

Gould, Elise, and Josh Bivens. "Opinion: Why a New Study Gives a Misleading View of Inequality in America." CNN, January 18, 2024. cnn.com/ 2024/01/17/opinions/inequality-earnings-economy-gould-bivens/index .html.

Gould, Jonathan S., and David E. Pozen. "Structural Biases in Structural Constitutional Law." *New York University Law Review* 97, no. 1 (April 2022).

Gourevitch, Alex. "Liberty and Democratic Insurgency: The Republican Case for the Right to Strike." In *Republicanism and the Future of Democracy,* edited by Geneviève Rousselière and Yiftah Elazar, 173–88. Cambridge University Press, 2019. doi.org/10.1017/9781108630153.010.

GovTrack.us. "With Kavanaugh Vote, the Senate Reaches a Historic Low in Democratic Metric." Medium, October 7, 2018. govtrackinsider.com/with -kavanaugh-vote-the-senate-reaches-a-historic-low-in-democratic-metric -dfb0f5fa7fa.

Gowan, Saoirse. "A Plan to Win Socialism in America." *Jacobin,* February 26, 2019. jacobin.com/2019/02/a-plan-to-win-socialism-in-america.

Graubard, Allen. "Ideas of Economic Democracy: Workers' Control and Public Rights." *Dissent,* 1984.

Green, Philip. "A Review Essay of Robert A. Dahl's 'Democracy and Its Critics'." *Social Theory and Practice* 16, no. 2 (1990).

Greenberg, Jon. "Most Republicans Still Falsely Believe Trump's Stolen Election Claims." Politifact, June 4, 2022. politifact.com/article/2022/jun/14/most -republicans-falsely-believe-trumps-stolen-ele.

Greenblatt, Alan. "The US Almost Tore Itself Apart to Get to 50 States. Can DC Make It 51?" *Vox,* September 18, 2019. vox.com/the-highlight/2019/9/18/ 20863026/dc-statehood-george-floyd-puerto-rico-statehood.

Greenhouse, Linda. "Ruth Bader Ginsburg, Supreme Court's Feminist Icon, Is Dead at 87." *The New York Times,* September 18, 2020, sec. U.S. nytimes .com/2020/09/18/us/ruth-bader-ginsburg-dead.html.

Greenhouse, Steven. "How Walmart Persuades Its Workers Not to Unionize." *The Atlantic,* June 8, 2015. theatlantic.com/business/archive/2015/06/how -walmart-convinces-its-employees-not-to-unionize/395051.

——. " 'Old-School Union Busting': How US Corporations Are Quashing the New Wave of Organizing." *The Guardian,* February 26, 2023. theguardian .com/us-news/2023/feb/26/amazon-trader-joes-starbucks-anti-union -measures.

Grim, Ryan. "National Review Is Trying to Rewrite Its Own Racist History." *The Intercept,* July 5, 2020. theintercept.com/2020/07/05/national-review -william-buckley-racism.

Grumbach, Jacob M. *Laboratories Against Democracy: How National Parties*

Transformed State Politics. Princeton Studies in American Politics. Princeton University Press, 2022.

———. "Laboratories of Democratic Backsliding." *American Political Science Review,* December 1, 2022, 1–18. doi.org/10.1017/S0003055422000934.

Grumbach, Jacob M., and Ruth Berins Collier. "The Deep Structure of Democratic Crisis." *Boston Review,* January 6, 2022. bostonreview.net/articles/the-deep-structure-of-democratic-crisis.

Gunn, Paul. "Against Epistocracy." *Critical Review* 31, no. 1 (January 2, 2019): 26–82. doi.org/10.1080/08913811.2019.1609842.

Gurri, Adam. "Liberal Democracy and the Federal System." *Liberal Currents,* November 30, 2021. liberalcurrents.com/liberal-democracy-and-the-federal-system.

Gutelius, Beth, and Sanjay Pinto. "Handling Hardship: Data on Economic Insecurity Among Amazon Warehouse Workers," May 20, 2024. indigo.uic.edu/articles/report/Handling_Hardship_Data_on_Economic_Insecurity_Among_Amazon_Warehouse_Workers/25823068.

———. "Pain Points: Data on Work Intensity, Monitoring, and Health at Amazon Warehouse," October 29, 2023. indigo.uic.edu/articles/report/Pain_Points_Data_on_Work_Intensity_Monitoring_and_Health_at_Amazon_Warehouses/24435124.

Haas, Karen L. "Statistics of the Congressional Election from Official Sources for the Election of November 4, 2014." Office of the Clerk U.S. House of Representatives, March 9, 2015.

———. "Statistics of the Congressional Election of November 2, 2010." Office of the Clerk U.S. House of Representatives, June 3, 2011.

Hadero, Haleluya. "Amazon Argues That National Labor Board Is Unconstitutional, Joining SpaceX and Trader Joe's." Associated Press, February 16, 2024. apnews.com/article/amazon-nlrb-unconstitutional-union-labor-45933 1e9b77f5be0e5202c147654993e.

———. "Thousands of Drivers File Arbitration Claims Against Amazon for Unpaid Wages and Other Losses." Associated Press, June 11, 2024. apnews.com/article/amazon-delivery-drivers-flex-pay-4673f95e5a7a3055cb369f334f77895a.

Hallock, Betty. "Can Scent Be Democratized?" *The New York Times,* March 13, 2022. nytimes.com/2022/03/18/style/art-olfaction-institute-smell.html.

Hamilton, Alexander. "Conjectures About the New Constitution." University of Virginia Press, 1787. Founders Online. founders.archives.gov/documents/Hamilton/01-04-02-0139.

———. "The Federalist No. 1." In *The Federalist Papers,* edited by Garry Wills. Bantam Classic. Bantam Books, 1982.

———. "The Federalist No. 8." In *The Federalist Papers,* edited by Garry Wills. Bantam Classic. Bantam Books, 1982.

———. "The Federalist No. 9." In *The Federalist Papers,* edited by Garry Wills. Bantam Classic. Bantam Books, 1982.

———. "The Federalist No. 22." In *The Federalist Papers,* edited by Garry Wills. Bantam Classic. Bantam Books, 1982.

Hansen, Morris H. "Some History and Reminiscences on Survey Sampling." *Statistical Science* 2, no. 2 (1987): 180–90.

Harris, Jasmine E. "Why Buck v. Bell Still Matters." *Bill of Health* (blog), October 14, 2020. blog.petrieflom.law.harvard.edu/2020/10/14/why-buck-v-bell-still-matters.

Harsanyi, David. "We Must Weed out Ignorant Americans from the Electorate." *Washington Post,* May 20, 2016. washingtonpost.com/opinions/we-must-weed-out-ignorant-americans-from-the-electorate/2016/05/20/f66b3e18-1c7a-11e6-8c7b-6931e66333e7_story.html.

Hartill, Robin. "Who Owns Amazon? Largest Shareholders." *The Motley Fool,* March 23, 2024. fool.com/investing/how-to-invest/stocks/who-owns-amazon.

Harwood, John. "'Embarrassingly Naive': I Expected America to Stand Up for Democracy." *Zeteo,* November 7, 2024. zeteo.com/p/embarrassingly-naive-voters-trump-democracy.

Hawkings, David. "Wealth of Congress: Richer Than Ever, but Mostly at the Very Top." *Roll Call,* February 27, 2018. rollcall.com/2018/02/27/wealth-of-congress-richer-than-ever-but-mostly-at-the-very-top.

"Health at a Glance 2023: OECD Indicators." OECD, November 7, 2023. doi.org/10.1787/7a7afb35-en.

Heartland Signal. "GOP Candidate for Minnesota Secretary of State Kim Crockett, Who Would Be the State's Chief Election Officer, Says That People Requiring Assistance Because They Do Not Speak English or Are Disabled 'Raises the Question: Should They Be Voting?'" August 5, 2022. x.com/HeartlandSignal/status/1555641109036007424.

Hegre, Håvard. "Democracy and Armed Conflict." *Journal of Peace Research* 51, no. 2 (March 2014). doi.org/10.1177/0022343313512852.

Hendricks, Bracken, Rhiana Gunn-Wright, and Sam Ricketts. "The Greatest Mobilization Since WWII." *Democracy Journal* 56, no. Spring (2020). democracyjournal.org/magazine/56/the-greatest-mobilization-since-wwii/.

Hersher, Rebecca. "D.C. Votes Overwhelmingly to Become 51st State." NPR, November 9, 2016, sec. The Two-Way. npr.org/sections/thetwo-way/2016/11/09/501412360/d-c-votes-overwhelmingly-to-become-51st-state.

Hertel-Fernandez, Alexander. "Collective Action, Law, and the Fragmented Development of the American Labor Movement." In *The American Political Economy: Politics, Markets, and Power,* edited by Alexander Hertel-Fernandez, Jacob S. Hacker, Kathleen Thelen, and Paul Pierson, 1–48. Cambridge Studies in Comparative Politics. Cambridge University Press, 2021. doi.org/10.1017/9781009029841.001.

Higgins, Eoin. "Peter Thiel, Trump's Man in Silicon Valley." *Rolling Stone,* February 23, 2025. rollingstone.com/politics/politics-features/owned-book-peter-thiel-trump-tech-silicon-valley-1235276868/.

Hill, Steven. "Periscope: Misdiagnosing the Vital Signs of Democracy." Substack newsletter. *DemocracySOS* (blog), June 8, 2022. democracysos.substack.com/p/misdiagnosing-the-vital-signs-of.

"Historical Background and Development of Social Security." Social Security Administration, n.d. ssa.gov/history/briefhistory3.html.

Hobbes, Thomas. *De Cive.* Edited by Sterling P. Lamprecht. xxxi, 211 pages. 1642. Appleton-Century-Crofts, 1949. catalog.hathitrust.org/Record/10245 6627.

Hoffman, Beatrix. "Health Care Reform and Social Movements in the United States." *American Journal of Public Health* 93, no. 1 (January 2003): 75–85. doi.org/10.2105/AJPH.93.1.75.

Hogarth, Paul. "Michigan House Holds Hearing to Join NPVIC, One Step Closer to Electing POTUS by Popular Vote." Daily Kos. Accessed March 10, 2023. dailykos.com/stories/2023/3/8/2156756/-Michigan-House-holds -hearing-to-join-NPVIC-one-step-closer-to-electing-POTUS-by-popular -vote.

Holton, Woody. *Unruly Americans and the Origins of the Constitution.* Hill and Wang, 2007.

Horowitz, Juliana Menasce, and Kim Parker. "How Americans View Their Jobs." Pew Research Center, March 30, 2023. pewresearch.org/social-trends/ 2023/03/30/how-americans-view-their-jobs.

Horwitz, Sari. "Getting a Photo ID so You Can Vote Is Easy. Unless You're Poor, Black, Latino or Elderly." *Washington Post,* May 23, 2016, sec. Courts & Law. washingtonpost.com/politics/courts_law/getting-a-photo-id-so-you -can-vote-is-easy-unless-youre-poor-black-latino-or-elderly/2016/05/23/ 8d5474ec-20f0-11e6-8690-f14ca9de2972_story.html.

Hounshell, Blake. "Scholars Ask Congress to Scrap Winner-Take-All Political System." *The New York Times,* September 19, 2022, sec. U.S. nytimes.com/ 2022/09/19/us/politics/redistricting-gerrymandering.html.

"How to Form a Union." More Perfect Union, September 5, 2022. perfectunion .us/how-to-form-a-union.

Huddy, Leonie. "The Group Foundations of Democratic Political Behavior." *Critical Review* 30, no. 1–2 (April 3, 2018): 71–86. doi.org/10.1080/089138.1 .2018.1466857.

Huremović, Damir. "Brief History of Pandemics (Pandemics Throughout History)." *Psychiatry of Pandemics,* May 16, 2019, 7–35. doi.org/10.1007/978-3 -030-15346-5_2.

Imamura, David. "The Rise and Fall of Redistricting Commissions: Lessons from the 2020 Redistricting Cycle." *Human Rights* 48, no. 1. Accessed March 8, 2023. americanbar.org/groups/crsj/publications/human_rights_magazine _home/economics-of-voting/the-rise-and-fall-of-redistricting -commissions.

"In Divided Washington, Americans Have Highly Negative Views of Both Parties' Leaders." Pew Research Center, April 7, 2023. pewresearch.org/ politics/2023/04/07/in-divided-washington-americans-have-highly -negative-views-of-both-parties-leaders.

"Income Inequality." OECD Data. Organisation for Economic Co-operation and Development, 2024. data.oecd.org/inequality/income-inequality .htm.

Ingham, Sean. *Rule by Multiple Majorities: A New Theory of Popular Control.* Cambridge University Press, 2018. doi.org/10.1017/9781108683821.

Ingham, Sean, and Frank Lovett. "Republican Freedom, Popular Control, and Collective Action." *American Journal of Political Science* 63, no. 4 (October 2019): 774–87. doi.org/10.1111/ajps.12439.

Itkowitz, Colby, and Clara Ence Morse. "How Kamala Harris Shifted Democrats' Message from 'Democracy' to 'Freedom.'" *The Washington Post,* August 20, 2024. washingtonpost.com/politics/2024/08/20/kamala-harris-freedom-democracy-biden.

Izaguirre, Rosmery, and Caitlin Oprysko. "Business Donors Overwhelmingly Bet on the GOP. Here's Where It Paid Off." *Politico,* November 24, 2024. politico.com/news/2024/11/24/business-election-donations-republicans-00191072.

Jacobs, Alan M., J. Scott Matthews, Timothy Hicks, and Eric Merkley. "Whose News? Class-Biased Economic Reporting in the United States." *American Political Science Review* 115, no. 3 (August 2021): 1016–33. doi.org/10.1017/S0003055421000137.

Jäger, Simon, Shakked Noy, and Benjamin Schoefer. "Codetermination and Power in the Workplace." *Journal of Law and Political Economy* 3, no. 1 (September 28, 2022). doi.org/10.5070/LP63159039.

Jamieson, Dave. "Amazon Spent $14 Million on Anti-Union Consultants in 2022." *The Huffington Post,* March 31, 2023. huffpost.com/entry/amazon-anti-union-spending-2022_n_6426fd1fe4b02a8d518e7010.

——. "The Life and Death of an Amazon Warehouse Temp." *The Huffington Post,* October 21, 2015. highline.huffingtonpost.com/articles/en/life-and-death-amazon-temp.

Jefferson, Thomas. "Thomas Jefferson to James Madison." University of Virginia Press, September 6, 1789. founders.archives.gov/documents/Madison/01-12-02-0248.

Jeffries, Hakeem. *The ABCs of Democracy.* First edition. Grand Central Publishing, 2024.

Johnson, Dave. "Massive Amazon Warehouses Are Used to Ship and Store Open-Box, Refurbished, and Returned Products," November 15, 2023. businessinsider.com/amazon-warehouse.

Johnson, David V. "Explanation for What?" *The Baffler,* December 2016. thebaffler.com/salvos/explanation-for-what-johnson.

Jones, Jeffrey M. "Record Low in U.S. Satisfied With Way Democracy Is Working," January 5, 2024. news.gallup.com/poll/548120/record-low-satisfied-democracy-working.aspx.

Jurecic, Quinta. "The Supreme Court Case That's All About Donald Trump." *The Atlantic,* November 29, 2022. theatlantic.com/ideas/archive/2022/11/moore-v-harper-scotus-elections-amicus-brief/672281.

Kamarck, Elaine, and John Kudak. "How to Get Rid of the Electoral College." *Brookings Institution* (blog), December 9, 2020. brookings.edu/blog/fixgov/2020/12/09/how-to-get-rid-of-the-electoral-college.

Kant, Immanuel. "An Answer to the Question: What Is Enlightenment?" In

Perpetual Peace, and Other Essays on Politics, History, and Morals, translated by Ted Humphrey. Hackett Pub. Co., 1988. archive.org/detai s/perpetualpeaceot00kant.

Kaswan, Mark J. "Property, Ownership and Employee Ownership: Employee Control in ESOPs." *Journal of Participation and Employee Ownership* 5, no. 1 (May 31, 2022): 14–31. doi.org/10.1108/JPEO-11-2020-0028.

Kazin, Michael. *What It Took to Win: A History of the Democratic Party.* Farrar, Straus and Giroux, 2022.

Keith, Tamara. "At the Site of Trump's Jan. 6 Rally, Harris Makes Her Closing Pitch for the Campaign." NPR, October 29, 2024, sec. Politics. npr.org/2024/10/28/nx-s1-5169210/kamala-harris-donald-trump-jan-6-speech.

Kelaidis, Katherine. "What the Great Plague of Athens Can Teach Us Now." *The Atlantic,* March 23, 2020. theatlantic.com/ideas/archive/2020/03/great-plague-athens-has-eerie-parallels-today/608545/.

Kelly, Jamie Terence. *Framing Democracy: A Behavioral Approach to Democratic Theory.* Princeton University Press, 2012.

Kelly, Kim. *Fight Like Hell: The Untold History of American Labor.* Paperback edition. One Signal Publishers/Atria, 2023.

Kelly, Nathan J., and Jana Morgan. "Hurdles to Shared Prosperity: Congress, Parties, and the National Policy Process in an Age of Inequality." In *The American Political Economy: Politics, Markets, and Power,* edited by Alexander Hertel-Fernandez, Jacob S. Hacker, Kathleen Thelen, and Paul Pierson, 1–48. Cambridge Studies in Comparative Politics. Cambridge University Press, 2021. doi.org/10.1017/9781009029841.001.

Kennedy, John F. "Statement by the President Upon Receiving a Report on Collective Bargaining and Industrial Peace," May 1, 1962. The American Presidency Project. presidency.ucsb.edu/documents/statement-the-president-upon-receiving-report-collective-bargaining-and-industrial-peace.

Kent, Ana Hernández, and Lowell R. Ricketts. "The State of U.S. Wealth Inequality." The Institute for Economic Equity, May 3, 2024. stlouisfed.org/institute-for-economic-equity/the-state-of-us-wealth-inequality.

Kerr, Camille. "A Brief, Visual Guide to Understanding Employee Ownership Structures." Democracy at Work Institute, 2015. institute.coop/resources/brief-guide-understanding-employee-ownership-structures.

Khan, Mishal. "At Work and Under Watch: Surveillance and Suffering at Amazon and Walmart Warehouses." Oxfam, April 10, 2024.

Khanna, Congressman Ro. "Rep. Ro Khanna on How Term Limits Would Restore 'Stability and Impartiality' to the Supreme Court," July 6, 2022. khanna.house.gov/media/editorials/rep-ro-khanna-how-term-limits-would-restore-stability-and-impartiality-supreme.

Kiely, Eugene. "Durbin and the Filibuster 'Myth.'" FactCheck.org (blog), January 23, 2018. factcheck.org/2018/01/durbin-filibuster-myth.

Kim, Soo Rin. "Just 12 Megadonors Accounted for 7.5% of Political Giving over Past Decade, Says Report." ABC News. Accessed February 14, 2023. abcnews.go.com/Politics/12-megadonors-accounted-75-political-giving-past-decade/story?id=77189636.

King, Martin Luther, Jr. "Speech to AFL-CIO's Fourth Constitutional Convention," December 11, 1961. University of Maryland. umdlabor.weebly.com/uploads/2/9/3/9/29397087/speech_transcript.pdf.

King, Rufus. "Notes of Rufus King in the Federal Convention of 1787." The Avalon Project. Accessed January 7, 2023. avalon.law.yale.edu/18th_century/king.asp#1.

Kinnard, Meg. "A Comprehensive Look at DOGE's Firings and Layoffs so Far." Associated Press, February 21, 2025. apnews.com/article/doge-firings-layoffs-federal-government-workers-musk-d33cdd7872d64d2bdd8fe70c28652654.

Klarman, Michael J. "Foreword: The Degradation of American Democracy—and the Court." *Harvard Law Review* 134, no. 1 (November 2020). doi.org/10.2139/ssrn.3671830.

———. *The Framers' Coup: The Making of the United States Constitution.* Oxford University Press, 2016.

Klein, Ezra. "How Politics Makes Us Stupid." *Vox,* April 6, 2014. vox.com/2014/4/6/5556462/brain-dead-how-politics-makes-us-stupid.

———. "The Definitive Case for Ending the Filibuster." *Vox,* October 1, 2020. vox.com/21424582/filibuster-joe-biden-2020-senate-democrats-abolish-trump.

———. *Why We're Polarized.* Avid Reader Press, 2020.

Klocksiem, Justin. "Epistocracy Is a Wolf in Wolf's Clothing." *The Journal of Ethics* 23, no. 1 (March 2019): 19–36. doi.org/10.1007/s10892-019-09279-1.

Knight, Heather, and Kate Selig. "A Constitutional Convention? Some Democrats Fear It's Coming." *The New York Times,* December 16, 2024, sec. U.S. nytimes.com/2024/12/16/us/a-constitutional-convention-some-democrats-fear-its-coming.html.

Kochan, Thomas A. "Worker Voice, Representation, and Implications for Public Policies." Task Force on the Work of the Future. MIT, July 2020. mitsloan.mit.edu/shared/ods/documents?PublicationDocumentID=8289.

Koerth, Maggie. "How Money Affects Elections." *FiveThirtyEight* (blog), September 10, 2018. fivethirtyeight.com/features/money-and-elections-a-complicated-love-story.

Kolata, Gina. "'Chaos and Confusion' at the Crown Jewel of American Science." *The New York Times,* March 24, 2025. nytimes.com/2025/03/24/health/nih-doge-trump.html.

Kroll, Andy. "Meet the Fortune 500 Companies Funding the Political Resegregation of America." *Mother Jones.* Accessed February 15, 2023. motherjones.com/politics/2014/11/rslc-redistricting-fortune-500-political-resegregation.

Krueger, Patrick M., Kathryn Dovel, and Justin T. Denney. "Democracy and Self-Rated Health across 67 Countries: A Multilevel Analysis." *Social Science & Medicine* 143 (October 2015): 137–44. doi.org/10.1016/j.socscimed.2015.08.047.

Kuttner, Robert. "Neoliberalism: Political Success, Economic Failure." *The American Prospect,* June 25, 2019. prospect.org/economy/neoliberalism-political-success-economic-failure.

"Labor Unions and the Middle Class." U.S. Department of the Treasury, August

2023. home.treasury.gov/system/files/136/Labor-Unions-And-The-Middle
-Class.pdf.

Lafuente, Sara. "Dual Majorities for Firm Governments." In *Democratize Work: The Case for Reorganizing the Economy*, edited by Isabelle Ferreras, Julie Battilana, and Dominique Méda, translated by Miranda Richmond Mouillot. The University of Chicago Press, 2022. doi.org/10.7208/chicago/9780226819631.001.0001.

Lanard, Noah. "Labor Law Is Stuck in 1947. It's No Surprise Companies Keep Winning." *Mother Jones*, May 10, 2021. motherjones.com/politics/2021/05/labor-law-is-stuck-in-1947-its-no-surprise-companies-keeps-winning.

Landemore, Hélène. *Democratic Reason: Politics, Collective Intelligence, and the Rule of the Many*. Princeton University Press, 2017.

———. "Democratize Firms . . . Why, and How?" In *Democratize Work: The Case for Reorganizing the Economy*, edited by Isabelle Ferreras, Julie Battilana, and Dominique Méda, translated by Miranda Richmond Mouillot. The University of Chicago Press, 2022. doi.org/10.7208/chicago/9780226819631.001.0001.

———. *Open Democracy: Reinventing Popular Rule for the Twenty-First Century*. Princeton University Press, 2020.

Landemore, Hélène, and Jason Brennan. *Debating Democracy: Do We Need More or Less?* Oxford University Press, 2021.

Largey, Matt. "The Bad Grade That Changed The U.S. Constitution." NPR, May 5, 2017, sec. National. npr.org/2017/05/05/526900818/the-bad-grade-that-changed-the-u-s-constitution.

Laurison, Daniel, Hana Brown, and Ankit Rastogi. "Voting Intersections: Race, Class, and Participation in Presidential Elections in the United States 2008–2016." *Sociological Perspectives* 65, no. 4 (August 1, 2022): 768–89. doi.org/10.1177/07311214211059136.

Lax, Jeffrey R., and Justin H. Phillips. "The Democratic Deficit in the States." *American Journal of Political Science* 56, no. 1 (2012): 148–66.

Lee, Frances E., and Bruce Ian Oppenheimer. *Sizing up the Senate: The Unequal Consequences of Equal Representation*. University of Chicago Press, 1999.

Lemar, Anika Singh. "The Public Hearing Process for New Housing Is Broken. Here's How to Fix It." *Brookings Institution* (blog), May 4, 2022. brookings.edu/articles/the-public-hearing-process-for-new-housing-is-broken-heres-how-to-fix-it.

Lemieux, Pierre. "Mencken's Theory of Democracy." *Regulation*, Winter 2024-2025. cato.org/regulation/winter-2024-2025/menckens-theory-democracy.

Levinson, Sanford. *An Argument Open to All: Reading the Federalist in the Twenty-First Century*. Yale University Press, 2017.

———. *Framed: America's Fifty-One Constitutions and the Crisis of Governance*. Oxford University Press, 2012.

———. *Our Undemocratic Constitution: Where the Constitution Goes Wrong (and How We the People Can Correct It)*. Oxford University Press, 2008.

Levitsky, Steven, and Daniel Ziblatt. *Tyranny of the Minority: Why American Democracy Reached the Breaking Point*. First edition. Crown, 2023.

Levitt, Justin. "A Comprehensive Investigation of Voter Impersonation

Finds 31 Credible Incidents out of One Billion Ballots Cast." *Washington Post,* August 6, 2014. washingtonpost.com/news/wonk/wp/2014/08/06/a -comprehensive-investigation-of-voter-impersonation-finds-31-credible -incidents-out-of-one-billion-ballots-cast.

Li, Michael. "The GOP's Redistricting Loophole," February 6, 2023. brennancenter.org/our-work/analysis-opinion/gop-redistricting-loophole.

Li, Michael, and Chris Leaverton. "Gerrymandering Competitive Districts to Near Extinction." Brennan Center for Justice, August 11, 2022. brennancenter .org/our-work/analysis-opinion/gerrymandering-competitive-districts -near-extinction.

"Life Expectancy at Birth." OECD Data. Organisation for Economic Co-operation and Development, 2024. data.oecd.org/healthstat/life-expectancy -at-birth.htm#indicator-chart.

Lincoln, Abraham. "Gettysburg Address." In *Collected Works of Abraham Lincoln,* edited by Roy P. Basler, 9th ed., 1953.

Lind, Dara. "Ruth Bader Ginsburg Is in the Hospital with 3 Broken Ribs." *Vox,* November 8, 2018. vox.com/2018/11/8/18075262/ruth-bader-ginsburg-rbg -hospital-age.

Lindsey, Robert. "Lowered Confidence in Nation: Its Effect on Spending and Votes." *The New York Times,* October 28, 1975.

Lippmann, Walter. *Public Opinion.* 1922. Free Press, 1997.

———. *The Phantom Public.* 1927. Reprint, Transaction Publishers, 1993.

Liptak, Adam. "U.S. Voting for Judges Perplexes Other Nations." *The New York Times,* May 25, 2008, sec. World. nytimes.com/2008/05/25/world/americas/ 25iht-judge.4.13194819.html.

Lowndes, Vivien, and Marie Paxton. "Can Agonism Be Institutionalised? Can Institutions Be Agonised? Prospects for Democratic Design." *The British Journal of Politics and International Relations* 20, no. 3 (August 2018): 693–710. doi.org/10.1177/1369148118784756.

Lowry, Rich. "The Left's Foolhardy Attack on the Senate." *The Salt Lake Tribune,* October 9, 2018. sltrib.com/opinion/commentary/2018/10/10/rich -lowry-lefts.

Lupia, Arthur, and John G. Matsusaka. "Direct Democracy: New Approaches to Old Questions." *Annual Review of Political Science* 7, no. 1 (May 17, 2004): 463–82. doi.org/10.1146/annurev.polisci.7.012003.104730.

Luttig, J. Michael. "There Is Absolutely Nothing to Support the 'Independent State Legislature' Theory." *The Atlantic,* October 3, 2022. theatlantic.com/ ideas/archive/2022/10/moore-v-harper-independent-legislature-theory -supreme-court/671625.

Machiavelli, Niccolò. *Discourses on Livy.* Translated by Harvey C. Mansfield and Nathan Tarcov. University of Chicago Press, 1998.

Mackie, Gerry. *Democracy Defended.* Cambridge University Press, 2003. doi .org/10.1017/CBO9780511490293.

Mackin, Christopher. "Ferreras and the Economic Democracy Debate." In *Democratizing the Corporation: The Bicameral Firm and Beyond,* edited by Isabelle Ferreras, Tom Malleson, and Joel Rogers. The Real Utopias Project. Verso, 2024.

Mader, George. "Binding Authority: Unamendability in the United States Constitution—A Textual and Historical Analysis." *Marquette Law Review* 99, no. 4 (2016).

Madison, James. "James Madison to Thomas Jefferson." University of Virginia Press, March 19, 1787. Founders Online. founders.archives.gov/documents/Madison/01-09-02-0169.

——. "The Federalist No. 10." In *The Federalist Papers*, edited by Garry Wills. Bantam Books, 1982.

——. "The Federalist No. 14." In *The Federalist Papers*, edited by Garry Wills. Bantam Books, 1982.

——. "The Federalist No. 37." In *The Federalist Papers*, edited by Garry Wills. Bantam Books, 1982.

——. "The Federalist No. 39." In *The Federalist Papers*, edited by Garry Wills. Bantam Books, 1982.

——. "The Federalist No. 57." In *The Federalist Papers*, edited by Garry Wills. Bantam Books, 1982.

——. "The Federalist No. 58." In *The Federalist Papers*, edited by Garry Wills. Bantam Books, 1982.

——. "The Federalist No. 62." In *The Federalist Papers*, edited by Garry Wills. Bantam Books, 1982.

——. "The Federalist No. 63." In *The Federalist Papers*, edited by Garry Wills. Bantam Books, 1982.

——. "Vices of the Political System of the United States." National Archives, April 1787. Founders Online. founders.archives.gov/documents/Madison/01-09-02-0187.

Madland, David. "How to Promote Sectoral Bargaining in the United States." Center for American Progress Action, July 10, 2019. americanprogressaction.org/article/promote-sectoral-bargaining-united-states.

——. "Wage Boards for American Workers." Center for American Progress, April 9, 2018. americanprogress.org/article/wage-boards-american-workers.

——. "Workers' Boards: Frequently Asked Questions." Center for American Progress, April 9, 2018. americanprogress.org/article/wage-boards-american-workers.

Madland, David, and Alex Rowell. "How State and Local Governments Can Strengthen Worker Power and Raise Wages." Center for American Progress Action, May 2, 2017. americanprogressaction.org/article/state-local-governments-can-strengthen-worker-power-raise-wages.

Madland, David, and Malkie Wall. "What Is Sectoral Bargaining?" Center for American Progress Action, March 2, 2020. americanprogressaction.org/article/what-is-sectoral-bargaining.

Madland, David, Karla Walter, and Ross Eisenbrey. "Right-to-Work 101." Center for American Progress Action, February 12, 2012. americanprogress.org/article/right-to-work-101.

Mahler, Jonathan, and Jim Rutenberg. "How Rupert Murdoch's Empire of Influence Remade the World." *The New York Times Magazine*, April 3, 2019.

nytimes.com/interactive/2019/04/03/magazine/rupert-murdoch-fox-news
-trump.html.

"Majority of Americans Say Trump Should Be Prosecuted on Federal Criminal Charges Linked to 2020 Election, Quinnipiac University National Poll Finds; DeSantis Slips, Trump Widens Lead in GOP Primary." Quinnipiac, August 16, 2023. poll.qu.edu/poll-release?releaseid=3877.

Malinksy, Gili. "In the U.S., You Can Legally 'Be Fired for Any Reason or No Reason at All'—Here's Why." CNBC, December 7, 2022. cnbc.com/2022/ 12/07/us-at-will-employment.html.

Malleson, Tom. *After Occupy: Economic Democracy for the 21st Century.* York: Oxford University Press, 2015.

——. "Beyond Electoral Democracy." *Jacobin,* May 29, 2018. jacobin.com/ 2018/05/legislature-lot-electoral-democracy-real-utopias.

——. "Making the Case for Workplace Democracy: Exit and Voice as Mechanisms of Freedom in Social Life." *Polity* 45, no. 4 (October 2013): 604–29. doi.org/10.1057/pol.2013.20.

Malleson, Tom, and Joel Rogers. "Introduction." In *Democratizing the Corporation: The Bicameral Firm and Beyond,* edited by Isabelle Ferreras, Tom Malleson, and Joel Rogers. The Real Utopias Project. Verso, 2024.

Maloy, J. S. "Book Review: Democracy for Realists: Why Elections Do Not Produce Responsive Government, by Christopher H. Achen & Larry M. Bartels." *Political Theory* 48, no. 2 (April 2020): 255–60. doi.org/10.1177/0090591719868432.

Mansbridge, Jane. "Rethinking Representation." *American Political Science Review* 97, no. 4 (2003).

——. "The Evolution of Political Representation in Liberal Democracies: Concepts and Practices." In *The Oxford Handbook of Political Representation in Liberal Democracies,* edited by Robert Rohrschneider and Jacques Thomassen. Oxford University Press, 2020.

Marbury v. Madison, No. 5 U.S. 137 (1803).

Marchese, David. "The Interview: Curtis Yarvin Says Democracy Is Done. Powerful Conservatives Are Listening." *The New York Times,* January 18, 2025. nytimes.com/2025/01/18/magazine/curtis-yarvin-interview.html.

Mares, Isabela. "A Discussion of Christopher H. Achen and Larry M. Bartels' Democracy for Realists: Why Elections Do Not Produce Responsive Government." *Perspectives on Politics* 15, no. 1 (March 2017): 159–60. doi.org/ 10.1017/S1537592716004266.

Maruf, Ramishah. "More than 15,000 Amazon Contract Drivers File Legal Claims Asking for Compensation for Overtime and Unpaid Wages." CNN, June 12, 2024. cnn.com/2024/06/11/business/amazon-contract -workers-file-legal-claims/index.html.

Mason, J. W. "The Economy During Wartime." *Dissent,* 2017. dissentmagazine .org/article/second-world-war-economy-mark-wilson-destructive -creation-review.

Matthews, Dylan. "Europe Could Have the Secret to Saving America's Unions." *Vox,* April 17, 2017. vox.com/policy-and-politics/2017/4/17/15290674/ union-labor-movement-europe-bargaining-fight-15-ghent.

——. "Sinclair Broadcast Group, the Pro-Trump, Conservative Company Taking over Local News, Explained." *Vox*, April 3, 2018. vox.com/2018/4/3/17180020/sinclair-broadcast-group-conservative-trump-david-smith-local-news-tv-affiliate.

——. "The Case for Massively Expanding the US House of Representatives, in One Chart." *Vox*, June 4, 2018. vox.com/2018/6/4/17417452/congress-representation-ratio-district-size-chart-graph.

——. "Workers Don't Have Much Say in Corporations. Why Not Give Them Seats on the Board?" *Vox*, April 6, 2018. vox.com/2018/4/6/17086720/poll-corporate-board-democracy-worker-council-codetermination-union-labor.

Mattioli, Dana, and Esther Fung. "The Biggest Delivery Business in the U.S. Is No Longer UPS or FedEx." *The Wall Street Journal*, November 27, 2023. wsj.com/business/amazon-vans-outnumber-ups-fedex-750f3c04.

Mayer, Jane. "State Legislatures Are Torching Democracy." *The New Yorker*, August 15, 2022. newyorker.com/magazine/2022/08/15/state-legislatures-are-torching-democracy.

Mayer, Robert. "Is There a Moral Right to Workplace Democracy?" *Social Theory and Practice* 26, no. 2 (2000): 301–25.

Mazoue, Aude. "Explainer: How Do France's Legislative Elections Work?" France 24, May 11, 2022. france24.com/en/france/20220511-explainer-how-do-france-s-legislative-elections-work.

McConnell, Mitch. "The Filibuster Plays a Crucial Role in Our Constitutional Order." *The New York Times*, August 22, 2019, sec. Opinion. nytimes.com/2019/08/22/opinion/mitch-mcconnell-senate-filibuster.html.

McCormick, John P. "The New Ochlophobia?: Populism, Majority Rule, and Prospects for Democratic Republicanism." In *Republicanism and the Future of Democracy*, edited by Geneviève Rousselière and Yiftah Elazar, 130–51. Cambridge University Press, 2019. doi.org/10.1017/9781108630153.008.

McCullough, David. *1776*. Simon and Schuster, 2005.

McFadden, Robert D. "Diversity of Americans Expressed Across Land." *The New York Times*, July 5, 1976. nytimes.com/1976/07/05/archives/diversity-of-americans-expressed-across-land.html?searchResultPosition=228.

McFaul, Michael. "The Tragic Success of Global Putinism." *The Atlantic*, March 10, 2025. theatlantic.com/international/archive/2025/03/tragic-success-global-putinism/681976/.

McGann, Anthony J. *The Logic of Democracy: Reconciling Equality, Deliberation, and Minority Protection*. University of Michigan Press, 2006.

McGaughey, Ewan. "Democracy in America at Work: The History of Labor's Vote in Corporate Governance." *Seattle University Law Review* 42, no. 2 (2019). digitalcommons.law.seattleu.edu/sulr/vol42/iss2/18.

——. "Five Principles of Economic Democracy." In *Democratizing the Corporation: The Bicameral Firm and Beyond*, edited by Isabelle Ferreras, Tom Malleson, and Joel Rogers. The Real Utopias Project. Verso, 2024.

McHenry, James. "Papers of Dr. James McHenry on the Federal Convention of 1787." Government Printing Office, 1927. The Avalon Project. avalon.law.yale.edu/18th_century/mchenry.asp.

McMaster, John Bach, and Frederick D. Stone, eds. *Pennsylvania and the Federal Constitution, 1787-1788.* Historical Society of Pennsylvania, 1888.

McNicholas, Celine, Margaret Poydock, and Lynn Rhinehart. "How the PRO Act Restores Workers' Right to Unionize." Economic Policy Institute, February 4, 2021. epi.org/publication/pro-act-problem-solution-chart.

McNicholas, Celine, Margaret Poydock, Samantha Sanders, and Ben Zipperer. "Employers Spend More than $400 Million per Year on 'Union-Avoidance' Consultants to Bolster Their Union-Busting Efforts." Economic Policy Institute, March 29, 2023. epi.org/publication/union-avoidance.

McNicholas, Celine, Margaret Poydock, and John Schmitt. "Workers Are Winning Union Elections, but It Can Take Years to Get Their First Contract." Economic Policy Institute, May 1, 2023. epi.org/publication/union-first-contract-fact-sheet.

Media Matters for America. "Ben Shapiro: The Right to Vote Should Require 'Some Sort of Minimum Level of Knowledge,'" February 3, 2020. mediamatters.org/ben-shapiro/ben-shapiro-right-vote-should-require-some-sort-minimum-level-knowledge.

Medium. "Letter to Congress on Ending Single Member Congressional Districts and Adopting Proportional Representation," September 19, 2022. medium.com/@scholars-redistricting-reform/open-letter-to-congress-to-end-single-member-congressional-districts-and-adopt-proportional-97ad1cf6aa2e.

Menand, Louis. "American Democracy Was Never Designed to Be Democratic." *The New Yorker,* August 15, 2022. newyorker.com/magazine/2022/08/22/american-democracy-was-never-designed-to-be-democratic-eric-holder-our-unfinished-march-nick-seabrook-one-person-one-vote-jacob-grumbach-laboratories-against-democracy.

———. "Everybody's an Expert." *The New Yorker,* November 27, 2005. newyorker.com/magazine/2005/12/05/everybodys-an-expert.

———. "The Rise and Fall of Neoliberalism." *The New Yorker,* July 17, 2023. newyorker.com/magazine/2023/07/24/the-rise-and-fall-of-neoliberalism.

Meyerson, Harold. "Democracy, Deshmocracy: Mega-Financiers Are Flocking to Trump." *The American Prospect,* May 30, 2024. prospect.org/api/content/75daf520-1ebc-11ef-a0f7-12163087a831.

———. "Restoring Workers' Freedoms." *The American Prospect,* January 30, 2023. prospect.org/labor/2023-01-30-restoring-worker-freedom-noncompete.

Milanovic, Branko. "Milton Friedman and Labor-Managed Enterprises." *Global Inequality* (blog), n.d. glineq.blogspot.com/2020/10/milton-friedman-and-labor-managed.html?m=1.

Mill, John Stuart. *On Liberty and Considerations on Representative Government.* Edited by R. B. McCallum. 1861. Reprint, Basil Blackwell, 1948. gutenberg.org/files/5669/5669-h/5669-h.htm.

———. *Principles of Political Economy.* Longmans, Green, and Company, 1848. oll.libertyfund.org/title/mill-principles-of-political-economy-ashley-ed.

Miller, Claire Cain. "The World 'Has Found a Way to Do This': The U.S. Lags on Paid Leave." *The New York Times,* June 22, 2023. nytimes.com/2021/10/25/upshot/paid-leave-democrats.html.

Miller, James. *Can Democracy Work?* Farrar, Straus and Giroux, 2018.

Miller, Julie. "'A Republic If You Can Keep It': Elizabeth Willing Powel, Benjamin Franklin, and the James McHenry Journal." Webpage. *Unfolding History: Manuscripts at the Library of Congress* (blog), January 6, 2022. blogs .loc.gov/manuscripts/2022/01/a-republic-if-you-can-keep-it-elizabeth -willing-powel-benjamin-franklin-and-the-james-mchenry-journal.

Millhiser, Ian. "The Case Against the Supreme Court of the United States." *Vox*, June 25, 2022. vox.com/2022/6/25/23181976/case-against-the-supreme-court -of-the-united-states.

———. "The Danger the Supreme Court Poses to Democracy, in Just Two Numbers." *Vox*, October 26, 2020. vox.com/2020/10/26/21534358/supreme-court -amy-coney-barrett-constitution-anti-democratic-electoral-college-senate.

———. "Democracy in America Is a Rigged Game." *Vox*, June 15, 2022. vox.com/ the-highlight/23066920/democracy-juneteenth-in-america-is-a-rigged -game.

———. "How America Lost Its Commitment to the Right to Vote." *Vox*, July 21, 2021. vox.com/22575435/voting-rights-supreme-court-john-roberts-shelby -county-constitution-brnovich-elena-kagan.

———. "The Overwhelming Strength of the Case Against Trump, in One Number." *Vox*, February 14, 2021. vox.com/2021/2/14/22282760/trump -impeachment-senate-malapportionment-76-million-acquital-conviction -capitol.

———. "The Supreme Court Leaves the Voting Rights Act Alive—but Only Barely." *Vox*, July 1, 2021. vox.com/2021/7/1/22559046/supreme-court-voting-rights -act-brnovich-dnc-samuel-alito-elena-kagan-democracy.

Miranda, Leticia, Nicole Nguyen, and Ryan Mac. "Here Are the Most Outrageous Incentives Cities Offered Amazon in Their HQ2 Bids." BuzzFeed News, November 15, 2018. buzzfeednews.com/article/leticiamiranda/ amazon-hq2-finalist-cities-incentives-airport-lounge.

Mishel, Lawrence. "Introduction—The Goliath in the Room: How the False Assumption of Equal Worker–Employer Power Undercuts Workplace Protections." *Journal of Law and Political Economy* 3, no. 1 (September 28, 2022). doi.org/10.5070/LP63159027.

———. "Not So Free to Contract: The Law, Philosophy, and Economics of Unequal Workplace Power." Economic Policy Institute. *Working Economics Blog* (blog), October 13, 2022. epi.org/blog/not-so-free-to-contract-the -law-philosophy-and-economics-of-unequal-workplace-power.

Monbiot, George. "Neoliberalism—the Ideology at the Root of All Our Problems." *The Guardian*, April 15, 2016. theguardian.com/books/2016/apr/ 15/neoliberalism-ideology-problem-george-monbiot.

Montanaro, Domenico. "Biden Endorses Reforming The Senate Filibuster. Here's What That Means." NPR, March 18, 2021, sec. Politics. npr.org/2021/03/ 18/978420540/biden-endorses-reforming-the-senate-filibuster-heres-what -that-means.

Morris, G. Elliott. "Roe v Wade and the End of Majority Rule in America." *Politics by the Numbers* (blog), May 8, 2022. gelliottmorris.substack.com/p/roe -v-wade-and-the-end-of-majority.

Morris, Kevin, and Coryn Grange. "Large Racial Turnout Gap Persisted in 2020 Election," August 6, 2021. brennancenter.org/our-work/analysis-opinion/large-racial-turnout-gap-persisted-2020-election.

Mouffe, Chantal. "Deliberative Democracy or Agonistic Pluralism?" *Social Research* 66, no. 3 (1999): 745–58.

———. *The Democratic Paradox.* Repr. Radical Thinkers. Verso, 2009.

———. *The Return of the Political.* Verso, 1993.

Müller, Jan-Werner. *Democracy Rules.* Farrar, Straus and Giroux, 2021.

Myers, Adam. "Is the U.S. Senate Unusually Undemocratic?" *Medium* (blog), October 9, 2020. adammyersprov.medium.com/is-the-u-s-senate-unusually-undemocratic-a5978e9b2abc.

Mygind, Niels, and Thomas Poulsen. "Employee Ownership—Pros and Cons—a Review." *Journal of Participation and Employee Ownership* 4, no. 2 (November 26, 2021): 136–73. doi.org/10.1108/JPEO-08-2021-0003.

Nadeem, Reem. "Americans Who Mainly Get Their News on Social Media Are Less Engaged, Less Knowledgeable." *Pew Research Center's Journalism Project* (blog), July 30, 2020. pewresearch.org/journalism/2020/07/30/americans-who-mainly-get-their-news-on-social-media-are-less-engaged-less-knowledgeable.

Naidu, Suresh, and Michael Carr. "If You Don't Like Your Job, Can You Always Quit? Pervasive Monopsony Power and Freedom in the Labor Market." *Journal of Law and Political Economy* 3, no. 1 (September 28, 2022). doi.org/10.5070/LP63159035.

Nanda, Seema. "Mandatory Arbitration Won't Stop Us from Enforcing the Law." *U.S. Department of Labor Blog* (blog), March 20, 2023. blog.dol.gov/2023/03/20/mandatory-arbitration-wont-stop-us-from-enforcing-the-law.

Narea, Nicole. "Poll: Most Americans Support a Path to Citizenship for Undocumented Immigrants." *Vox,* February 4, 2021. vox.com/policy-and-politics/2021/2/4/22264074/poll-undocumented-immigrants-citizenship-stimulus-biden.

National Archives. "Articles of Confederation," April 9, 2021. archives.gov/milestone-documents/articles-of-confederation.

National Archives. "Declaration of Independence: A Transcription," November 1, 2015. archives.gov/founding-docs/declaration-transcript.

National Archives. "What Is the Electoral College?," August 27, 2019. archives.gov/electoral-college/about.

National Center for Employee Ownership. "The Rights of ESOP Participants," April 5, 2012. nceo.org/articles/rights-esop-participants.

National Conference of State Legislatures. "Voter ID Laws." Accessed February 13, 2023. ncsl.org/elections-and-campaigns/voter-id.

National Popular Vote. "9.16 Myths About Interstate Compacts and Congressional Consent," January 19, 2019. nationalpopularvote.com/section_9.16.

National Popular Vote. "Map of General-Election Campaign Events and TV Ad Spending by 2020 Presidential Candidates," September 7, 2020. nationalpopularvote.com/map-general-election-campaign-events-and-tv-ad-spending-2020-presidential-candidates.

National Popular Vote. "Status of National Popular Vote Bill in Each State," November 11, 2016. nationalpopularvote.com/state-status.

Naylor, Brian. "Read Trump's Jan. 6 Speech, A Key Part of Impeachment Trial." NPR, February 10, 2021, sec. Politics. npr.org/2021/02/10/966396848/read-trumps-jan-6-speech-a-key-part-of-impeachment-trial.

NDVoices. "Statewide Results," November 12, 2020. results.sos.nd.gov/ResultsSW.aspx?text=All&type=SW&map=CTY&eid=313.

Neale, Thomas H. "The Article V Convention to Propose Constitutional Amendments: Contemporary Issues for Congress." Congressional Research Service, March 29, 2016. sgp.fas.org/crs/misc/R42589.pdf.

Neff, Timothy, and Victor Pickard. "Funding Democracy: Public Media and Democratic Health in 33 Countries." *The International Journal of Press/Politics,* December 13, 2021, 194016122110602. doi.org/10.1177/19401612211060255.

Newport, Frank. "Average American Remains OK With Higher Taxes on Rich." Gallup, August 12, 2022. news.gallup.com/opinion/polling-matters/396737/average-american-remains-higher-taxes-rich.aspx.

Nicholls, Flynn. "Donald Trump's Victory Speech in Full: Transcript." *Newsweek,* November 6, 2024. newsweek.com/donald-trump-victory-speech-full-transcript-1981234.

Nippel, Wilfried. *Ancient and Modern Democracy: Two Concepts of Liberty?* Translated by Keith Tribe. 1st ed. Cambridge University Press, 2016. doi.org/10.1017/CBO9781139107297.

Noah, Timothy. "For Wall Street Billionaires, This Election Is About One Thing." *The New Republic,* May 29, 2024. newrepublic.com/article/182015/wall-street-billionaires-support-trump-tax-cuts.

Norris, Pippa. *Why American Elections Are Flawed (and How to Fix Them).* 1st ed. Cornell University Press, 2017. jstor.org/stable/10.7591/j.ctt1n7qkxz

"Notes on the Debates in the Federal Convention." The Avalon Project. Accessed May 12, 2025. avalon.law.yale.edu/subject_menus/debcont.asp.

Numéro. "How Jacob Elordi Democratizes Men's Handbags." December 13, 2024. numero.com/en/fashion/how-does-jacob-elordi-democratize-mens-handbags/.

Nunes da Costa, Marta. "Creating the People as 'One'? On Democracy and Its Other." *Theoria* 63, no. 149 (2016).

Nwanevu, Osita. "American Democracy Is Broken. Can Proportional Representation Fix It?" *The New Republic,* March 7, 2022. newrepublic.com/article/165557/proportional-representation-fix-the-house.

———. "Bernie Sanders's Walmart Speech May Offer a Preview of Larger Labor Proposals." *The New Yorker,* June 7, 2019. newyorker.com/news/our-columnists/bernie-sanderss-walmart-speech-may-offer-a-preview-of-larger-labor-proposals.

———. "D.C. Statehood Is a Test of Biden's Political Courage." *The New Republic,* June 26, 2020. newrepublic.com/article/158312/joe-biden-dc-statehood-2020.

———. "Democracy's Moment of Reckoning." *The New Republic,* May 13, 2021. newrepublic.com/article/162272/republican-voter-suppression-texas-democracy-reckoning.

———. "If Jeff Bezos Makes Washington the Second Headquarters of Amazon." *The New Yorker,* November 3, 2018. newyorker.com/news/news-desk/if-jeff-bezos-makes-washington-the-second-headquarters-of-amazon.

———. "Infrastructure Spending Can Save Local Journalism." *The New Republic,* April 8, 2021. newrepublic.com/article/161976/infrastructure-democrats-save-local-journalism.

———. "Joe Manchin Wants to Pass a Popular Gun Control Bill That Will Save Lives, but He Loves the Filibuster More." *The New Republic,* March 5, 2021. newrepublic.com/article/161605/manchin-gun-background-checks-filibuster.

———. "Maybe Making Election Day a National Holiday Wouldn't Really Work." *Slate,* November 3, 2016. slate.com/news-and-politics/2016/11/an-election-day-holiday-might-not-increase-turnout-studies-demonstrate.html.

———. "Murder the Filibuster and Never Look Back." *The New Republic,* January 19, 2021. newrepublic.com/article/160946/biden-democrats-filibuster-nuclear-option.

———. "Musk's Rampage through Government Shows Us How We Can Finally Close the Book on What Trumpism Is All about." The Guardian, February 18, 2025. theguardian.com/commentisfree/2025/feb/18/musks-rampage-through-government-shows-us-how-we-can-finally-close-the-book-on-what-trumpism-is-all-about.

———. "The Case for Giving Workers Ownership Rights." *The New Republic,* December 22, 2020. newrepublic.com/article/160528/workplace-democracy-pandemic-economic-crisis.

———. "The Corporations Funding the End of Democracy." *The New Republic,* January 6, 2021. newrepublic.com/article/160800/corporate-money-trump-gop-coup.

———. "The Democratic Party Has a Fatal Misunderstanding of the QAnon Phenomenon." *The New Republic,* February 5, 2021. newrepublic.com/article/161266/qanon-classism-marjorie-taylor-greene.

———. "The Ridiculous War-Gaming of the 2020 Election." *The New Republic,* September 14, 2020. newrepublic.com/article/159352/wargaming-2020-election-trump-biden.

———. "The Right to Run." *Slate,* October 22, 2014. slate.com/news-and-politics/2014/10/age-of-candidacy-laws-should-be-abolished-why-18-year-olds-should-be-able-to-run-for-public-office.html.

———. "The Vexing Question of Puerto Rican Statehood." *The New Republic,* April 30, 2021. newrepublic.com/article/162222/puerto-rico-statehood-velasquez-aoc.

———. "The Willful Blindness of Reactionary Liberalism." *The New Republic,* July 6, 2020. newrepublic.com/article/158346/willful-blindness-reactionary-liberalism.

———. "Trump Isn't the Only One to Blame for the Capitol Riot." *The New York Times,* January 4, 2022, sec. Opinion. nytimes.com/2022/01/04/opinion/capitol-riot.html.

Oakes, John B. "Conscience of the Nation." *The New York Times,* November 11, 1975.

Ober, Josiah. *The Rise and Fall of Classical Greece.* Princeton University Press, 2016.

O'Connell, Jonathan. "Amazon Receives 238 Proposals for Second Headquarters." *The Washington Post,* October 23, 2017. washingtonpost.com/news/business/wp/2017/10/23/amazon-receives-238-proposals-for-second-headquarters/.

O'Donovan, Caroline, and Leticia Miranda. "New York City Offered Amazon More Than $1.5 Billion in Incentives for HQ2." BuzzFeed News, November 13, 2018. buzzfeednews.com/article/leticiamiranda/amazon-second-headquarters-new-york-arlington.

Okwerekwu, Jennifer A., James B. McKenzie, Katherine A. Yates, Renee M. Sorrentino, and Susan Hatters Friedman. "Voting by People with Mental Illness." *Journal of the American Academy of Psychiatry and the Law Online,* October 31, 2018, JAAPL.003780-18. doi.org/10.29158/JAAPL.003780-18.

Ongweso, Edward. "Amazon Calls Warehouse Workers 'Industrial Athletes' in Leaked Wellness Pamphlet," June 1, 2021. vice.com/en/article/epnvp7/amazon-calls-warehouse-workers-industrial-athletes-in-leaked-wellness-pamphlet.

Oppenheimer, Danny, and Mike Edwards. *Democracy Despite Itself: Why a System That Shouldn't Work at All Works so Well.* MIT Press, 2012.

Orth, Taylor. "Three-Quarters of Americans Think the Federal Minimum Wage Is Too Low," December 1, 2022. today.yougov.com/topics/politics/articles-reports/2022/12/01/most-americans-think-minimum-wage-is-too-low.

Orts, Eric W. "The Path to Give California 12 Senators, and Vermont Just One." *The Atlantic,* January 2, 2019. theatlantic.com/ideas/archive/2019/01/heres-how-fix-senate/579172/.

O'Shea, Tom. "In the Interests of All." *Aeon,* October 2, 2023. aeon.co/essays/for-socialism-and-freedom-the-life-of-eugene-debs.

———. "Radical Republicanism and the Future of Work." *Theory & Event* 24, no. 4 (2021): 1050–67. doi.org/10.1353/tae.2021.0058.

———. "Wage Slavery: A Neo-Roman Account." *European Journal of Political Theory,* October 17, 2024, 14748851241289254. doi.org/10.1177/14748851241289254.

———. "What Is Economic Liberty?" *Philosophical Topics* 48, no. 2 (2020): 203–22.

"Our Common Purpose: Reinventing American Democracy for the 21st Century." American Academy of Arts and Sciences, 2020. amacad.org/ourcommonpurpose/report.

Ovetz, Robert. *We the Elites: Why the US Constitution Serves the Few.* 1st ed. Pluto Press, 2022.

Oyez. "*Reynolds v. Sims.*" Accessed January 24, 2023. oyez.org/cases/1963/23.

"Pack the Union: A Proposal to Admit New States for the Purpose of Amending the Constitution to Ensure Equal Representation." *Harvard Law Review* 133, no. 3 (January 2020): 1049–70.

Page, Benjamin I., and Martin Gilens. *Democracy in America? What Has Gone*

Wrong and What We Can Do About It: With a New Afterword. The University of Chicago Press, 2020.

Paine, Thomas. *Common Sense.* In *Collected Writings.* The Library of America. 1776. Reprint, Library of America, 2009.

———. *Rights of Man.* In *Collected Writings.* The Library of America. 1776. Reprint, Library of America, 2009.

Palder, Darcy. "America's Unique Kind of Disenfranchisement." *Foreign Policy* (blog), November 5, 2020. foreignpolicy.com/2020/11/05/america-ex-felon-disenfranchisement-democracies.

Palladino, Lenore. "Economic Democracy at Work: Why (and How) Workers Should Be Represented on US Corporate Boards." In *Democratizing the Corporation: The Bicameral Firm and Beyond,* edited by Isabelle Ferreras, Tom Malleson, and Joel Rogers. The Real Utopias Project. Verso, 2024.

———. "The Potential Benefits of Employee Equity Funds in the United States." *Journal of Participation and Employee Ownership* 5, no. 1 (May 31, 2022): 56–78. doi.org/10.1108/JPEO-08-2020-0023.

Panetta, Grace, and Brent D. Griffiths. "Republicans' Next Big Play Is to 'Scare the Hell out of Washington' by Rewriting the Constitution. And They're Willing to Play the Long Game to Win." Business Insider, July 31, 2022. businessinsider.com/constitutional-convention-conservatives-republicans-constitution-supreme-court-2022-7.

Pareene, Alex. "Abolish States." Substack newsletter. *The AP (Alex Pareene) Newsletter* (blog), February 5, 2022. theap.substack.com/p/abolish-states.

Parker, Ashley, and Philip Rucker. "Trump Taps Kushner to Lead a SWAT Team to Fix Government with Business Ideas." *Washington Post,* March 6, 2017. washingtonpost.com/politics/trump-taps-kushner-to-lead-a-swat-team-to-fix-government-with-business-ideas/2017/03/26/9714a8b6-1254-11e7-ada0-1489b735b3a3_story.html.

Pateman, Carole. "Participatory Democracy Revisited." *Perspectives on Politics* 10, no. 1 (2012).

Paxton, Marie. *Agonistic Democracy: Rethinking Political Institutions in Pluralist Times.* Routledge Advances in Democratic Theory 11. Routledge, 2021.

Pek, Simon. "Learning from Cooperatives to Strengthen Economic Bicameralism." In *Democratizing the Corporation: The Bicameral Firm and Beyond,* edited by Isabelle Ferreras, Tom Malleson, and Joel Rogers. The Real Utopias Project. Verso, 2024.

Perry, Andre M., Hannah Stephens, and Manann Donoghoe. "Black Wealth Is Increasing, but so Is the Racial Wealth Gap." Brookings, January 9, 2024. brookings.edu/articles/black-wealth-is-increasing-but-so-is-the-racial-wealth-gap.

Peters, Cameron. "Bernie Sanders Just Made the Progressive Case for Joe Biden." *Vox,* August 18, 2020. vox.com/2020/8/18/21373190/bernie-sanders-progressive-case-for-joe-biden-democratic-national-convention-transcript.

Pettit, Philip. *On the People's Terms: A Republican Theory and Model of Democracy.* Cambridge University Press, 2012.

Phelps, Hailey. "When Interstates Paved the Way." *Econ Focus,* no. Second/Third Quarter (2021). richmondfed.org/publications/research/econ_focus/2021/ q2-3/economic_history.

Phillips, Matt. "The Rich Now Own a Record Share of Stocks." *Axios,* January 10, 2024. axios.com/2024/01/10/wealthy-own-record-share-stock-marke .

Picchi, Aimee. "Union: Walmart Shut 5 Stores over Labor Activism." CBS, n.d. cbsnews.com/news/union-walmart-shut-5-stores-over-labor-activism/.

Piccone, Ted. "Democracy and Civil War." Democracy and Security Dialogue Policy Brief Series. The Brookings Institution, September 2017. brookings .edu/research/democracy-and-civil-war.

———. "Democracy and Violent Crime." Democracy and Security Dialogue Policy Brief Series. The Brookings Institution, September 2017. brookings .edu/research/democracy-and-violent-crime-2.

Pierce, Olga, Justin Elliott, and Theodoric Meyer. "How Dark Money Helped Republicans Hold the House and Hurt Voters." ProPublica, December 2 , 2012. propublica.org/article/how-dark-money-helped-republicans-hold-the -house-and-hurt-voters.

Pitkin, Hanna Fenichel. *The Concept of Representation.* University of California Press, 1972.

Plato. *The Republic of Plato.* Translated by Francis MacDonald Cornford. Oxford University Press, 1941.

"Political Independents: Who They Are, What They Think." Pew Research Center, March 2019. pewresearch.org/politics/2019/03/14/political-independents -who-they-are-what-they-think.

Politico. "Corporations Gave $10M to Election Objectors after Pledging to Cut Them Off," January 6, 2023. politico.com/news/2023/01/06/corporations -election-objectors-donations-00076668.

Poloni-Staudinger, Lori, and Michael R. Wolf. *American Difference: A Guide to American Politics in Comparative Perspective.* Second Edition. CQ Press, an imprint of SAGE Publications, Inc, 2020.

"Population, Total | Data." World Bank. Data Bank. Accessed January 20, 2023. data .worldbank.org/indicator/SP.POP.TOTL?most_recent_value_desc=true.

Porter, Eduardo. "Should the Feds Guarantee You a Job?" *The New York Times,* February 18, 2021, sec. Business. nytimes.com/2021/02/18/business/ economy/job-guarantee.html.

"Potential Years of Life Lost." OECD Data. Organisation for Economic Co-operation and Development, 2024. data.oecd.org/healthstat/potential-years -of-life-lost.htm#indicator-chart.

Potts, Monica. "Turnout Was High Again. Is This The New Normal?" *FiveThirty Eight* (blog), November 15, 2022. fivethirtyeight.com/features/turnout -was-high-again-is-this-the-new-normal.

"Poverty Rate." OECD Data. Organisation for Economic Co-operation and Development, 2024. data.oecd.org/inequality/poverty-rate.htm#indicator-chart.

Press, Alex N. "The Teamsters Organized Some Amazon Delivery Workers. What Happens Next Is Complicated." *Jacobin,* April 28, 2023. jacobin .com/2023/04/amazon-teamsters-delivery-workers-union-organizing-dfs -bts-dax8.

Frice, Steven D. *Endangered Phrases: Intriguing Idioms Dangerously Close to Extinction.* Skyhorse Publishing, 2011.

Friest, Maura. "Why Children Should Be Allowed to Vote." *Public Affairs Quarterly* 30, no. 3 (2016): 215–38.

"Primed for Pain: Amazon's Epidemic of Workplace Injuries." Strategic Organizing Center, May 2021. thesoc.org/wp-content/uploads/2021/02/PrimedForPain.pdf.

Princeton University Alumni. "James Madison Medal." Accessed December 26, 2022. alumni.princeton.edu/our-community/awards/james-madison-medal.

Prokop, Andrew. "Sotomayor: Supreme Court Racial Gerrymandering Ruling Comes at 'Serious Costs to Our Democracy.'" *Vox,* June 25, 2018. vox.com/policy-and-politics/2018/6/25/17500918/supreme-court-texas-gerrymandering-abbott-v-perez.

———. "The Supreme Court Just Said Federal Courts Can't Stop Partisan Gerrymandering." *Vox,* June 27, 2019. vox.com/policy-and-politics/2019/6/27/18681923/supreme-court-gerrymandering-partisan-rucho-common-cause.

———. "Why Some Democrats Are Quietly Unhappy with the House's Big Voting Rights Bill." *Vox,* April 5, 2021. vox.com/22346812/voting-rights-bill-hr1-for-the-people-act.

Quackenbush, Casey. "A Tea-Party Veteran Has a Plan to Upend the Constitution." Intelligencer, June 13, 2023. nymag.com/intelligencer/2023/06/the-dark-money-behind-mark-mecklers-convention-of-states.html.

Quote Investigator. "Dialogue Origin: 'What Do You Think of Western Civilization?' 'I Think It Would Be a Good Idea,'" April 23, 2013. quoteinvestigator.com/2013/04/23/good-idea.

Rahman, K. Sabeel. *Democracy Against Domination.* Oxford University Press, 2017.

Rahman, K. Sabeel, and Kathleen Thelen. "The Role of the Law in the American Political Economy." In *The American Political Economy: Politics, Markets, and Power,* edited by Alexander Hertel-Fernandez, Jacob S. Hacker, Kathleen Thelen, and Paul Pierson, 76–102. Cambridge Studies in Comparative Politics. Cambridge University Press, 2021. doi.org/10.1017/9781009029841.003.

Rana, Aziz. *The Constitutional Bind: How Americans Came to Idolize a Document That Fails Them.* 1st ed. University of Chicago Press, 2024.

Reed, Lawrence W. "Why the Polish-Lithuanian Commonwealth's Legacy of Liberty Is Worthy of Our Appreciation Today." *Foundation for Economic Education* (blog), October 7, 2020. fee.org/articles/why-the-polish-lithuanian-commonwealth-s-legacy-of-liberty-is-worthy-of-our-appreciation-today.

Reinhart, RJ. "Faith in Elections in Relatively Short Supply in U.S." Gallup, February 13, 2020. news.gallup.com/poll/285608/faith-elections-relatively-short-supply.aspx.

Reiss, Julian. "Expertise, Agreement, and the Nature of Social Scientific Facts or: Against Epistocracy." *Social Epistemology* 33, no. 2 (March 4, 2019): 183–92. doi.org/10.1080/02691728.2019.1577513.

"Republic." In *Merriam-Webster*. Accessed October 15, 2022. merriam-webster
.com/dictionary/republic.

Repucci, Sarah, and Amy Slipowitz. "Freedom in the World 2022: The Global
Expansion of Authoritarian Rule." Freedom House, 2022. freedomhouse
.org/report/freedom-world/2022/global-expansion-authoritarian-rule.

Reston, James. "Dangers of Pessimism." *The New York Times,* April 2, 1975.
nytimes.com/1975/04/02/archives/dangers-of-pessimism-washington
.html.

Reuters. "Corporate America Pledges Donations for Trump's Inauguration."
December 17, 2024, sec. United States. reuters.com/world/us/corporate
-america-pledges-donations-trump-inauguration-2024-12-17.

Reuters. "The Republicans Who Voted to Overturn the Election." February 4,
2021. reuters.com/graphics/USA-TRUMP/LAWMAKERS/xegpbedzdvq.

Rhinehart, Lynn, and Celine McNicholas. "Shortchanged—Weak Anti-
Retaliation Provisions in the National Labor Relations Act Cost Workers
Billions." Economic Policy Institute, April 22, 2021. epi.org/publication/
shortchanged-weak-anti-retaliation-provisions-in-the-national-labor
-relations-act-cost-workers-billions.

Riccardi, Nicholas, and Linley Sanders. "Americans Are Widely Pessimistic
About Democracy in the United States, an AP-NORC Poll Finds." Associated Press, July 14, 2023. apnews.com/article/poll-democracy-partisanship
-trump-biden-trust-221f2b4f6cf9805f766c9a8395b9539d.

Riccardi, Nicholas, and Thomas Beaumont. "Democrats' Win in Wisconsin
Court Race Also Is a Big Loss for Elon Musk." Associated Press, April 2,
2025. apnews.com/article/wisconsin-supreme-court-elon-musk-81f71cdda
271827ae281a77072a26bad.

Richardson, Heather Cox. "When Adding New States Helped the Republicans."
The Atlantic, September 19, 2019. theatlantic.com/ideas/archive/2019/09/
when-adding-new-states-helped-republicans/598243.

Riker, William H. *Liberalism Against Populism: A Confrontation Between the
Theory of Democracy and the Theory of Social Choice.* Waveland Press,
1982.

Roberts, Siobhan. "Mathematicians Are Deploying Algorithms to Stop Gerrymandering." *MIT Technology Review*. Accessed March 4, 2023. technology
review.com/2021/08/12/1031567/mathematicians-algorithms-stop
-gerrymandering.

Robinhood. "About Us." Accessed December 25, 2024. robinhood.com/us/en/
about/legal.

Rogers, Brishen. "Libertarian Corporatism Is Not an Oxymoron" 94, no. 7
(June 14, 2016). texaslawreview.org/libertarian-corporatism-is-not-an
-oxymoron.

Romano, Aja. "'Protect RBG' Memes Capture Cultural Anxiety over the
Supreme Court." *Vox,* November 8, 2018. vox.com/culture/2018/11/8/
18075770/ruth-bader-ginsburg-memes-hospitalization-notorious-rbg.

Romeo, Nick. "How Mondragon Became the World's Largest Co-Op." *The
New Yorker,* August 27, 2022. newyorker.com/business/currency/how
-mondragon-became-the-worlds-largest-co-op.

Romero, Paul D., and Julie M. Whittaker. "A Brief Examination of Union Membership Data." Congressional Research Service, June 16, 2023. sgp.fas.org/crs/misc/R47596.pdf.

Roof, Tracy. *American Labor, Congress, and the Welfare State, 1935-2010.* Johns Hopkins University Press, 2011.

Roosevelt, Franklin Delano. "Fireside Chat," September 6, 1936. presidency.ucsb.edu/documents/fireside-chat-18.

Roosevelt, Theodore. "Special Message," January 1, 1909. The American Presidency Project. presidency.ucsb.edu/documents/special-message-368.

Rorty, Richard. *Achieving Our Country: Leftist Thought in Twentieth-Century America.* The William E. Massey Sr. Lectures in the History of American Civilization 1997. Harvard University Press, 2001.

Rose, Joel. "Despite Concerns About Border, Poll Finds Support for More Pathways to Citizenship." NPR, May 20, 2021, sec. National. npr.org/2021/05/20/998248764/despite-concerns-about-border-poll-finds-support-for-more-pathways-to-citizenshi.

Rosenfeld, Jake, Patrick Denice, and Jennifer Laird. "Union Decline Lowers Wages of Nonunion Workers," August 30, 2016. epi.org/publication/union-decline-lowers-wages-of-nonunion-workers-the-overlooked-reason-why-wages-are-stuck-and-inequality-is-growing.

Rothwell, Jonathan, and Steve Crabtree. "Not Just a Job: New Evidence on the Quality of Work in the United States." Gallup, 2019. luminafoundation.org/wp-content/uploads/2019/11/not-just-a-job-new-evidence-on-the-quality-of-work-in-the-united-states.pdf.

Rousseau, Jean-Jacques. "The Social Contract." In *The Social Contract and Other Later Political Writings,* edited by Victor Gourevitch. 1762. Reprint, Cambridge University Press, 1997.

Royden, Laura, and Michael Li. "Extreme Maps." Brennan Center for Justice, May 9, 2017. brennancenter.org/our-work/research-reports/extreme-maps.

Rubenstein, Dana. "Ocasio-Cortez Takes on the Amazon Fight in New York." *Politico,* November 22, 2018. politico.com/story/2018/11/22/amazon-hq-2-new-york-alexandria-ocasio-cortez-1012546.

Rubin, April. "Trump Set to Be the First Republican Candidate to Win the Popular Vote in 20 Years." *Axios,* November 6, 2024. axios.com/2024/11/06/trump-popular-vote-republican-candidates.

Rubin, Jennifer. "A 'Republic If We Can Keep It.' Perhaps We Cannot." *The Washington Post,* November 6, 2024. washingtonpost.com/opinions/2024/11/06/trump-election-americans-blame-democracy/.

Rush, Benjamin. " 'Address to the People of the United States.' " In *Friends of the Constitution: Writings of the "Other" Federalists, 1787–1788,* edited by Colleen A. Sheehan and Gary L. McDowell, 1998. oll.libertyfund.org/title/mcdowell-friends-of-the-constitution-writings-of-the-other-federalists-1787-1788.

Russell, Kyle. "Stepping Into the NFT Frontier: Where Creativity Meets Innovation." *Milwaukee Journal Sentinel,* March 28, 2024. jsonline.com/story/

special/contributor-content/2024/03/28/stepping-into-the-nft-frontier
-where-creativity-meets-innovation/73130926007.

Sabl, Andrew. "The Two Cultures of Democratic Theory: Responsiveness, Democratic Quality, and the Empirical-Normative Divide." In *Reclaiming
Representation: Contemporary Advances in the Theory of Political Representation,* edited by Mónica Brito Vieira. Routledge, 2017.

Saenz, Arlette. "Joe Biden Announces He Is Running for President in 2020 "
CNN, April 25, 2019. cnn.com/2019/04/25/politics/joe-biden-2020-president/
index.html.

Sainato, Michael. "Accidents at Amazon: Workers Left to Suffer after Warehouse
Injuries." *The Guardian,* July 30, 2018. theguardian.com/technology/2018/
jul/30/accidents-at-amazon-workers-left-to-suffer-after-warehouse
-injuries.

———. "Doge's Attack on Social Security Causing 'Complete, Utter Chaos', Staff
Says." *The Guardian,* April 6, 2025. theguardian.com/us-news/2025/apr/
06/musk-doge-social-security.

———. "Revealed: Amazon Employees Are Left to Suffer after Workplace Injuries." *The Guardian,* April 2, 2019. theguardian.com/technology/2019/apr/
02/revealed-amazon-employees-suffer-after-workplace-injuries.

———. " 'They Are Breaking the Law': Inside Amazon's Bid to Stall a Union
Drive." *The Guardian,* April 3, 2024. theguardian.com/technology/2024/
apr/03/amazon-union-warehouse-california.

———. " 'They're More Concerned About Profit': Osha, DoJ Take on Amazon's
Grueling Working Conditions." *The Guardian,* n.d. theguardian.com/
technology/2023/mar/02/amazon-safety-citations-osha-department-of
-justice.

Sally Yates Speaks at 2020 DNC. ABC News, n.d. youtube.com/watch?v=3e
-Wkg9dZDk.

Salzer, Rebecca, and Jocelyn Kiley. "Majority of Americans Continue to Favor
Moving Away from Electoral College." *Pew Research Center* (blog). Accessed March 10, 2023. pewresearch.org/fact-tank/2022/08/05/majority-of
-americans-continue-to-favor-moving-away-from-electoral-college/.

Sanders, Bernie. *It's OK to Be Angry About Capitalism.* Edited by John Nichols.
First edition. Crown, 2023.

Sang-Hun, Choe. "The Impeachment of South Korea's President, Explained." *The
New York Times,* December 14, 2024. nytimes.com/2024/12/14/world/
asia/south-korea-impeachment-yoon-explained.html.

Sargent, Greg. "The Campaign for D.C. Statehood Just Got a Big Boost." *The
Washington Post,* May 24, 2021. washingtonpost.com/opinions/2021/05/
24/dc-statehood-constitutional-letter.

Saward, Michael. "Democracy and Citizenship: Expanding Domains." In *The
Oxford Handbook of Political Theory,* edited by John S. Dryzek, Bonnie
Honig, and Anne Phillips. Oxford University Press, 2009.

Scheiber, Noam. "Amazon Argues Labor Board Is Unconstitutional." *The
New York Times,* February 15, 2024. nytimes.com/2024/02/15/business/
economy/amazon-labor-nlrb.html.

——. "Amazon Is Cracking Down on Union Organizing, Workers Say." *The New York Times,* December 8, 2023. nytimes.com/2023/12/08/business/economy/amazon-union-workers.html.

Schickler, Eric. *Racial Realignment: The Transformation of American Liberalism, 1932–1965.* Princeton Studies in American Politics: Historical, International, and Comparative Perspectives. Princeton University Press, 2016.

Schlozman, Kay Lehman, Sidney Verba, and Henry E. Brady. *The Unheavenly Chorus: Unequal Political Voice and the Broken Promise of American Democracy.* Second printing, and First paperback printing. Princeton University Press, 2013.

——. *Unequal and Unrepresented: Political Inequality and the People's Voice in the New Gilded Age.* Princeton University Press, 2018.

Schneider, Howard, and Chris Kahn. "Majority of Americans Favor Wealth Tax on Very Rich: Reuters/Ipsos Poll." *Reuters,* January 10, 2020, sec. reboot-live. reuters.com/article/us-usa-election-inequality-poll-idUSKBN1Z9141.

Schott, Bryan. "Jan. 6 Report Sheds New Details About Sen. Mike Lee's Efforts to Help Trump Overturn 2020 Election." *The Salt Lake Tribune,* December 23, 2022. sltrib.com/news/politics/2022/12/23/jan-6-report-sheds-new-details/.

Schouten, Fredreka, David Wright, and Alex Leeds Matthews. "Musk Spent More than a Quarter-Billion Dollars to Elect Trump, Including Funding a Mysterious Super PAC, New Filings Show." CNN, December 6, 2024. cnn.com/2024/12/05/politics/elon-musk-trump-campaign-finance-filings/index.html.

Schulte, Gabriela. "Poll: 79 Percent Support Federal Jobs Program for the Unemployed." *The Hill,* July 10, 2020. thehill.com/hilltv/what-americas-thinking/506777-poll-79-support-federal-jobs-program-for-the-unemployed/.

Schumacher, Shannon, and Aidan Connaughton. "From Voter Registration to Mail-in Ballots, How Do Countries around the World Run Their Elections?" *Pew Research Center* (blog). Accessed February 12, 2023. pewresearch.org/fact-tank/2020/10/30/from-voter-registration-to-mail-in-ballots-how-do-countries-around-the-world-run-their-elections.

Schumpeter, Joseph A. *Capitalism, Socialism and Democracy.* Routledge, 2005.

Schweickart, David. *After Capitalism.* 2. ed. New Critical Theory. Rowman & Littlefield, 2011.

Scott, Dylan. "9 Questions About Budget Reconciliation You Were Too Afraid to Ask." *Vox,* January 25, 2021. vox.com/22242476/senate-filibuster-budget-reconciliation-process.

Seifter, Miriam. "Countermajoritarian Legislatures." *Columbia Law Review* 121, no. 6 (2021): 1733–1800.

"75 Years of the GI Bill: How Transformative It's Been." U.S. Department of Defense, January 19, 2019. defense.gov/News/Feature-Stories/Story/article/1727086/75-years-of-the-gi-bill-how-transformative-its-been/.

Shabo, Vicki. "Explainer: Paid and Unpaid Leave Policies in the United States,"

May 3, 2024. newamerica.org/better-life-lab/briefs/explainer-paid-and-unpaid
-leave-policies-in-the-united-states.

Shah, Seema, and Alexander Hudson. "The Global State of Democracy 2024."
Global State of Democracy Inititative. International Institute for Democracy and Electoral Assistance, 2024. sveltekit-prerender/gsod/2024.

Shapiro, Ian, ed. *The Real World of Democratic Theory*. Princeton University
Press, 2011.

——. *The State of Democratic Theory*. Princeton University Press, 2003.

Shepherd, Tyler. "First Class Service, First Class Results: The Premium Exper-
ence of Amazon Automation." *USA Today*, December 11, 2024. usatoday
.com/story/special/contributor-content/2024/12/11/first-class-service
-first-class-results-the-premium-experience-of-amazon-automation/
76920874007.

Shimabukuro, Jon O., and Gerald Mayer. "The National Labor Relations Act
(NLRA): Union Representation Procedures and Dispute Resolution."
Congressional Research Service, December 11, 2013. crsreports.congress
.gov/product/pdf/RL/RL32930/37.

Shimabukuro, Jon O., and Julie M. Whittaker. "Federal Labor Relations Statutes:
An Overview." Congressional Research Service, September 5, 2014.

Shine, Tom. "47% of Congress Members Millionaires—a Status Shared by Only
1% of Americans." ABC News. Accessed February 14, 2023. abcnews.go
.com/blogs/politics/2011/11/47-of-congress-members-millionaires
-a-status-shared-by-only-1-of-americans.

Shrider, Emily A., and John Creamer. "Poverty in the United States: 2022."
United States Census Bureau, September 12, 2023. census.gov/library/
publications/2023/demo/p60-280.html.

Singer, Natasha. "The Democratization of Plastic Surgery." *The New York Times*,
August 17, 2007. nytimes.com/2007/08/17/business/worldbusiness/17int
-surgery.4.7159164.html?searchResultPosition=20.

Skelley, Geoffrey. "Few Americans Who Identify As Independent Are Actually Independent. That's Really Bad for Politics." *FiveThirtyEight* (blog),
April 15, 2021. fivethirtyeight.com/features/few-americans-who
-identify-as-independent-are-actually-independent-thats-really-bad
-for-politics.

——. "How the House Got Stuck at 435 Seats." *FiveThirtyEight*, August 12,
2021. fivethirtyeight.com/features/how-the-house-got-stuck-at-435-seats".

Skinner, Quentin. "Classical Liberty and the Coming of the English Civil War."
In *Republicanism: A Shared European Heritage*, 10. Cambridge University
Press, 2002.

Smith, Carl. "Can New Technology Tools Keep Redistricting Honest and Fair."
Governing, September 16, 2021. governing.com/now/can-new-technology
-tools-keep-redistricting-honest-and-fair.

Solitro, Joey. "Amazon Eyes $2 Trillion Market Cap as CEO Talks AI, Cost
Cuts." *Kiplinger's Personal Finance*, April 11, 2024. kiplinger.com/investing/
stocks/amazon-eyes-dollar2-trillion-market-cap-as-ceo-talks-ai-cost-cuts.

Somin, Ilya. *Democracy and Political Ignorance: Why Smaller Government Is*

Smarter. 2nd ed. Stanford Law Books, an imprint of Stanford University Press, 2016.

Soon, Valerie. "Review of 'Against Democracy.'" *Essays in Philosophy* 19, no. 1 (2018): 1603. doi.org/10.7710/1526-0569.1603.

"Speech to the House of Commons." United Kingdom: Hansard Parliamentary Debates, November 11, 1947. hansard.parliament.uk/commons/1947-11 -11/debates/ab1e1152-6b4a-4d04-ac38-954df6634b08/ParliamentBill #206.

Stancil, Kenny. "80% of US Voters Want Congress to Enact National Paid Family Leave: Poll." *Common Dreams,* September 23, 2022. commondreams.org/ news/2022/09/23/80-us-voters-want-congress-enact-national-paid-family -leave-poll.

"State Population Totals and Components of Change: 2020-2022." United States Census Bureau. Accessed February 7, 2023. census.gov/data/tables/time -series/demo/popest/2020s-state-total.html.

"Statement and Return Report for Certification: General Election 2024." New York City Board of Elections, December 3, 2024. vote.nyc/page/election -results-summary-2024.

"Statewide Results." South Dakota Secretary of State. Accessed April 21, 2025. electionresults.sd.gov/resultsSW.aspx?type=SWR&map=CTY.

"Statewide Results." North Dakota Secretary of State. Accessed April 21, 2025. results.sos.nd.gov/ResultsSW.aspx?text=All&type=SW&map=CTY.

Steckelberg, Aaron, and Chiqui Esteban. "Over 4 Million Americans Don't Have Anyone to Vote for Them in Congress." *The Washington Post,* September 28, 2017. washingtonpost.com/graphics/2017/national/fair -representation.

Stevens, Laura. "Amazon to Raise Its Minimum U.S. Wage to $15 an Hour." *The Wall Street Journal,* October 2, 2018. wsj.com/articles/amazon-to-raise-its -minimum-u-s-wage-to-15-an-hour-1538476027.

Stock Analysis. "Biggest U.S. Employers." n.d. stockanalysis.com/list/most -employees.

Stonberg, Stephen. "Cryptocurrencies Are Democratizing the Financial World. Here's How." World Economic Forum, January 22, 2021. weforum.org/ stories/2021/01/cryptocurrencies-are-democratising-the-financial-world -heres-how.

Stone, Peter. "Elon Musk's Conflicts of Interest 'Should Scare Every American', Experts Say." *The Guardian,* February 27, 2025. theguardian.com/us-news/ 2025/feb/27/elon-musk-conflicts-of-interest.

Strine, Leo E., Jr., Aneil Kovvali, and Oluwatomi O. Williams. "Lifting Labor's Voice: A Principled Path Toward Greater Worker Voice and Power Within American Corporate Governance." *Faculty Scholarship at Penn Carey Law,* February 24, 2021. scholarship.law.upenn.edu/faculty_scholarship/ 2256.

Stuessy, Meghan M. "Regular Vetoes and Pocket Vetoes: In Brief." Congressional Research Service, August 2, 2016.

Sultan, Niv M. "Election 2016: Trump's Free Media Helped Keep Cost Down."

OpenSecrets, April 13, 2017. opensecrets.org/news/2017/04/election-2015 -trump-fewer-donors-provided-more-of-the-cash.

Svirnovskiy, Gregory. "Paid Leave Is Incredibly Popular—Even with Republicans." *Vox,* June 7, 2021. vox.com/2021/6/7/22380427/poll-paid-leave -popular-democrats-republicans-covid-19.

Tankersley, Jim. "The Real Reason the American Economy Boomed After World War II." *The New York Times,* August 6, 2020. nytimes.com/2020/08/06/ sunday-review/middle-class-prosperity.html.

Taylor, Alan. *American Revolutions: A Continental History, 1750–1804.* First published as a Norton paperback. W. W. Norton & Company, 2017.

Taylor, Astra. *Democracy May Not Exist, but We'll Miss It When It's Gone.* Metropolitan Books, 2019.

Taylor, Steven L., Matthew Soberg Shugart, Arend Lijphart, and Bernard Grofman. *A Different Democracy: American Government in a Thirty-One-Country Perspective.* Yale University Press, 2014.

Tharoor, Ishaan. "Other Countries Use Ranked-Choice Voting. Has Its Moment in the U.S. Arrived?" *Washington Post,* June 23, 2021. washingtonpost .com/world/2021/06/23/ranked-choice-voting-global.

"The 2019 State of the First Amendment." Freedom Forum Institute, 2019. freedomforuminstitute.org/wp-content/uploads/2019/06/SOFArepot 2019.pdf.

The Annenberg Public Policy Center of the University of Pennsylvania. "Americans' Civics Knowledge Increases During a Stress-Filled Year" September 14, 2021. annenbergpublicpolicycenter.org/2021-annenberg -constitution-day-civics-survey.

The Constitution of Sweden: The Fundamental Laws and the Riksdag Act. The Riksdag Administration, n.d.

"The Distribution of Household Income, 2019." Congressional Budget Office, November 2022. cbo.gov/publication/58781.

The Global Social Mobility Report 2020: Equality, Opportunity and a New Economic Imperative. Cologny/Geneva, Switzerland: World Economic Forum, 2020.

"The Impact of Voter Suppression on Communities of Color." Brennan Center for Justice, January 10, 2022. brennancenter.org/our-work/research -reports/impact-voter-suppression-communities-color.

The New York Times. "Elect Joe Biden, America." October 6, 2020. nytimes .com/2020/10/06/opinion/joe-biden-2020-nytimes-endorsement.html.

The Washington Post. "Our Democracy in Peril." September 22, 2020. washington post.com/opinions/2020/08/21/our-democracy-in-peril-editorial-board -series.

The White House. "A Proclamation on Day of Remembrance: 10 Years After The 2012 Sandy Hook Elementary School Shooting," December 14, 2022. whitehouse.gov/briefing-room/presidential-actions/2022/12/14. a -proclamation-on-day-of-remembrance-10-years-after-the-2012-sandy -hook-elementary-school-shooting.

"The Workplace Democracy Plan." Friends of Bernie Sanders, n.d. berniesanders .com/issues/workplace-democracy.

"Third Episode about Mr. Isaac Woodard, Jr." *Orson Welles Commentaries*, August 11, 1946. Indiana University Libraries. orsonwelles.indiana.edu/items/show/2172.

Thomas, George. "'America Is a Republic, Not a Democracy' Is a Dangerous—and Wrong—Argument." *The Atlantic*, November 2, 2020. theatlantic.com/ideas/archive/2020/11/yes-constitution-democracy/616949.

Thucydides. *The Landmark Thucydides: A Comprehensive Guide to the Peloponnesian War.* Edited by Robert B. Strassler. Translated by Richard Crawley. Free Press, 2008.

Tocqueville, Alexis de. *Democracy in America.* Translated by Henry Reeve. Project Gutenberg, 1840.

Todd, Sarah. "Are Starbucks and Chipotle Union-Busting by Closing Stores?" *Quartz*, July 27, 2022. qz.com/2191767/are-starbucks-and-chipotle-union-busting-by-closing-stores.

Tomasky, Michael. "Can the Monster Be Elected?" *The New York Review of Books*, July 14, 2016. nybooks.com/articles/2016/07/14/can-the-monster-be-elected.

Totenberg, Nina. "The Landmark Voting Rights Act Faces Further Dismantling at the Supreme Court." NPR, October 4, 2022, sec. Law. npr.org/2022/10/04/1126619000/voting-rights-act-supreme-court.

Toussaint, Kristin. "For Years, the NLRB Has Been Too Toothless to Enforce Labor Laws. Is That Finally Changing?" *Fast Company*, April 12, 2024. fastcompany.com/91090679/nlrb-unfair-labor-practices-labor-laws.

Trickey, Erick. "Where Did the Term 'Gerrymander' Come From?" *Smithsonian Magazine*, June 20, 2017. smithsonianmag.com/history/where-did-term-gerrymander-come-180964118.

Tucker, Todd N. "Fixing the Senate: Equitable and Full Representation for the 21st Century." Roosevelt Institute, 2019. rooseveltinstitute.org/publications/fixing-the-senate-equitable-full-representation-21st-century.

Tumulty, Karen. "The Great Society at 50." *The Washington Post*, May 17, 2014. washingtonpost.com/wp-srv/special/national/great-society-at-50.

Tung, Irene, and Yannet Lathrop. "A Good Living: Amazon Can and Must Make a Middle-Income Livelihood Possible for the People Who Work in Its Warehouses." National Employment Law Project, September 26, 2023.

"2000 Election Results for President." Federal Election Commission. Accessed January 26, 2023. fec.gov/introduction-campaign-finance/election-and-voting-information/federal-elections-2000/president2000/.

"2020 General Election Official State Canvass Results." South Dakota Secretary of State, 2020. sdsos.gov/elections-voting/assets/2020GeneralStateCanvassFinal&Certificate.pdf.

"2021 State of the Sector Worker Cooperatives in the U.S." Democracy at Work Institute and the U.S. Federation of Worker Cooperatives, April 2022. democracy.institute.coop/2021-worker-cooperative-state-sector-report.

Uggen, Christopher, Ryan Larson, Sarah Shannon, and Robert Stewart. "Locked Out 2022: Estimates of People Denied Voting Rights." The Sentencing Project, October 26, 2022. sentencingproject.org/reports/locked-out-2022-estimates-of-people-denied-voting-rights.

Umbers, Lachlan Montgomery. "Democratic Legitimacy and the Competence Objection." *Res Publica* 25, no. 2 (May 2019): 283–93. doi.org/10.1007/s11158-018-9395-4.

"Unemployment Compensation: Federal-State Partnership." U.S. Department of Labor, May 2024. oui.doleta.gov/unemploy/pdf/partnership.pdf.

"Union Members—2023." Bureau of Labor Statistics, January 23, 2024. bls.gov/news.release/pdf/union2.pdf.

United States Census Bureau. "The District of Columbia Gained More Than 87,000 People in 10 Years." Accessed February 7, 2023. census.gov/library/stories/state-by-state/district-of-columbia-population-change-between-census-decade.html.

United States Senate. "Seven-Year Senate Terms?" Accessed December 30, 2022. senate.gov/artandhistory/history/minute/Seven_Year_Senate_Terms.htm.

United States Senate. "The Virginia Plan." Accessed December 26, 2022. senate.gov/civics/common/generic/Virginia_Plan_item.htm.

Urbinati, Nadia. "Democracy and Republicanism: A Difficult Partnership." In *Republicanism and the Future of Democracy,* edited by Geneviève Rousselière and Yiftah Elazar, 152–70. Cambridge University Press, 2019. doi.org/10.1017/9781108630153.009.

——. "The Democratic Tenor of Political Representation." In *Reclaiming Representation: Contemporary Advances in the Theory of Political Representation,* edited by Mónica Brito Vieira. Routledge, 2017.

"U.S. Census Bureau QuickFacts: California." U.S. Census Bureau. Accessed January 20, 2023. census.gov/quickfacts/CA.

"U.S. Census Bureau QuickFacts: Oklahoma City City, Oklahoma." Accessed January 24, 2023. census.gov/quickfacts/oklahomacitycityoklahoma.

"U.S. Census Bureau QuickFacts: Wyoming." U.S. Census Bureau. Accessed January 20, 2023. census.gov/quickfacts/WY.

Van Reybrouck, David. *Against Elections: The Case for Democracy.* Translated by Liz Waters. The Bodley Head, 2016.

Vanderbilt University. "Vanderbilt Unity Poll Explains Why Democracy May Take Center Stage in This Week's Presidential Debate—and the Campaign More Broadly," July 25, 2024. news.vanderbilt.edu/2024/06/25/vanderbilt-unity-poll-june-2024.

Vasilogambros, Matt. "The Messy Politics of Voter Purges." Stateline. Pew, October 25, 2019. pew.org/2Ndx2vh.

Vergara, Camila. *Systemic Corruption: Constitutional Ideas for an Anti-Oligarchic Republic.* Princeton University Press, 2020.

——. "Towards Material Anti-Oligarchic Constitutionalism." *Revus,* no. 46 (January 5, 2022). doi.org/10.4000/revus.8133.

Vieira, Mónica Brito. "Introduction." In *Reclaiming Representation: Contemporary Advances in the Theory of Political Representation,* edited by Mónica Brito Vieira. Routledge, 2017.

——. "Performative Imaginaries: Pitkin versus Hobbes on Political Representation." In *Reclaiming Representation: Contemporary Advances in the The-*

ory of Political Representation, edited by Mónica Brito Vieira. Routledge, 2017.

Waldron, Jeremy. "Democracy." In *The Oxford Handbook of Political Philosophy,* edited by David Estlund. Oxford University Press, 2012.

Walmart. "Location Facts," July 31, 2024. corporate.walmart.com/about/location -facts.

Walsh, Matt. "In Order to Save America, We Must Legally Prevent Oblivious People from Voting," March 8, 2016. theblaze.com/contributions/in -order-to-save-america-we-must-legally-prevent-oblivious-people-from -voting.

Warren, Mark E. "Democracy and the State." In *The Oxford Handbook of Political Theory,* edited by John S. Dryzek, Bonnie Honig, and Anne Phillips. Oxford University Press, 2009.

Warren, Mercy Otis. "Observations on the New Constitution, and on the Federal and State Conventions by a Columbian Patriot." In *Pamphlets on the Constitution of the United States 1787–1788,* edited by Paul Leicester Ford, 1888. oll.libertyfund.org/title/ramsay-pamphlets-on-the-constitution-of -the-united-states-1787-1788?html=true.

Watson, Betsy Cribb. "What Is a Tea Towel?" *Yahoo Life,* August 31, 2019. yahoo .com/lifestyle/tea-towel-201047008.html.

Webster, Noah. "Miscellaneous Remarks on Divizions of Property . . . in the United States." In *The Founders' Constitution,* edited by Philip B. Kurland and Ralph Lerner, 1986. press-pubs.uchicago.edu/founders/documents/ v1ch15s44.html.

Wegman, Jesse. "Will We Ever Amend the Constitution Again?" *The New York Times,* August 4, 2021. nytimes.com/2021/08/04/opinion/amend-constitution .html.

Weisman, Jonathan. "In Congress, Republicans Shrug at Warnings of Democracy in Peril." *The New York Times,* June 14, 2021, sec. U.S. nytimes.com/2021/ 06/14/us/politics/democracy-in-peril.html.

Westbrook, Robert B. *John Dewey and American Democracy.* N.Y.: Cornell University Press, 1991.

Western, Bruce, and Jake Rosenfeld. "Unions, Norms, and the Rise in U.S. Wage Inequality." *American Sociological Review* 76, no. 4 (August 2011): 513–37. doi.org/10.1177/0003122411414817.

Westneat, Danny. "The WA GOP Put It in Writing That They're Not into Democracy." *The Seattle Times,* April 24, 2024. seattletimes.com/seattle -news/politics/the-wa-gop-put-it-in-writing-that-theyre-not-into -democracy.

"What Percentage of Americans Own Stock?" Gallup, May 24, 2023. news.gallup .com/poll/266807/percentage-americans-owns-stock.aspx.

White, Marian. "Top 300 Largest Cities in the United States by Population 2022." Moving.com, July 26, 2022. moving.com/tips/largest-cities-in-us/.

Whitman, Walt. *Democratic Vistas, and Other Papers.* Fredonia Books, 2002.

Wiefek, Nancy, Corey Rosen, and Timothy Garbinsky. "Promoting Employee Ownership: A Look at the States." *Journal of Participation and Employee*

Ownership 2, no. 3 (December 9, 2019): 183–89. doi.org/10.1108/JPEO-09 -2019-0024.

Wike, Richard, and Janell Fetterolf. "Satisfaction with Democracy Has Declined in Recent Years in High-Income Nations." Pew Research Center, June 13, 2024. pewresearch.org/short-reads/2024/06/18/satisfaction-with-democracy -has-declined-in-recent-years-in-high-income-nations.

Wike, Richard, Janell Fetterolf, Maria Smerkovich, Sarah Austin, Sneha Gubbala, and Jordan Lippert. "Representative Democracy Remains a Popular Ideal, but People Around the World Are Critical of How It's Working." Pew Research Center, February 28, 2024. pewresearch.org/global/2024/02/28/ representative-democracy-remains-a-popular-ideal-but-people-around -the-world-are-critical-of-how-its-working.

Wike, Richard, Laura Silver, Shannon Schumacher, and Aidan Connaughton. "Many in U.S., Western Europe Say Their Political System Needs Major Reform," March 31, 2021. pewresearch.org/global/2021/03/31/many-in-us -western-europe-say-their-political-system-needs-major-reform.

Wile, Rob. "Biden Administration Bans Noncompete Agreements, Setting up Legal Showdown with Business Groups." NBC News, April 23, 2024. nbcnews.com/business/business-news/biden-administration-bans -noncompete-agreements-setting-legal-showdown-rcna149069.

Williamson, Kevin. "Summer Reading Recommendations—National Review Contributors Weigh In." *National Review,* July 22, 2016. nationalreview.com/ 2016/07/summer-reading-recommendations-national-review-contributors

———. "Two Cheers for Democracy." nationalreview.com/corner/two-cheers-for -democracy.

Williamson, Molly Weston. "The State of Paid Family and Medical Leave n the U.S. in 2024." Center for American Progress, January 17, 2024. americanprogress.org/article/the-state-of-paid-family-and-medical-leave -in-the-u-s-in-2024.

———. "The State of Paid Sick Time in the U.S. in 2024." Center for American Progress, January 17, 2024. americanprogress.org/article/the-state-of-paid -family-and-medical-leave-in-the-u-s-in-2024.

Wilson, James Lindley. *Democratic Equality.* Princeton University Press, 2019.

Wilson, Steven, William Koerber, and Evan Brassell. "2020 Population of U.S. Island Areas Just Under 339,000." Census.gov. Accessed February 7, 2023. census.gov/library/stories/2021/10/first-2020-census-united-states-island -areas-data-released-today.html.

Wilson, Woodrow. "Address at the Fairgrounds Auditorium in Billings, Montana," September 11, 1919. The American Presidency Project. presidency .ucsb.edu/documents/address-the-fairgrounds-auditorium-billings -montana.

Wines, Michael. "Deceased G.O.P. Strategist's Hard Drives Reveal New Details on the Census Citizenship Question." *The New York Times,* May 30, 2019, sec. U.S. nytimes.com/2019/05/30/us/census-citizenship-question-hofeller.html.

Winship, Scott. "Understanding Trends in Worker Pay over the Past 50 Years." American Enterprise Institute, May 2024.

Witko, Christopher, Jana Morgan, Nathan J. Kelly, and Peter K. Enns. *Hijacking the Agenda: Economic Power and Political Influence.* Russell Sage Foundation, 2021.

Wolf, Martin. *The Crisis of Democratic Capitalism.* Penguin Press, 2023.

Wolf, Zachary B. "Republicans Won the Popular Vote, but They're Not Used to This Feeling." CNN, December 17, 2022. cnn.com/2022/12/17/politics/popular-vote-midterms-what-matters/index.html.

Wolin, Sheldon S. "Democracy: Electoral and Athenian." *PS: Political Science and Politics* 26, no. 3 (1993).

Woodhouse, A.S.P. "Puritanism and Democracy." *The Canadian Journal of Economics and Political Science* 4, no. 1 (February 1938): 1. doi.org/10.2307/136751.

Woolrych, Austin. "The Cromwellian Protectorate: A Military Dictatorship?" *History* 75, no. 244 (June 1990). jstor.org/stable/24420972.

"Workers Lose Billions in Unpaid Wages Every Year." National Employment Law Project, July 11, 2023. nelp.org/app/uploads/2023/07/Workers-Lose-Billions-Unpaid-Wages-Every-Year.pdf.

Wright, Gerald C. "A Discussion of Christopher H. Achen and Larry M. Bartels' Democracy for Realists: Why Elections Do Not Produce Responsive Government." *Perspectives on Politics* 15, no. 1 (March 2017): 161–62. doi.org/10.1017/S1537592716004278.

Yankelovich, Daniel. "The Status of Ressentiment in America." *Social Research* 42, no. 4 (1975): 760–77.

Yaptangco, Ariana. "Latte Makeup, Strawberry Girl, Glazed Donut Skin: How Food Changed the Way We Think About Beauty." *Glamour,* October 5, 2023. glamour.com/story/food-beauty-trends.

Yates, Robert. "Notes of the Secret Debates of the Federal Convention of 1787," 1927. The Avalon Project. avalon.law.yale.edu/18th_century/yates.asp.

Yglesias, Matthew. "American Democracy Is Doomed." *Vox,* March 2, 2015. vox.com/2015/3/2/8120063/american-democracy-doomed.

——. "Elizabeth Warren Has a Plan to Save Capitalism." *Vox,* August 15, 2018. vox.com/2018/8/15/17683022/elizabeth-warren-accountable-capitalism-corporations.

Young, Kevin A., Tarun Banerjee, and Michael Schwartz. "Capital Strikes as a Corporate Political Strategy: The Structural Power of Business in the Obama Era." *Politics & Society* 46, no. 1 (March 2018): 3–28. doi.org/10.1177/0032329218755751.

Yourish, Karen, Larry Buchanan, and Denise Lu. "The 147 Republicans Who Voted to Overturn Election Results." *The New York Times,* January 7, 2021, sec. U.S. nytimes.com/interactive/2021/01/07/us/elections/electoral-college-biden-objectors.html.

Zakaria, Fareed. "Democrats Need to Focus on the Gut, Not the Head." *Washington Post,* December 1, 2016, sec. Opinions. washingtonpost.com/opinions/democrats-need-to-focus-on-the-gut-not-the-head/2016/12/01/dfbe7782-b803-11e6-a677-b608fbb3aaf6_story.html.

Zelinger, Julie. "Meet the Most Impressive Woman on Forbes' Female Billionaire List." *Mic,* March 2, 2015. mic.com/articles/111622/meet-the-most-impressive-woman-on-forbes-female-billionaire-list.

NOTES

Introduction

xi **We have frequently printed:** Whitman, *Democratic Vistas,* p. 37.

xi **In 2019, Joe Biden began his run for the presidency with an announce-ment:** Saenz, "Joe Biden Announces He Is Running for President in 2020."

xi **"This administration," former president Barack Obama warned:** Collinson, "Obama Issues a Dire Warning About American Democracy in Stunning Rebuke of Trump."

xi **"This election," Bernie Sanders said in his own speech:** Peters, "Bernie Sanders Just Made the Progressive Case for Joe Biden."

xi **"Speaking at a political convention is something I never expected to be doing":** *Sally Yates Speaks at 2020 DNC.*

xii **In September,** *The Washington Post*'s **editorial board:** Editorial Board, "Our Democracy in Peril."

xii **Biden,** *The New York Times* **editorial board agreed:** Editorial Board, "Elect Joe Biden, America."

xii **"Our democracy," Biden told the country that day:** Detrow, "Biden: Democracy 'Under Unprecedented Assault' As Pro-Trump Extremists Occupy Capitol."

xii **By one count, Biden used the word "democracy":** Itkowitz and Morse, "How Kamala Harris Shifted Democrats' Message from 'Democracy' to 'Freedom' "; Biden, "Remarks by President Biden in Statement to the American People."

xii **"He is the person," she warned voters:** Keith, "At the Site of Trump's Jan. 6 Rally, Harris Makes Her Closing Pitch for the Campaign."

xii **Trump was reelected with not only an Electoral College majority:** Rubin, "Trump Set to Be the First Republican Candidate to Win the Popular Vote in 20 Years."

xiii **And, troublingly, many who did:** Fields and Sanders, "Democracy Was a Motivating Factor for Both Harris and Trump Voters, but for Very Different Reasons."

xiii **In a poll from Vanderbilt University:** "Vanderbilt Unity Poll Explains Why Democracy May Take Center Stage in This Week's Presidential Debate—and the Campaign More Broadly."

xiii **After all, most Republicans believed:** Agiesta and Edwards-Levy, "CNN Poll: Percentage of Republicans Who Think Biden's 2020 Win Was Illegitimate Ticks Back Up Near 70%."

xiii **"Now it is up to Congress to confront":** Naylor, "Read Trump's Jan. 6 Speech, A Key Part of Impeachment Trial."

xiii **Eight Republican senators and 139 House Republicans:** Yourish, Buchanan, and Lu, "The 147 Republicans Who Voted to Overturn Election Results."

xiii **In the days and weeks prior:** Corasaniti, Yourish, and Collins, "How Trump's 2020 Election Lies Have Gripped State Legislatures."

xiii **According to a survey:** Levitsky and Ziblatt, *Tyranny of the Minority,* pp. 119, 125.

xiii **Undeterred, industry and corporate political action committees (PACs) donated:** von Allmen, "Corporations Have Given over $100 Million to the Sedition Caucus."

xiv **Overall in the 2024 presidential race:** Izaguirre and Oprysko, "Business Donors Overwhelmingly Bet on the GOP. Here's Where It Paid Off."

xiv **And Trump also earned:** Noah, "For Wall Street Billionaires, This Election Is About One Thing."

xiv **"What possibly could have produced":** Meyerson, "Democracy, Deshmocracy."

xiv **Having given more than:** Schouten, Wright, and Matthews, "Musk Spent More than a Quarter-Billion Dollars to Elect Trump"; Kinnard, "A Comprehensive Look at DOGE's Firings and Layoffs So Far"; Nwanevu, "Musk's Rampage through Government Shows Us How We Can Finally Close the Book on What Trumpism Is All About."

xiv **Whole agencies:** Goodwin, "Elon Musk's DOGE Has Worked Quickly to Cut Federal Agencies."

xiv **Federal scientific research:** Kolata, "'Chaos and Confusion' at the Crown Jewel of American Science."

xiv **And government services:** Sainato, "Doge's Attack on Social Security Causing 'Complete, Utter Chaos', Staff Says."

xv **Meanwhile, Musk companies:** Stone, "Elon Musk's Conflicts of Interest 'Should Scare Every American', Experts Say."

xv **Evidently unsatisfied:** Epstein, "Liberal Wins Wisconsin Court Race, Despite Musk's Millions"; Riccardi and Beaumont, "Democrats' Win in Wisconsin Court Race Also Is a Big Loss for Elon Musk."

xv **In early 2024, Gallup reported 71 percent dissatisfaction:** Jones, "Record Low in U.S. Satisfied with Way Democracy Is Working."

xv **Only 19 percent of Americans:** Fetterolf and Ramones, "72% of Americans Say the U.S. Used to Be a Good Example of Democracy, but Isn't Anymore"; Corasaniti, Igielnik, and Baker, "Voters Are Deeply Skeptical About the Health of American Democracy."

xvi **"Democracy is a bad idea":** Campbell, "Charlie Kirk: 'Democracy Is a Bad Idea.'"

xvi **Robert Welch, the candy magnate:** Berman, *Minority Rule,* p. 230.

xvi **"Democracy," Utah senator Mike Lee wrote:** Beauchamp, "Sen. Mike Lee's Tweets Against 'Democracy,' Explained."

xvii **On any given day:** "Unleashing the Power of AI to Democratize Creativity for Everyone"; Russell, "Stepping Into the NFT Frontier."

xvii **A post might inform you:** Stonberg, "Cryptocurrencies Are Democratizing the Financial World. Here's How"; Shepherd, "First Class Service, First Class Results."

xvii **"Social media,"** *Glamour* **adds:** Yaptangco, "Latte Makeup, Strawberry Girl, Glazed Donut Skin."

xvii **In the financial pages:** "Wheels Up."

xviii *Forbes* **has doubts:** Gollan, "Is Democratization of Private Jets Dead?"

xviii **On space tourism,** *Smithsonian* **has fewer:** Fishman, "The Future of Zero-Gravity Living Is Here."

xviii **A luxury magazine tells you:** Courtney, "A Brief History of Ferrari Supercars, from the 288 GTO to the F80."

xviii **In** *Southern Living,* **an article:** Watson, "What Is a Tea Towel?"

xviii *The New York Times,* **for its part:** Glusac, "The Democratization of Airport Lounges"; Singer, "The Democratization of Plastic Surgery"; Gallagher, "Leigh Perkins, Who Built Orvis Into a Lifestyle Brand, Dies at 93."

xviii **"Can Scent Be Democratized?":** Hallock, "Can Scent Be Democratized?"

xviii **From 2020 to 2024, one in five elections:** Shah and Hudson, "The Global State of Democracy 2024."

xviii **Surveys tell us that many countries:** Wike and Fetterolf, "Satisfaction with Democracy Has Declined in Recent Years in High-Income Nations"; Wike et al., "Representative Democracy Remains a Popular Ideal, but People Around the World Are Critical of How It's Working."

xix **A week after the 2024 election:** Jeffries, *The ABCs of Democracy.*

xix **In** *Democracy in America:* Tocqueville, *Democracy in America.*

xxi **What we tend to forget:** "Declaration of Independence."

xxi **Life, liberty, and the pursuit of "Happiness":** Conklin, "The Origins of the Pursuit of Happiness."

xxii **That language is derived from:** Foner, *The Second Founding,* p. xx.

1. The Meaning of Democracy

3 **For instance, Robert Dahl:** Dahl, "What Political Institutions Does Large-Scale Democracy Require?"

3 **Today, Freedom House:** Repucci and Slipowitz, "Freedom in the World 2022."

4 **Similarly, the Economist Intelligence Unit:** "Democracy Index 2021," "Democracy Index 2023," "Democracy Index 2024."

4 **Around 28 percent of countries:** Ibid.

5 **Anthropologists believe early human bands:** Mansbridge, "The Evolution of Political Representation in Liberal Democracies."

5 **From there, the historical record suggests:** Taylor, *Democracy May Not Exist, but We'll Miss It When It's Gone,* p. 238.

5 **But the word** *democracy* **itself:** Miller, *Can Democracy Work?,* p. 28; Ober, *The Rise and Fall of Classical Greece,* p. 307; Cartledge, *Democracy: A Life,* p. 3.

5   Historians believe democracy in Greece: Cartledge, *Democracy: A Life*, pp. 50–52; Ober, *The Rise and Fall of Classical Greece*, pp. 135–37; Miller, *Can Democracy Work?*, p. 22.

5   Then, in the sixth and fifth: Miller, *Can Democracy Work?*; Ober, *The Rise and Fall of Classical Greece*; Cartledge, *Democracy: A Life*.

6   The structure and nature of Athenian democracy: Thucydides, *The Landmark Thucydides*.

7   "The people" who ruled in Athens: Miller, *Can Democracy Work?*, pp. 29, 35, 51; Dahl, *Democracy and Its Critics*, p. 22.

7   And even the supposed equality: Miller, *Can Democracy Work?*, p. 29.

7   Moreover, though Athens lacked: Dahl, *Democracy and Its Critics*, p. 21

7   Plato, for instance, described: Plato, *The Republic of Plato*, pp. 273–94.

7   But while democracy in Athens: Cartledge, *Democracy: A Life*, pp. 216–25.

7   The word *democracy* managed: Miller, *Can Democracy Work?*, p. 49; Cartledge, *Democracy: A Life*, p. 265.

8   As the philosopher Joshua Cohen: Cohen and Sabel, "Directly Deliberative Polyarchy."

8   The best plain-English version: Lincoln, "Gettysburg Address."

8   For most of the last eighty: Foa and Mounk, "When Democracy Is No Longer the Only Path to Prosperity."

8   Research tells us that: Bollyky et al., "The Relationships Between Democratic Experience, Adult Health, and Cause-Specific Mortality in 170 Countries between 1980 and 2016"; Krueger, Dovel, and Denney, "Democracy and Self-Rated Health across 67 Countries"; Franco, Álvarez-Dardet, and Ruiz, "Effect of Democracy on Health."

9   And many scholars also believe: Piccone, "Democracy and Violent Crime"; Piccone, "Democracy and Civil War"; Hegre, "Democracy and Armed Conflict."

9   The classical scholar Josiah Ober: Ober, *The Rise and Fall of Classical Greece*.

9   The share of world GDP: Foa and Mounk, "When Democracy Is No Longer the Only Path to Prosperity."

10   Although Americans tend to associate: Price, *Endangered Phrases*, p. 45.

10   Before we overthrew our own king: Taylor, *American Revolutions*.

10   And back in Ancient Greece: Plato, *The Republic of Plato*.

11   This was part of Thomas Paine's: Paine, *Common Sense*.

11   A century and a half later: Dewey, *The Public and Its Problems*, p. 206.

12   Rather than being: Wilson, *Democratic Equality*, p. 17.

12   For Dewey, one of: Dewey, *The Ethics of Democracy*, p. 25.

12   And as the philosopher: Rorty, *Achieving Our Country*, p. 30.

13   The poet Walt Whitman: Whitman, *Democratic Vistas*, p. 23.

14   this specific dynamic: Shapiro, *The State of Democratic Theory*, p. 88.

15   The political scientist Carole Pateman, in fact: Pateman, "Participatory Democracy Revisited."

16   In *Democracy and Its Critics*: Dahl, *Democracy and Its Critics*, pp. 31–32.

16   During the English Civil War, for instance: Woodhouse, "Puritanism and Democracy"; Dahl, *Democracy and Its Critics*, p. 32.

18 As the political scientist Corey Brettschneider: Brettschneider, *Democratic Rights,* pp. 20–22.

18 Of all the rules: Dahl, *Democracy and Its Critics,* pp. 135–40.

20 In a passage of his *Politics:* Aristotle, *Politics;* Taylor, *Democracy May Not Exist, But We'll Miss It When It's Gone,* p. 197.

20 "Participatory democratic theory is": Pateman, "Participatory Democracy Revisited."

21 And although direct political participation: Lemar, "The Public Hearing Process for New Housing Is Broken."

21 "New and demanding opportunities to participate": Elliott, *Democracy for Busy People,* p. 7.

21 As the theorist Hannah Pitkin: Pitkin, *The Concept of Representation,* pp. 1-10, 222.

22 "The English people thinks it is free": Rousseau, "The Social Contract."

22 A provision of the Magna Carta: Mansbridge, "The Evolution of Political Representation in Liberal Democracies."

22 After all, as the political scientist Hélène Landemore: Landemore, *Open Democracy,* pp. 68–74.

22 This insight is one of: Landemore, *Open Democracy.*

23 "Since all cannot, in a community": Mill, *On Liberty and Considerations on Representative Government,* p. 151; Dahl, "What Political Institutions Does Large-Scale Democracy Require?"

23 As Robert Dahl recognized: Dahl, *Democracy and Its Critics,* pp. 29–30.

23 As the historian Jan-Werner Müller argues: Müller, *Democracy Rules,* p. 51.

23 And beyond offering arenas: Disch, "Toward a Mobilization Conception of Democratic Representation."

23 And though it's true: Elliott, *Democracy for Busy People,* p. 122.

23 Some theorists, among them Nadia Urbinati: Urbinati, "The Democratic Tenor of Political Representation."

24 For many Americans at the time: Klarman, *The Framers' Coup,* p. 176; Pitkin, *The Concept of Representation,* p. 149.

24 "Leadership, emergency action, action": Pitkin, *The Concept of Representation,* pp. 162–63, 234.

25 "Not simply a form of politics": Cohen, *Philosophy, Politics, Democracy,* p. 160.

25 When they accomplish this: Wilson, *Democratic Equality,* pp. 158-59.

25 "[Deliberative democrats]," the political scientist Ian Shapiro: Shapiro, *The State of Democratic Theory,* p. 22.

26 Theorists such as Philip Green: Green, "*Democracy and Its Critics* by Robert A. Dahl."

26 Similarly, the progressive activist: Taylor, *Democracy May Not Exist, But We'll Miss It When It's Gone,* pp. 2, 13.

2. Democracy's Critics

28 "Above all": Frum, "Trump Won. Now What?"

28 "If you're accustomed": Harwood, "Embarrassingly Naïve."

28 **"Felon and President-elect":** Rubin, "A 'Republic If We Can Keep It.' Perhaps We Cannot."

28 **In 2023, Pew:** "In Divided Washington, Americans Have Highly Negative Views of Both Parties' Leaders."

28–29 **It would surely tickle:** Lemieux, "Mencken's Theory of Democracy."

29 **In Plato's *Republic*, Socrates:** Plato, *The Republic of Plato*, p. 191.

29 **"They do not understand," Socrates sighs:** Plato.

30 **"There are plenty of people":** Williamson, "Two Cheers for Democracy."

30 **"The typical citizen drops":** Schumpeter, *Capitalism, Socialism and Democracy*, p. 262.

31 **"Every man whose business it is":** Lippmann, *Public Opinion*, p. 73.

31 **In 2014, the liberal commentator:** Klein, "How Politics Makes Us Stupid"; Johnson, "Expanation for What?"

31 **Released in the thick:** Tomasky, "Can the Monster Be Elected?"; Williamson, "Summer Reading Recommendations—*National Review* Contributors Weigh In."

31 **CNN's Fareed Zakaria:** Zakaria, "Democrats Need to Focus on the Gut, Not the Head"; "The Best Books of 2016"; Achen and Bartels, *Democracy for Realists*.

32 **As Achen and Bartels describe it:** Achen and Bartels, *Democracy for Realists*, p. 1; Bartels, "Uninformed Votes."

32 **As he suggests, surveys:** Achen and Bartels, *Democracy for Realists*, p. 10; Brennan, *Against Democracy*.

33 **"If your only reason to follow":** Somin, *Democracy and Political Ignorance*.

33 **"For most, leisure time":** Achen and Bartels, *Democracy for Realists*, p. 9.

34 **In his 2016 book *Against Democracy*:** Brennan, *Against Democracy*, p. 3.

34 **In one experiment summarized:** Brennan, *Against Democracy*, pp. 38, 44

34 **And, as Achen and Bartels write:** Achen and Bartels, *Democracy for Realists*, pp. 299, 311.

35 **Brennan, going further:** Brennan, *Against Democracy*, pp. 8, 142.

35 **Take this passage, for instance:** Brennan, *Against Democracy*, pp. 27–28.

36 **Brennan writes, for instance:** Brennan, *Against Democracy*, p. 26; "America's Knowledge Crisis: A Survey of Civic Literacy."

36 **He writes, based on a poll:** Brennan, *Against Democracy*, p. 29; "Americans' Civics Knowledge Increases During a Stress-Filled Year."

37 **He writes that "less than 30":** Brennan, *Against Democracy*, p. 29; "The 2019 State of the First Amendment."

37 **"Voters generally know who":** Brennan, *Against Democracy*, p. 26; "America's Knowledge Crisis: A Survey of Civic Literacy."

37 **And in its 2022 Survey:** "ABA Survey of Civic Literacy 2022."

37 **Achen and Bartels write themselves:** Achen and Bartels, *Democracy for Realists*, pp. 39–40; Brennan, *Against Democracy*, pp. 35–36.

38 **Researchers have found, for instance:** Beattie, "Theory, Media, and Democracy for Realists."

38 **In a paper responding:** Achen and Bartels, "Government for the People."

38 **As Hélène Landemore notes:** Aristotle, *Politics*, p. 99; Landemore, *Democratic Reason*, p. 59.

39 Even Machiavelli—author of *The Prince:* Machiavelli, *Discourses on Livy,* pp. 157–58; Landemore, *Democratic Reason,* p. 64.

39 Nicolas de Condorcet, an influential mathematician: Estlund, *Democratic Authority,* p. 15.

40 Importantly though, that bit of math doesn't work out: Estlund, *Democratic Authority;* Landemore, *Democratic Reason,* pp. 71–74, 147–56.

40 We know, for instance, that when: Oppenheimer and Edwards, *Democracy Despite Itself,* pp. 186–94.

40 There's also the concept of: Landemore, *Democratic Reason,* pp. 97–98.

42 Achen and Bartels spend much: Achen and Bartels, *Democracy for Realists,* pp. 146–76.

42 In July 1916, four people: Achen and Bartels, *Democracy for Realists,* pp. 118–28.

43 From the attacks: Achen and Bartels, *Democracy for Realists,* pp. 128–45.

43 These findings on the 1916 shark attacks: Fowler and Hall, "Do Shark Attacks Influence Presidential Elections?"

43 And as Achen and Bartels admit: Achen and Bartels, *Democracy for Realists,* pp. 119–20.

43 After correcting an important: Fowler and Hall, "Do Shark Attacks Influence Presidential Elections?"

44 "For most people": Achen and Bartels, *Democracy for Realists,* p. 266.

45 Paraphrasing Achen and Bartels: Brennan and Landemore, *Debating Democracy,* pp. 35–36.

45 "Today the parties": Klein, *Why We're Polarized,* p. 136.

45 There are more self-described independents: Gallup, "Party Affiliation."

45 Importantly, most of those: "Political Independents: Who They Are, What They Think"; Skelley, "Few Americans Who Identify As Independent Are Actually Independent."

46 Moreover, as ideologically polarized: Abramowitz, *The Great Alignment,* pp. 112–13.

46 *Democracy for Realists* highlights: Fowler, "Partisan Intoxication or Policy Voting?"; Achen and Bartels, *Democracy for Realists,* p. 44.

46 Brennan tries to undermine: Brennan, *Against Democracy,* pp. 41–42.

47 And while it's true: Landemore and Brennan, *Debating Democracy,* pp. 35–36.

47 *Democracy for Realists,* for instance: Achen and Bartels, *Democracy for Realists,* pp. 246–58.

47 As evidence: Achen and Bartels, *Democracy for Realists,* pp. 250–52, 257.

48 The most the book: Achen and Bartels, *Democracy for Realists,* p. 252.

48 "When coalitions shift": Achen and Bartels, *Democracy for Realists,* p. 266.

49 The afterword to the paperback: Achen and Bartels, *Democracy for Realists,* pp. 335–44.

49 As you may have noticed by now: Ahlstrom-Vij, "Is Democracy an Option for the Realist?"

49 Instead, things like: Achen and Bartels, *Democracy for Realists,* pp. 142–43, 153, 175.

49 "Most of the time": Achen and Bartels, *Democracy for Realists,* p. 294.

50 **In a chapter examining:** Achen and Bartels, *Democracy for Realists,* p. 73.

50 **"Democracy, as we practice it":** Brennan, *Against Democracy,* p. 230.

50 **In *Considerations on Representative Government:*** Mill, *On Liberty and Considerations on Representative Government,* pp. 217–21.

51 **The pundit Ben Shapiro:** Media Matters, "Ben Shapiro: The Right to Vote Should Require 'Some Sort of Minimum Level of Knowledge'"; Walsh, "In Order To Save America, We Must Legally Prevent Oblivious People From Voting"; Goldberg, "Literacy Tests"; Harsanyi, "We Must Weed out Ignorant Americans from the Electorate."

51 **"If the argument":** Brennan, *Against Democracy,* p. 144.

52 **"These tests were":** Brennan, *Against Democracy,* pp. 18, 223–24.

52 **Research on political knowledge:** Brennan, *Against Democracy,* p. 226.

53 **Brennan doesn't say much:** Brennan, *Against Democracy,* pp. 55, 227.

54 **This is despite the fact:** Gunn, "Against Epistocracy"; Soon, "Review of 'Against Democracy'"; Nwanevu, "The Democratic Party Has a Fatal Misunderstanding of the QAnon Phenomenon."

54 **For one vast and influential study:** Menand, "Everybody's an Expert."

55 **Jason Brennan references:** Brennan, *Against Democracy,* p. 193.

55 **Among economists, for instance:** Brennan, *Against Democracy,* p. 193.

55 **On the same grounds:** Lippmann, *Public Opinion,* pp. 31, 401.

55 **In fact, one of the earliest:** Bass, "The Athenian Plague"; Huremović, "Brief History of Pandemics"; Kelaidis, "What the Great Plague of Athens Can Teach Us Now."

58 **It's an example of:** Mackie, *Democracy Defended,* pp. 5–8.

60 **Decades ago:** Mackie, *Democracy Defended,* pp. 78–83.

62 **In his 1982 book:** Riker, *Liberalism Against Populism,* pp. 236–38; Mackie, *Democracy Defended,* pp. 31–43.

62 **Democracy, by Riker's lights:** Riker, *Liberalism Against Populism,* p. 244; Mackie, *Democracy Defended,* pp. 31–43.

62 **It would be difficult:** Mackie, *Democracy Defended,* pp. 10, 23–26.

63 **Some of those irrationalities:** Mackie, *Democracy Defended,* pp. 435–40.

64 **"We operate strategically":** Dowding "Can Populism Be Defended?"

64 **As Mackie points out:** Mackie, *Democracy Defended,* pp. 435–36.

64 **Another reason not:** Mackie, *Democracy Defended,* pp. 409–25, 440–43.

64 **Mackie makes:** Mackie, *Democracy Defended,* p. 70.

65 **Some democratic theorists have argued:** McGann, *The Logic of Democracy,* p. 25.

65 **But the evidence that cycles:** Mackie, *Democracy Defended;* Shapiro, *The Real World of Democratic Theory,* pp. 72–73.

66 **The political scientist Sean Ingham:** Ingham, *Rule by Multiple Majorities,* pp. 1-4.

67 **What Ingham contends:** Ingham, *Rule by Multiple Majorities,* p. 91.

70 **Needless to say:** Higgins, "Peter Thiel, Trump's Man in Silicon Valley"; McFaul, "The Tragic Success of Global Putinism"; Marchese, "The Interview: Curtis Yarvin Says Democracy Is Done."

3. The Shape of Democracy

74 **Liberalism is an ideology:** Nwanevu, "The Willful Blindness of Reactionary Liberalism."

74 **In a telling:** Kant, "An Answer to the Question: What Is Enlightenment?"; Cavallar, "Kant's Judgment on Frederick's Enlightened Absolutism"; Dahms, "Diligent Bureaucrats and the Expulsion of Jews from West Prussia, 1772–1786."

75 **Again, as Corey Brettschneider:** Brettschneider, *Democratic Rights,* pp. 20–22.

76 **And some of those rights:** Brettschneider, *Democractic Rights,* pp. 43–49; Christiano, *The Constitution of Equality,* pp. 92–93, 139–54.

77 **But while power devolved:** Cartledge, *Democracy: A Life,* pp. 247–63.

78 **That ambiguity suited Rome's:** Cartledge, *Democracy: A Life,* pp. 247–63; North, "Politics and Aristocracy in the Roman Republic."

78 **Republican governments since Rome:** Pettit, *On the People's Terms,* p. 6; Woolrych, "The Cromwellian Protectorate: A Military Dictatorship?"; Reed, "Why the Polish-Lithuanian Commonwealth's Legacy of Liberty Is Worthy of Our Appreciation Today."

79 **Freedom for republicans:** Pettit, *On the People's Terms,* pp. 1–2.

79 **The fundamental injustice of slavery:** Skinner, "Classical Liberty and the Coming of the English Civil War," p. 10; O'Shea, "Wage Slavery."

80 **Above and beyond any specific:** O'Shea, "In the Interests of All."

80 **While some liberals:** Beaumont, "Phillip Pettit, Republicanism"; Pettit, *On the People's Terms,* p. 2.

81 **To ensure that states:** Cartledge, *Democracy: A Life,* pp. 254–63.

81 **Republican theorist John McCormick:** McCormick, "The New Ochlophobia?"

82 **"It is the proper function":** O'Shea, "Radical Republicanism and the Future of Work."

82 **"Greek oligarchs":** McCormick, "The New Ochlophobia?"

82 **In fact, as we've already seen:** Pettit, *On the People's Terms,* pp. 173–74, 222; Machiavelli, *Discourses on Livy,* pp. 157–58.

83 **But republicans in the second tradition:** McCormick, "The New Ochlophobia?"

84 **In his work:** Pettit, *On the People's Terms,* p. 82.

85 **"We could say":** Mouffe, "Deliberative Democracy or Agonistic Pluralism?"

85 **"Contestation," as the theorist Marie Paxton:** Paxton, *Agonistic Democracy,* p. 37.

86 **"The 'other' is no longer seen":** Mouffe, "Deliberative Democracy or Agonistic Pluralism?"

86 **Doing so, as Mouffe writes:** Mouffe, *The Return of the Political,* p. 48; Paxton, *Agonistic Democracy,* p. 8.

87 **"The concern . . . is that":** Paxton, *Agonistic Democracy,* p. 3.

89 **This is why some democratic theorists:** Christiano, *The Constitution of Equality,* p. 274.

89 **Philip Pettit argues:** Pettit, *On the People's Terms,* p. 112.

90 **In the 1980s:** Dahl, *A Preface to Economic Democracy*, pp. 54–55.

91 **In recent years, that reality:** Anderson, *Private Government*, pp. 37–38.

92 **In short, the modern workplace:** O'Shea, "Radical Republicanism and the Future of Work."

94 **At the time of writing, there are eighteen:** Forbes, "The World's Real-Time Billionaires."

95 **In the late nineteenth and early twentieth:** Mill, *Principles of Political Economy;* Frega, Herzog, and Neuhäuser, "Workplace Democracy—The Recent Debate."

96 **"As it gains practical":** Dewey, *The Ethics of Democracy*, p. 1.

4. A Republic Kept

103 **At the close:** Miller, "'A Republic If You Can Keep It.'"

105 **There were no women deliberating:** Klarman, *The Framers' Coup*, pp. 257–303, 63–31; Levinson, *Framed*, pp. 38, 183; Millhiser, "Democracy in America Is a Rigged Game."; Taylor, *American Revolutions*, pp. 379–82.

106 **Benjamin Rush, a famed:** Klarman, *The Framers' Coup*, p. 2.

106 **In Federalist 37:** Klarman, *The Framers' Coup*, p. 1; Madison, "The Federalist No. 37."

106 **The idea that the Constitution:** Klarman, *The Framers' Coup*, pp. 2–10.

107 **Although quill pens:** Taylor, *American Revolutions*, pp. 361–62; Miller, *Can Democracy Work?*, p. 97.

107 **The revolution also triggered:** Taylor, *American Revolutions*, pp. 3, 361–63; Klarman, *The Framers' Coup*, p. 75.

108 **The Articles of Confederation:** Klarman, *The Framers' Coup*, pp. 13–15, 41–45.

108 **Congress likewise lacked:** Taylor, *American Revolutions*, pp. 316–18; Klarman, *The Framers' Coup*, pp. 11–21.

108 **And by 1783:** Klarman, *The Framers' Coup*, pp. 27–28.

108 **Even in victory:** Klarman, *The Framers' Coup*, p. 11; Taylor, *American Revolutions*, p. 349.

108 **Meanwhile, state governments:** Klarman, *The Framers' Coup*, pp. 11–12, 48–72.

109 **In the absence:** Klarman, *The Framers' Coup*, pp. 11–12, 21–24; Taylor, *American Revolutions*, pp. 349–50.

109 **And, like Congress:** Klarman, *The Framers' Coup*, pp. 76–77; Holton, *Unruly Americans*, p. 29.

109 **Yet as far as:** Klarman, *The Framers' Coup*, pp. 83–84; Holton, *Unruly Americans*, p. 29.

109 **The supposed spending habits:** Holton, *Unruly Americans*, p. 49.

109 **One woman who happened:** Taylor, *American Revolutions;* Holton, *Unruly Americans*, p. 88.

110 **But as more and more:** Klarman, *The Framers' Coup*, pp. 81–83; Taylor, *American Revolutions*, p. 365.

110 **By the mid-1780s:** Taylor, *American Revolutions*, pp. 368–70; Klarman, *The*

Framers' Coup, p. 88; Ovetz, *We the Elites*, pp. 56, 64–65; Holton, *Unruly Americans*, pp. 8–9.

110 **These campaigns:** Klarman, *The Framers' Coup*, pp. 76–77.

110 **But while most states:** Fishkin and Forbath, *The Anti-Oligarchy Constitution*, pp. 47–48; Klarman, *The Framers' Coup*, pp. 73–90.

110 **By then, out in the state's:** Fishkin and Forbath, *The Anti-Oligarchy Constitution*, pp. 47–49; Klarman, *The Framers' Coup*, pp. 90–91.

111 **In January 1787:** Taylor, *American Revolutions*, pp. 368–69; Klarman, *The Framers' Coup*, pp. 91–92.

111 **While Shays' Rebellion:** Taylor, *American Revolution*, pp. 369–70; Klarman, *The Framers' Coup*, pp. 97–98.

111 **All this sent:** Taylor, *American Revolutions*, pp. 370–72; Klarman, *The Framers' Coup*, pp. 92–96.

111 **The rise of paper:** Klarman, *The Framers' Coup*, pp. 83–86.

112 **One fellow Virginian:** Klarman, *The Framers' Coup*, p. 86.

112 **In August 1786:** Klarman, *The Framers' Coup*, p. 100.

112 **In a February 1787 letter:** Klarman, *The Framers' Coup*, pp. 100–101.

113 **In September 1786:** Klarman, *The Framers' Coup*, pp. 101–10.

113 **Initially, leaders in several states:** Klarman, *The Framers' Coup*, pp. 108–20.

113 **All were at least:** Taylor, *American Revolutions*, pp. 375–76; Klarman, *The Framers' Coup*, p. 247.

113 **Obviously, and as noted:** Taylor, *American Revolutions*, pp. 375–76.

114 **In fact, Rhode Island:** Taylor, *American Revolutions*, pp. 374–75; Klarman, *The Framers' Coup*, p. 248; Dahl, *How Democratic Is the American Constitution?*, pp. 1–2.

114 **That suspicion was:** Klarman, *The Framers' Coup*, pp. 246–54.

114 **Yet unbeknownst:** Klarman, *The Framers' Coup*, pp. 141–44.

114 **In the very first speech:** Holton, *Unruly Americans*, p. 5.

115 **The terms of the convention's:** Klarman, *The Framers' Coup*, pp. 127–32; "James Madison Medal."

115 **The Virginia Plan introduced:** The Virginia Plan Senate Historical Office, "The Virginia Plan"; Klarman, *The Framers' Coup*, pp. 133–44.

116 **Madison had also:** Klarman, *The Framers' Coup*, pp. 139–40.

116 **Most delegates:** Klarman, *The Framers' Coup*, pp. 147–53.

117 **The convention also:** Klarman, *The Framers' Coup*, pp. 215–18; Holton, *Unruly Americans*, pp. 197–98.

117 **Even with those shorter:** Holton, *Unruly Americans*, p. 188.

117 **Such a veto:** "Notes on the Debates in the Federal Convention: July 21"; Klarman, *The Framers' Coup*, pp. 218–22.

117 **For the same reason:** Klarman, *The Framers' Coup*, pp. 155–58; Holton, *Unruly Americans*, pp. 182–86; Madison, "James Madison to Thomas Jefferson," March 19, 1787.

118 **In the end:** Klarman, *The Framers' Coup*, pp. 159–64; *Marbury v. Madison*.

118 **Beyond ditching the federal veto:** Klarman, *The Framers' Coup*, p. 170; "Notes on the Debates in the Federal Convention: May 31."

119 **These detractors aside:** Klarman, *The Framers' Coup*, pp. 170–71.

119 **"The election may":** Klarman, *The Framers' Coup*, p. 171; "Founders Online."

119 **Even so, Madison also:** Klarman, *The Framers' Coup*, pp. 172–73, 206.

120 **A few weeks into:** Klarman, *The Framers' Coup*, pp. 153–54.

120 **Naturally, Madison:** "Notes on the Debates in the Federal Convention: June 18, July 14"; Klarman, *The Framers' Coup*, pp. 184–85; Ovetz, *We the Elites*, p. 4.

121 **Opponents of equal:** Yates, "Notes of the Secret Debates of the Federal Convention of 1787."

121 **Most, including Madison:** Klarman, *The Framers' Coup*, pp. 185–86.

121 **To that point:** Yates, "Notes of the Secret Debates of the Federal Convention of 1787: June 29"; Klarman, *The Framers' Coup*, p. 202; Levitsky and Ziblatt, *Tyranny of the Minority*, pp. 154–56.

122 **James Wilson put the:** Klarman, *The Framers' Coup*, pp. 184–86; "Notes on the Debates in the Federal Convention: June 29."

122 **In response, the small states:** Klarman, *The Framers' Coup*, pp. 188–91; "Notes on the Debates in the Federal Convention: June 9, June 29."

122 **As Paterson's comments suggest:** "Notes on the Debates in the Federal Convention"; Klarman, *The Framers' Coup*, pp. 193–94; Dahl, *How Democratic Is the American Constitution?*, pp. 14–15; Yates, "Notes of the Secret Debates of the Federal Convention of 1787: June 30."

124 **At the outset:** Klarman, *The Framers' Coup*, pp. 194–95.

124 **That tie was broken:** Klarman, *The Framers' Coup*, pp. 195–201.

125 **Separately and infamously:** Klarman, *The Framers' Coup*, pp. 269–76; Holton, *Unruly Americans*, pp. 18–89.

125 **As far as the Senate was concerned:** Klarman, *The Framers' Coup*, p. 201.

125 **The equally apportioned Senate:** Holton, *Unruly Americans*, p. 193.

125 **"In framing a system":** "Notes on the Debates in the Federal Convention: June 26"; Senate Historical Office, "Seven-Year Senate Terms?"

126 **These remarks echoed:** Yates, "Notes of the Secret Debates of the Federal Convention of 1787."

126 **Delegates at the convention:** "Notes on the Debates in the Federal Convention: July 19"; Klarman, *The Framers' Coup*, pp. 227–28.

126 **But his support:** "Notes on the Debates in the Federal Convention: July 19."

126 **Most delegates disagreed:** Klarman, *The Framers' Coup*, p. 228; Levitsky and Ziblatt, *Tyranny of the Minority*, pp. 156–58.

127 **As with the question of apportionment:** Klarman, *The Framers' Coup*, pp. 230–31.

128 **The Founders fully:** Holton, *Unruly Americans*, p. 180; Chemerinsky, *No Democracy Lasts Forever*, p. 30; Levitsky and Ziblatt, *Tyranny of the Minority*, pp. 153–54.

128 **"It is an undisputed fact":** Warren, "Observations on the New Constitution, and on the Federal and State Conventions by a Columbian Patriot."

129 **The Constitution's Federalist supporters:** Klarman, *The Framers' Coup*, pp. 243, 312–16.

129 **In practice, the composition:** Klarman, *The Framers' Coup*, p. 406; "Notes on the Debates in the Federal Convention: August 31."

129 But the Anti-Federalists: "Notes on the Debates in the Federal Convention: September 15."

130 At Virginia's ratifying convention: Elliot, "The Debates in the Convention of the Commonwealth of Virginia."

130 Virginia's Patrick Henry: Elliot, "The Debates in the Convention of the Commonwealth of Virginia."

131 In the end, of course: Klarman, *The Framers' Coup*, pp. 453, 516–30, 546–95.

132 "The contemporary efforts": Dobski, "America Is a Republic, Not a Democracy."

132 The conservative interpretation: Beauchamp, "Sen. Mike Lee's Tweets Against 'Democracy,' Explained."

133 Again, three delegates: Klarman, *The Framers' Coup*, p. 162.

133 In Federalist 22: Hamilton, "The Federalist No. 22."

134 The power given: Madison, "The Federalist No. 62."

135 "In a democracy": Madison, "The Federalist No. 14."

135 Still, as Madison explains: Madison, "The Federalist No. 39."

135 But in Federalist 10: Madison, "The Federalist No. 10."

136 A key benefit: Madison, "The Federalist No. 10."

136 And though he was: Madison, "The Federalist No. 63."

137 While representation *could*: Madison, "The Federalist No. 10."

138 While Madison and the other: Klarman, *The Framers' Coup*, pp. 138, 410; Holton, *Unruly Americans*, p. 109; "Notes on the Debates in the Federal Convention: August 22"; Madison, "The Federalist No. 18."

139 And in Federalist 10: Madison, "The Federalist No. 10."

139 The lexicographer: Webster, "Miscellaneous Remarks on Divizions of Property . . . in the United States"; Fishkin and Forbath, *The Anti-Oligarchy Constitution*, p. 33.

140 Instead, Madison's position: Madison, "The Federalist No. 10"; Taylor, *Democracy May Not Exist, But We'll Miss It When It's Gone*, p. 65.

141 Again, fears that: Hamilton, "Conjectures About the New Constitution"; Ovetz, *We the Elites*, p. 25.

141 "It is in vain": Madison, "The Federalist No. 10."

141 Madison also hoped: Pitkin, *The Concept of Representation*, pp. 194–96; Fishkin and Forbath, *The Anti-Oligarchy Constitution*, p. 61; Levinson, *Framed*, pp. 92–93.

142 Mass democratic politics: Madison, "The Federalist No. 10"; Ovetz, *We the Elites*, p. 38; Holton, *Unruly Americans*, p. 10.

142 Beyond being a more convenient: Pitkin, *The Concept of Representation*, pp. 195–96.

143 Against charges: Madison, "The Federalist No. 57."

143 Though the Constitution: Holton, *Unruly Americans*, p. 196; Klarman, *The Framers' Coup*, p. 178.

144 Madison also didn't mention: King, "Notes of Rufus King in the Federal Convention of 1787"; Lee and Oppenheimer, *Sizing up the Senate*, p. 30.

144 There had also been: Klarman, *The Framers' Coup*, pp. 182–83, 210; King, "Notes of Rufus King in the Federal Convention of 1787."

144 **Though most of that:** Klarman, *The Framers' Coup,* p. 372.

144 **As Madison wrote in Federalist 63:** Madison, "The Federalist No. 63."

145 **It should be remembered here:** Hansen, "Some History and Reminiscences on Survey Sampling."

145 **As Madison pointed out:** Klarman, *The Framers' Coup,* p. 175; "Notes on the Debates in the Federal Convention: June 12."

145 **Unlike some state constitutions:** Klarman, *The Framers' Coup,* p. 175; Holton, *Unruly Americans,* p. 199; Pitkin, *The Concept of Representation,* p. 149.

145 **All in all, the kind of republicanism:** Miller, *Can Democracy Work?,* pp. 92–93; Rush, "'Address to the People of the United States.'"

147 **In the decades immediately:** Klarman, *The Framers' Coup,* p. 622.

147 **The emergence of partisanship:** Klarman, *The Framers' Coup,* pp. 628–29; Taylor, *American Revolutions,* pp. 424–26; Dahl, *How Democratic Is the American Constitution?,* pp. 77–78.

148 **While electors were:** Klarman, *The Framers' Coup,* pp. 622–23; Dahl, *How Democratic Is the American Constitution?,* p. 82; McCarthy, "How the Electoral College Became Winner-Take-All."

148 **With time, even the:** Dahl, *How Democratic Is the American Constitution?,* pp. 19–20, 27–28; Klarman, *The Framers' Coup,* pp. 623–25.

5. Toward a Democratic Politics

149 **Much of what *is* here:** Brennan Center, "Annotated Guide to the For the People Act of 2021."

150 **In 1812:** Trickey, "Where Did the Term 'Gerrymander' Come From?"

150 **But there are two basic strategies:** Page and Gilens, *Democracy in America?;* Chemerinsky, *No Democracy Lasts Forever,* p. 69.

151 **After the 2010 Census:** Chang, "The Man Who Rigged America's Election Maps"; Chemerinksy, *No Democracy Lasts Forever,* pp. 70–71; Levitsky and Ziblatt, *Tyranny of the Minority,* pp. 180–81.

151 **But by 2017, one analysis:** Royden and Li, "Extreme Maps."

151 **It has been allowed:** Prokop, "The Supreme Court Just Said Federal Courts Can't Stop Partisan Gerrymandering."

151 **But it should also:** Page and Gilens, *Democracy in America?,* pp. 161–62; Klarman, "Foreword"; Hill, "Periscope: Misdiagnosing the Vital Signs of Democracy."

152 **Together, that reality and gerrymandering:** Page and Gilens, *Democracy in America?,* pp. 161–62; Wolf, "Republicans Won the Popular Vote, but They're Not Used to This Feeling."

152 **In 2012, for instance:** Page and Gilens, *Democracy in America?,* p. 162.

152 **In 2022, on the other hand:** Wolf, "Republicans Won the Popular Vote, but They're Not Used to This Feeling."

152 **That's largely a product:** Skelley, "How the House Got Stuck at 435 Seats"; Bouk, "House Arrest."

153 **That's the highest ratio:** DeSilver, "U.S. Population Keeps Growing, but

House of Representatives Is Same Size as in Taft Era"; Matthews, "The Case for Massively Expanding the US House of Representatives, in One Chart."

153 **Behind the average:** Skelley, "How the House Got Stuck At 435 Seats."

153 **Through a variety:** Page and Gilens, *Democracy in America?*, pp. 174–76.

154 **The most obvious remedy for partisan gerrymandering:** Drutman, "What We Know About Redistricting and Redistricting Reform."

154 **Twenty states have tried to address:** Imamura, "The Rise and Fall of Redistricting Commissions"; "Annotated Guide to the For the People Act of 2021."

154 **But the results of those commissions:** Imamura, "The Rise and Fall of Redistricting Commissions."

155 **Electoral reformers have proposed:** "Ranked Choice Voting Information."

156 **It's a more complex system:** "Evaluating the Effects of Ranked-Choice Voting"; Drutman, *Breaking the Two-Party Doom Loop,* pp. 180–83; Tharoor, "Other Countries Use Ranked-Choice Voting."

156 **This is where having:** Nwanevu, "American Democracy Is Broken."

157 **Multi-winner elections:** "Letter to Congress on Ending Single Member Congressional Districts and Adopting Proportional Representation."

158 **True proportional representation:** Drutman, *Breaking the Two-Party Doom Loop,* pp. 183–90; Mazoue, "Explainer."

159 **In one important way:** Taylor et al., *A Different Democracy.*

159 **One particularly important rule:** Levitsky and Ziblatt, *Tyranny of the Minority,* p. 163.

159 **In 1957, Strom:** Glass, "Congress Passes Civil Rights Act Aug. 29, 1957."

159 **The mere threat:** Chemerinsky, *No Democracy Lasts Forever,* p. 51.

160 **Spending and revenue bills:** Scott, "9 Questions About Budget Reconciliation."

160 **Thanks to the filibuster:** Nwanevu, "Murder the Filibuster and Never Look Back"; Nwanevu, "Joe Manchin Wants to Pass a Popular Gun Control Bill."

160 **Though the filibuster:** Klein, "The Definitive Case for Ending the Filibuster."

161 **In 2018, for example:** Kiely, "Durbin and the Filibuster 'Myth.'"

161 **Similarly, in 2019:** Davis, "Senate Pulls 'Nuclear' Trigger to Ease Gorsuch Confirmation"; McConnell, "The Filibuster Plays a Crucial Role."

161 **As political scientist Sarah Binder:** Binder, "Statement of Sarah A. Binder, Department of Political Science, George Washington University."

161 **Hamilton is crystal clear:** Hamilton, "The Federalist No. 22"; Levinson, *An Argument Open to All,* pp. 80–81.

161 **Although the Founders:** Madison, "The Federalist No. 58"; Levinson, *An Argument Open to All,* pp. 219–20; Levitsky and Ziblatt, *Tyranny of the Minority,* pp. 160–61.

162 **That line of thought:** "A Proclamation on Day of Remembrance"; Nwanevu, "Joe Manchin Wants to Pass a Popular Gun Control Bill."

162 **In theory, states:** Levitsky & Ziblatt, *Tyranny of the Minority,* p. 175.

163 **But our largest state:** Chemerinsky, *No Democracy Lasts Forever,* p. 10; "QuickFacts"; "Population, Total | Data."

163 **Mathematically, because both:** Taylor et al., *A Different Democracy*, p. 99.

163 **one 2014 analysis:** Eidelson, "The Majoritarian Filibuster."

164 **An analysis of filibusters:** Eidelson, "The Majoritarian Filibuster."

164 **Moreover, the special powers:** Taylor et al., *A Different Democracy*, p. 207.

164 **In 2020, for instance:** Millhiser, "The Danger the Supreme Court Poses to Democracy, in Just Two Numbers"; "With Kavanaugh Vote, the Senate Reaches a Historic Low in Democratic Metric."

164 **Similarly, in 2021:** Millhiser, "The Overwhelming Strength of the Case Against Trump, in One Number."

164 **If current population trends continue:** Bump, "In About 20 Years, Half the Population Will Live in Eight States."

164 **And those inequities:** Lee and Oppenheimer, *Sizing Up the Senate*, pp. 54–8-, 96–120.

165 **"Why should Los Angeles":** Lowry, "The Left's Foolhardy Attack on the Senate."

166 **Residents of Oklahoma City:** White, "Top 300 Largest Cities in the United States by Population 2022"; "U.S. Census Bureau QuickFacts"; "Census Profile."

167 **Instead they represent:** *"Reynolds v. Sims."*

168 **"There can be no":** Yates, "Notes of the Secret Debates of the Federal Convention of 1787."

168 **One suggestion, endorsed:** Montanaro, "Biden Endorses Reforming The Senate Filibuster."

168 **But this wouldn't be:** Nwanevu, "Democracy's Moment of Reckoning."

169 **Equal apportionment in the Senate:** "Pack the Union."

169 **The most obvious tweak:** "Pack the Union."

169 **In 2018, Michigan:** Dingell, "I Served in Congress Longer Than Anyone."

169 **About two-thirds:** "Field Listing—Legislative Branch."

170 **In fact, if we're absolutely set:** Malleson, "Beyond Electoral Democracy."

170 **Deliberative experiments:** Fishkin, *Democracy When the People Are Thinking*, pp. 79–91, 111–40, 157–80; Gerwin, *Citizens' Assemblies: Guide to Democracy That Works.*

171 **On five occasions:** "FEDERAL ELECTIONS 2016: Election Results for the U.S. President, the U.S. Senate and the U.S. House of Representatives"; "2000 Election Results for President"; Kamarck and Kudak, "How to Get Rid of the Electoral College."

172 **The states and the District of Columbia:** "What Is the Electoral College?"

172 **Consequently, while California's:** Durran, "Whose Votes Count the Least in the Electoral College?"

173 **What's more, nearly:** "Map of General-Election Campaign Events and TV Ad Spending by 2020 Presidential Candidates."

174 **As loudly as Republicans might denigrate:** Nwanevu, "Trump Isn't the Only One to Blame for the Capitol Riot."

174 **Among peer nations:** Taylor et al., *A Different Democracy*, p. 262.

174 **In the aftermath:** DeSilver, "Among Democracies, U.S. Stands out in How It Chooses Its Head of State."

175 **Fortunately, reformers:** Nwanevu, "The Ridiculous War-Gaming of the 2020 Election."

176 **The Constitution requires:** Ovetz, *We the Elites,* p. 104.

178 **While peer countries:** Rahman and Thelen, "The Role of the Law in the American Political Economy."

179 **"Justices love referenda":** Klarman, "Foreword."

179 **In 2022, the court's:** Chemerinsky, *No Democracy Lasts Forever,* p. 79.

180 **That decision was no:** Harris, "Why Buck v. Bell Still Matters"; Millhiser, "The Case against the Supreme Court of the United States."

180 **While judicial review:** Rahman and Thelen, "The Role of the Law in the American Political Economy."

180 **But in practice:** Rahman and Thelen, "The Role of the Law in the American Political Economy."

181 **The last years of liberal justice:** Lind, "Ruth Bader Ginsburg Is in the Hospital with 3 Broken Ribs"; Romano, "'Protect RBG' Memes Capture Cultural Anxiety over the Supreme Court"; Bronner and Rakich, "Advantage, GOP"; Greenhouse, "Ruth Bader Ginsburg, Supreme Court's Feminist Icon, Is Dead at 87."

182 **Terms of ten to fifteen years:** Diamond, "Saving Democracy—Realistically."

182 **The same might be said about a proposal:** Epps and Sitaraman, "How to Save the Supreme Court."

182 **Epps and Sitaraman:** Epps and Sitaraman, "How to Save the Supreme Court."

184 **When the role and design:** Taylor et al., *A Different Democracy;* Gould and Pozen, "Structural Biases in Structural Constitutional Law"; Hacker et al., "The American Political Economy."

184 **Japan and the European nations:** Yglesias, "American Democracy Is Doomed."

185 **In fact, there are more than four million:** Steckelberg and Esteban, "Over 4 Million Americans Don't Have Anyone to Vote for Them in Congress"; Wilson, Koerber, and Brassell, "2020 Population of U.S. Island Areas Just Under 339,000"; "The District of Columbia Gained More Than 87,000 People in 10 Years."

185 **The residents of American Samoa:** Frost, "The Only U.S. Territory Without U.S. Birthright Citizenship."

185 **The majority of these Americans:** Steckelberg and Esteban, "Over 4 Million Americans Don't Have Anyone to Vote for Them in Congress."

185 **In 2016, for instance, Congress created:** Cheatham and Roy, "Puerto Rico: A U.S. Territory in Crisis."

185 **And in the District of Columbia:** Delgadillo, Kurzius, and Sadon, "The Past, Present, and (Potential) Future of D.C. Statehood, Explained."

186 **Although D.C. boasts:** Delgadillo, Kurzius, and Sadon, "State Population Totals and Components of Change."

186 **In the District's case:** Hersher, "D.C. Votes Overwhelmingly to Become 51st State"; Greenblatt, "The US Almost Tore Itself Apart to Get to 50 States."

186 **Dozens of scholars:** Sargent, "The Campaign for D.C. Statehood Just Got a Big Boost."

186 **But it's less clear:** Nwanevu, "The Vexing Question of Puerto Rican Statehood."

187 **Americans are asked:** Poloni-Staudinger and Wolf, *American Difference*, pp. 238–39.

187 **And beyond the frequency:** Liptak, "U.S. Voting for Judges Perplexes Other Nations."

187 **"Most American voters":** Taylor et al., *A Different Democracy,* pp. 131–32.

187 **Though turnout:** DeSilver, "Turnout in U.S. Has Soared in Recent Elections."

187 **And turnout for nonpresidential elections:** Page and Gilens, *Democracy in America?,* p. 57.

188 **In the recent:** Potts, "Turnout Was High Again."

188 **In primary and state and local elections:** Klarman, "Foreword."

188 **While most countries:** Poloni-Staudinger and Wolf, *American Difference*, pp. 239–40; Schumacher and Connaughton, "From Voter Registration to Mail-in Ballots, How Do Countries around the World Run Their Elections?"

188 **Many other countries:** Page and Gilens, *Democracy in America?*, pp. 61–62; Poloni-Staudinger and Wolf, *American Difference,* p. 240; DeSilver, "Weekday Elections Set the U.S. Apart from Many Other Advanced Democracies."

188 **In 2022, 4.6 million Americans:** Uggen et al., "Locked Out 2022"; Palder, "America's Unique Kind of Disenfranchisement."

188 **The poor and racial minorities:** Horwitz, "Getting a Photo ID so You Can Vote Is Easy"; "The Impact of Voter Suppression on Communities of Color"; Laurison, Brown, and Rastogi, "Voting Intersections"; Schlozman, Verba, and Brady, *The Unheavenly Chorus,* pp. 152–54; Morris and Grange, "Large Racial Turnout Gap Persisted in 2020 Election."

188 **While proponents of these laws:** Levitt, "A Comprehensive Investigation of Voter Impersonation Finds 31 Credible Incidents out of One Billion Ballots Cast."

189 **The rarity of fraud:** Klarman, "Foreword."

189 **Ten states now strictly:** Totenberg, "The Landmark Voting Rights Act Faces Further Dismantling at the Supreme Court"; Vasilogambros, "The Messy Politics of Voter Purges"; Corasaniti, "Voting Rights and the Battle Over Elections"; "Voter ID Laws."

189 **Though they're discussed:** Nwanevu, "The Right to Run."

190 **As far as basic:** Millhiser, "How America Lost Its Commitment to the Right to Vote."

190 **The John Lewis Voting Rights Advancement Act:** Brennan Center, "Annotated Guide to the For the People Act of 2021"; Brennan Center, "Key Differences Between the For the People Act and the Freedom to Vote Act"; Brennan Center, "The John Lewis Voting Rights Advancement Act."

190 **The For the People Act also contained:** "Our Common Purpose Reinventing American Democracy for the 21st Century"; Brennan Center, "An-

notated Guide to the For the People Act of 2021"; Diamond, "Saving Democracy—Realistically"; Nwanevu, "Maybe Making Election Day a National Holiday Wouldn't Really Work."

91 **While early voting:** "Democracy"; Nwanevu, "Maybe Making Election Day a National Holiday Wouldn't Really Work."

92 **But most countries:** Diamond, "Saving Democracy—Realistically"; "Our Common Purpose Reinventing American Democracy for the 21st Century"; Levinson, *Framed;* Schlozman, Verba, and Brady, *The Unheavenly Chorus,* pp. 558–60.

93 **In James Fishkin's deliberative polls:** Lupia and Matsusaka, "Direct Democracy"; Demsas, "Community Input Is Bad, Actually"; Fishkin, *Democracy When the People Are Thinking,* pp. 69–91, 160–66.

93 **Of the twelve thousand:** Wegman, "Will We Ever Amend the Constitution Again?"

93 **The last of the seventeen:** Calabresi and Teachout, "Interpretation"; Largey, "The Bad Grade That Changed The U.S. Constitution."

94 **In fact, one of the major defects:** Chemerinsky, *No Democracy Lasts Forever,* p. 37; Mader, "Binding Authority: Unamendability in the United States Constitution."

94 **First, a proposed:** Neale, "The Article V Convention to Propose Constitutional Amendments: Contemporary Issues for Congress."

94 **These rules make:** Levinson, *Our Undemocratic Constitution,* pp. 161–63; Taylor et al., *A Different Democracy,* pp. 78–81.

95 **At the very least:** Wegman, "Will We Ever Amend the Constitution Again?"

95 **The French:** Elkins, Ginsburg, and Melton, *The Endurance of National Constitutions.*

95 **Political tumults:** Taylor et al., *A Different Democracy,* p. 67.

95 **In 1789, Thomas Jefferson:** Jefferson, "Founders Online," September 6, 1789.

96 **The federal Constitution:** Gurri, "Liberal Democracy and the Federal System."

96 **A 2018 survey:** Grumbach, *Laboratories Against Democracy,* p. 75.

97 **The progressive Supreme Court justice:** Grumbach, *Laboratories Against Democracy,* p. 4.

97 **State legislatures:** Lax and Phillips, "The Democratic Deficit in the States."

98 **What's more:** Grumbach, *Laboratories Against Democracy,* p. 77.

98 **And once elected:** Nwanevu, "Infrastructure Spending Can Save Local Journalism"; Pareene, "Abolish States."

98 **Democratically troubling too:** Badger, "Blue Cities Want to Make Their Own Rules."

98 **These are among:** Grumbach, *Laboratories Against Democracy.*

98 **Still, the states abound:** Gurri·, "Liberal Democracy and the Federal System"; Scholzman, Verba, and Brady, *The Unheavenly Chorus,* p. 47; Levinson, *Framed,* pp. 120, 123–24.

99 **But a tremendous amount:** Dunn, "Most Americans Support a $15 Federal Minimum Wage"; Orth, "Three-Quarters of Americans Think the Federal

Minimum Wage Is Too Low"; Narea, "Poll: Most Americans Support a Path to Citizenship for Undocumented Immigrants."

199 **All of that said:** Bronner and Rakich, "Advantage, GOP"; Gould and Pozen, "Structural Biases in Structural Constitutional Law."

200 **In fact, as data journalist G. Elliot Morris:** Bronner and Rakich, "Advantage, GOP."

200 **The 2020 election:** Levitsky and Ziblatt, *Tyranny of the Minority*, p. 176; Liasson, "Democrats Increasingly Say American Democracy Is Sliding Toward Minority Rule."

200 **The specific policies:** Chait, "The Filibuster Is Living on Borrowed Time."

201 **As if that weren't enough:** Bronner and Rakich, "Advantage, GOP"; Klarman, "Foreword."

201 **None of this is to say:** "FEDERAL ELECTIONS 2004 Election Results for the U.S. President, the U.S. Senate and the U.S. House of Representatives"; Cohn, "2022 Review"; Haas, "Statistics of the Congressional Election from Official Sources for the Election of November 4, 2014"; Haas, "Statistics of the Congressional Election of November 2, 2010."

201 **"The idea of democracy":** Weisman, "In Congress, Republicans Shrug at Warnings of Democracy in Peril."

201 **Really, the admission:** Greenblatt, "The US Almost Tore Itself Apart to Get to 50 States. Can DC Make It 51?"; Richardson, "When Adding New States Helped the Republicans."

202 **There are other:** "Pack the Union: A Proposal to Admit New States for the Purpose of Amending the Constitution to Ensure Equal Representation."

202 **As we've seen:** "All the Ways Trump Tried to Overturn the Election—and How It Could Happen Again—Washington Post"; Li, "The GOP's Redistricting Loophole"; Corasaniti and Epstein, "Map by Map, G.O.P. Chips Away at Black Democrats' Power"; Wines, "Deceased G.O.P. Strategist's Hard Drives Reveal New Details on the Census Citizenship Question"; Daley, "The Secret Files of the Master of Modern Republican Gerrymandering"; Epstein and Corasaniti, "Republicans Push Crackdown on Crime Wave That Doesn't Exist."

202 **Republican losses:** Prokop, "Why Some Democrats Are Quietly Unhappy with the House's Big Voting Rights Bill."

203 **Upon losing:** "All the Ways Trump Tried to Overturn the Election—and How It Could Happen Again—Washington Post"; Yourish, Buchanan, and Lu, "The 147 Republicans Who Voted to Overturn Election Results."

203 **In the year after the attack:** Greenberg, "Most Republicans Still Falsely Believe Trump's Stolen Election Claims."

203 **"Minority rule":** Bronner and Rakich, "Advantage, GOP."

203 **The party's gerrymandering campaign:** Nwanevu, "The Corporations Funding the End of Democracy"; Kroll, "Meet the Fortune 500 Companies Funding the Political Resegregation of America"; Meyer, "How Dark Money Helped Republicans Hold the House and Hurt Voters"; Daley, "The House the GOP Built."

204 **In January 2023:** "Corporations Gave $10M to Election Objectors after Pledging to Cut Them Off."

205 **As far as campaign spending:** Klarman, "Foreword"; Page and Gilens, *Democracy in America?*, pp. 113–14; Rahman and Thelen, "The Role of the Law in the American Political Economy."

206 **the federal elections in 2020:** Evers-Hillstrom, "Most Expensive Ever."

206 **According to one study:** Page and Gilens, *Democracy in America?*, pp. 96–97; Klarman, "Foreword."

206 **And in 2016:** Page and Gilens, *Democracy in America?*, pp. 104–5.

206 **Altogether, the more than $3 billion:** Kim, "Just 12 Megadonors Accounted for 7.5% of Political Giving over Past Decade."

207 **In 2016, Congressman Rick Nolan:** "Are Members of Congress Becoming Telemarketers?"

207 **In 2016, for instance, Hillary:** Sultan, "Election 2016"; Koerth, "How Money Affects Elections"; Press, "Donald Trump and Hillary Clinton's Final Campaign Spending Revealed."

208 **In an influential 2003 paper:** Ansolabehere, de Figueiredo, and Snyder Jr., "Why Is There So Little Money in U.S. Politics?"

208 **While they might not:** Page and Gilens, *Democracy in America?*, pp. 111–12, 120–21.

209 **One 2021 study:** Witko et al., *Hijacking the Agenda*, pp. 107–8, 127–28.

209 **In 2011, nearly half:** Schlozman, Verba, and Brady, *Unequal and Unrepresented*, p. 156.

209 **As with campaign donations:** Page and Gilens; Witko et al., *Hijacking the Agenda*.

210 **"The prevalence":** Page and Gilens, *Democracy in America?*, p. 140.

210 **It should be remembered:** Shine, "47% of Congress Members Millionaires"; Hawkings, "Wealth of Congress"; Evers-Hillstrom, "Most Expensive Ever"; Bonica and Grumbach, "Old Money: Campaign Finance and Gerontocracy in the United States."

211 **Many of our international peers:** Neff and Pickard, "Funding Democracy"; Nadeem, "Americans Who Mainly Get Their News on Social Media Are Less Engaged, Less Knowledgeable."

211 **That's particularly worrying:** Mahler and Rutenberg, "How Rupert Murdoch's Empire of Influence Remade the World"; Matthews, "Sinclair Broadcast Group, the Pro-Trump, Conservative Company Taking over Local News, Explained."

211 **On the latter point:** Jacobs et al., "Whose News?"

212 **Upon his election:** Young, Banerjee, and Schwartz, "Capital Strikes as a Corporate Political Strategy."

214 **Some of the solutions:** "Annotated Guide to the For the People Act of 2021."

215 **Obama's decision:** "Annotated Guide to the For the People Act of 2021"; Page and Gilens, *Democracy in America?; "*Democracy."

215 **And in the long view:** Page and Gilens, *Democracy in America?*, p. 187.

6. Toward a Democratic Economy

218 **And as Elizabeth Anderson:** Anderson, *Private Government*.

219 **"If we allow":** Roosevelt, "Special Message," January 1, 1909.

219 **In 1919, Woodrow Wilson:** Wilson, "Address at the Fairgrounds Auditorium in Billings, Montana," September 11, 1919.

219 **"All American workers":** Roosevelt, "Fireside Chat," September 6, 1936.

220 **And John F. Kennedy:** Kennedy, "Statement by the President Upon Receiving a Report on Collective Bargaining and Industrial Peace," May 1, 1962.

220 **In a 1961 address:** King Jr., "Speech to AFL-CIO's Fourth Constitutional Convention," December 11, 1961.

220 **"In places, circumstances":** Ferreras, "Democratizing the Corporation: The Proposal of the Bicameral Firm."

221 **One difference between states and firms:** Mayer, "Is There a Moral Right to Workplace Democracy?"

221 **Opponents of economic democracy:** Arneson, "Democratic Rights at National and Workplace Levels"; Mayer, "Is There a Moral Right to Workplace Democracy?"

221 **People need to work:** Malleson, *After Occupy,* pp. 29–30.

222 **Defenders of the firm-state:** Mayer, "Is There a Moral Right to Workplace Democracy?"

222 **Anderson acknowledges:** Anderson, *Private Government,* pp. 67–68.

223 **Additionally, the state and the firm:** Frega, "Against Analogy."

225 **"The rationale":** Breen, "Freedom, Republicanism, and Workplace Democracy."

225 **John Dewey made:** Ellerman and Gonza, "Less-Known Supporters of Workplace Democracy."

226 **America left the Great Depression:** Alperovitz, *What Then Must We Do?,* p. 121.

226 **Beyond that:** Mason, "The Economy During Wartime"; Hendricks, Gunn-Wright, and Ricketts, "The Greatest Mobilization Since WWII"; English, "How U.S. Infrastructure Plans Shrank in Ambition"; Phelps, "When Interstates Paved the Way."

226 **The GI Bill:** "75 Years of the GI Bill: How Transformative It's Been"; Alperovitz, *What Then Must We Do?,* p. 12.

226 **The Social Security Act:** Tumulty, "The Great Society at 50"; Alperovitz, *What Then Must We Do?,* p. 12; *"Unemployment Compensation: Federal-State Partnership"; "Historical Background And Development of Social Security."*

226 **The fights for civil rights:** Tankersley, "The Real Reason the American Economy Boomed After World War II."

227 **In 1935, the National Labor Relations Act:** Shimabukuro and Whittaker, "Federal Labor Relations Statutes: An Overview"; Shimabukuro and Mayer, "The National Labor Relations Act (NLRA): Union Representation Procedures and Dispute Resolution"; Kazin, *What It Took to Win,* pp. 174–75.

227 **union membership spiked:** Romero and Whittaker, "A Brief Examination of Union Membership Data."

227 **In 1935, about 13 percent:** Romero and Whittaker, "A Brief Examination of Union Membership Data."

227 **Beyond getting:** Alperovitz, *What Then Must We Do?,* pp. 13–14; Hoffman,

"Health Care Reform and Social Movements in the United States"; Kazin, *What It Took to Win*, pp. 175–90; 226–28.

227 **After 1935, organizers:** "AFL-CIO Labor Commission on Racial and Economic Justice Report"; Kelly, *Fight Like Hell;* Bivens et al., "Unions Promote Racial Equity"; Boris and Orleck, "Feminism and the Labor Movement"; Kazin, *What It Took to Win*, pp. 175–87; Grumbach and Collier, "The Deep Structure of Democratic Crisis."

227 **According to one 2021 paper:** Farber et al., "Unions and Inequality over the Twentieth Century."

227 **And while union families:** Rosenfeld, Denice, and Laird, "Union Decline Lowers Wages of Nonunion Workers"; Western and Rosenfeld, "Unions, Norms, and the Rise in U.S. Wage Inequality"; "Labor Unions and the Middle Class"; Farber et al., "Unions and Inequality over the Twentieth Century."

228 **In 1947:** Lanard, "Labor Law Is Stuck in 1947."

228 **But American workers:** Madland, Walter, and Eisenbrey, "Right-to-Work 101"; Hertel-Fernandez, "The American Political Economy."

228 **Similarly, unions:** Rogers, "Libertarian Corporatism Is Not an Oxymoron."

229 **And disempowering unions:** Kuttner, "Neoliberalism: Political Success, Economic Failure"; Menand, "The Rise and Fall of Neoliberalism."

229 **Though the productivity:** Winship, "Understanding Trends in Worker Pay over the Past 50 Years."

229 **From 1979 to 2022:** Gould and Bivens, "Opinion: Why a New Study Gives a Misleading View of Inequality in America."

229 **And the nation's top:** Gould and Bivens, "Opinion: Why a New Study Gives a Misleading View of Inequality in America."

229 **These are among the reasons:** "Income Inequality."

229 **The top 10 percent of American households:** Kent and Ricketts, "The State of U.S. Wealth Inequality."

230 **Between 2007 and 2016 alone:** Bruenig, "Social Wealth Fund for America."

230 **That owed largely:** Phillips, "The Rich Now Own a Record Share of Stocks"; "What Percentage of Americans Own Stock?"

230 **Off of Wall Street:** Perry, Stephens, and Donoghoe, "Black Wealth Is Increasing, but So Is the Racial Wealth Gap."

230 **From its peak:** Romero and Whittaker, "A Brief Examination of Union Membership Data"; "Union Members—2023."

230 **According to one estimate:** Farber et al., "Unions and Inequality over the Twentieth Century."

230 **According to another:** Western and Rosenfeld, "Unions, Norms, and the Rise in U.S. Wage Inequality."

230 **In 2020, the World Economic Forum:** *The Global Social Mobility Report 2020: Equality, Opportunity and a New Economic Imperative;* "Poverty Rate"; "Health at a Glance 2023"; "Potential Years of Life Lost."

231 **Although the Wagner Act:** McNicholas et al., "Employers Spend More than $400 Million per Year on 'Union-Avoidance' Consultants."

232 **And even when companies:** Toussaint, "For Years, the NLRB Has Been Too Toothless to Enforce Labor Laws. Is That Finally Changing?"; Rhinehart and McNicholas, "Shortchanged—Weak Anti-Retaliation Provisions in the National Labor Relations Act Cost Workers Billions."

232 **That weakness has:** Greenhouse, "'Old-School Union Busting': How US Corporations Are Quashing the New Wave of Organizing"; Picchi, "Union: Walmart Shut 5 Stores over Labor Activism"; Todd, "Are Starbucks and Chipotle Union-Busting by Closing Stores?"

232 **In 2018, a study:** Toussaint, "For Years, the NLRB Has Been Too Toothless to Enforce Labor Laws."; McNicholas, Poydock, and Schmitt, "Workers Are Winning Union Elections, but It Can Take Years to Get Their First Contract."

232 **"Workers often have":** Battilana, "Introduction: For a Fairer, More Democratic, Greener Society."

233 **On average:** Miller, "The World 'Has Found a Way to Do This': The U.S. Lags on Paid Leave."

233 **Instead, federal law:** Shabo, "Explainer: Paid and Unpaid Leave Policies in the United States."

233 **Certain states and localities:** Williamson, "The State of Paid Family and Medical Leave in the U.S. in 2024"; Williamson, "The State of Paid Sick Time in the U.S. in 2024."

233 **While surveys show:** Eren et al., "Job Satisfaction 2023"; Horowitz and Parker, "How Americans View Their Jobs."

233 **In one 2019 survey:** Rothwell and Crabtree, "Not Just a Job: New Evidence on the Quality of Work in the United States."

233 **Workers who speak out:** Andrias and Hertel-Fernandez, "Ending At-Will Employment: A Guide for Just Cause Reform"; Malinksy, "In the U.S., You Can Legally 'Be Fired for Any Reason or No Reason at All'—Here's Why."

234 **And even workers fired:** Nanda, "Mandatory Arbitration Won't Stop Us from Enforcing the Law"; Colvin, "The Growing Use of Mandatory Arbitration."

234 **That makes it easier:** "Workers Lose Billions in Unpaid Wages Every Year."

234 **much of all this:** Mishel, "Introduction—The Goliath in the Room"; Naidu and Carr, "If You Don't Like Your Job, Can You Always Quit?"

235 **According to the Federal Trade Commission:** Wile, "Biden Administration Bans Noncompete Agreements, Setting up Legal Showdown with Business Groups"; Casarino and Sarkisian, "The FTC's Effort for a Non-Compete Ban."

235 **This "fissuring" of the workforce:** Dukes and Streeck, *Democracy at Work*, p. 79.

235 **That goes a long way:** Block and Sachs, "Clean Slate for Worker Power: Building a Just Economy and Democracy."

235 **Companies of the "gig economy":** Dukes and Streeck, *Democracy at Work*, pp. 86–87.

237 **In July 2021:** Aleem, "Amazon Workers Deserve More than Jeff Bezos' Trite Post-Space 'Thank You'"; Hartill, "Who Owns Amazon? Largest Shareholders"; *Forbes*, "The World's Real-Time Billionaires."

238 **At a market capitalization:** Solitro, "Amazon Eyes $2 Trillion Market Cap

as CEO Talks AI, Cost Cuts"; "Biggest U.S. Employers"; Tung and Lathrop, "A Good Living: Amazon Can and Must Make a Middle-Income Livelihood Possible."

238 **And though Amazon:** Di Pizio, "People Think Amazon Is an E-Commerce Company."

238 **In sprawling warehouses:** Mattioli and Fung, "The Biggest Delivery Business in the U.S. Is No Longer UPS or FedEx"; Johnson, "Massive Amazon Warehouses Are Used to Ship and Store Open-Box, Refurbished, and Returned Products."

238 **While Amazon touts:** Day and Soper, "Amazon Has Turned a Middle-Class Warehouse Career Into a McJob"; Tung and Lathrop, "A Good Living: Amazon Can and Must Make a Middle-Income Livelihood Possible for the People Who Work in Its Warehouses"; Stevens, "Amazon to Raise Its Minimum U.S. Wage to $15 an Hour."

239 **"Wages often tick":** Gutelius and Pinto, "Handling Hardship: Data on Economic Insecurity Among Amazon Warehouse Workers."

239 **In 2023, a survey:** Gutelius and Pinto, "Handling Hardship: Data on Economic Insecurity Among Amazon Warehouse Workers."

239 **That helps explain why:** Day and Soper, "Amazon Has Turned a Middle-Class Warehouse Career Into a McJob"; Brown, "Despite Now Offering $15 Minimum Wage, Amazon Still a Top Employer of SNAP Recipients in Many States."

239 **Those warehouse workers:** Khan, "At Work and Under Watch."

240 **Long shifts are the product:** Khan, "At Work and Under Watch."

240 **In the 2023 survey:** Khan, "At Work and Under Watch."

240 **Unsurprisingly, given the pace:** "Primed for Pain: Amazon's Epidemic of Workplace Injuries."

240 **In 2021 for instance:** Gutelius and Pinto, "Pain Points: Data on Work Intensity, Monitoring, and Health at Amazon Warehouse"; Gutelius and Pinto, "Handling Hardship: Data on Economic Insecurity Among Amazon Warehouse Workers."

240 **In a pamphlet:** Ongweso, "Amazon Calls Warehouse Workers 'Industrial Athletes' in Leaked Wellness Pamphlet."

241 **At the time of writing:** Chapman and Hadero, "Amazon Labor Union Members Vote Overwhelmingly in Favor of an Affiliation with the Teamsters."

241 **In 2022 alone:** Jamieson, "Amazon Spent $14 Million On Anti-Union Consultants in 2022."

241 **And sometimes the company:** Sainato, " 'They Are Breaking the Law': Inside Amazon's Bid to Stall a Union Drive"; Scheiber, "Amazon Is Cracking Down on Union Organizing, Workers Say."

241 **All told, though:** Day and Soper, "Amazon Has Turned a Middle-Class Warehouse Career Into a McJob."

241 **Amazon has also:** Goldstein, "How Amazon's Outsourcing Facilitates Union Busting"; Goldberg and Smiley, "Three Paths for Labor after Amazon"; Jamieson, "The Life and Death of an Amazon Warehouse Temp"; Press, "The Teamsters Organized Some Amazon Delivery Workers."

241 **And Amazon's "delivery service partners":** Sainato, "Accidents at Amazon Workers Left to Suffer After Warehouse Injuries"; Sainato, "Revealed: Amazon Employees Are Left to Suffer After Workplace Injuries"; Press, "The Teamsters Organized Some Amazon Delivery Workers"; Goldstein, "How Amazon's Outsourcing Facilitates Union Busting."

241 **It also gets a key:** Goldstein, "How Amazon's Outsourcing Facilitates Union Busting"; Press, "The Teamsters Organized Some Amazon Delivery Workers."

241 **In June 2024:** Hadero, "Thousands of Drivers File Arbitration Claims Against Amazon for Unpaid Wages and Other Losses"; Maruf, "More than 15,000 Amazon Contract Drivers File Legal Claims Asking for Compensation for Overtime and Unpaid Wages."

242 **The NLRB determines:** "Breaking Down the NLRB Decision in Atlanta Opera."

242 **It should thus:** Hadero, "Amazon Argues That National Labor Board Is Unconstitutional"; Scheiber, "Amazon Argues Labor Board Is Unconstitutional."

242 **Amazon's announcement:** O'Connell, "Amazon Receives 238 Proposals for Second Headquarters"; Nwanevu, "If Jeff Bezos Makes Washington the Second Headquarters of Amazon."

242 **That public stunt:** Creswell, "Cities' Offers for Amazon Base Are Secrets Even to Many City Leaders."

243 **But those jobs:** Rubenstein, "Ocasio-Cortez Takes on the Amazon Fight in New York"; Cohn, "Amazon Reveals the Truth on Why It Nixed New York and Chose Virginia for Its HQ2."

243 **Virginia had offered Amazon:** Armus, "Amazon HQ2 Was Supposed to Add Jobs Last Year. It Shed Them Instead."

243 **In recent years:** McNicholas, Poydock, and Rhinehart, "How the PRO Act Restores Workers' Right to Unionize."

244 **Federal labor law:** Brown, "The PRO Act Is Critically Important."

244 **And workers should:** Palladino, "Economic Democracy at Work."

244 **As Harvard Law's:** Block and Sachs, "Clean Slate for Worker Power."

245 **What's more:** Block and Sachs, "Clean Slate for Worker Power."

245 **It should also:** Block and Sachs, "Clean Slate for Worker Power."

245 **While these policies:** Greenhouse, "How Walmart Persuades Its Workers Not to Unionize"; "Location Facts."

245 **Historically, unions have:** Madland, "How to Promote Sectoral Bargaining in the United States."

246 **Policymakers could also:** Block and Sachs, "Clean Slate for Worker Power"; Madland and Rowell, "How State and Local Governments Can Strengthen Worker Power and Raise Wages"; Matthews, "Europe Could Have the Secret to Saving America's Unions."

246 **Sectoral bargaining has:** Block and Sachs, "Clean Slate for Worker Power."

246 **But perhaps most:** Madland and Rowell, "How State and Local Governments Can Strengthen Worker Power and Raise Wages."

247 **the federal government established:** Western and Rosenfeld, "Unions, Norms, and the Rise in U.S. Wage Inequality."

247 **And in recent years:** Glass and Madland, "Momentum for Worker Standards Boards Continues To Grow."

248 **One such reform would be:** Jäger, Noy, and Schoefer, "Codetermination and Power in the Workplace."

248 **Contrary to what skeptics:** Madland, "Wage Boards for American Workers"; Jäger, Noy, and Schoefer, "Codetermination and Power in the Workplace."

248 **The fear that:** Palladino, "Economic Democracy at Work: Why (and How) Workers Should Be Represented on US Corporate Boards"; Block and Sachs, "Clean Slate for Worker Power."

249 **In some countries:** Jäger, Noy, and Schoefer, "Codetermination and Power in the Workplace."

249 **Germany's system:** "German Codetermination ('Mitbestimmung')"; Matthews, "Workers Don't Have Much Say in Corporations. Why Not Give Them Seats on the Board?"; Dammann and Eidenmueller, "Codetermination."

249 **And, as with work councils:** Jäger, Noy, and Schoefer, "Codetermination and Power in the Workplace."

249 **While codetermination:** Battilana, "Introduction: For a Fairer, More Democratic, Greener Society"; Ferreras, "Democratizing the Corporation"; Block and Sachs, "Clean Slate for Worker Power"; McGaughey, "Democracy in America at Work."

249 **In 2018:** Matthews, "Workers Don't Have Much Say in Corporations"; Strine Jr., Kovvali, and Williams, "Lifting Labor's Voice."

249 **This was followed by:** Dammann and Eidenmueller, "Taming the Corporate Leviathan."

250 **Under the Baldwin:** Dammann and Eidenmueller, "Codetermination"; Jäger, Noy, and Schoefer, "Codetermination and Power in the Workplace."

250 **Still, granting workers:** Dammann and Eidenmueller, "Taming the Corporate Leviathan."

251 **According to Rutgers professor:** Blasi, Freeman, and Kruse, *The Citizen's Share*, p. 82.

251 **And at some private companies:** Blasi, Freeman, and Kruse, *The Citizen's Share*, pp. 82–97.

251 **For years now:** Palladino, "Economic Democracy at Work"; Wiefek, Rosen, and Garbinsky, "Promoting Employee Ownership."

251 **About 6,500 companies:** Case and Quarrey, "Turning Employees into Owners"; Ellerman, "Fallacies About Corporations"; Nwanevu, "The Case for Giving Workers Ownership Rights."

251 **And research suggests:** Case and Quarrey, "Turning Employees into Owners"; Mygind and Poulsen, "Employee Ownership—Pros and Cons."

251 **While some might:** Palladino, "Economic Democracy at Work"; Blasi, Freeman, and Kruse, *The Citizen's Share*, pp. 181–82.

252 **Moreover, companies with:** Wiefek, Rosen, and Garbinsky, "Promoting Employee Ownership."

252 **From a democratic perspective:** "The Rights of ESOP Participants."

252 **Yet they can be structured differently:** Kaswan, "Property, Ownership and Employee Ownership."

252 **In 2019:** "Corporate Accountability and Democracy"; Palladino, "The Po-

tential Benefits of Employee Equity Funds in the United States"; Nwanevu, "The Case for Giving Workers Ownership Rights."

252 **At the same time:** Boolchandani, "When ESOPs Go Wrong."

253 **In plainer terms:** Golshan, "Bernie Sanders's Plan to Reshape Corporate America, Explained."

253 **And their ownership:** Palladino, "The Potential Benefits of Employee Equity Funds in the United States."

253 **As far-reaching:** Nwanevu, "Bernie Sanders's Walmart Speech May Offer a Preview of Larger Labor Proposals."

253 **The worker-cooperative:** "2021 STATE OF THE SECTOR WORKER COOPERATIVES IN THE U.S."

254 **Consider Spain's Mondragon:** Romeo, "How Mondragon Became the World's Largest Co-Op."

254 **In general, cooperatives:** Malleson, *After Occupy,* pp. 40–41; Romeo, "How Mondragon Became the World's Largest Co-Op."

255 **And more worker-ownership centers:** Blasi, Kruse, and Freeman, "Broad-Based Employee Stock Ownership and Profit Sharing"; "Corporate Accountability and Democracy."

256 **"As business interests":** McGaughey, "Five Principles of Economic Democracy."

Conclusion

259 **"I have written":** Lippmann, *Public Opinion,* p. 411.

259 **Many years ago:** "Dialogue Origin: 'What Do You Think of Western Civilization?' 'I Think It Would Be a Good Idea.'"

261 **To that end:** Quackenbush, "A Tea-Party Veteran Has a Plan to Upend the Constitution"; Panetta and Griffiths, "Republicans' Next Big Play."

261 **What's more:** "Stopping a Dangerous Article V Convention."

262 **we are already at or above:** Knight and Selig, "A Constitutional Convention?"

264 **Thomas Paine:** Paine, *Rights of Man;* Taylor, *Democracy May Not Exist, But We'll Miss It When It's Gone,* p. 283.

264 **And even as they defended:** Hamilton, "The Federalist No. 1."

265 **"The earth":** Jefferson, "Thomas Jefferson to James Madison."

266 **"Giving the world":** "Third Episode about Mr. Isaac Woodard, Jr."

266 **"We have it":** Paine, *Common Sense.*

INDEX

ABOUT THE AUTHOR

OSITA NWANEVU is a contributing editor at *The New Republic*, a columnist at *The Guardian*, and the Democratic Institutions fellow at the Roosevelt Institute. He is a former staff writer at *The New Republic*, *The New Yorker*, and *Slate*, and his work has also appeared in *The New York Times*, *The New York Review of Books*, *The Nation*, *Harper's Magazine*, *Columbia Journalism Review*, *In These Times*, and *Gawker*. This is his first book. He lives in Baltimore, Maryland.

01 14
J